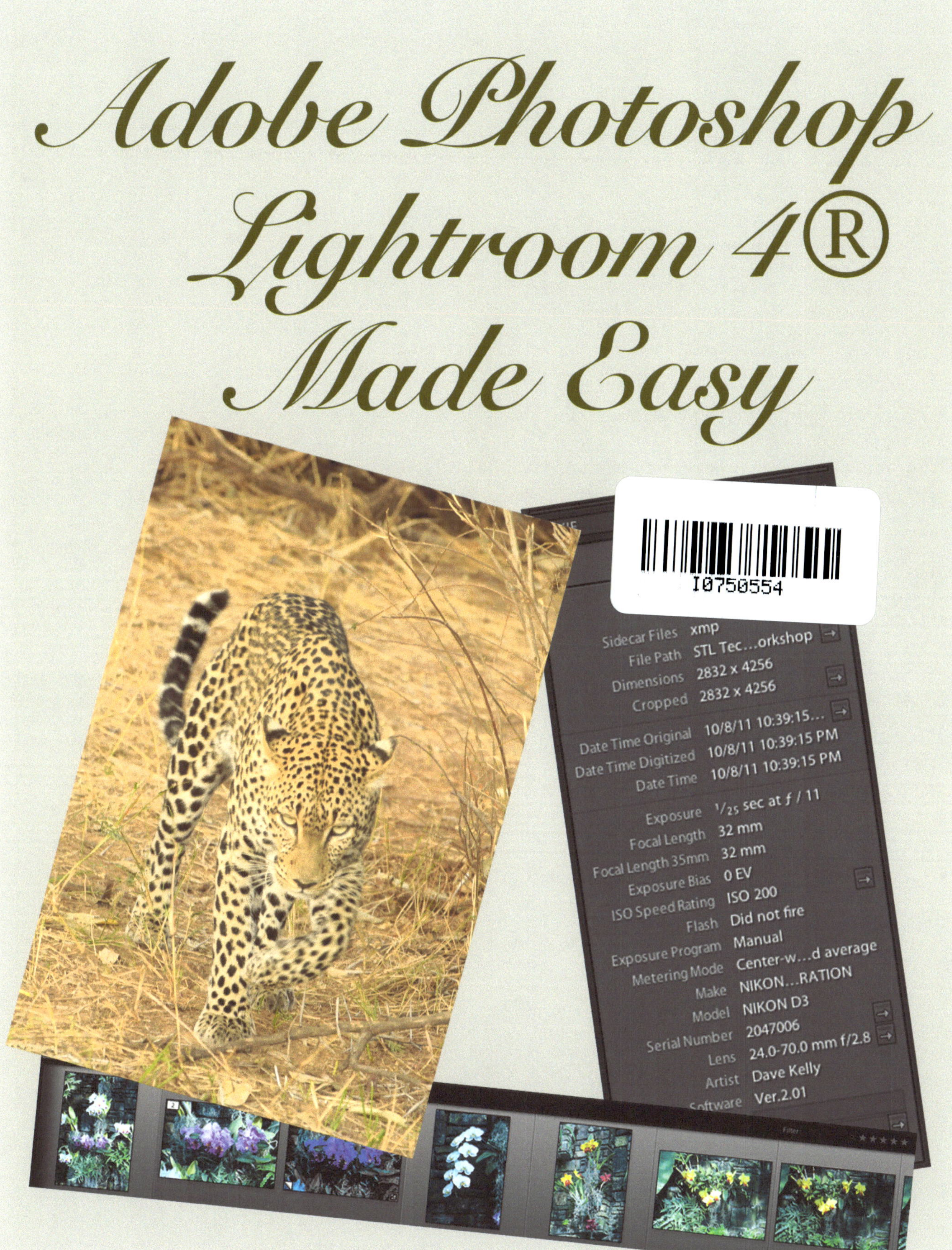
Adobe Photoshop
Lightroom 4®
Made Easy
I0750554
Sidecar Files xmp
File Path STL Tec…orkshop
Dimensions 2832 x 4256
Cropped 2832 x 4256
Date Time Original 10/8/11 10:39:15…
Date Time Digitized 10/8/11 10:39:15 PM
Date Time 10/8/11 10:39:15 PM
Exposure 1/25 sec at f / 11
Focal Length 32 mm
Focal Length 35mm 32 mm
Exposure Bias 0 EV
ISO Speed Rating ISO 200
Flash Did not fire
Exposure Program Manual
Metering Mode Center-w…d average
Make NIKON…RATION
Model NIKON D3
Serial Number 2047006
Lens 24.0-70.0 mm f/2.8
Artist Dave Kelly
Software Ver.2.01

*ISBN-13: 978-0615692609 (Custom Universal)
ISBN-10: 0615692605*

For
Peach

# About This Book

Photography is becoming the fastest growing hobby in America. People retiring, looking for something to occupy their time, mothers and fathers of new born babies, growing kids, kids involved in sports, music, spelling bees, any number of activities, people looking for a new career, people looking to turn a hobby into a career are all looking to photography as a possibility. Camera manufacturers are turning out more and more sophisticated cameras that are easier to use, smaller in size and less expensive with more and more unique algorithms to reduce noise. Camera phones now come with large megapixel sensors. Lenses are becoming better and better with vibration reduction or image stabilization, tilt shift, shorter focal lengths for wider angles and longer focal lengths to bring the subject in closer. The advent of the digital world in photography has eliminated the darkroom with all it's smelly chemicals and has given people the ability to develop and print their own images on their own computer and printer. The result is the digital camera pays for itself over time because it has eliminated buying of film and paying for developing images. People who do take their images to the camera store for developing only take the ones the want developed.

All this has lead to more people taking more pictures and the problem of what to do with them, how to organize them so they can be easily found. The Library module of Adobe Photoshop Lightroom 4® is far more than just a file browser, it is the best asset management program available to photographers today and it's easy to use. This book will take you step by step completely through every thing the Library module has to offer. The goal is to make it easy for you to import, organize, find, email and export your images. There are even some tricks to placing develop settings on images in the Library module without having to go to the Develop module as well as how to edit video in the Library module. The Develop module offers the ability to birng out the best in your images. New algorithms offer better image development and there are some new techniques available. The output modules have increase with a Map and Book module added. The Slideshow, Print and Web modules remain the same, but are enhanced by the new techniques available in the Library and Develop modules. Most people who use Lightroom® barely scratch the surface, with this book you'll learn how to go far deeper easily and have fun doing it.

**What this book is not**

All of the books written about Lightroom® contain a great deal of both practical and technical information about the software. This book was not part of the race to be the first book published about Lightroom®4. Most of those books were based on the public beta version of Lightroom®4. This book is also not a rehash of a previous version of Lightroom® with a "What's New" section added and the new effects sliders added. It is also not a book to show off my images or what I can do with my images. In fact, you will find very few of my images in this book

.

**What this book is**

This book is a fresh look at Lightroom®4 based on the final software not the public beta version. There are some new sections added in the final software that were not in the beta version. An example is the Color section in the Lens Correction panel of the Develop module which you will not find in the early books. These new sections are all covered in this book. In this book you will find information not available in any other book or video tutorial. Things you will find in this book are efficient ways to organize your images, and why, with the exception of Smart Collections, all the images in your collections should be Virtual Copies and why each Collection should have new Virtual Copies. You'll also find how to determine when there is loss of detail (clipping) in images even when it doesn't show with the Clipping warnings turned on and how to get rid of that loss of detail. Another new technique is how to change colors in the Tone Curve panel and how to use the Tone Curve panel to remove clipping . These are only a few of the new techniques available.

This book is created to sit with the photographer at the computer and guide her or him through the various techniques of organizing, developing, creating books, slideshows prints and web galleries on their own images. It uses easy to understand language with bullet points for each technique.

A book like this is not possible without learning from other people. First, I'd like to thank the students who have taken my classes, they were the impetus for this book. One of the most frequently asked questions was is there a short concise book that will teach how to organize and develop my images. Second, I'd like to thank Julieanne Kost, whom I've never met, but I feel like I know because I've watched all her video tutorials, read her blog and attended her presentations at Photoshop World. In studying to become an Adobe Certified Instructor, her tutorials were the most helpful. Third, I'd like to thank Matt Klosklowski and Scott Kelby at Kelby Training, their tutorials were also very helpful. Finally I'd like to thank Sangara Singh whose Examaid programs I feel prepared me well to jump through all of Adobe's hoops in meeting the requirements to become an Adobe Certified Instructor. A lot of the basics you will read in this book came from learning from others. Most of the practical suggestions you'll find are mine, arrived at by trying different things that made sense to me. Hope you enjoy it and that this book helps you to conquer Adobe Photoshop Lightroom 4®

Dave Kelly

# Contents

## The Map Module 146



## The Book Module 152

# The Library Module

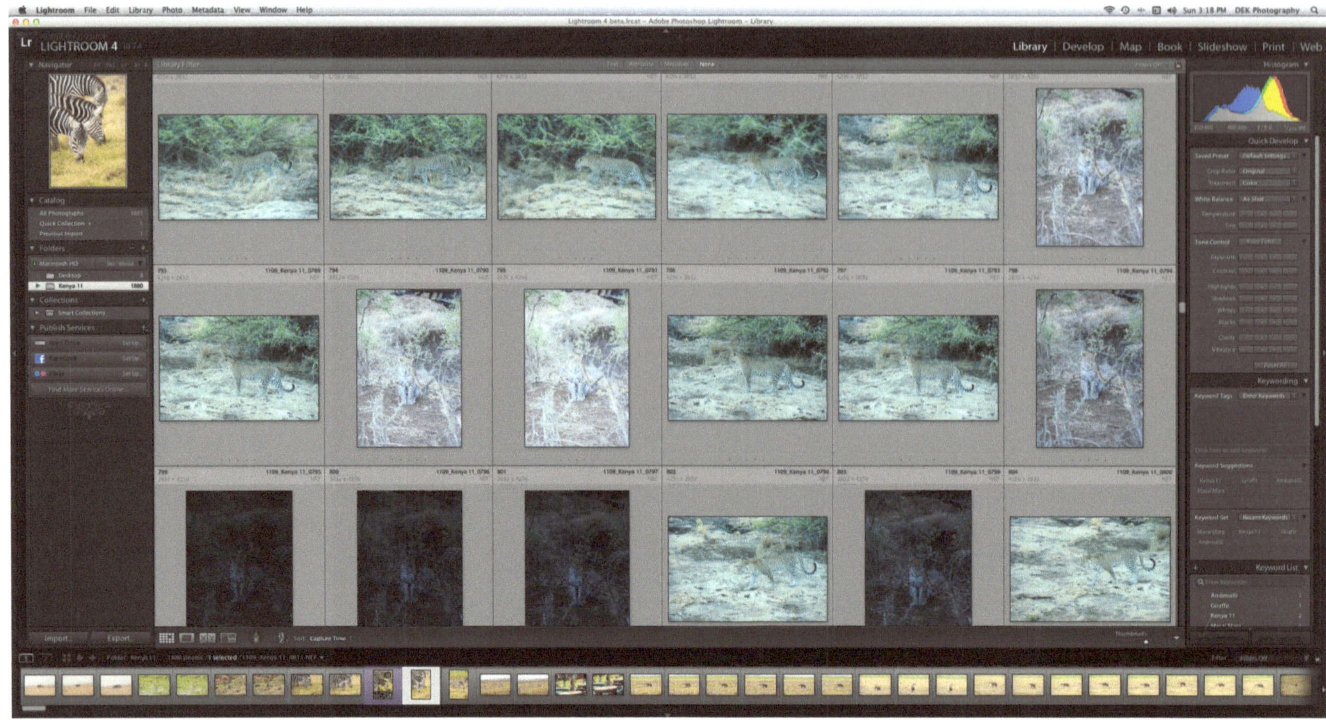


Figure 1

Of the seven Lighroom® modules, the Library module is probably the most powerful. Not only is it a browser for your images, it is a total asset management module. Many people fail to take advantage of all that the Library module has to offer, so, briefly here is what you can accomplish with the Library module:

- ► Organize your images into catalogs, folders, collections and stacks.
- ► Create duplicate images on a second hard drive during import.
- ► Add your images directly to your catalog using tethered capture, bypassing the memory card.
- ► Create custom naming templates and apply them during import.
- ► Rename individual images or all images in a folder after import.
- ► Create Import presets.
- ► Create metadata presets and apply them during import.
- ► Apply metadata presets to individual images or all images in a folder after import.
- ► Apply Lightroom® develop presets or user created presets during import.
- ► Classify images as picks or rejects.
- ► Rate images with stars.
- ► Label images with colors.
- ► Keyword images both during and after import.
- ► Show metadata on the images.
- ► Zoom in, zoom out to various magnification levels.
- ► Compare two images or groups of images on the same screen.
- ► Group images by key words.
- ► Create Collections of images from different Folders
- ► Stack similar images and save space on the desktop.
- ► Find images by ratings, color labels, flags, keywords and metadata with the Library Filter Bar.
- ► Sort images by different aspects after import.
- ► Create virtual copies.
- ► Find missing folders or individual images.

- ► Rotate and flip images.
- ► Sync develop settings from one image to another.
- ► View an impromptu slide show.
- ► Select images from Lightroom® or from your hard drive.
- ► Work seamlessly with an external editing program such as Photoshop®.
- ► Export images to CD/DVDs, hard drives or plug-in programs.
- ► Apply Photoshop® actions as droplets that take your images back to Photoshop® and run the actions to make the images ready to go up on the web.

If you are going to learn how to take advantage of all the Library module of Lightroom® has to offer, it's time to get started.

## The Screen Setup  (Figure 1)

By default, the Library module opens when you start Lightroom® for the first time.  Every time you open Lightroom® after the first time, Lighroom® will open in the module in which you were working when you closed it the last time.  To open the Library module from one of the other modules, do one of the following:

- Click with the cursor on the word Library in the Module Picker on the top left of the screen.
- Hold down the Command and Option (Macintosh) or Control and Alt (PC) keys and press the number one (1) key on the keyboard.
- Press one of the Library module's keyboard shortcuts (Grid view Loupe view, Compare view, Survey view, etc. to be discussed later).
- From the Window menu in the menu bar at the top of the screen, select Library module.

Once the Library module is open, familiarize yourself with the screen setup.

### The Menus

Across the top of the screen you will find on the left side, eight menus in the menu bar, File, Edit, Library, Photo, Metadata, View, Window and Help.  In addition, if you are using a Macintosh computer, the word Lightroom® will precede File in the menu bar.  Clicking with the cursor on any of these menus will display a drop down menu with which you can accomplish various tasks or select various tools.

TIP:  It is labor intensive to keep going back to the menus and making selections from the drop down menus.  Almost every choice in the drop down menus has a keyboard shortcut listed to the right of the choice in the menu.  It is much more efficient and will speed up your categorizing and editing your images to use the keyboard shortcuts.  To see all the keyboard shortcuts hold down the Command (Macintosh), Control (PC) key and press the forward slash (/) key on the keyboard.  Doing this will bring up a pop up screen with all the keyboard shortcuts for the module in which you are working.  This is a quick way to find and learn the keyboard shortcuts you use most often.

Below this menu bar is a black bar, the left side of which has the Identity Plate and the right side of which has the Module Picker for the seven modules, ***Library, Develop, Map, Book, Slideshow, Print and Web.***

## The Identity Plate (Figure 2)

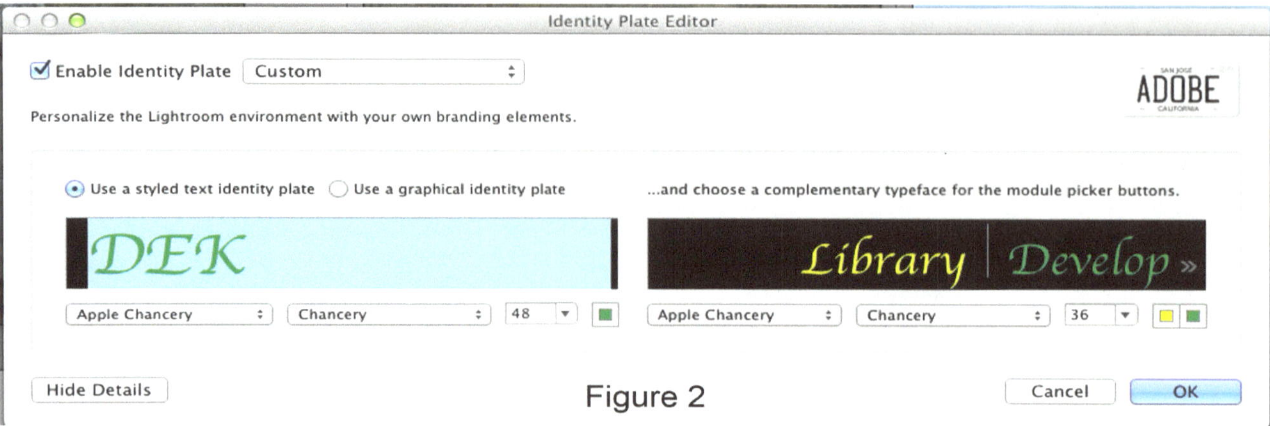

Figure 2

The identity Plate says Adobe Photoshop Lightroom®4 in white letters on the black bar when you first open Lightroom®. In addition, the seven modules in the Module Picker are also in white letters on the right side of the black bar. You might want to personalize the Identity Plate to make Lightroom® more your own by placing your name, the name of your company or a logo in the Identity Plate. Learning how to change the Identity Plate will come in handy in the other modules. To change the Identity Plate, do the following:

- Click with the cursor on Lightroom® at the top of the left of the screen on the Macintosh or click with the cursor on the Edit menu on the PC. From the drop down menu that appears, click with the cursor on "Identity Plate Setup". This will bring up the Identity Plate Editor dialog box (Figure 2.)
- Choose between a styled text Identity Plate or a graphical Identity Plate.
- If your have a graphical logo, click with the cursor in the circle in front of Use Graphical Identity Plate to place a check mark in the circle.
- Choose the image of your logo and drag it into the Identity Plate box.
- If you choose a styled text Identity Plate, choose the font from the drop down menu located below the text box for the Identity Plate.
- In the blank to the right of the font, choose whether you want the letters to be regular, bold or black.
- In the next box to the right, choose the font size from the drop down menu next to the fonts menu.
- Choose the color for the font from the color wheel that appears when you click with the cursor in the box beneath the right side of the Identity Plate.

TIP: You can also change the font, font size and color of the seven modules in the Module Picker to match the Identity Plate by following the same procedure with the boxes under the Module Picker. The difference is that there are two boxes for colors. The first box will be the color of the active module, the second color will be for the inactive modules.

Once you have the Identity Plate and Module Picker fonts and colors you like, do the following:

- Click with the cursor in the box at the top of the Identity Plate Editor dialog box to bring up a drop down menu.
- From this menu select "Save as."
- In the "Save Identity Plate as" dialog box that appears, name your new Identity Plate and click with the cursor on the Save button.
- Next, place a check mark in the box at the top of the Identity Plate Editor dialog box labeled "Enable Identity Plate" by clicking in the box with the cursor.
- Finally, click with the cursor on the OK button at the bottom right of the Identity Plate Editor dialog box.

Your new personalized Identity Plate will appear at the top of all seven modules. This may seem like a small thing, but it comes in very handy in the output modules when your are sending images, slide shows or web pages to a client or some one else. You can also have as many Identity Plates as you like and they can be used for adding information to slideshows and prints.

## The Image Window

In the very center of the screen is the image window. This is where all your images can be seen. There are multiple views of your images available. They are as follows:

- Grid view, all the images in the current catalog, folder or collection are visible on screen in the image window.
- Loupe view, only the image you have selected will be visible in this main image window.
- Compare view, two selected images are visible for comparison on the screen.
- Survey view, multiple selected image are visible on the screen.

To switch between the various views, do the following:

- ► With one image selected go to the view menu and from the drop down menu select the view you want, Grid or Loupe.
- ► Alternatively use the keyboard shortcuts, press the G key on the keyboard for the Grid view or the E key on the keyboard for the Loupe view.
- ► If two images are selected in the Grid view or the Filmstrip, select the Compare view from the View drop down menu or use the keyboard short cut, press the C key on the keyboard.
- ► If more than two images are selected in the Grid view or Filmstrip, select Survey view from the View drop down menu or use the keyboard shortcut, press the N key on the keyboard.
- ► Another way to access the different views is to use the icons on the Toolbar. There is one icon for each of the views. All you have to do is select the image or images and click with the cursor on the appropriate icon in the toolbar (Figure 3).

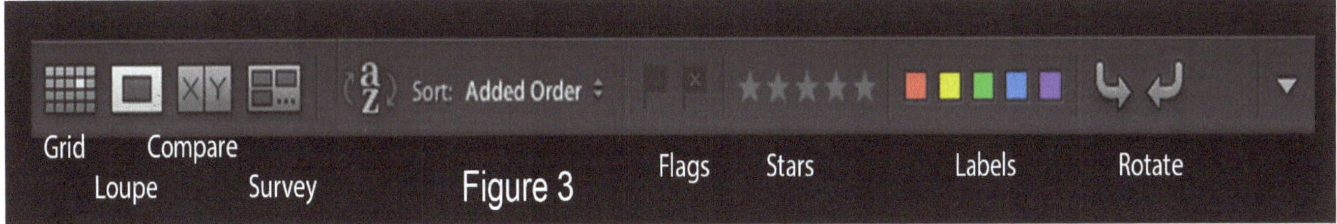

Figure 3

TIP: The different views come in very handy when you are trying to make a decision about which image you like the best.

## The Compare View

When in the Compare view, the first image you select will have the word "Select" at the top right of the image. The second image you selected will have the word "Candidate" at the top left of the image. When in the Compare view the toolbar will change and at the right side there will be several new icons in the toolbar in addition to the view icons. These icons work as follows

- The compare view icon will be highlighted.
- To the right of the view icons will be the word "Compare".
- To the right of the word "Compare will be a padlock icon, with the padlock closed. You can click with the cursor on either image and they will both be magnified to the same magnification level.
- Open the padlock by clicking on it with the cursor, and then click on either image and only that image will be magnified.
- To the right of the padlock icon is a slider bar which can be used to move the image or images through the various levels of magnification from Fit to Fill to any magnification from 1:4 all the way up to 11:1.
- On the right side of the toolbar are four more icons and the word "Done".
- The first of these icons is a split box with and X and Y in it and a top arrow pointing right and a bottom arrow pointing left. Clicking on this icon with the cursor will exchange the positions of the two images, the Select will become the Candidate and the Candidate will be come the Select.
- The second icon is also a box in which there is an X and Clicking with the cursor on this icon moves the Candidate into the select box and places the next image to the right in the Filmstrip into the Candidate box.
- The next two icons to the right are left and right pointing arrows. Clicking on either of these arrows leaves the Select image the same and makes the Candidate the next image to the right or left of the Candidate.
- Finally, clicking with the cursor on the "Done" button at the right end of the toolbar will close the compare view and brings the final Selected image up full screen.

**The Survey View**

In the Survey view, the Toolbar changes again. The word "Compare" changes to the word "Survey" and has a right and left pointing arrow next to it. The other icons which were on the right side of the toolbar in the Compare view are no longer present. However, when you hover your cursor over one of the images in the Survey view, an X will appear in the bottom right corner of the image. Clicking with the cursor on the X will eliminate the image from the screen and the remaining image will be enlarged on the screen. You can continue clicking on the X of each image until you have the image you feel is the best from the group.

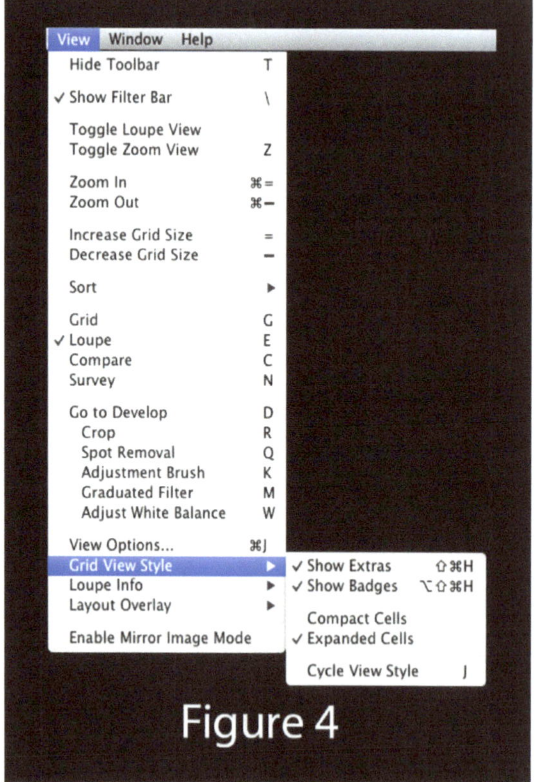

Figure 4

## Compact and Expanded Cells in the Grid view

It is possible to show information about the image in both the Grid view and the Loupe view. In the Grid view, you have a choice of Compact cells or Expanded Cells (Figure 4). To find out what information you can see in the cells in the Grid view, do the following:

- Go to the View menu at the top of the screen and from the drop down menu choose "View Options" or use the keyboard short cut, hold down the Command (Macintosh), Control (PC) key and press the J key on the keyboard ( Figure 4).
- In the Library View Options popup menu, select "Grid" At the top of the dialog box (Figure 5).
- In the first options blank, "Show Grid Options", click on the double pointed arrow at the right side of the blank and

choose “Compact Cells”.

- In the section labeled “Compact Cell Extras”, place a check mark in the boxes in front of “Top label” and “Bottom Label”. To the right of these labels is a blank the right side of which has a double pointed arrow.
- Click with the cursor on this double pointed arrow and from the drop down menu choose what information you want to show in the top label and the bottom label. For example, choose the Exposure and ISO for the top label and the Lens setting for the bottom label (Figure 5)
- Go back to the top blank and change to Expanded Cells.
- Go down to the Expanded Cell Extras section of the Library View Options popup dialog box, place check marks in the boxes to show Header with Labels and Show Rating Footer.
- In the Header, you have four blanks for the information that can be seen on the top of the images in the Expanded Cell.

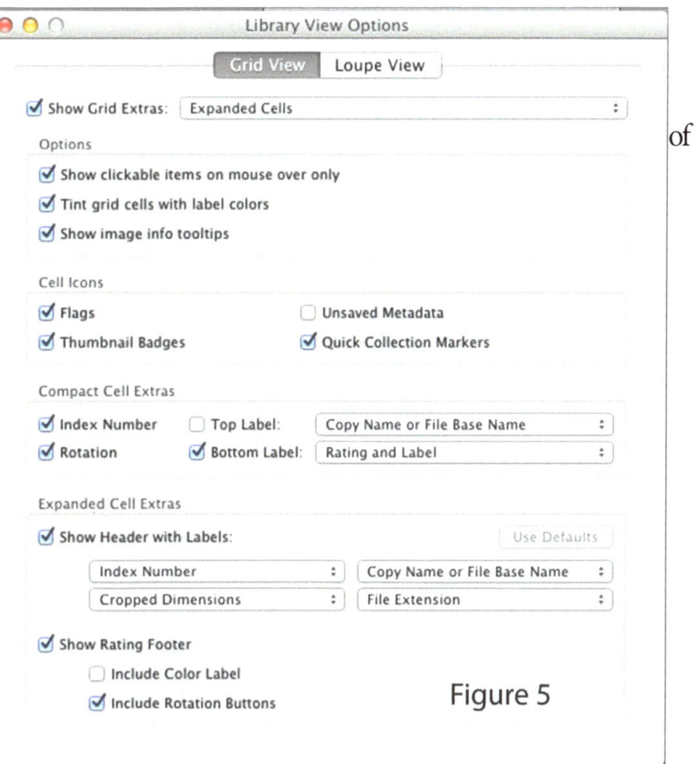

Figure 5

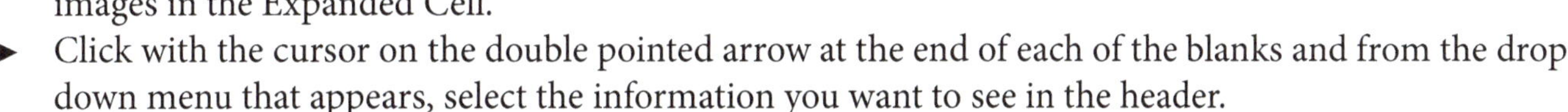

- Click with the cursor on the double pointed arrow at the end of each of the blanks and from the drop down menu that appears, select the information you want to see in the header.
- In the footer of the Expanded Cell, you can see ratings and color labels as well as rotation arrows if you choose to turn these on by clicking with the cursor in the boxes in front of these choices.

In both of the Compact and Expanded Cell views you can choose to see Cell icons such as flags, thumbnail badges, the Quick Collection icon, more on these later. In order to see the icons, badges and Quick collection icon you need to place a check mark in the boxes in front of these choices in the “Cell Icons” section of the Library View Options dialog box. In order to see the choices you have made in the Compact or Expanded Cell views as well as the Cell Icons, after you have made your choices and closed the Library View Options dialog box, you need to go back to the View menu and from the drop down menu choose “Grid View Style”. (Figure 4) From the menu that appears choose whether you want to see the Compact Cells or the Expanded Cells and then click with the cursor on “Show Extras” and “Show Badges”. Now all the icons, badges and information you chose to be shown on the Compact or Expanded Cells will show up in the Grid view.

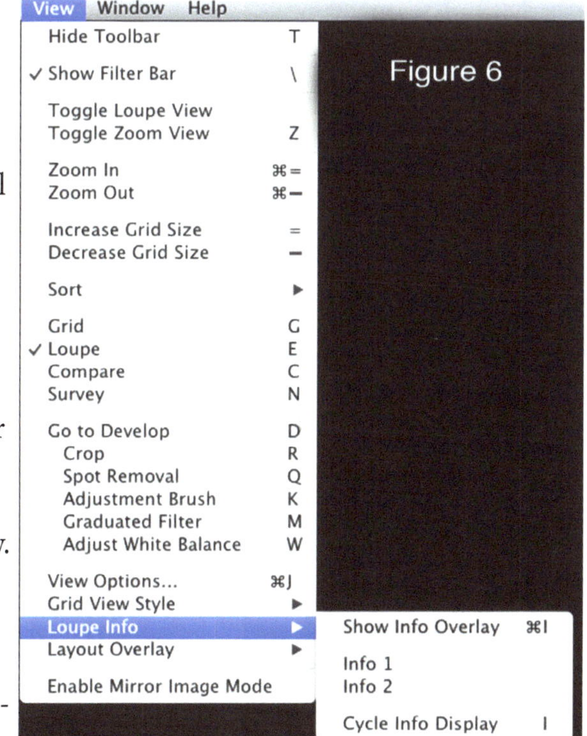

Figure 6

## Info In the Loupe View

In the Loupe view, you also have a choice of what informa-

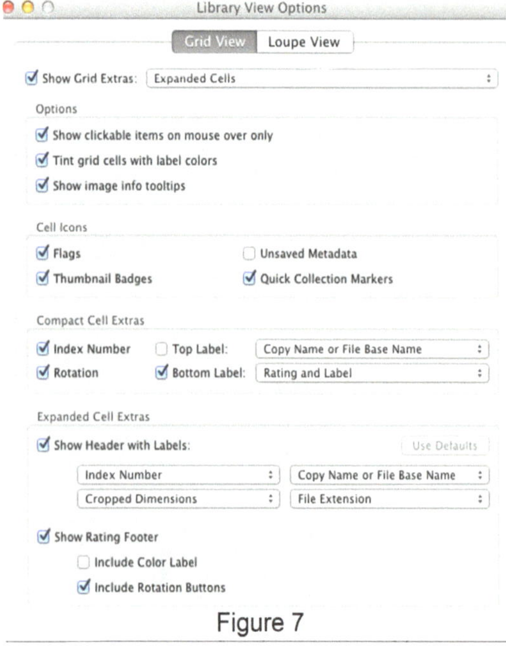

Figure 7

tion can be seen in the image. The information you choose to show on the images in the Loupe view will also be on the image in the Develop module. To choose the information you want to see on the image in the Loupe view, do the following:

- ► From the View menu at the top of the screen, choose "View Options" or use the keyboard shortcut, hold down the Command (Macintosh), Control (PC) key and press the J key on the keyboard (Figure 6).
- ► At the top of the Library View Options popup menu dialog box, select "Loupe" (Figure 7).
- ► There are two sections, labeled Loupe Info 1 and Loupe Info 2. Each has three blanks into which you can place information.
- ► To place your choice of what information is to be seen in these blanks, click with the cursor on the double pointed arrow at the right side of each blank and choose the information for each blank by clicking with the cursor on your choice from the drop down menu.
- ► Once you have made your choices, go to the top of the Library View Options dialog box and choose which info you want displayed when the image comes up in the loupe view, Info 1 or Info 2.

TIP: You can cycle through the different Loupe views on the screen, including not seeing the Loupe Info by pressing the I key on the keyboard. You can also choose to show the info 1 or 2 briefly by checking the box under each info selection that says "Show briefly when the photo changes".

# The Left Side Panels

## The Navigator Panel

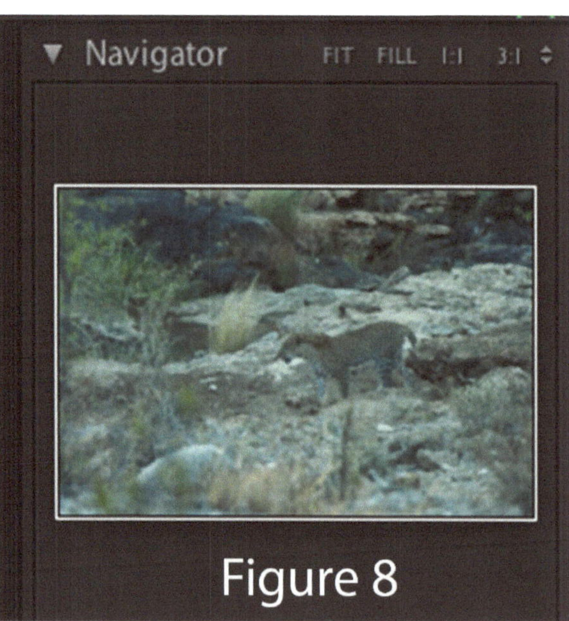

Figure 8

To the left of the Image Window is a column of panels, this is where Lightroom® keeps track of your images and shows you where your images are located. At the top of the column is the Navigator window. (Figure 8) Any image you have selected will appear in the Navigator window. The word Navigator appears on the left side in the header bar of this panel. To the right of the word Navigator there are four choices for seeing the image magnified, Fit, Fill, 1:1 and a drop down menu that will let you see the image magnified to any size between 1:4 all the way up to 11:1. To choose the magnification, simply click with the cursor on the size you would like to see the image or click on the drop down arrow to the right and click with the cursor on your choice of magnification. Each time you choose a magnification above Fill, a white rectangle will appear in the image in the Navigator window showing you what part of the image it is at which you are looking. You can close the Navigator window, as you can any of the panels by clicking with the cursor on either the down pointing arrow to the left of the word Navigator or just clicking anywhere in the header bar of the Navigator panel. The last magnification level you choose will be the one that is used when you click with the cursor on the image in the Loupe view.

## The Catalog

Below the Navigator window are the panels by which Lightroom® organizes your images. The first panel is the Catalog panel. Only one catalog can be open in Lightroom® at a time. To open another catalog, you will have to go to the File menu at the top left of the screen and choose either "Open Catalog" or "Open Recent" from the drop down menu. When you select another catalog you would like to open, Lightroom® will ask you if you want to relaunch Lightroom®. If you choose to relaunch Lightroom®, you will be asked if you would like to backup the current catalog. If you choose to backup the current catalog, Lightroom® will back up the catalog, close the current catalog and relaunch itself and open with the new catalog. The Catalog Contains the following:

- Preview information for all the images in the Catalog.
- The Location of the folders and number of files in each folder, and all the files on the computer and external hard drives that have been imported into Lightroom®.
- Module settings for each of the seven Lightroom®4 modules.
- Metadata, keywords, ratings and labels for all the files.
- Information for all the Collections of images you have created.

In the Catalog panel are four sections, All Photographs, Quick Collection, Previous Import and Missing Photographs. To the right of each of these choices is a number indicating how many images there are in each of these sections. You can see the missing images by clicking with the cursor on the Missing Photographs section of the Catalog panel. You can go to the Library menu at the top of the page and select "Find Missing Photos" and Lightroom® will first show you all the missing photographs on screen and then will scan your computer and any connected hard drives in an effort to find the missing photos.

One of the things you need to decide about your Catalog is, do you want to have just one Catalog with all your images in it or do you want multiple catalogs? In previous versions of Lightroom® the catalog tended to slow down as more and more images were added. Starting with Lightroom®3 that has not been a problem, Lightroom®3 and 4 catalogs are capable of handling vast amounts of images. The reasons a Catalog slows down are more dependent on the computer than increasing numbers of images. The things that affect how fast or slow Lightroom® runs on a computer are the following:

- Computer CPU speed.
- Amount of RAM.
- The Drive speed is too slow.
- The size of the images you have is very large.

Lightroom® 4 seems to be able to handle tens of thousands of images without noticeably slowing down.

The advantage of having just one catalog is it simplifies the workflow and makes it easy to search for just one image because the entire Catalog can be searched at one time. Also, you can create collections of images from any one of your folders. At some point, Lightroom® may start to slow down. To improve the performance and possibly speed up Lightroom®, do the following:

- Go to the File menu at the top left of the screen.
- From the drop down menus, select "Optimize Catalog".
- A dialog box will appear telling you when the Catalog was last optimized and that optimizing may improve the performance.
- Also, it will tell you that you will not be able to use Lightroom® during the optimization process.
- Ignore the warning and click with the cursor on "Optimize".
- Lightroom® will optimize your catalog and tell you when it is finished optimizing with a pop up window

on the main screen.

The advantage to having multiple catalogs is that you can place different types of images in separate Catalogs. For example, you might have one catalog for business and one for personal or for family. Some professional photographers have one for weddings, one for portraits and one for personal. Others have one catalog for each
year. The disadvantage to multiple catalogs is that to go from one to the other you need to relaunch Lightroom® every time you switch catalogs. While not hard to do, it does take some time. Of course, the decision as to how many catalogs is up to you and how you want to organize your images.

One other thing to decide is where to locate your catalog. By default, Lightroom® places a Catalog in the Pictures folder on your hard drive for a Macintosh computer and on a PC the Catalog is in My Pictures. My suggestion is to not have your catalog located on your computer's hard drive, but instead, locate it on a large external hard drive. There are several reasons for this, first, you will not be taking up space on your computer's hard drive and second, when your computer's had drive fails or if you get a new computer it will be easy for Lightroom® to locate the images when you first open Lightroom® on the new computer. A third reason is that if you are working with both a desktop computer and a laptop, you can move the hard drive from one to the other and always have access to your images. If you do put your catalog on an external hard drive, make sure that the hard drive you choose for your images is included when you backup your computer system.

Lightroom® comes with a default catalog which will be located on the same drive as the one on which you installed Lightroom®. The easiest way to place the catalog on a different hard drive is to do the following:

- From the File drop down menu select "New Catalog".
- A dialog box entitled "Create Folder with New Catalog" will appear on screen.
- In the box that says "Save As:" give your new catalog a name.
- Below the "Save As:" box is a box that allows you to choose where you want the new catalog.
- Click with the cursor on the drop down menu and select the drive for the new catalog.
- Click with the cursor on "Create" at the bottom right of the dialog box.
- Your new catalog will be on the hard drive you chose and will open.

Another important thing to decide about your catalog is how often you want it backed up. Choosing this and some other things are done in the Catalog Settings. Catalog Settings are found under the word Lightroom® at the top left of the screen on the Macintosh and under the Edit menu at the top of the screen on the PC. When you bring up the Catalog Settings dialog box, you can set up how often Lightroom® backs up your catalog under the "General" heading. Also under the General heading you will find the date your catalog was created, the date of the last backup, the date of the last optimization and the size of the catalog. The backup setting is at the bottom of the General settings dialog box and has a drop down menu from which you can choose how often to backup your catalog.

Other choices in the Catalog Settings dialog box are for file handling. Here you can choose the size and quality of your previews and when to discard 1:1 previews and Metadata, which deals with where develop settings are recorded. In most cases, the default settings are more than adequate.

## The Folders Panel

Below the Catalog panel is the Folders panel. Each time you import images into Lightroom®, you will import them into a folder. You can have as many folders as you need in a catalog. You can create a folder and name it during the import of images (more on how to do this later during the discussion on importing). As in the Catalog panel, Lightroom® will list the number of images in each folder to the right of the folder name.

Lightroom® will remember every image imported into the Catalog and where it was placed during import, on your computer's hard drive on an external hard drive. All of the places you have images that have been imported into the Lightroom® catalog on the computer will be listed in the Folders panel. If you have images on an external hard drive that is not connected to the computer, Lightroom® will still show the external hard drive in the Folders panel, but the folders on that hard drive will have a question mark (?) beside them indicating Lightroom® cannot locate them. If the hard drive is reconnected to the computer Lightroom will recognize them and remove the question mark from the folders. If you move a folder outside of Lightroom®, for example off your computer's hard drive and onto an external hard drive, you will break the connection to Lightroom® and Lightroom® will not know where the images are located. To find the folder you moved, do the following:

- ▶ Control (Macintosh) Right (PC) click with the cursor on the name of the missing folder.
- ▶ From the menu that appears, choose "Find Missing Folder".
- ▶ Lightroom® will bring up all the drives connected to your computer.
- ▶ Navigate to the drive to which you moved the folder and select the folder.
- ▶ With the missing folder highlighted, click with the cursor on "Choose" at the bottom right of the dialog box.
- ▶ Lightroom® will re-establish the connection to the missing folder.

Another common situation occurs when you get a new computer and install Lightroom® or when you upgrade to a new version of Lightroom® on your present computer (upgrading from Lightroom 3® to 4, for example). When you first open Lightroom® on the new computer, Lightroom® will not know where your images are. To establish a connection to the images in Lightroom® on the new computer you can do the following:

- ▶ Under the File menu select "Open Catalog" from the drop down menu.
- ▶ Lighroom® will bring up a dialog box called "Open" which lists all the devices connected to your computer.
- ▶ Navigate to the hard drive on which your catalog is located and highlight it to select it.
- ▶ Click with the cursor on "Open" at the bottom right of the dialog box.
- ▶ The connection between Lightroom® and the catalog will be established.
- ▶ All of the folders will be just as they were in the catalog on the old computer.

## The Collections Panel

The next panel down is the Collections panel and is one of the real strengths of Lightroom®. This panel is one for which you will find multiple uses. The Collection panel is available in all seven modules of Lightroom®4, however, the Library module is the only one in which you can create a collection from images that are in different folders. In all the other modules you can create a collection that is specific to that module. For example, you can create a collection in the book module of the images you want in your book. Once created, that book collection will show up in the collections panel and have a different icon specific to the Book module. In addition, when you hover your cursor over the collection, a right pointing arrow will appear at the end of the bar for that collection. If you click with the cursor on the right pointing arrow, Lightroom® will open the book module and your images will be as you left them in the book project. The same is true for the other output modules, Slideshow, Print and Web. The Collections panel is the most useful panel in organizing your images, more on this later.

## The Publish Services Panel

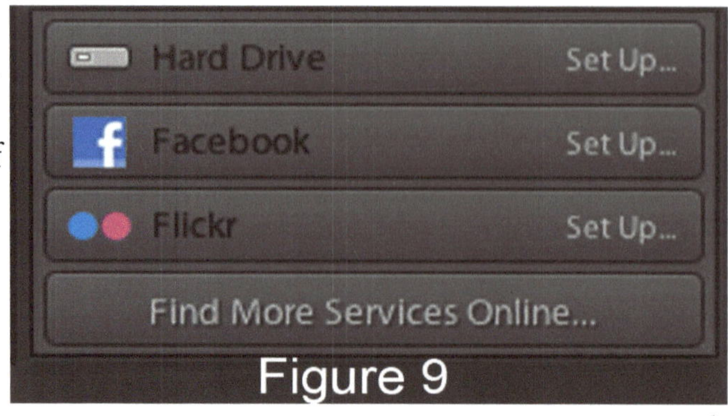

Figure 9

The final panel in the left side column is the Publish panel (Figure 9). Here you can place images to be uploaded to file sharing sites such as Facebook®, Smugmug® and Flickr®. You can also move images to one of your hard drives. To use the Publish Services, do the following:

- ► Set up your file sharing account in Lightroom®, choose Flickr® for example (Figure 10).
- ► Choose to rename your images or use your file name.
- ► Resize your image to 72 dpi and 500 to 700 pixels on the longest side.
- ► Set the output sharpening for "Screen".
- ► Minimize the Metadata.
- ► Put a watermark on your image if you want to do that.
- ► Select your privacy settings.

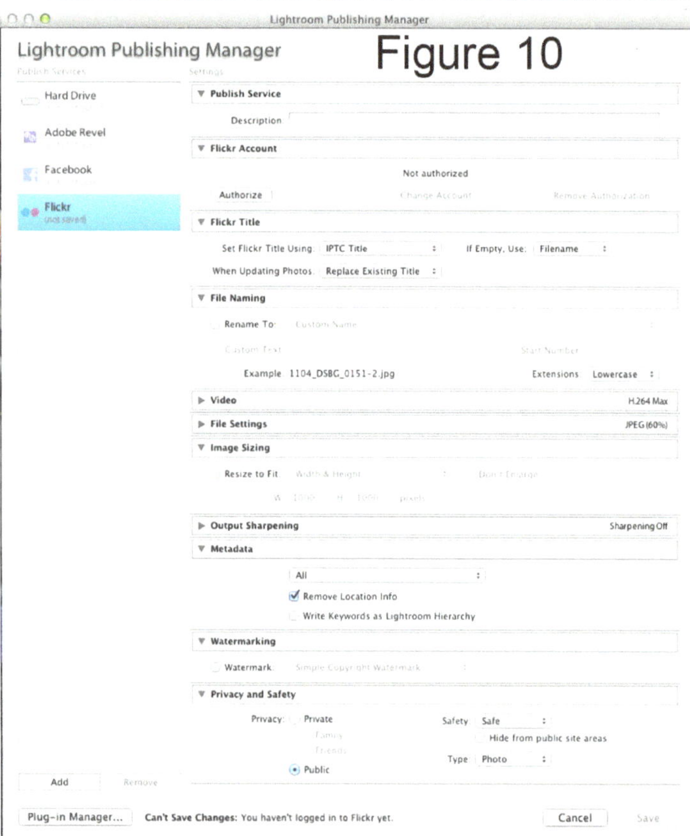

Figure 10

Once you have your file sharing account set up, The name you have chosen for your photostream will show up next to the name of the file sharing site. (Figure 11) Do the following to upload images to the file sharing site:

- ► Sign in to your account.
- ► Drag the images you want to publish to the photostream (Yellow arrow, Figure 11).
- ► Click with the cursor on the Photostream and then on the "Publish" button at the top right of the screen.

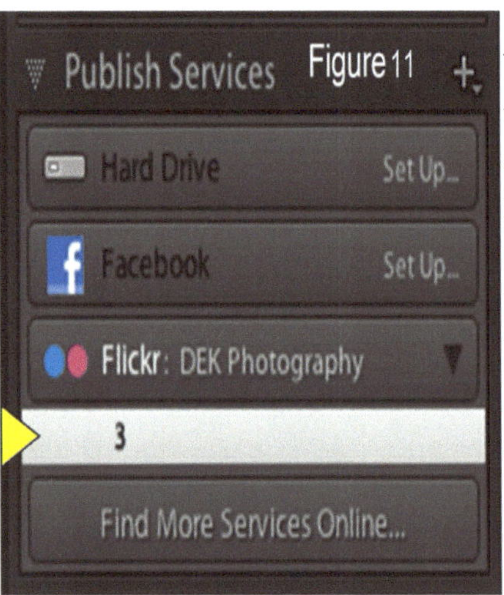

Figure 11

You only have to set up your account and indicate sizes, etc. one time. After the setup, you only have to drag your images to the Photostream. You can drag as many images as you like to the Photostream, Lightroom® will keep them ready until you are ready to publish them. Selecting "Publish" will cause all the images in the Photostream to be uploaded to the photo sharing site. The next time you go into the Publish Services, Lightroom® will indicate which images are published at the top of the screen. Also, if some one posts a comment about one of your images, that comment will appear in Lightroom® on the bottom right of the screen under the Comments panel.

Finally, at the bottom of the left column are two buttons, one is for importing your images into Lightroom® and the other for exporting your images. Importing and exporting images will be discussed in another section.

## The Toolbar

Below the image window is the Toolbar. In the Toolbar are several icons for the different image views, classifying images, adjusting magnification of the images, rotating images, flagging images, rating images, labeling images and showing an impromptu slide show. The icons that you can choose to show in the Tool Bar are as follows:

- View modes, Grid, Loupe, Compare, Survey that have already been discussed.
- The Painter tool (Blue circle, Figure 12) for placing information on your images (Grid view only).

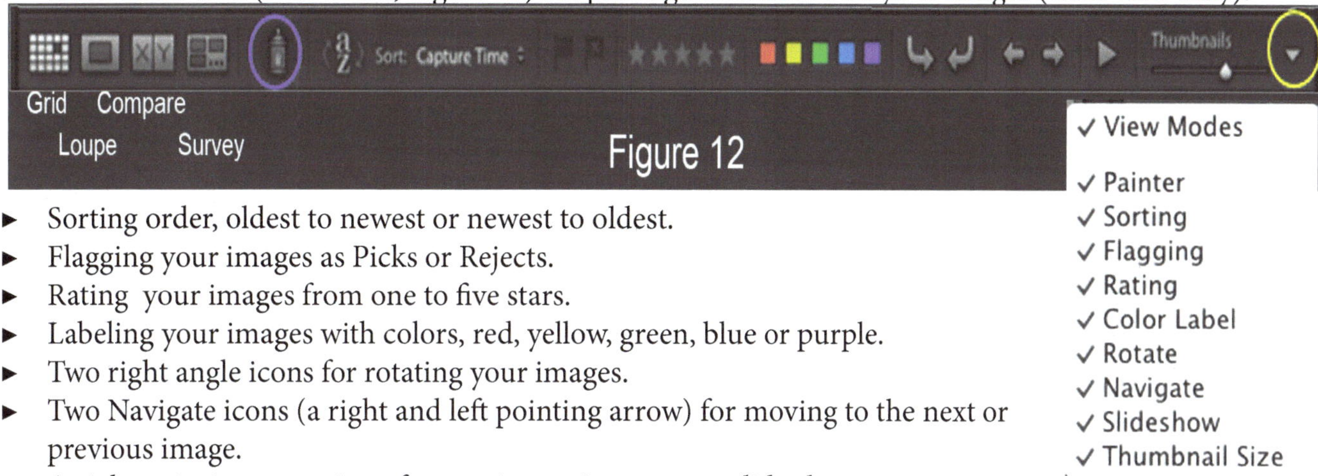


Figure 12

- Sorting order, oldest to newest or newest to oldest.
- Flagging your images as Picks or Rejects.
- Rating your images from one to five stars.
- Labeling your images with colors, red, yellow, green, blue or purple.
- Two right angle icons for rotating your images.
- Two Navigate icons (a right and left pointing arrow) for moving to the next or previous image.
- A right pointing arrow icon for starting an impromptu slide show.
- A zoom slider for increasing or decreasing the size of thumbnails on the screen in Grid view.

Not all of these icons may be visible in the Tool Bar when you open Lightroom®. To either add or remove one of these icons, do the following:

- Click with the cursor on the down pointing arrow at the right side of the Tool Bar (Yellow circle, Figure 12).
- A pop up menu will appear with all the icons available in the Toolbar will appear (Figure 12).
- Select the name of the icon you want to add to the Tool Bar.
- Place a check mark in front of the name of the icon by clicking on the name with the cursor.
- Select the name of any icon with a check mark in front of it, the check will disappear and the icon will be removed from the Toolbar.

Depending on how big your screen is, you may not have room for all the icons on the Tool Bar. Select only the ones you use most often to show on the Toolbar. How to use these icons will be discussed in different sections where their use is needed.

TIP: Some of the icons on the toolbar can be eliminated by using keyboard shortcuts instead. For example, you can remove the zoom slider that increases or decreases the size of the thumbnails from the Toolbar and use the equal key (=) to increase the size of the thumbnails or the minus key (-) to decrease the size of the thumbnails. You can eliminate the Navigation arrows by using the left and right arrow keys on the keyboard. There are keyboard shortcuts for the flag ratings, the P key for a Pick, the X key for a Reject and the U key for an unflagged image, star ratings, the 1 through 5 keys and four of the color labels (red, yellow green, and blues), the 6 through 9 keys

TIP: The Painter Tool (Blue Circle, Figure 12) is one of the most versatile tools in Lightroom®. It is only present in the Toolbar in the Library Module Grid view. To activate the Painter Tool, do one of the following:

- Click with the cursor on the Painter Tool icon on the Toolbar.

- Use the Keyboard shortcut, Option, Command K (Macintosh), Alt, Control K (PC).
- From the Metadata drop down menu at the top of the page, select "Enable Painting".

Once the Painter Tool is active, a double pointed arrow will appear to the right of the tool in the Toolbar. If you click with the cursor on this double pointed arrow a drop down menu will appear from which you can choose what you want painted on an image. The choices are, keywords, labels, flags, ratings, metadata and settings. You can also choose to rotate an image or place it in the Quick Collection. To use the Painter Tool, do the following:

- Select the image or images on which you want to paint.
- Activate the Painter tool.
- From the drop down menu choose what you want to paint on the image or images.
- When you hover the cursor over a selected image the cursor will turn into the Painter Tool.
- Hover the Painter Tool cursor over the image or one of the selected images.
- Press the cursor once and the attribute you chose will be on all of the selected images.
- To remove the attribute, hover the Painter Tool cursor over the image a second time.
- Hold down the Option (Macintosh), Alt (PC) key and the Painter Tool cursor turns into an eraser.
- Press the cursor and the previously painted attribute will be removed from the selected image.

## The Filmstrip

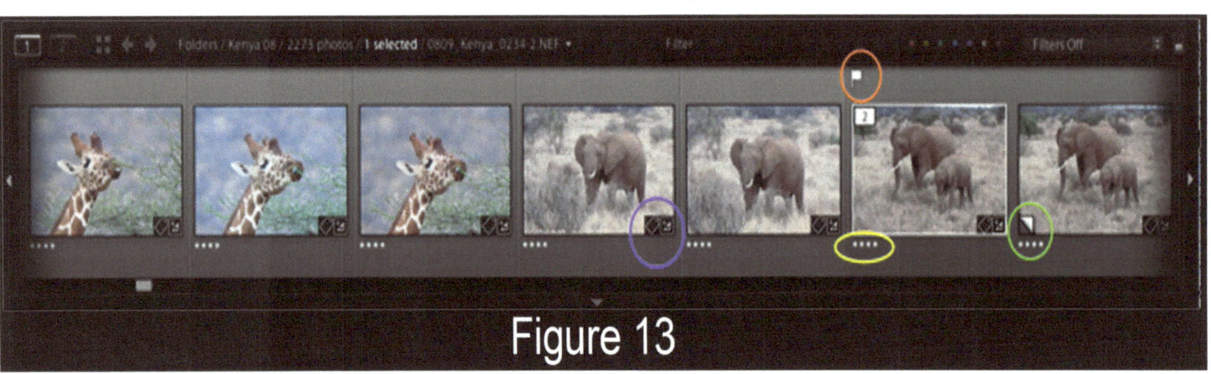
Figure 13

At the bottom of the screen is the Filmstrip. (Figure 13) It contains all the images in the current folder or collection on which you're working as well as any images you've edited in an external editing program such as Photoshop.

The following can be shown on images in the Filmstrip:

- Flags (Red Circle, Figure 13).
- Rating stars (Yellow Ellipse, Figure 13).
- Color labels.
- Badges indicating the image has Keywords attached (Blue Circle, Figure 13).
- Badges indicating the image has been edited in Lightroom®.
- Badges indicating the image has GPS coordinates in the Metadata.
- Images edited in an external editing program and saved back to Lightroom.
- Virtual Copies (Green Circle, Figure 13).

In order to have Lightroom® show the above in the Filmstrip, you have to go into Lightroom® preferences which are found by clicking with the cursor on the word Lightroom® at the top left of the screen on the Macintosh or the Edit menu on the PC. Choose the Interface preferences and make sure that the items you want to show in the images in the Filmstrip are checked. You can also have the images in the Filmstrip show in the Navigator window on mouse over

The images edited in an external editing program and saved back to Lightroom will, by default, have "-Edit. tiff" attached at the end of the file name and will be stacked next to the original. They will no longer be RAW files. In addition, any files of which you've made virtual copies (more on this later) will also be in the Filmstrip next to the original.
At the top of the Filmstrip, there is a black bar which has several useful items, they are as follows in order from left to right:

- Icons, labeled 1 and 2 for using two screens or monitors.
- An icon that will take you back to the Grid mode of the Library Module.
- A backward pointing arrow, clicking on which will take you to the previous panel, module or folder in which you were working.
- A forward pointing arrow, clicking on which will take you back to the panel, module or folder you just left.
- Text which tells you the name of the folder/collection in which you are working.
- Text telling you how many images are in that folder/collection.
- Text telling you the filename of the image on which you are currently working.

At the end of the filename of the image on which you are working you will find a down pointing arrow. Clicking on this arrow will bring up a drop down menu that allows you to do any of the following:

- See all the images in your catalog in the Grid mode of the Library module.
- Go to the Quick Collection in the Library Module.
- See the images from the last import.
- Go to any of the recent folders or collections (resources) on which you've worked.
- Add images to your Favorites.
- Clear all your recent sources (Folders or Collections).

When you are in another module, this feature makes it very easy to switch folders while remaining in the current module without having to go back into the Library Module.

On the right side of this same bar above the Filmstrip is a same filter bar as the one in the Library Filter Bar (More on this later). By clicking on the down pointing arrow you can choose what you want shown in the filmstrip, badges, rating, and labels. When you choose any one of these selections, Lightroom® will show all the images in the filmstrip that meet the criteria you've selected. For example, if you select "Flagged" from the drop down menu, only those images that you've flagged as picks or rejects will appear in the filmstrip. If you select "Filters Off" from the drop down menu all of the images in the current folder or collection will appear in the filmstrip. Selecting camera info, default columns, exposure info, will not make any visible change in the filmstrip. However, if you hover the cursor over an image in the filmstrip, the exposure info and camera info will appear.

## The Right Side Panels

To the right of the Image Window is another column of six panels, they are:

- The Histogram Panel
- The Quick Develop panel
- The Keywording panel
- The Keyword List panel
- The Metadata panel
- The Comments panel

## The Histogram

In the Library Module, the Histogram (Figure 14)simply gives you information about the selected image. The Histogram shows you the distribution of the tones in the image and tells you if there is any loss of detail in either the highlights or the shadows. The highlights are on the right side of the Histogram and the shadows are on the left side. As long as the histogram is not climbing the wall on either the right or left side as if it's trying to escape the frame, you know you have all the details in both the highlights and shadows. If the histogram is climbing the wall on the right side, you know you have lost detail in the highlights, climbing the wall on the left sides means loss of detail in the shadows. This is called clipping and it may or may not be important, depending on where the clipping is located in the image.

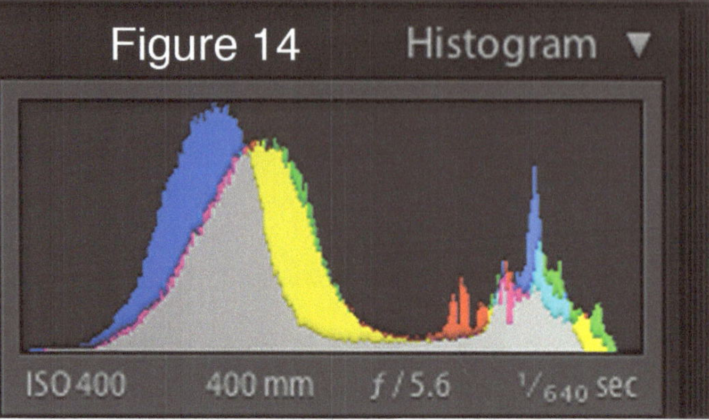


Below the Histogram image is a bar that tells you the ISO sensitivity, the focal length of the lens used to create the image, the aperture opening of the lens and the shutter speed.

## The Quick Develop Panel

The next panel down below the Histogram is the Quick Develop panel (Figure 15). This panel allows you to make quick changes in your image without going to the Develop Module. The things you can accomplish in the Quick Develop panel are as follows:

- Apply any of the Saved Presets (more on saved presets later). Default or user created develop presets that are available in the Lightroom® Presets panel in the Develop module.
- Change the white balance.
- Apply an Auto Tone Correction which is what Lightroom® feels is the right exposure for the image.
- Change any of the effects in the Tone Control section of the Quick Develop panel, the Exposure, Contrast, Highlights, Shadows, Whites, Blacks, Clarity or Vibrance of the image.

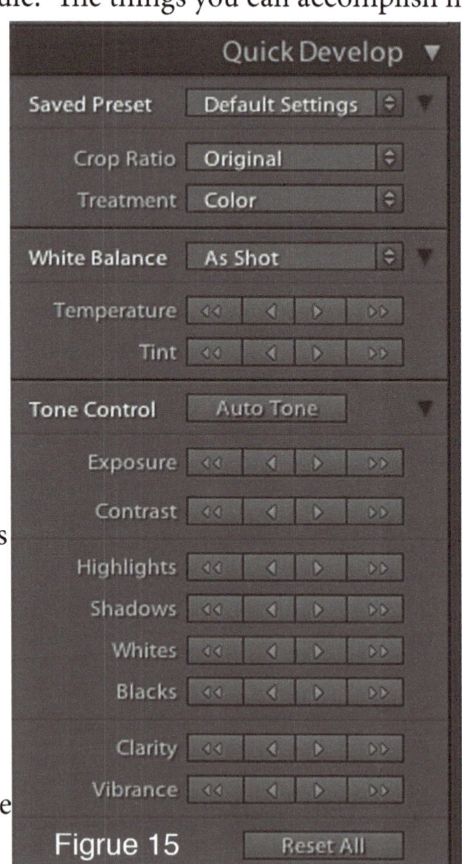


To change any of the effects in the Tone Control section of the Quick Develop panel, do the following:

- Click with the cursor on either the single or double pointed arrows in the bars next to the name of the effect you want to change.
- Clicking with the cursor on the single pointed arrow makes a change in the exposure of one third of a stop.
- Clicking with the cursor on the double pointed arrow makes a change in the exposure of one full stop.
- With the Exposure effect, clicking on the right pointing arrows lightens the image. Clicking on the left pointed arrows darkens the image.

- Clicking with the cursor on the single pointed arrow will make a 5% change in any of the other effects in the Tone Control section of the Quick Develop panel.
- Clicking with the cursor on the double pointed arrow will make a 20% change in any of the other effects in the Tone Control section of the Quick Develop panel.
-

With any of the effects, clicking on the right pointing arrows increases the effect, clicking on the left pointing arrows decreases the effect.

I believe there are much better, more accurate and quicker ways to edit an image in the Develop module of Lightroom®. For that reason, I never use the Quick Develop panel to edit an image. The only time I would use the Quick Develop panel is when I'm making a presentation to a group using their projector and my images appear too dark or too light on the screen. In that case, I can go to the Edit menu at the top left of the screen, choose "Select All" from the drop down menu and use the Exposure buttons in the Quick Develop panel to lighten or darken all my images for the presentation.

However, the Quick Develop panel allows you to make changes in video you've imported into Lightroom® and this will be discussed when we get to the section on video.

## The Keywording Panel

The Keywording panel is one of the most important in the Library Module. By embedding keywords in your images they will be easier for you to find. Also, if you keyword your images correctly in detail and put them up on the web, there is a greater chance stock photography companies and advertising agencies will also find them.

## The Keyword List Panel

One of the things that Lightroom® does that makes it easy to apply keywords to your images is to keep a list of every keyword you have applied to any image. When you go to apply keywords to a new image, Lightroom® will suggest keywords from the list. Lightroom® will base the keyword suggestions from the list when you apply the first keyword. Keywords from other images with the same keyword you apply will be automatically suggested.

## The Metadata Panel

As soon as you press the shutter release button on your camera down to create your image, metadata called EXIF metadata is embedded in your image by your camera. EXIF metadata consists of the following:

- The Camera brand, model and serial number.
- The Exposure setting (shutter speed and Aperture), ISO Sensitivity setting.
- The size of the file in pixels.
- Whether the flash fired.
- Any exposure compensation.
- The exposure mode (manual, aperture priority, shutter priority, Program).
- Metering mode (Spot, center weighted, matrix/evaluative).
- Lens and focal length used.
- The date and time the image was taken.
- The version of the camera firmware.
- GPS coordinates if your camera is GPS equipped.

When you import your image into Lightroom®, the filename, type of file (RAW, JPEG, tiff), folder name, file size, and metadata status are added to the metadata by Lightroom®.

To this metadata you can add other metadata such as your copyright, contact information and information about the image. The easiest way to do this is to create a metadata template that can be applied during import or added after import. Discussion of creating a metadata template will come later.

### The Comments Panel

If you publish your images to a file sharing site such as Facebook®, Flickr®k, etc. You can set up Lightroom® to receive comments from people who view your images online. The comments will automatically show up in Lightroom® if any one leaves a comment for you on the file sharing site. You can also use this panel to place your own comments about your image on the file sharing site.

## Getting Started

Now that you know where every thing is on the screen, it's time to get started using Lightroom®. The first thing to do is make sure you have an understanding of how Lightroom® manages your images.

### The Catalog

Everyone is anxious to get started importing images into Lightroom® so they can see them and start developing them. However, there are a few decisions to make and a preset and template to set up before you start importing. The first decision is how you want your images stored. By default, Lightroom® comes with a catalog called Lightroom® 4 Catalog.Ircat. If you plan to use only one catalog, this will be fine. What you need to decide is if you want to use only one catalog. The advantages and disadvantages of working with only one catalog have already been discussed as has where to locate your Catalog.

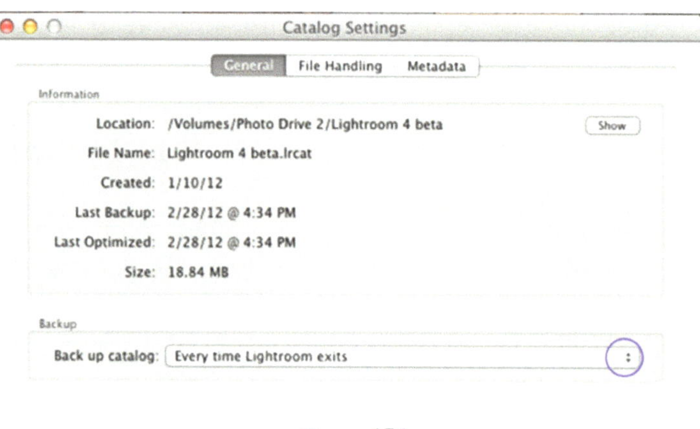

Figure 15A

Once you have made the decision about how many catalogs you want and where you want them on your computer, go to Catalog settings. To find Catalog Settings, click with the cursor on the word Lightroom® (Macintosh) or the Edit menu (PC) and from the drop down menu select Catalog Settings. This will bring up the Catalog Settings dialog box. (Figure 15A) There are three Catalog settings, General, File Handling and Metadata. The General settings are mostly informational. They tell you the name of your catalog, where it is located on your computer, the date it was created, the size of the catalog and when the last time it was backed up and optimized. The box at the bottom of General settings is very important. It is where you determine how often you want the catalog backed up. Click with the cursor on the double pointed arrow at the left of the "Back up catalog" blank (Blue circle, Figure 15A)and from the drop down menu choose how often you want to back up your catalog. If you do a lot of developing images, it's probably a good idea to back up your catalog every time Lightroom® closes. There is less chance of losing your work that way.

In the File Handling section of Catalog Settings, there is only one decision to make and that is how often Lightroom® discards one to one previews. To explain, when images are first imported into Lightroom®, they come in as JPEG and are converted to RAW images after import, unless you tell Lightroom® to import them as one to one images (more on this in the Import section). One to one images take up a lot of room on a hard drive and to save room on the hard drive it is a good idea to let Lightroom discard the one to one images and keep the JPEG thumbnails which will be turned back into RAW images when brought up on screen in the Develop module. The default setting for discarding one to one files is 30 days. This can be changed if you feel you'll be working on the images more than 30 days. The default settings for the other choices under the File Handling section of Catalog Settings are fine.

The final section of Catalog Settings deals with metadata which will be important when looking for images. I believe it is very important to have all the metadata possible included with your files in Lightroom®. So place checks in all of the first three choices regarding writing metadata to the images. I'm not sure that it is important to know the date and time I made changes to an image, so I don't have the last check box turned on. It may not be that important to have all the metadata in the image when you export images, but more on that later.

Finally, it goes without saying that you should back up your computer and all your external hard drives on a regular basis. Not only do computer hard drives fail, external hard drives also fail.

## The Folders Panel

The second panel on the left side of the image window is the Folders panel. This is where Lightroom® keeps track of all the images you have imported into Lightroom®. The confusing thing to a lot of people is understanding that your images are not really in Lightroom® as you think of them being in Photoshop® when you open an image on which you want to work. When you import images into Lightroom®, you put them into a folder on one of your hard drives. By importing them into Lightroom®, Lightroom® knows where they are and keeps a list of the folder locations on the left side of the image window in the Folders panel. When you open a folder by clicking on the name of the folder with the cursor, Lightroom® shows you all the images in that folder. In the Library module, you can organize or classify your images with flags, star ratings, labels or keyword them from either the Grid or Loupe views or from the Filmstrip (more on this process shortly). What you are really doing is giving Lightroom® a set of instructions that Lightroom® stores for you in Lightroom®. If you close Lightroom® or move to another folder, you don't have to save anything, Lightroom® has already saved the instructions for you and the next time you open the folder, the organization/classification, flags, ratings, etc. will still be there on the images.

Another neat thing about Lightroom® is that you don't have to have the hard drive on which your images are located attached to Lightroom® to be able to organize or classify your images, you can apply flags, ratings, etc. to the images. If the hard drive isn't connected to Lightroom®, it will still be listed in the left panel, but grayed out and with a question mark in the header bar. Lightroom will still show you the images in all the folders of the not connected hard drive and you can still apply flags, ratings, etc. and even organize them into collections, but you will not be able to take them to the Develop module to work on them. When you attach the missing external hard drive to your computer, Lightroom® will know they are back.

You can also move folders from one hard drive to another and you should always do that from within Lightroom®. If you move a folder from one hard drive to another by navigating to the folder you want to move and then moving it to another hard drive outside Lightroom®, you will have broken the connection for that folder in Lightroom® and Lightroom® will not know where that folder is now located. To move a folder from one hard drive to another inside Lightroom®, do the following:

- ► In the Library module, select the folder you want to move and highlight it by clicking on it with the cursor.
- ► Drag the folder to the new location on another hard drive.
- ► A warning message will appear telling you that if you make this move it cannot be undone.
- ► While it sounds pretty scary, ignore this message, the move can be undone by simply dragging the folder back to its original location.

If you have moved folders from outside Lightroom®, do the following to find your images:

- ► Hold down the Control key and click with the cursor on the name of the missing folder (Macintosh), Right click with the cursor on the missing folder (PC).
- ► From the pop up menu select "Find Missing Folder.
- ► The Finder (Macintosh), Explorer (PC) window will appear on screen.
- ► Navigate to the location of the missing folder.
- ► Click with the cursor on the missing folder to highlight it.
- ► Click with the cursor on the Choose button at the bottom right of the dialog box.
- ► Lightroom® will re-establish the connection to the missing folder.

# Before You Import Images

## Creating a Filename Template

Before you start importing your images, there are a couple of things that you should do. The first of these is to create a filenaming template. There are two places to create a Filename Template in Lightroom®. The first is in the Rename Photos section of the Library menu and the second is in the File Renaming section of the Import dialog box . To create a file naming template from either the Library menu or the Import Dialog box, do the following:

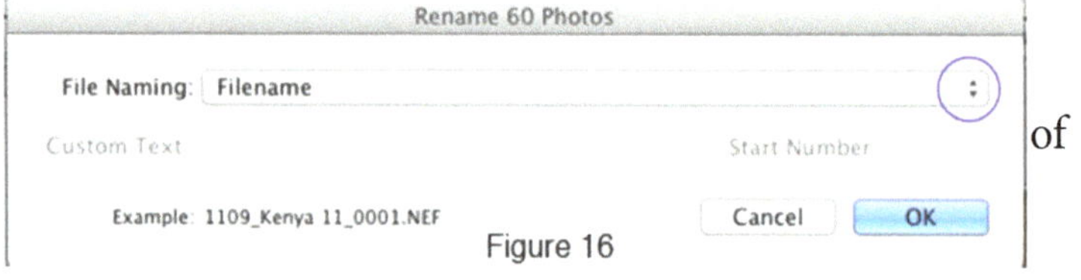

Figure 16

- ► From the Library drop down menu select "Rename Photos...".
- ► In the dialog box that comes up, click with the cursor on the double pointed arrow at the end of the File Naming blank (Blue Circle, Figure 16).
- ► From the menu that appears, select the last choice, "Edit...".
- ► Alternatively, from the File Renaming section in the Import Dialog box, (you'll see this shortly in the Importing discussion) place a check mark in the Rename files box at the top of the section by clicking in the box with the cursor.
- ► Click with the cursor on the double pointed arrow at the right side of the Template blank.
- ► From the drop down menu that appears, select "Edit".
- ► With either of these methods, the Filename Template Editor box will appear on the screen (Figure 17).
- ► Create your own filename using the choices in the different sections of the Filename Template Editor.

TIP: The Filename Template Editor has multiple Filename presets from which you can choose. You can see them by clicking on the double pointed arrow at the end of the Presets blank at the top of the Filename Template Editor. The next box down is a blank box where your filename will appear. Below the blank box are four sections; Image Name, Sequence and Date, Metadata and Custom. Each section has two choices with double pointed arrows at the end of the blank for each choice, followed by a button that says "Insert".

Clicking on the double pointed arrow at the end of one of the blanks will give you choices of what you can have in your filename. All you have to do is make a choice and click with the cursor on the Insert button at the end of the line and your choice will appear in the blank box. You can use any combination of the choices from all the boxes.

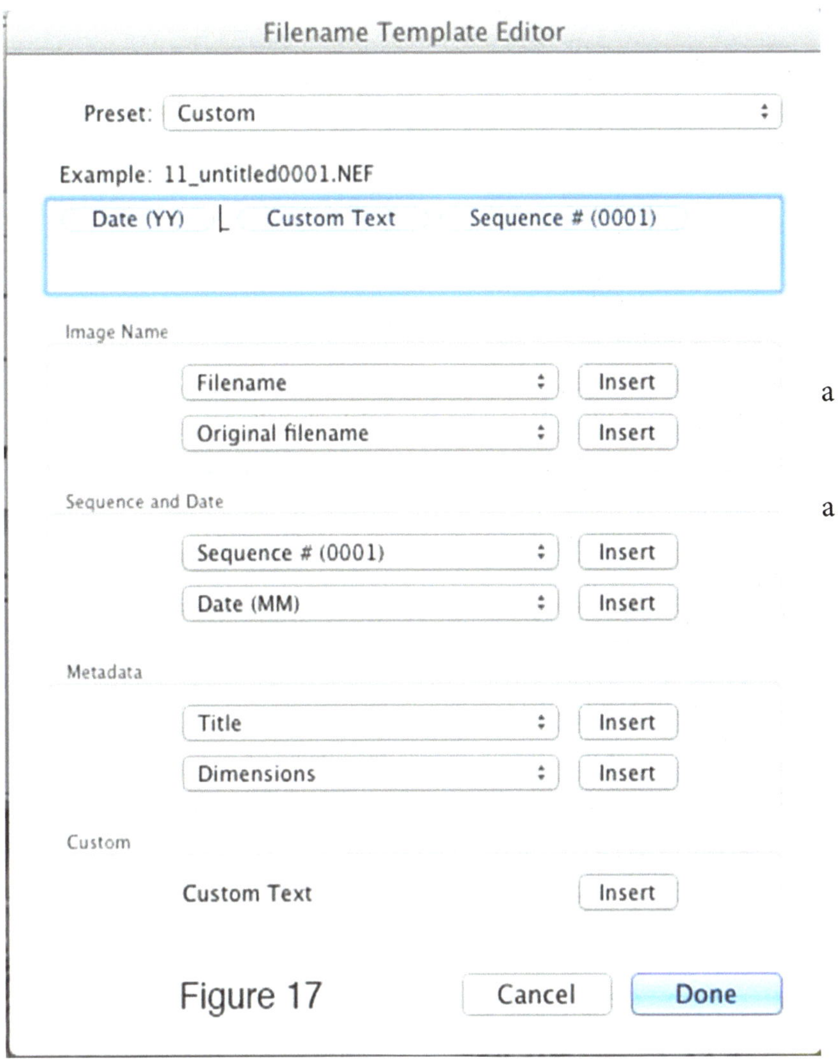

The following is an example of creating custom filename:

- Start by choosing a date in the Sequence and Date section, such as year.
- From the Date choices in the drop down menu, choose a two digit year (YY.)
- Click with the cursor on the Insert button at the end of the Sequence and Date section.
- In the blank box "Date (YY)" will appear in the Example blank of the Filename Template Editor dialog box.
- Place an underscore (_) next "Date (YY)_".
- From the bottom section, Custom Text, click with the cursor on the Insert box "Date (YY)_ Custom Text"
- Place another underscore (_) after the Custom Text "Date (YY)_Custom Text_" will now appear in the Example box in the Filename Template Editor dialog box.
- From the Sequence section insert a four digit sequence (0001) "Date(YY)_Custom Text_Sequence#0001" will now appear in the Filename Template Editor dialog box.
- Press the Insert button at the end of the Sequence line.
- The Custom Filename Template will appear in the Example blank of the Filename Template Editor dialog box. (Figure 17)
- An example of your custom File Name will be shown above the blank box.
- Click the double pointed arrow at the end of the Presets blank at the top of the Filenaming Template Editor. (Blue circle, Figure 17)
- From the drop down menu select "Save Current Settings as a New Preset".
- Give the new Filename Template a name in the New Preset dialog box that pops up on screen
- Click with the cursor on the Create button at the bottom right of the New Preset dialog box.
- Click with the cursor on the Done button at the bottom right of the Filenaming Template Editor.

Figure 17

Your new filename will now be available for renaming images during and after import. When importing images, click with the cursor in the box at the top of the Rename images section of the Import Dialog box and then click with the cursor on the double pointed arrow at the right side of the Template blank. The custom Filename Template will be listed along with the Lightroom® filename templates. Choose your custom filename and fill in the Custom Text section. (More on this in the Import discussion) To rename images after the images have been imported into Lightroom®, do the following:

- Select the images you want to rename or if you want to rename all the images in a folder, choose "Select All" from the Edit drop down menu or use the keyboard shortcut, hold down the Command (Macintosh), Control (PC) key and press the A key on the Keyboard.
- Open the Library menu at the top of the screen and from the drop down menu that appears, choose "Rename Photos".
- A Rename Photos dialog box will appear on screen and at the top of the box Lightroom® will tell you how many photos are to be renamed (Figure 16).
- Click with the cursor on the double pointed arrow on the right side of the File Naming blank (Blue circle, Figure 16).
- From the drop down menu choose your custom Filename Template.
- Enter the appropriate text in the Custom Text blank.
- Place the Start Number you wish Lightroom® to use when renaming the images.
- A progress bar will appear at the top left of the screen and move left to right as the images are renamed.

## Creating a Metadata Preset

The next task you should do before importing your images is create a metadata preset which can be applied to your images during import or after import. There are two places in the Library module you can create a metadata preset, from the Metadata menu at the top of the page and under the "Apply During Import" section of the Import window. To create a metadata preset do the following:

- From the Metadata menu drop down list, select "Edit Metadata Presets"(Figure 18) OR,
- From the "Apply During Import" panel of the Import dialog box, in the Metadata section, click on the double pointed arrow next to the word Metadata and select either "New" or "Edit Presets" from the drop down menu (Yellow circle, Figure 19).
- With either of these choices, the Edit Presets dialog box or the New Presets dialog box will appear, these two boxes are identical (Figure 20).
- Place a check mark in the box titled "IPTC Copyright" and a check mark in the box titled "IPTC Creator".
- Fill out the blanks in the section titled "IPTC Copyright" to embed your copyright in the image metadata.
- Fill out the blanks in the section titled "IPTC Creator" to embed your contact information in the image metadata.

Metadata View Window Help
Set Keyword Shortcut... ⌥⇧⌘K
Toggle Shortcut Keyword ⇧K
Enable Painting ⌥⌘K
Keyword Set ▶
Color Label Set ▶
Show Metadata for Target Photo Only
Copy Metadata... ⌥⇧⌘C
Paste Metadata ⌥⇧⌘V
Sync Metadata...
Enable Auto Sync ⌥⇧⌘A
**Edit Metadata Presets...**
Edit Capture Time...
Revert Capture Time to Original
Save Metadata to Files ⌘S
Read Metadata from Files
Update DNG Previews & Metadata
Import Keywords...
Export Keywords...
Purge Unused Keywords

Figure 18

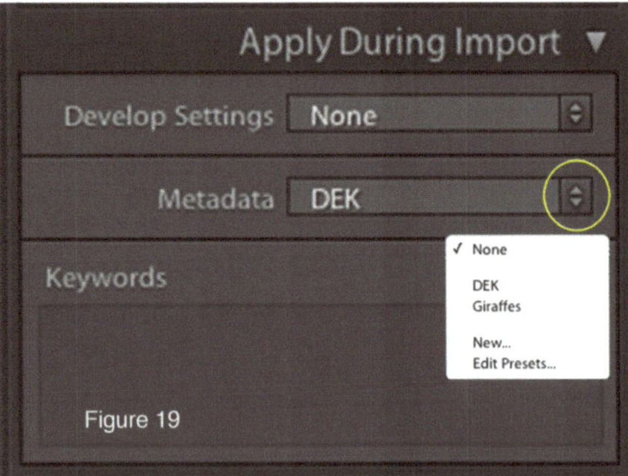

Figure 19

- Click on the double pointed arrow next to the word "Custom at the top of the page and select "Save Current Settings as a New Preset.
- Name the new preset and click with the cursor on the word "Done" at the bottom right of the dialog box.
- Your new metadata preset will now be available to apply during import or add later to your images.

TIP: All of the other panels in the Edit Presets or New Preset dialog box pertain to individual images. If you want to add the information into the metadata at a later time, select the image and choose "Edit Metadata Presets" from the Metadata drop down menu and you'll be able to fill out the other panels for the image you have selected. Adding things like a title and/or caption will be important in the output modules, the Book, Slideshow, Print and Web modules. Other things that you might want to add to metadata later are keywords or a description of the image, etc.

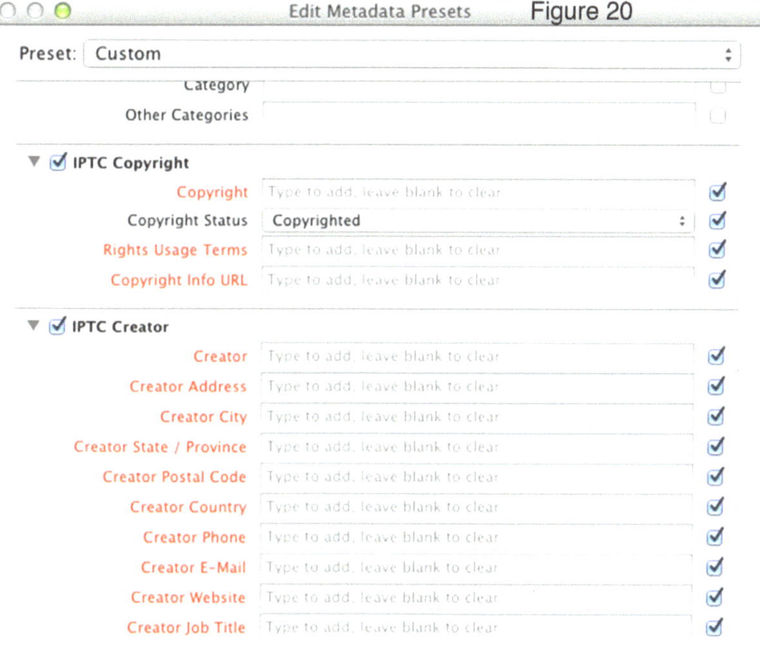

Figure 20

TIP: When filling out the IPTC Creator panel in the Edit or New Metadata Preset dialog box, it is probably best not to add your phone number. If some one on another continent discovers your image and wants to talk to you about it, and if there is a seven hour time difference between where you are and where they are it might not be a convenient time to talk, especially if it's in the middle of the night where you are.

# Importing Images

You can import images into Lightroom® from anywhere on your computer or from a memory card in a card reader or in your camera. By default, Lightroom® opens the Import Dialog screen when it detects a memory card in a card reader. (Figure 21) You can turn this feature off by going to the Lightroom® Preferences under the word Lightroom® on the Macintosh or under the Edit menu on a PC. In the General Preferences you will find a box that says "Show import dialog when a memory card is detected". If you uncheck the box in front of this choice, Lightroom® will not automatically open the Import Dialog when a memory card is detected. With the box unchecked or if you want to import images from your hard drive or an external hard

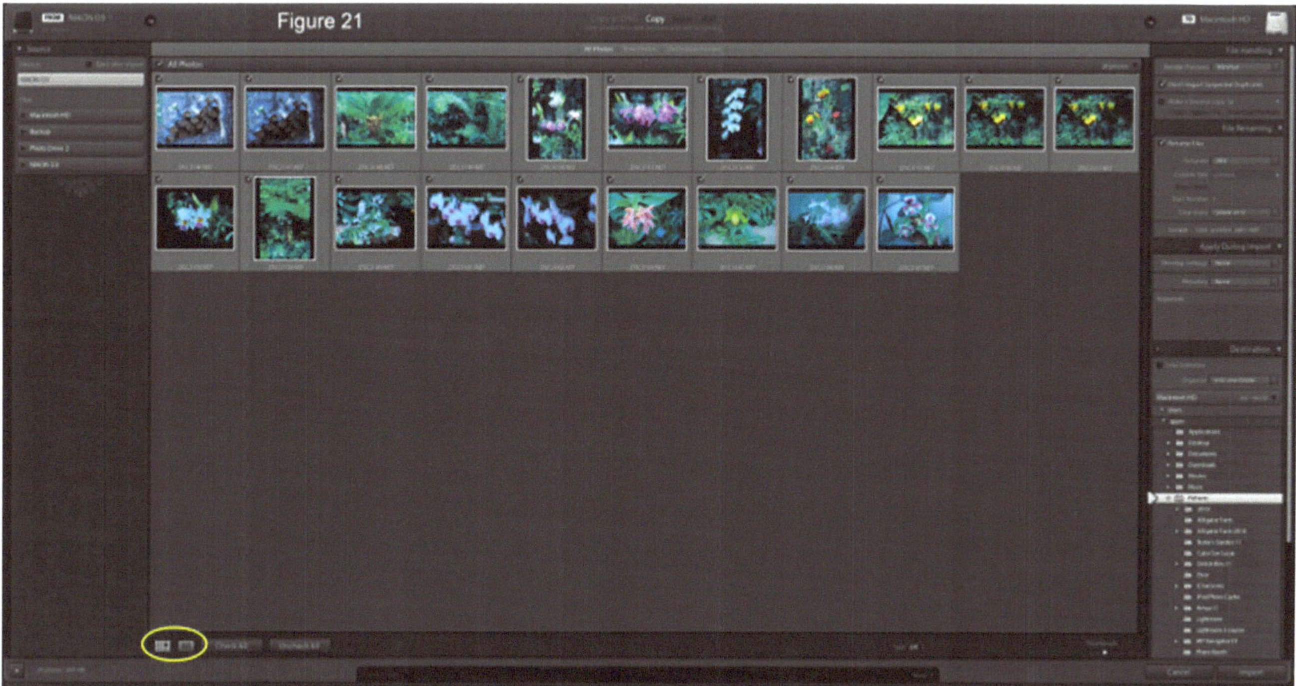
Figure 21

drive there are several ways to open the Import dialog screen. To open the Import Dialog Screen, do one of the following:

- Under the File Menus select Import Photos.
- Use the Keyboard shortcut, hold down the Shift and Command keys (Macintosh), Shift and Control keys (PC) and press the I key on the keyboard.
- Click with the cursor on the Import button at the bottom left of the page.
- Simply drag the folder into Lightroom and the Import dialog box will automatically open.

With the Import Dialog screen open (Figure 21) the first thing you must do is select a source for the images you want to import. At the top left of the Import dialog box you will see "Select a Source" with a double pointed arrow next to it. Clicking with the cursor on this double pointed arrow will give you a drop down menu with two sections, Files and Recent. (Figure 22) Under the Files section will be listed Desktop, Pictures (if you have a file named pictures), Movies and Other Source. If you choose Desktop or Pictures, Lightroom® will show you on the Import dialog screen, all the images from those two places that can be imported into Lightroom®. If you choose "Other Source", Lightroom® will bring up a dialog box that shows you all the places on your computer from which you can import images.

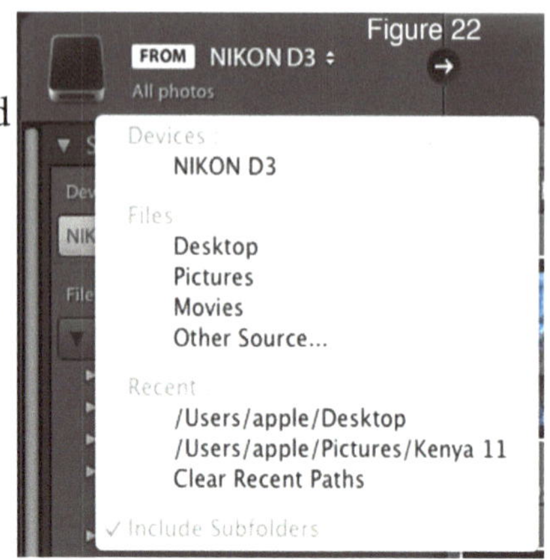

Figure 22

In the column on the left side of the screen in the Import Dialog Box, under the heading "Source", Lightroom® lists all the folders on your computer's hard drive or any external hard drive where files exist that have already imported into Lightroom®.

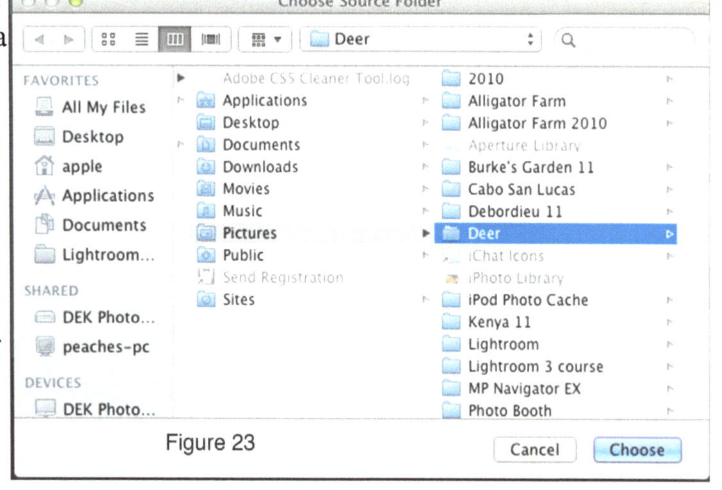

Figure 23

Clicking with the cursor on "Other Source" at the top left of the Import dialog screen will bring up a pop up menu (Figure 23) in which you can navigate to your images on the computer's hard drive or an external hard drive or on a memory card in a card reader (if you have turned off the default that allows Lightroom® to automatically open the Import dialog box when it detects a memory card) and select the images you want to import into Lightroom®. The selected images will appear in the center of the screen as thumbnails in the Import Dialog screen. (Figure 21) Each thumbnail will have a checkbox in the upper left corner indicating it will be imported. If you do not want to import all the images you can uncheck any that you don't want to import. If you are not sure about an image, at the bottom left of the screen are two icons, one is for the Grid view and the other is for the Loupe view. (Yellow ellipse, Figure 21) You can select the image you are not sure you want to import by clicking on it with the cursor and then click with the cursor on the Loupe view icon at the bottom of the screen to bring it up full screen. You can also use the keyboard shortcut, the E key, to bring the image up full screen in the Loupe view and the G key to go back to the Grid View in the Import Dialog screen. Make your decision about importing the image and either uncheck the box or leave it checked. If you only want to import some of the images, do the following:

- Click with the cursor on the "Uncheck All" button at the bottom left of the Import dialog box.
- Click with the cursor on an image you want to import to highlight it.
- To select a group of adjacent images for import, hold down the Shift key and click with the cursor on

the last image of a group of adjacent images you want to import.

- To import a group of images that are not adjacent, hold down the Command (Macintosh), Control (PC) key and click on any images that are not adjacent images you want to import.
- With all the images you want to import selected, click with the cursor in the box at the top left of any of the selected images.
- A check mark will appear in the box at the top left of all the images you selected and they will be imported into Lightroom®.

Next, at the top, center of the Import Dialog Screen you have four choices for importing your images, they are:

- Copy as DNG which converts the images to Adobe®'s proprietary digital negative format, embeds the metadata into the file, moves it to the location you choose (more on this shortly) and adds the images to the Catalog.
- Copy, which copies the file to the designated location and adds the images to the Catalog
- Move, which moves the files from their current location on your computer to the designated location and adds them to the Catalog.
- Add, which adds the images to the catalog without moving them from their current location.

TIP: When you have images on a memory card, your only choice will be Copy photos to a new location and add to the Catalog.
TIP: The option to Move photos from one location to another is probably not a good choice. Should there be a power failure or some other event that could disrupt the moving of the images, you take a chance on losing them. There are much easier ways to move images in Lightroom®. If the images are on your computer, but not in Lightroom® choose "Copy to a New Location and Add to Catalog". The images will remain in their location, but will be added to a new location in Lightroom®. Once the images are safely in Lightroom, there will be two copies of them on your computer. You can then go back to the original location and delete the folder of images in that location to gain more room on your drive. If the images are on your computer, but not in Lightroom® and you want to leave them in their current location, then choose "Add to the Catalog". The images will remain in their location, but will be added to Lightroom®.

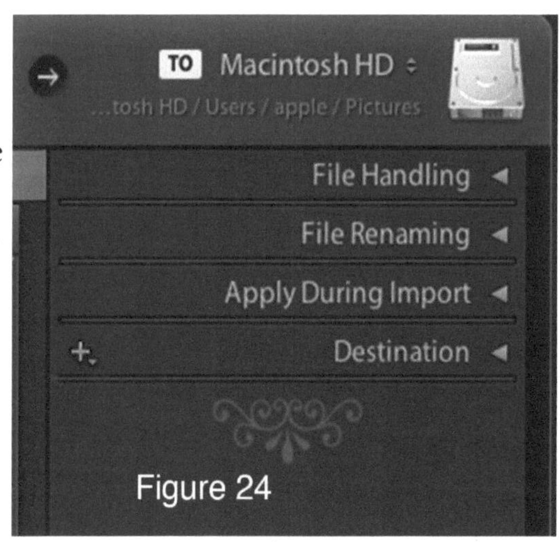

Figure 24

After you have selected the source of your images and decided how you want to import them, the next step is to decide where you want to put the images you are importing. At the top of the right column is the word "To" and to the right of that is listed the last place to which you imported images. (Figure 24) Usually it is the name of a drive and underneath the drive name is the path to the folder where you imported the images. To the right of the name of the hard drive is a double pointed arrow. Clicking with the cursor on this double pointed arrow gives you the choice of Desktop, Pictures, Movies and Other Destination. Choosing Other Destination will open up a dialog box listing all the places on your computer that you can put the images you are importing. If the images are to go into a new folder, then you need to navigate to the hard drive to which you would like to import your images. Selecting the hard drive will open up that drive with a list of all the folders on that drive. At the bottom left of this dialog box will be a button that says "New Folder". Clicking with the cursor on the New Folder button will open a New Folder dialog box asking you to name the folder and then create it. The new named folder will then show up in the list of folders on that drive. Make sure the new folder is highlighted in the list of folders in the Choose Destination dialog box and click with the cursor on the Choose button at the bottom right of the Choose Destination dialog box. The new destination for your images should now be listed at the top of the right column of panels.

If you already have a folder containing images that have been imported into Lightroom® and into which you want to import new images, that folder will be listed in the Destination panel (Figure 25), the bottom panel in the column of panels on the right side of the screen. In that case, all you need to do it open the Destination panel by clicking with the cursor on the header bar of the Destination panel and select the folder to which you want to import your images. Clicking with the cursor on the folder will highlight the folder and the name of the folder will be listed as the destination at the top of the right column of panels.

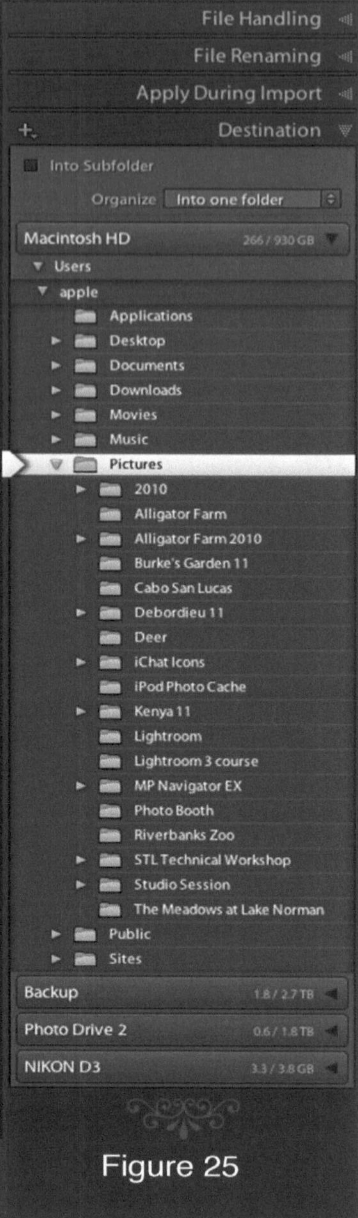

Figure 25

On the right side of the screen is a column containing four panels. In addition to the Destination panel at the bottom of the column, they are; File Handling, File Renaming and Apply During Import. Before going to the top three panels it is a good idea to open the Destination panel and make sure the folder to which you have chosen to import your images is highlighted. Next, open the File Handling panel. (Figure 26) The first choice to make in this panel is how to import the previews of your images. The choices are; Minimal, Embedded with Sidecar, Standard and 1:1. The fastest way to import your images into Lightroom® is to choose Minimal. If you don't mind waiting hours or days, depending on how many images need to be imported then, choose one of the other three choices. Importing your images in anything other than Minimal will also take up more room on your hard drive. When you choose minimal, the preview image you see in the Grid mode is a JPEG. When you bring the image up into the Loupe view or move it to the Develop module, the image will take a few seconds to load and come up as a RAW file and it will Fit the screen.

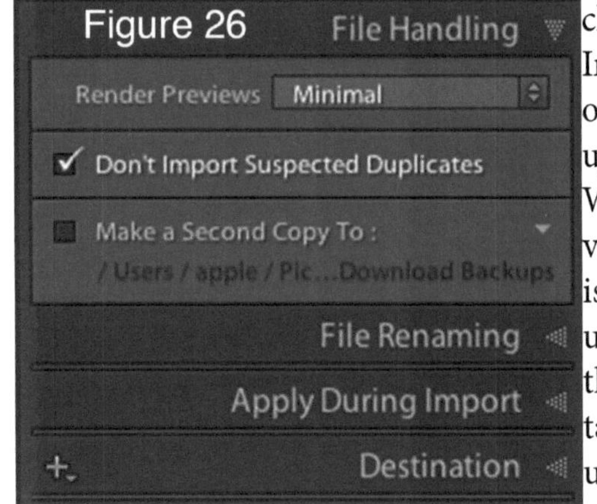

Figure 26

TIP: To save room on your hard drives, you can have Lightroom® discard the 1:1 previews after a certain amount of time. To do this, go to Catalog Settings, found in the drop down menu under the word Lightroom® on the Macintosh or in the drop down Edit menu on the PC. The File Handling section of the Catalog Settings dialog box gives you the option of deleting the 1:1 previews after so many days.

The second choice in the File Handling panel is "Don't Import Suspected Duplicates". If you place a check mark in the box by clicking in it with the cursor, any images on your card or in a folder you are importing from a hard drive will be grayed out in the Import dialog screen. If you leave the box unchecked then none of the images will be grayed out and Lightroom® will import any image checked in the Import dialog box.

The third choice in the File Handling panel is "Make a second copy to". This is one of the neat features of

Lightroom®, it allows you to not only import your images to one of your hard drives, but, at the same time, import a second copy to another hard drive. This can be particularly valuable if you are out in the field importing images to a laptop and making a second copy to an external hard drive and you want to import your images to your larger desktop (more on this later) when you get home. To make a second copy all you have to do is place a check mark in the box in front of "Make a Second Copy to:" and tell Lightroom® where to place the second copy. To do this, click with the cursor on the down pointing arrow on the right side of the panel and select "Choose Folder". Navigate to the folder and select it. The name of the folder where the second copy of the images will go will show up in the box below "Make a Second Copy To:".

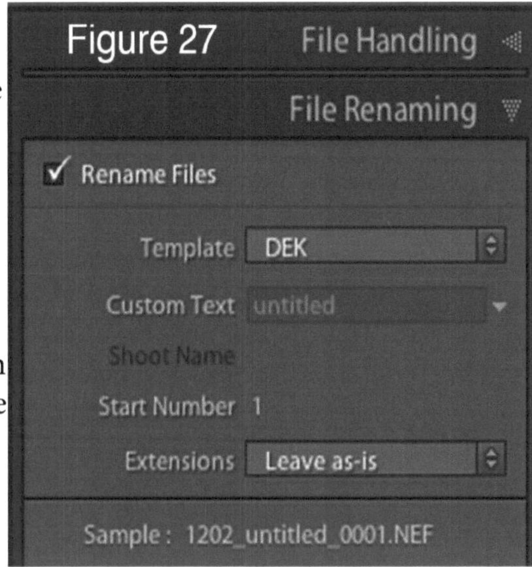


The second panel in the column on the right side of the screen is File Renaming. Activate this panel by placing a check mark in the File Renaming box. (Figure 27) Lightroom has several renaming templates from which to choose. Click with the cursor on the double pointed arrow on the right side of the blank labeled "Template" to see the Lightroom® file naming presets. You will also find the custom file naming template you created in this list. You can choose any one of the templates including your own. If you do choose your own then you will need to put custom text in the box beneath the template. If you only have one card from one camera, then choose your custom file naming template, choose a number with which to start and all the images will be imported with your custom filename in the order in which you created the images.

TIP: If you have multiple cards with images to be imported and you don't know the order in which you used them and/or you photograph with two cameras, then do not rename the files on import. Import the files using the filename the camera assigned them. The reason for this suggestion is, if you have photographed with two different cameras and used them both for photographing the same subject, it will be easier to organize the images and rename them after import. For example, if you are photographing a lion as it walks toward you with a 400mm lens and as he gets closer you put down the camera with the 400mm lens and pick up the camera with a 70-200mm lens on it to continue photographing as he continues to get closer, the images will not be in the proper order when you import them. After you have imported all the images off all the cards, do the following:

- Go to the Edit menu and from the drop down menu choose "Select All" or use the keyboard shortcut, hold down the Command (Macintosh), Control (PC) key and press the A key on the keyboard.
- Go to the toolbar and from the drop down "Sort" menu select Capture Time.
- Lightroom will place all the images in the order they were created. That means the lion images shot with the two cameras will be right together in the Grid view.
- Again, go to the Edit menu and from the drop down menu choose "Select All" or use the keyboard shortcut, Command/Control A.
- Go to the Library menu and from that drop down menu select "Rename Photos".
- The Rename Photos dialog box (Figure 16) will come up and you will be able to choose your custom filename from the drop down menu at the end of the File Naming box.
- Add the custom text in the box below the file name and choose a number from which to start. Your images will then all be in order and numbered from the first to the last one.

The third panel in the column of panels on the right side of the screen is Apply During Import. (Figure 28)

At the top of the panel is a blank for applying a Develop Settings preset. The Develop Settings presets are found in the Develop module and there are quite a few of them. So, if you are familiar with the develop settings presets and you know you want your images imported with one of them or you have created your own develop settings preset and want to apply it to the images as they are imported into Lightroom®, you can select it in this box and all the images will be imported with that preset. Otherwise, select None for this box. Below the develop settings box is a blank for applying metadata to the images as they are imported. If you have not created a Metadata Preset, none will be available and you will need to create one. Once created, you can choose to apply the custom metadata preset containing your copyright and creator information to the images as they are imported into Lightroom®. You will find your custom metadata template by clicking with the cursor on the double pointed arrow at the end of the metadata blank. It will be in the drop down menu along with the choice to create a new metadata template, edit a metadata template you have already created or apply none. It is a good idea to apply your custom metadata template with your copyright and creator information when you import your images. Finally, in this panel you can apply a keyword by typing it in the keyword box at the bottom of the panel. Unless the images are all of the same thing, a person, for example, I think it's a good idea to put the location or name of the shoot in as a keyword. It's just one more thing that will help you find your images later.

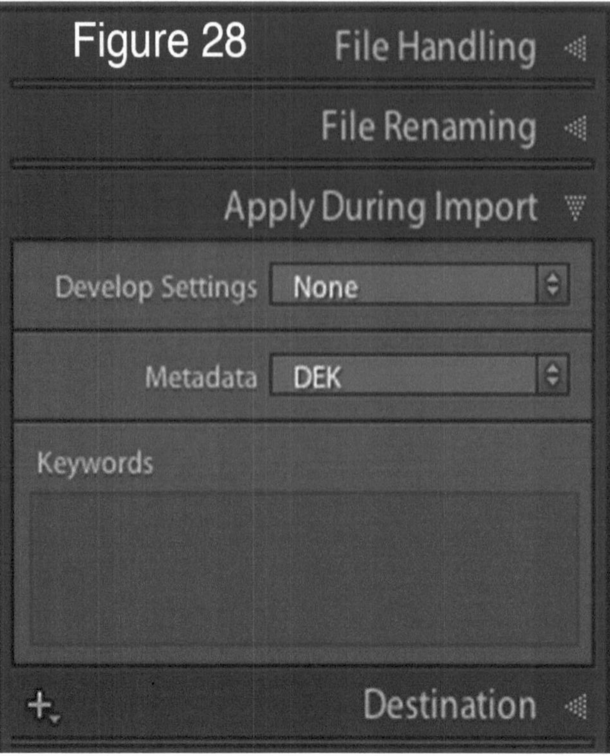


Once you have chosen the source of your import, decided how to import them, determined their destination, and made your choices in the File handling, File Renaming and Apply During Import panels, you are ready to import the images into Lightroom®. All you have to do now is click with the cursor on the Import button at the bottom right of the screen. Lightroom® will start importing the images. First, a progress bar will appear on the top left of the screen showing you approximately how far along in the import Lightroom® is. As images are imported they will appear as thumbnails on the main screen. While they are being imported, if there is one you want to see in the Loupe view, select it and bring it up full screen by using the keyboard shortcut, the E key or click with the cursor on the Loupe view icon in the toolbar or go to the view menu and from the drop down menu select Loupe or just double click with the cursor on the image. When Lightroom® is finished importing it will let you know by playing a sound. You can choose the sound it plays. To select the sound, go to Lighroom® Preferences and select the sound you want from the Completion Sounds section of the General Preferences.

Now that you know about all of the choices in the Import dialog box, what follows is a step by step sequence for importing your images:

- Select the source where your images are located from a folder on your computer or a memory card in a card reader.
- With the images on the main screen, select the images you want to import or don't want to import by checking or unchecking to box in the top left corner of each image.
- Select "Copy to a new location and add to the Catalog" for images on your computer but not in Lightroom®.
- Copy to a new location and add to the Catalog is your only choice when importing from a memory card.
- Select "Add to the Catalog without moving" if the images are on your computer where you want them,

but not in Lightroom®.

- Select a destination for the images either in a folder that already exists in Lightroom® or by creating a new folder on your computer.
- For rendering previews, choose Minimal.
- Place a check in the checkbox for "Don't import duplicates".
- Choose to import a second copy and set up a destination for the second copy.
- If you only have one card to import, rename the images with your custom filename, type custom text in the custom text box.
- Do not rename the files if you have more than one card to import or you have photographed with two cameras.
- Choose a develop settings preset if there is one you like, otherwise make sure "None" is the choice in the develop settings box.
- Choose to apply your custom Metadata Template from the metadata drop down menu at the end of the metadata blank.
- Type an appropriate keyword in the keyword box.
- Check in the Destination panel that the folder to which you want the images imported is highlighted.
- Click with the cursor on the Import button at the bottom right corner of the screen.
- Take a break while your images are imported..................;

# Organizing Images

Once your images are imported into Lightroom®, what's next? For most people the next step is to go through the images one at a time and find the best ones. If you are going to do that , why not organize them by classifying them while you are looking through them? Lightroom® has multiple ways to classify images and by classifying your images you will find it much easier to put them in Collections or organize presentations. With the multiple ways to classify images, you will be able to work out a way that is both easy and fast for you.

Organizing your images is the thing no one really wants to do, usually the reason is because it takes too much time. After you have imported your images, the desire is to get to developing them right away, but if you take the time to organize your images, you will save yourself a lot of time and trouble in the future. I know when I first return from a trip/workshop, I'm not going to develop any images the first day back. What I am going to do is organize them so that I can sort them, keyword them, put them in collections and make my life easier down the road.

In Lightroom® you can flag, rate or label images. What you are really doing is preparing the images to be easily found and picking out the best ones as well as getting rid of the poor ones. In the center of the Tool-

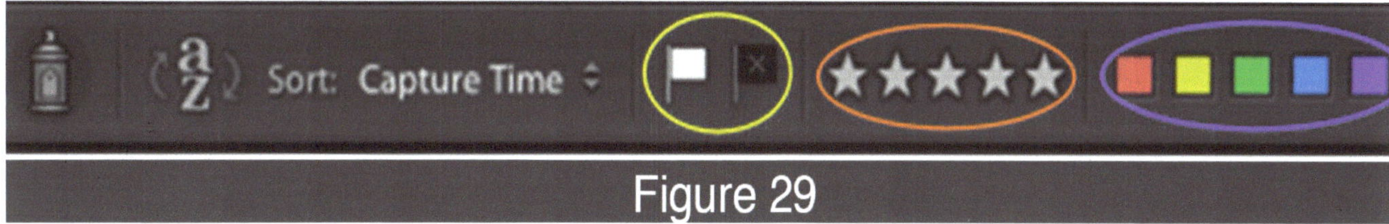

Figure 29

bar you will find the tools for classifying your images. (Figure 29) The first way to classify images in Lightroom® is to flag them. You can flag an image as a Pick or Reject or leave it unflagged. The toolbar has two flag icons, one is a white flag and the other is a black flag with an X in the flag.(Yellow ellipse, Figure 29) When you flag an image as a Pick a little white flag will appear in the upper left corner of the thumbnail in both the Grid view and in the Filmstrip. The Rejects will have black flags with an X on them in the upper left corner of the thumbnail in both the Grid view and the Filmstrip. The Picks should be what you think are

your best images, the ones on which you want to work first. To flag an image do the following:
To flag an image as a Pick:
- Select the image and do one of the following
- Press the P key on the keyboard, OR,
- Click with the cursor on the white flag icon in the toolbar.

To flag an image as a Reject:
- Select the image and do one of the following;
- Press the X key on the keyboard, OR,
- Click with the cursor on the black flag icon in the toolbar.

To change the Flag status:
- Hold down the Command (Macintosh), Control (PC) key and press the up or down arrow keys.
- Pressing the down arrow key once will change a Pick to Unflagged.
- Pressing the down arrow key a second time will make the image a Reject.
- Pressing the up arrow key will make a Reject unflagged.
- Pressing the up arrow key a second time will make the image a Pick.

TIP: It is much more simple to just use the P, U and X keys on the keyboard to flag or unflag an image.
To remove a flag
- Select the image on which there is a flag and do one of the following;
- Press the U key on the keyboard, OR,
- Click with the cursor on either the white or black flag icon in the toolbar, OR,
- Click with the cursor on the flag in the upper left corner of the image.

When you flag an image, a message will appear in the bottom of the screen telling you the image has been flagged as a Pick or Reject. If you remove a flag you will also get a message on the bottom of the screen telling you the flag has been removed. Note that you can also go to the Photo Menu at the top of the screen and from the drop down menu choose "Set Flag" and then select; Flagged, Unflagged or Rejected from the popup menu, but this seems labor intensive and takes too much time. After you have flagged all the rejects, the first way to get rid of them is to go to the Photo menu at the top of the screen and from the drop down menu choose "Delete Rejected Photos". all the rejected photos will appear on the screen to give you a last look at them and a pop up menu will ask you whether you want to remove them from the disk or just remove them from Lightroom®.

The second way to organize images is to rate them with stars. (Red ellipse, Figure 29) You can rate an image with from one to five stars. To rate the images with one to five stars, do the following:
- Select the image in the Grid view or Loupe view and do one of the following;
- Press any of the 1 through the 5 keys on the keyboard to place one to five stars on an image. Pressing the one key will place one star on the image, the two key will place two stars on the image, the three key will place three stars on the image, the four key, four stars and the five key, five stars.
- Alternatively, you can click with the cursor on the stars in the toolbar to apply the appropriate number of stars for each image.
- To increase or decrease the star rating, press the appropriate number on the keyboard.
- You can also increase the star rating by pressing the right bracket key (]) on the keyboard.
- Pressing the left bracket key ([) on the keyboard will decrease the star rating.
- Pressing the zero key on the keyboard will remove the star rating.

Again, it is much more simple to just use the number keys, 0 through 5 to rate or unrate an image.

My personal opinion is you would have to be an obsessive compulsive individual off your medication to want to go through all your images and rate them as to their quality from one to five stars. What would you do with a one star image? However, there is a way to use the stars and I'll get to that shortly. Again, you can waste your time and go to the Photo Menu at the top of the screen and from the drop down menu select "Set Rating" and then click on the appropriate number of stars in the popup menu

The third way to organize images is by using color labels (Blue ellipse, Figure 29). This makes more sense to me. For example, if you are a wedding photographer, you might label the bride Red, the groom Yellow (no pun intended here), the bridal party green, the family pictures Blue and the Reception Purple. Pressing the 6 key on the keyboard will place a red label on the image, pressing the seven key will place a yellow label on the image, the eight key will place **a** green label on the image, the nine key will place a blue label on the image. Labeling will certainly make the images easier to find. There is no ten key on the keyboard, but you can put a purple label on images by clicking with the cursor on the purple color on the Toolbar or with the Painter tool, more on this later. To label the images with colors do one of the following:

- ► Select an image in the Grid or Loupe view.
- ► Press the six through the nine keys on the keyboard to place the appropriate color label on an image.
- ► Use the Painter tool on the toolbar or click on the purple label on the toolbar to set the color purple because there is no ten key.
- ► Click with the cursor on the appropriate color in the toolbar to place the label on the image.

To remove a color label do one of the following:

- ► Select the image with the color label you want to remove and click with the cursor on the color label in the toolbar.
- ► If you have just placed the label on the image you can hold down the Command (Macintosh), Control (PC) and press the Z key on the keyboard.
- ► If you used the Painter tool to apply a color label, you can remove it by holding down the Option key (Macintosh), Alt key (PC) and when you hover the cursor over the image, the cursor turns into an eraser cursor
- ► Clicking on the image with the eraser cursor removes the color label.
- ► Go to the Photo menu at the top of the screen and from the drop down menu choices select Set Color Label.
- ► From the pop up menu that appears, select None.

.

The flags, stars and labels are not mutually exclusive. An image can be flagged, rated with stars and labeled with a color. There are Seventy-one combinations of Pick Flags, Star Ratings and Color Labels. Knowing this, you can work out a system using either the Flags, Stars and Labels alone or a combination of Flags, Stars and Labels that will let you find the images you want quickly. When I return from a trip to Africa for example, I usually have some where near 3000 images of all kinds of different animals, birds, etc. So what follows is my system for classifying my images, I call it the DEK One Pass System:

- ► Import all the images without renaming them, but with applying my custom metadata preset.
- ► After import, sort them by capture time so that the first image I shot is first.
- ► Decide what animals the stars will represent, which animals will have color labels. For example, one star is an antelope, two stars is a bird, three stars is a cat, four stars is an elephant, giraffe, hippo, etc.
- ► Write down for what each star or color label stands.
- ► Set the magnification level for clicking with the cursor to 1:1.
- ► In the Library module bring up the first image in the loupe view, this allows me to see the image full screen and make a decision about it.
- ► If the image is what I think is one of the best I press the P key to flag it as a Pick.
- ► If the image is out of focus or for some other reason I don't like it I press the X key to flag it as a reject.
- ► Next I press the appropriate one through the nine key for the stars or labels.

- Next I press the right arrow key on the keyboard to move to the next image.
- The Painter tool is not available in the Loupe view in the Library module so I leave the images that will be labeled Purple (usually wildebeests, warthogs and zebras) without the purple label. However, I still look at them for Picks or Rejects and flag them appropriately.

TIP: If I needed another category I could use the Quick Collection, located in the Catalog panel on the left side of the screen. To add an image to the Quick Collection do one of the following:

- Press the keyboard shortcut, the B key on the keyboard.
- Click with the cursor on the small circle that appears in the upper right hand corner of an image when you hover the cursor over the image in the Grid view.
- From the Photo menu at the top of the screen select "Add to Quick Collection".
- With either method, the circle in the upper right hand corner of the image turns dark

To remove an image from the Quick Collection do one of the following:

- Select the image and press the keyboard shortcut, the B key on the keyboard.
- Select the image and click on the cursor on the dark circle in the upper right hand corner of the image.
- Select the image and from the Photo menu at the top of the screen select "Remove from Quick Collection."

The Quick Collection can also be saved as a regular Collection, to save it do the following:

- Hold down the Control key(Macintosh), and click with the cursor on the Quick Collection, Right Click (PC) on the Quick collection, OR,
- Use the Keyboard shortcut, hold down the Option and Command keys (Macintosh) Alt and Control keys (PC) and press the B key on the keyboard.
- From the popup menu choose "Save Quick Collection".
- The Save Quick Collection dialog box will appear on the screen.
- Give the new Collection a name in the blank.
- Place a check mark in the box in front of the text "Clear Quick Collection after Saving".
- Click with the cursor on the Save button at the bottom right of the Save Quick Collection dialog box.
- The Quick Collection will now be saved in the Collections panel.

The Quick Collection can also be cleared without saving, to do this, do the following:

- Control click (Macintosh), Right Click (PC) with the cursor on the Quick Collection.
- From the popup menu choose "Clear Quick Collection" OR,
- Use the keyboard Shortcut, hold down the Shift and Command Keys (Macintosh), the Shift and Control keys (PC) and press the B key on the keyboard.

TIP: You could also use the Quick Collection for images you are not sure about, in my case, images with two animals of different species, for example. You can also use the Quick Collection for your favorite images and then convert the Quick Collection to a regular Collection when you are done classifying all the images.

When I'm done flagging, rating or labeling all the images, I can use the Library Filter bar (more on this shortly) to bring up all the unrated, unlabeled images and place the purple label on them by selecting them all (Edit>Select All or Command/Control A), choosing the Painter tool from the Toolbar, and setting the Painter Tool to spray the purple label on the images. With all the images selected for the purple label, I only have to spray the purple label on one of them and all the selected images will be labeled purple, more on this when I get to the Library Filter Bar.

With this method, I just press the P, X, 1 through 9 and right arrow keys to go through all my images. When done then I go back to the Grid view and use the painter tool on the purple images. It is a very quick and efficient way to go through the images. The times I slow down from pushing keys on the keyboard is trying to decide if an image is a Pick. This is often when I use the one to one magnification to see the image in more detail. You could use this method in the Grid mode, especially if you have a large screen and can make the thumbnails very large, then you wouldn't have to wait to label the purple images with the Painter tool. However, it would slow you down to have to go to the mouse to spray purple on an image with the Painter tool.

TIP: You can eliminate the need to press the right arrow key by going to the Photo menu at the top of the screen and selecting "Auto Advance" from the drop down menu. Once you flag, rate or label an image Lightroom® 4 will automatically go to the next image. The reason I have Auto Advance turned off is that if I rate an image as a Pick it would automatically go to the next image and I want to rate it with a star or label. That means I would have to press the left arrow key to go back to the image to place stars or a label on it.

The next step is to get rid of all the rejected photos. To do this, go to the Photo Menu at the top of the page and from the drop down menu select "Remove rejected Photos". Lightroom® will bring up all the rejected photos to give you one more look at them and ask you if you want to remove them. Clicking with the cursor on "Remove" will take them out of Lightroom®. A second way to get rid of the rejected photos is with the Library Filter Bar and that will be covered next.

With the seventy-one combinations of flags, stars and labels the following is an example of using combinations for images of a family of four consisting of a father, mother, two children and a dog.

- Assign each member of the family a color, red for the wife, yellow for the husband, green for one child, blue for the other and purple for the dog (It's not a good idea to assign stars to family members, especially if one kid finds out the other has more stars).
- Images with only a color label will have only one member of the family in them.
- Place the color label of the oldest member of the family in the picture on the image if there are more than one member of the family in the image.
- If there are two members of the family in the picture place two stars on the image, three stars for three members in the image, etc.
- Place a Pick flag on the favorites.

Using a combination of Flags, Stars and Labels will allow you to quickly move through your images and classify them. However, once you decide on the combination you want to use, write it down and keep it by the computer as you move through the images. What you are really doing is making your images easily found using the Library Filter Bar. This really isn't very complicated and you are going to go through your images anyway, so why not press some keys while you are doing it and end up with all your images classified.

## The Library Filter Bar

At the top of the main window in the Grid view is the Library Filter Bar. If you don't see it then press the back slash key (\) or go to the View menu and select "Show Filter Bar" and it will appear. The Library Filter

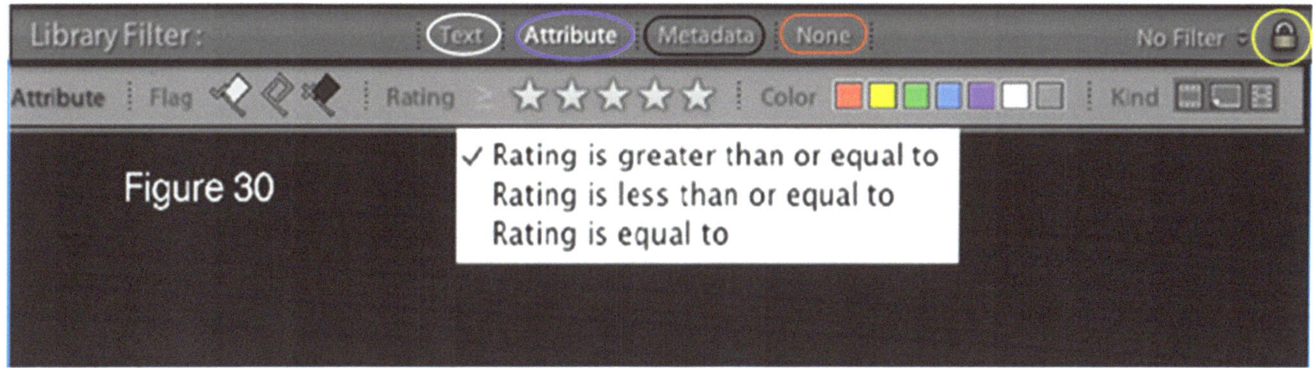

Figure 30

Bar is only available in the Grid View. If you are in the Loupe View when you press the Back Slash key, the Grid view will open with the Filter Bar on the top. This bar has four sections, Text, Attribute, Metadata and None. The Attribute section (Blue ellipse, Figure 30), the second section will probably be the one you use the most. It has sections for Flags, Stars and Labels. There are three icons for the flags, Picks, Rejects and a blank flag for images that have no flag,between the Picks and Rejects flags. If you click with the cursor on the icon next to the word "Rating" the Stars section has a choice of "Rating is greater than or equal to", "Rating is less than or equal to" and "Rating is equal to", followed by the five Stars. The Labels section has seven blocks, the red, yellow, green, blue and purple colors and then a block for a custom color and a block for unlabeled photos, ones with no color label. There are also three icons at the right side of the Attributes bar, these allow you to see only Master Photos, Virtual Copies or Movies. If you hover your cursor over each of the icons, Lightroom® will tell you for what each icon is.

TIP: When you bring up the Library Filter Bar, it may still be set for the last selections you made with it. If that's the case, click with the cursor on None (Red ellipse, Figure 30) on the top of the Filter Bar to clear any previous selections, then make your choices from the Attributes section.

Going back to the Library Filter bar the first choice for finding images is Text. (White ellipse, Figure 30) This section allows you to search for images using any text in any area of the image, filename, metadata, either IPTC or EXIF, keyword, caption, title or copy name. When you select Text in the Library Filter Bar three text blocks appear, the first two have double pointed arrows which, when you click on them with the cursor, give you a choice of parameters from which you can choose. (Figure 31) In the third text box you can type in what you are looking for. The first text box gives you a choice of keywords, metadata, filename, copy name, caption, title and any searchable field. The second text box, gives you variables such as "contains", "contains all", "contains words", "doesn't contain", "starts with" or "ends with", from which to choose. The third text box allows you to type in what you are looking for in the image. For example, if you were looking for images of lions, in the first text box you could select Keyword, in the second text box choose Contains and in the third text box type in "lion". Lightroom® would search the current folder, collection or the entire catalog and show you only images that had the keyword lion embedded in them.

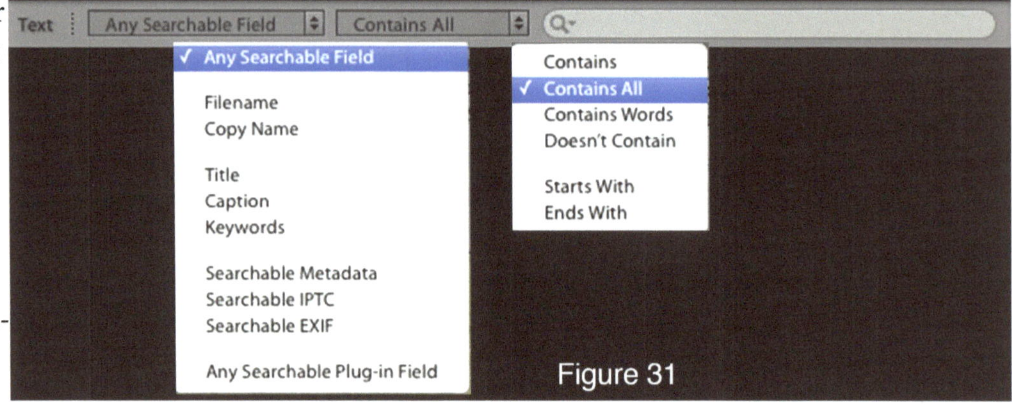

Figure 31

The third choice in the Library Filter bar is Metadata. (Black ellipse, Figure 30) By default, the metadata section of the Library Filter Bar opens with four sections. (Figure 32) These four columns can be changed to

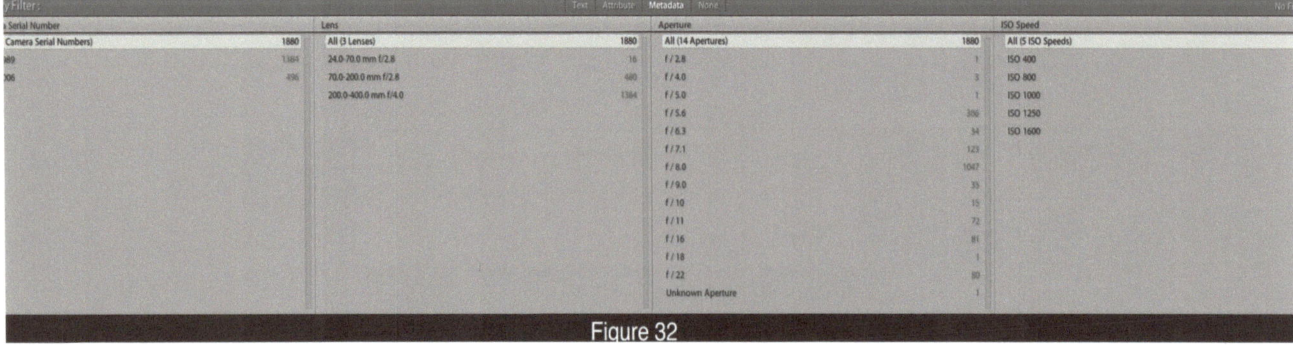
Figure 32

search any section of the metadata for the image. The default columns are Date, Camera, Lens and Label. You can change any of these columns to search using other metadata. To change the columns and get a custom metadata search field, do the following:
At the top right of the Library Filter Bar, you will see text that says by default "No Filter" next to a padlock. (Yellow circle, Figure 30) Click with the cursor on the double pointed arrow next to this text. In the drop down menu you will have a choice of metadata presets for the four columns;

- Camera info,
- Default columns,
- Location,
- Exposure info.

Selecting Camera info will bring up the following in the four columns:

- Camera brand,
- Lens type,
- Focal length,
- Flash state.

The Default columns have already been mentioned. Selecting Location will bring up columns for the following

- The country in which the image was created.
- The State/Province in which the image was created.
- The city in which the image was create.
- Images created in unknown locations.

Each section has two drop down menus at the top. The drop down menu on the left allows you to choose what metadata you want to show in that section. When you select one column, Lightroom® will tell you the number of images that match each selection on the right side of the column. Once you have made your selections, Lightroom® will bring up any images that match the selections. You can change the content of any one of the columns. To change the content of a column, do the following:

- Hover your cursor over the header bar of any column.
- A white double pointed arrow will appear next to the title of the column in the area of the Yellow circle, Figure 33.
- Click with the cursor on the white double pointed arrow.
- A menu will appear on screen with all of the metadata choices. (Figure 34)
- Select the new metadata content for the column from this menu.
- The new metadata choice with the number of images matching on the right side of the column will replace the previous choice of metadata.

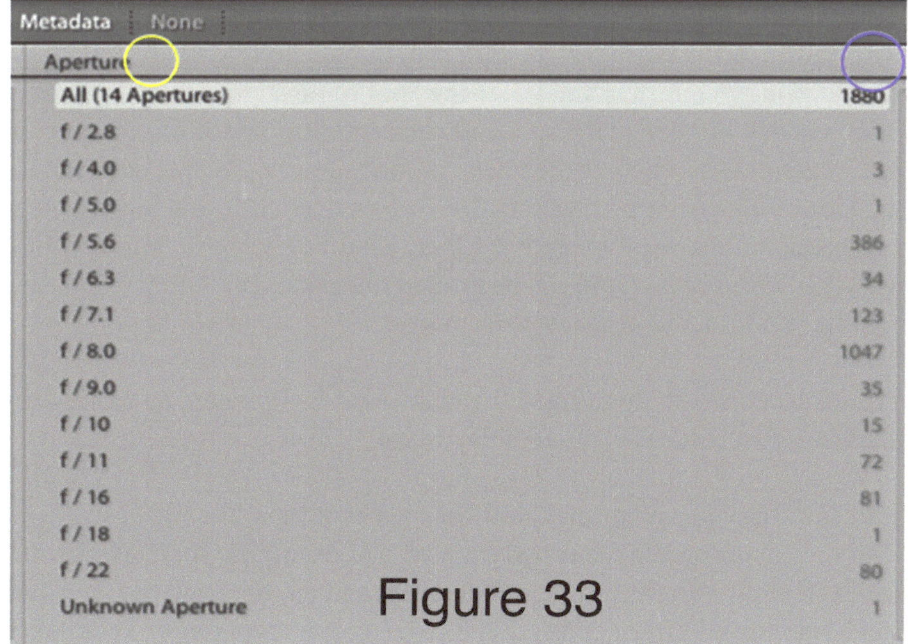

Figure 33

You can also add or remove a column to the Metadata section. To add or remove a column, do the following:

- Hover the cursor over the header bar of any of the columns.
- A double pointed arrow with a menu will appear on the right side of the column header bar in the area of the blue circle, Figure 33.
- Clicking with the cursor will bring up a menu that allows you to add or remove a column.
- Clicking with the cursor on "Add a Column" will add a column to the right of the column in which you are currently working.
- By default, this column will have "None" selected for the contents of the column on the left side of the header bar.
- Click with the cursor on the double pointed arrow to the right of "None" in the header bar of the column (The double pointed arrow will appear in the area of the yellow circle, Figure 33 when you hover your cursor over the word "None") and a drop down menu will give you your choice of showing any of the metadata in the new column (Figure 34).

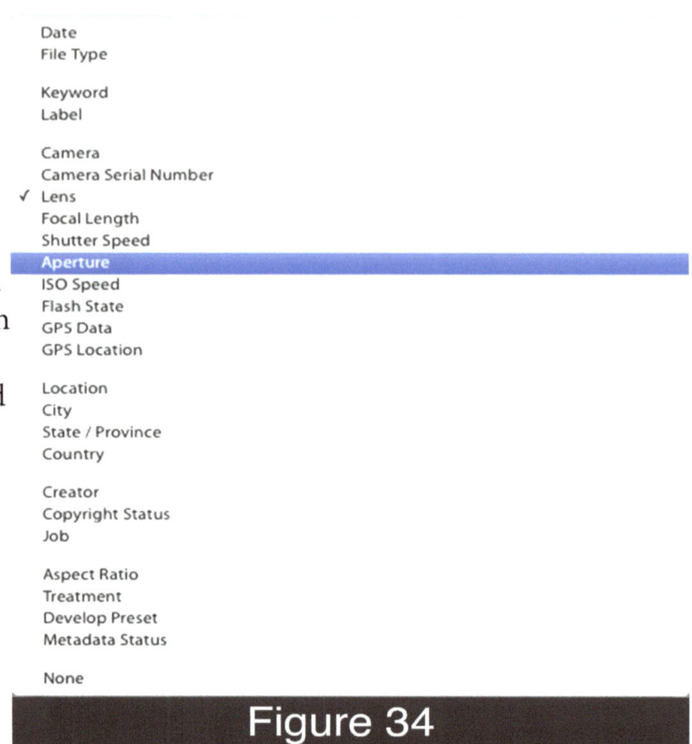

Figure 34

You can search your images using any of the metadata embedded in your images, including the IPTC metadata you added. This section of the Library Filter Bar can be very useful. This getting a little bit ahead of ourselves, but, for example, if you discover you have a spot on a lens, you can search for all the images taken with that lens on the same day. All you would have to do is put the date in one column and the lens in another column. Lightroom® will show you all the images taken with that lens on that day and only those images. If you find that all or just some of the images have a spot, what you can do next is select all of the images that have the spot on them and press the D key on the keyboard. This will move only the images with the spot on them to the Develop Module. The first image you selected will be on the main screen and all the other images will be in the Filmstrip. Make sure all the images are still selected and that the Auto-sync button in the bottom right corner of the screen is turned on. Get the Spot Removal Tool from the toolbar under the histogram, hover the Spot removal tool over the spot, adjust the size of the Spot Removal tool to match the size of the spot and click with the cursor on the spot. The spot in all the images will disappear regardless of whether the image is portrait or landscape. You can also accomplish the same thing in the Library Filter Bar by selecting the Text section, choosing searchable metadata in the first box, contains in the second box and typing in the focal length of the lens. This would also show you all the images taken with that lens, but it would not be limited to a date. The Library Filter Bar is a very valuable, versatile tool in helping you find and organize your images.

TIP: You can select anything in the embedded EXIF metadata to show in the columns as well as any IPTC metadata that you have added to the image.

TIP: You can open all of the selection choices at the same time by selecting one and then shift clicking with the cursor on the other two choices. For example, Open text, shift click with the cursor on Attributes and shift click with the cursor on Metadata and all three will be open at the top of the page in the finder bar. Opening all three choices at the same time in the Library Filter bar will allow you to really refine your search. For example, in the text field you could type in a keyword, in the Attributes field you could select all flagged images that were rated three stars and in the Metadata section you could select images that were taken on a date with a certain camera and lens at an ISO sensitivity setting. Lightroom® would then show you only the images that met those criteria on the screen.

The Library Filter Bar also makes it easy to delete images flagged as Rejects. This is the second way to bring up the rejected images before you delete them. To delete rejected images using the Library Filter Bar, do the following:

- Select the black flag with an X in it from the Attributes section of the Library Filter Bar.
- This will bring up only the images that have been flagged as rejects.
- Look them over to make sure they are the ones you want to delete.
- Go to the Photo menu at the top of the page and from the drop down menu, at the bottom select Delete Rejected Photos.
- Alternatively, hold down the Command (Macintosh), Control (PC) key and press the Delete (Macintosh), Backspace (PC) key on the keyboard.
- Either of these will bring up a dialog box asking you whether you want to delete the photos from the disk or just remove them from Lightroom®.
- Make your choice and click on it with the cursor.

If you delete the image from the disk, you will have no chance to bring it back into Lightroom® unless you still have the image on a card or CD/DVD and go through the Import process again. If you just remove it from Lightroom®, you can bring it back in by immediately holding down the Command key(Macintosh) Control key (PC) and pressing the Z key on the keyboard. The only other way to bring the image back into Lightroom® is to re-import it from its location on your hard drive.

With all the rejected images deleted, the remaining images are Picks, rated, labeled or images without any flags, rating or label. So, what's the next step in the workflow? The next step is to select all the images without a rating, label or flag and in my workflow, I use the Painter tool to label them with the purple color. To do that, do the following:

- In the Attribute section of the Library Filter Bar select the Middle flag.
- Click with the cursor on the equal to sign before the stars, but do not select any number for the stars.
- Choose the color block for the unlabeled photos (The last one, Gray).
- The only images on the screen will be unflagged, unrated and unlabeled.
- From the drop down Edit menu choose "Select All" or use the keyboard shortcut, hold down the Command (Macintosh), Control (PC) key and press the A key on the keyboard.
- Get the Painter tool from the toolbar by clicking on it with the cursor.
- Make sure the label Purple is chosen for the Painter tool.
- Hover the Painter tool (cursor) over one of the images and click with the cursor on the image.
- All of the selected images will now be labeled Purple.
- Finally, look through all the images now labeled Purple and flag any that deserve to be Picks.

When you are ready to start editing your images, select the white flag from the finder bar and it brings up all the images you flagged as Picks and you can start working on those images first.

The fourth choice in the Library Filter Bar is None. Whenever you want to change the parameters in the Library Filter Bar, you need to select None in the filter bar before you go to your next set of parameters. Otherwise, the first set will still be in use and Lightroom will be looking for images that meet both criteria when it looks for images to show you. It is a good idea to click with the cursor on None when you first start to use the Library Filter Bar.

## The Collections Panel

The Collections panel is one of the most powerful resources in the Library Module. It is where you can organize your images for ease in finding them, for presentations you are going to make, for books you want to print, for slide shows, for images you want to print and for images you want to include in a web gallery. In the Library module you can create Collections sets and Smart Collections as well as Collections that are specific to one of the other modules in Lightroom®. It is the only module that allows you to create collections of images from different folders. The Collections panel is present in all seven modules of Lightroom®, but is most useful in the Library module. In the Library module you can create a Collection, Smart Collection and/or a Collection Set. If you are putting together a collection of images for a presentation then you only need to create a Collection. A Collection Set is useful when you are creating multiple Collections of images from the same photo shoot or from different Folders. A Collection is useful when you are creating a collection of images from different Folders. A Smart Collection is an automated way of creating a Collection.

To create a Collection, do the following:

Figure 35

- In the Grid view, select a group of images from the Folder on which you are currently working and do one of the following three;
- Use the keyboard Shortcut, hold down the Command (Macintosh) Control (PC) and press the N key on the keyboard, OR,
- From the Library Menu at the top of the screen, select New Collection, OR
- Click with the cursor on the plus (+) sign (Blue Circle, Figure 35) on the right side of the header bar for Collections and from the menu that appears select "Create Collection...".
- A Create Collection dialog box will appear on screen (Figure 36).
- Name the new Collection in the top blank in the first section of the dialog box.
- In the second section of the dialog box, click with the cursor in the circle in front of the text "Top Level".
- Make sure the check box for "include selected photos" is checked in the third section.
- Click with the cursor on the Create button at the bottom right of the Create Collection dialog box

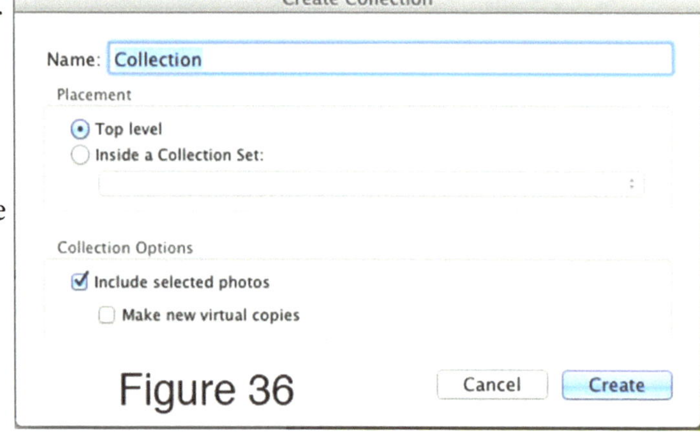

Figure 36

All of the selected photos will be in the named Collection in the Collections panel on the left side of the screen and to the right of the name of the collection will be the number of images in the collection. With the Collection created, you can add images to it from the same folder or a different folder. All you have to do is select the image and simply drag the image to the Collection. When you drag an image to the Collection, as you hover your cursor over the name of the Collection, the name will become highlighted. With the name of the Collection highlighted, when you release the cursor, the image will be added to the highlighted Collection. So, make sure the Collection to which you want to add the image is the one highlighted, not the one above or below. You can also make all the images Virtual Copies (More on Virtual Copies later) in the new Collection by placing a check mark in the box in front of the text "Make new virtual copies". Doing this will make all the images in the Collection Virtual copies and this will become important in the other Lightroom® modules.

## Collection Sets

Collection sets are useful if you would like to create multiple collections from the same photo shoot. For example, if you have photographed multiple animals on an African photo safari and want to place the different species in their own collection. To Create a Collection set, do the following:

- From the Library menu at the top of the screen, choose "New Collection Set" from the drop down menu, OR,
- Click with the cursor on the plus sign (+) in the header bar of the Collections panel (Blue circle, figure 35).
- From the pop up menu that appears select "Create Collection Set..."(Figure 35).
- A Create Collection Set dialog box will appear on screen (Figure 37).
- Name the Collection Set in the top blank.
- Make sure the circle in front of "Top level is selected.
- Click with the cursor on the Create button at the bottom right of the dialog box.

Create Collection Set
Name: Collection Set
Placement
Top level
Inside a Collection Set:
Cancel
Create

Figure 37

Once you have created a Collection Set, you can create Collections and place Collections in the Collection Set. There are two ways to do this. If you already have Collections created, you can select the Collection in the Collections panel on the left side of the screen and highlight it by clicking on it with the cursor. You can then drag the Collection to the newly created Collection Set. As you drag the cursor over the Collection Set, the Set will become highlighted. Release the cursor and the Collection will be inside the Collection Set and appear in the left column of panels underneath the newly created Collection Set. The following is an example of the second way to place a Collection inside a Collection Set:

- In the Library Filter Bar Attributes section select an Attribute, equal to three stars, for example (these are the Cats in my rating example).
- Lightroom® brings up only the images of cats.
- To make a collection of lions, select only lions from all the cats by clicking with the cursor on the first one and shift clicking on the last one if they are consecutive in the grid mode. For non-consecutive lion images hold down the Command (Macintosh), Control(PC) key and click with the cursor on the lion images.
- Once the lion images are selected use the keyboard shortcut for a new Collection, hold down the Command key (Macintosh), Control key(PC) and press the N key on the keyboard or click with the cursor on the plus (+) sign in the Collections header bar (Blue circle, Figure 35).

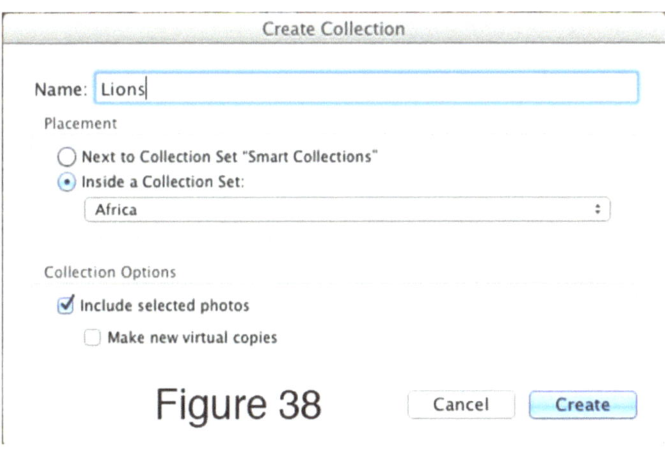


Figure 38

- Choose Create a Collection from the menu that appears (Figure 35).
- In the Create Collection dialog box name the Collection "Lions" in the top blank in the first section (Figure 38).
- In the second section of the Create Collection dialog box, click with the cursor in the circle in front of the text "Inside Collection Set".

- Click with the cursor on the double pointed arrow at the end of the blank for the Collection Set and from the menu that appears, choose the Collection Set, "Africa" in this case.
- Make sure the "Include Selected Photos" box is checked in the third section of the dialog box.
- Click with the cursor on the Create button at the bottom right of the dialog box.
- The Lions collection will now be inside the Africa Collection Set and listed underneath the Africa Set in the Collections panel on the left side of the screen.
- Go back to the Library Filter Bar and click on None in the header bar to remove the selection criteria.
- Go back to the Folders panel and click with the cursor on the Kenya folder again. This will bring up all the images in the folder.
- In the Attributes section of the Library Filter Bar, select equal to three stars again and this time select the leopards.
- Follow the same procedure for creating a collection of leopards under the Collection Set Africa.
- Continue until all the animals are in Collections under the Africa Collection Set.

TIP: New in Lightroom 4 is the ability to create Collection Sets inside other Collection sets. To do this, do the following:

- In the second section of the Create Collection Set dialog box(Figure 37), click with the cursor in the circle in front of the text "Inside a Collection Set" to activate the blank at the bottom of the box.
- The name of the first Collection Set (alphabetical order) you created will appear in the blank.
- Click with the cursor on the double pointed arrow at the end of this blank and all of your Collection Sets will appear in a drop down menu.
- Select the Collection Set into which you want to place your new Collection Set.
- The selected Collection Set will become the Top Level Collection Set.
- Click with the cursor on the Create button at the bottom right of the Create Collection Set dialog box.
- The new Collection Set will appear in the Collections panel on the left side of the screen underneath the Top Level Collection Set in which you chose to put it.

Placing a Collection Set inside another Collection Set gives you just a little more versatility in organizing your images. For example, if you have a Top Level Collection Set entitled Africa, you could put a Collection Set inside the Africa set called Cats. In the Cats Collection Set you could have separate Collections of Cheetahs, Leopards, Lions and Serval Cats. (Figure 38) The more you organize your images, the easier they become to find.

## Smart Collections

Creating Smart Collections is a way to automate organizing your images. To create a Smart Collection, do the following:

- From the Library menu select "New Smart Collection" OR
- Click with the cursor on the plus (+) sign on the right side of the Collections header bar and choose "Create Smart Collection" (Figure 35).
- The Create Smart Collection dialog box will appear on the screen (Figure 39).
- In the top blank in the Create Smart Collection dialog box that appears, name the new Smart

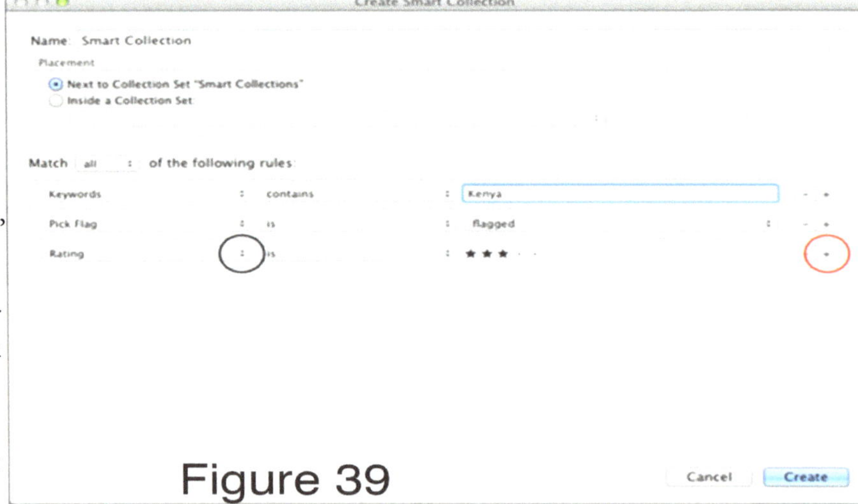

Figure 39

Collection to indicate what it is, Flagged for example.

- In the second section down, place a check mark in the appropriate circle to choose whether you want the Smart Collection to be a Top Level Smart Collection or whether you want to place it inside one of your Collection Sets.
- Below the second section is a blank for choosing whether you want to match Any, All or None of the Criteria you set up in the bottom section of the Create Smart Collection dialog box.
- The third section down is where you select the criteria for Lightroom® to match in creating a Smart Collection.
- By default there is one line at the top of the section with 3 blanks.
- The first blank has a double pointed arrow at the right end. Clicking on this double pointed arrow will show you a pop up window with all the choices Lightroom® will look for to match.
- Select the criteria you want to match.
- If you want to see only images from the current folder or last import, select Keyword in the first blank.
- In the second blank to the right you can choose how the first blank is matched. The choices in the second blank depend on the choice you made in the first blank. If you choose keyword in the first blank the choices in the second blank will be things like "Contains, Doesn't contain, Starts with, Ends with, etc".
- The choices in the third blank depend on the choices made in the first two blanks. For example if you chose Keywords, you can type the keyword in the third blank. If you want to see only images from the current folder or shoot, type in the keyword you embedded in all the image when you first imported them. If you Chose rating you can click with the cursor on the number of stars you want.
- At the end of the line with the three blanks are two boxes, one with a minus sign (-) and one with a plus sign (+).
- Clicking with the cursor on the plus (+) sign will add another line to the dialog box and allow you to select other criteria for Lightroom® to match in addition to matching the criteria in the first line. For example, in this second line, you could add Pick Flag from the drop down menu in the first box, "Is" in the second box and "Flagged in the third box. Lightroom would then place all images in the current Folder with the keyword embedded from the first line and flagged as Picks in the second line in the smart collection.
- Clicking on the plus (+) sign again will add a third line for another criteria for Lightroom® to match. For example if this time you chose Rating for the first box, "is "for the second box and three stars for the third box, (if you rated all your cats three stars,) Lightroom® would place all the cats from the current shoot or folder that have been flagged Picks into the Smart Collection.
- If you click with the cursor on the minus (-) sign at the end of the line, Lightroom® deletes the line
- Once you have set up the parameters Lightroom® is to look for in an image to add it to the Smart Collection, click with the cursor on the Create button at the bottom right of the dialog box.
- You will then have a Smart Collection with the images that matches all the criteria show up in the Collections panel in the left column of panels as if by magic.

Tip: You can select any flag, rating, label or any information from the embedded metadata for Lightroom® to use in adding images to the Smart Collection. For example, if you set up a Smart Collection of the images you flagged as picks when you were going through your images, flagging, rating or labeling, then when you finish, you will have a collection of all your best images ready to go for developing. If you wanted to see images taken with a certain shutter speed or ISO sensitivity setting, you can set up the Smart Collection using the Metadata section of the Library Filter Bar to add just those images. Smart Collections can be a real time saver for you.

Putting all your images in collections accomplishes a couple of things for you. First, when looking for an image you will not have to go through an entire folder looking for an image. If you know you want, for example, an image of a lion, select the lion collection. There will be fewer images to sort through. Also, with the images in Collections it is much easier to apply keywords, which will be discussed shortly.

The first collection you should probably create before you start flagging, rating and labeling your images is a Smart Collection of the images you flagged as picks. This will basically be your portfolio, the ones you want to develop first or the ones you want to put up on your website, or the ones you want to show a client. If you want to create a Smart Collection for images you flag as Picks, you can also place star ratings or color labels on the images as well. You can also go back and flag images as Picks after you have placed a star rating or color label on them. Any images flagged as Picks, either before or after you created a Smart Collection of images flagged as Picks will show up in the Flagged Smart collection. When you are done flagging, rating and labeling your images, the flagged images are there waiting for you already in the Smart Collection to start developing, you don't have to look for them. If you want to see images from just your most recent shoot or import, then add a second line to the Smart Collection using the keyword you embedded in the images when you imported them. Lightroom® will then show you only those flagged images with the keyword from the recent import. However, if you have a Smart Collection set up for Flagged images in your Catalog, then the images from the recent shoot or import will also be in that flagged images Smart Collection. This allows you to find all the images flagged as Picks in your entire Catalog.

## Keywording

After flagging, rating, labeling your images and then putting them in collections if you desire, the next step to good organization is keywording. Keywording is one of the most valuable things you can do not only because it helps you sort and find your images, but done correctly, it makes them easily discoverable by stock photography companies and advertising agencies.

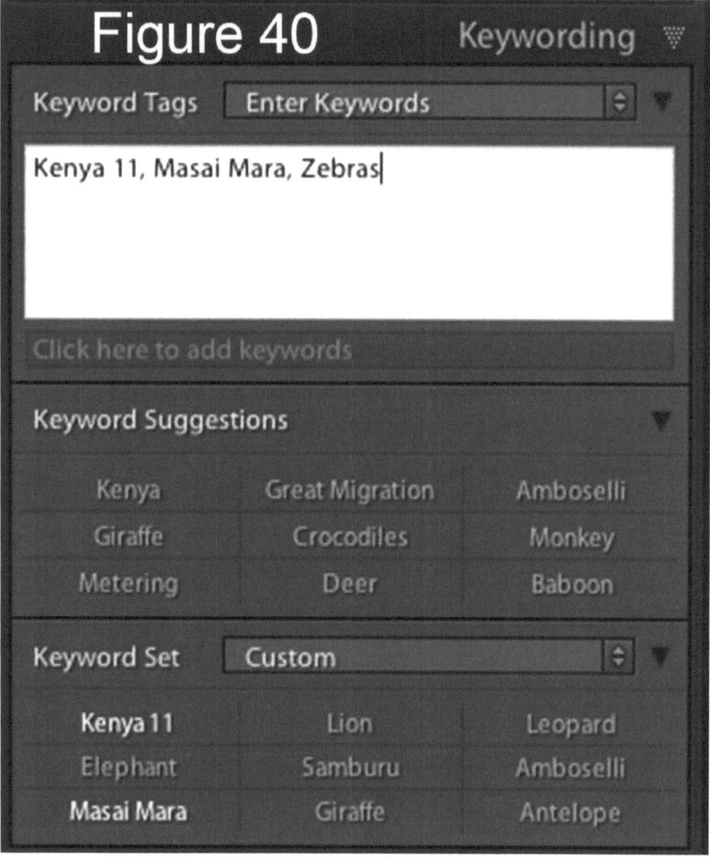


There are two panels for Keywords in the right side column of panels. The first one is for placing new Keywords on an image. (Figure 40) The second Keyword panel is a list of Keywords already in Lightroom's® memory and is for placing Keywords from that list on to your images. (Figure 41)

If you have your images in collections, then do the following if the images have no Keywords already embedded in them, except the keyword you embedded during import:

- Select a collection.
- Go to the edit menu and choose "Select all" or use the keyboard shortcut, hold down the Command (Macintosh),Control (PC) key and press the A key on the keyboard.
- Open the Keywording panel in the right column under the Quick Develop panel by clicking on the header bar.
- Click in the dark gray box under the Keyword Tags heading to activate it.
- The dark gray box will turn white and allow you to enter Keywords.
- In the box, type in the Keyword you want to embed in the images.
- Press the Return (Macintosh), Enter (PC) key on the keyboard.
- The Keyword will now be embedded in all the images in the Collection.

- A small banner will appear in the lower right corner of the image in the Grid view and in the Filmstrip.
- If you click with the cursor on this banner, Lightroom® will show you all the keywords embedded in the image.

Figure 41 Keyword List

Filter Keywords

| Keyword | Count |
|---|---|
| African birds | 18 |
| African mammals | 320 |
| Alligator Farm | 200 |
| Alligator Farm 11 | 563 |
| Alligator farm birds | 747 |
| Alligators | 1231 |
| Amboselli | 2 |
| Antelope | 280 |
| Baboon | 3 |
| Birds | 1067 |
| birds and reptiles | 5 |
| Bison | 633 |
| Botswana | 3074 |
| Cameras | 22 |
| Cats | 605 |
| Cheeta | 297 |
| Circle of confusion | 4 |
| Coyote | 633 |
| Crocodiles | 1 |
| Debordieu | 993 |
| Deer | 50 |
| DOF | 4 |
| Eagle | 633 |
| Elk | 633 |
| Giraffe | 2 |
| Great Migration | 4 |
| Ground squirrel | 633 |
| Hyena | 38 |
| Kenya | 2497 |
| ✓ Kenya 11 | 162 |
| Kenya mammals | 5 |
| Leopard | 129 |
| Lightroom course | 4 |
| Lion | 179 |
| mammals | 18 |
| Masai Mara | 2 |
| Metering | 4 |
| Monkey | 3 |
| Naples | 1 |
| Pronghorn | 633 |
| reptiles | 338 |
| Samburu | 3 |
| Shore birds | 484 |
| Wildebeest | 2 |
| Wolf | 633 |
| Yellowstone | 1 |
| ✓ Zebras | 3 |

If you want to embed a Keyword on an image or images that you have already placed on another image, then the Keyword will be in the Keyword list (Figure 41) in the Keyword panel, so do the following:

- Select an image or images or a Collection of images.
- If you select a Collection of images, from the Edit Menu choose "Select All" or use the keyboard shortcut, hold down the Command(Macintosh), Control(PC) key and press the A key on the keyboard.
- Open the Keyword List panel by clicking with the cursor on the header bar.
- Scroll down the Keyword list until you find the Keyword for which you are looking.
- Hover your cursor over the Keyword, a small black box will appear to the left of the Keyword.
- Click with the cursor in the box to the left of the Keyword.
- The Keyword will be embedded in your selected image or images.

While any keyword you place on an image will automatically be added to the Keyword list, there is a way to add a keyword to the list without applying it to an image. On the left side of the Keyword List header bar are plus (+) and minus (-) signs. (Yellow ellipse, Figure 41) Clicking with the cursor on this plus sign will bring up a Create Keyword Tag dialog box. (Figure 42) The top section is a blank for the new keyword. The second section is a larger blank is for synonyms. You can type in words synonymous with the new keyword. The third section has three check boxes for including the keyword on export. The last section at the bottom is a check box for applying the new keyword to any selected images. After typing in the new Keyword and any synonyms, place a check mark in the appropriate boxes for including the keyword on export, Export Containing Keywords and/or Export synonyms, then click with the cursor on the Create button at the bottom right of the Create Keyword Tag dialog box.

There are several other things to know about the Keywording panel. Under the box containing the Keywords (Figure 40) is a second grayed out bar that, if you look closely says "Click here to enter Keywords". If you click in the bar, it activates and turns white and you can enter Keywords. You can also activate this bar by opening the Photo menu at the top of the screen and from the drop down menu choosing "Add Keywords". When you type a keyword into this blank, and press the Return (Macintosh), Enter (PC) key, the Keyword you entered in the bar will move up to the Keyword box and be embedded in the images.

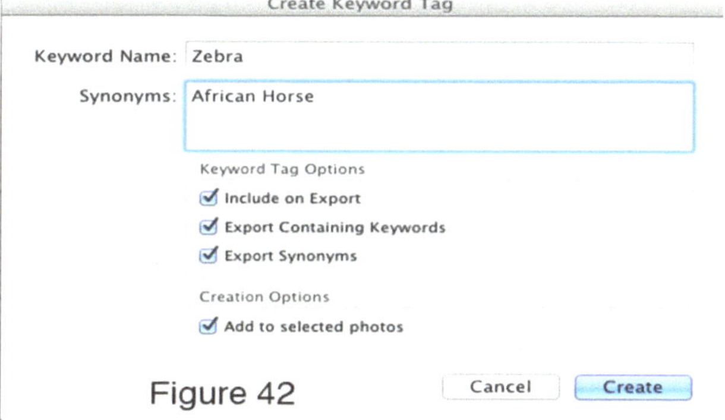


Figure 42

Below this second bar for adding Keywords (Figure 40) is another section titled Keyword Suggestions. When you enter a Keyword that is in Lightroom's® memory, Lightroom® will fill out the Keyword Suggestions box with other Keywords from the Keyword list that have been used on images that have the same keyword as the one you entered. To add a Keyword from this list of suggestions simply click with the cursor on one of the suggested Keywords and it will appear in the Keywording box and be embedded in the image or images selected. By the way, Lightroom® will arrange the Keywords in the Keywording box in alphabetical order.

Finally, below the Keyword Suggestions section of the Keywording panel (Figure 40) is a third section titled "Keyword Set". To the right on this bar is a box with a double pointed arrow. Clicking with the cursor on this double pointed arrow will do two things. First, it will show you some Keyword presets Lightroom already has in a pop up menu. (Figure 43) These presets are Outdoor Photography, Wedding Photography and Portrait Photography. Choosing any one of the presets will populate the box with Keywords Lightroom® thinks are appropriate for the topic. You can click with the cursor on any one of the Keywords in this section and it will become embedded in your selected image or images. You can create your own Keyword Set. To do this, do the following:

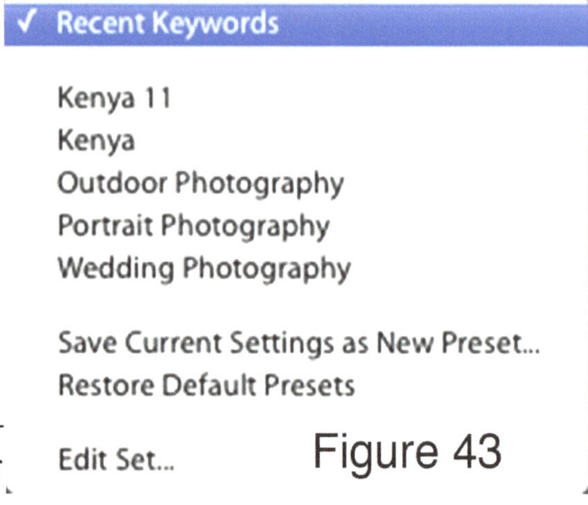

Figure 43

- In the Keyword Set section of the Keywording panel click with the cursor on the double pointed arrow at the end of the box containing the name of the keyword preset, OR,
- From the Metadata drop down menu at the top of the screen, select "Keyword Set".
- From the menu that appears, select "Edit".
- The result of either of these choices is a Keyword Set dialog box will appear with nine blanks with the keywords for the preset (Figure 44).
- Click with the cursor in the first box with a keyword in it and the word will be highlighted.
- Type a new Keyword in the box.
- Move to the next box and repeat the procedure typing in a new keyword for your Keyword Set.
- You are limited to nine keywords for a set.
- If you do not have nine keywords for your set, click with the cursor in the other boxes and press the delete key (Macintosh), backspace key (PC) to make the box empty.

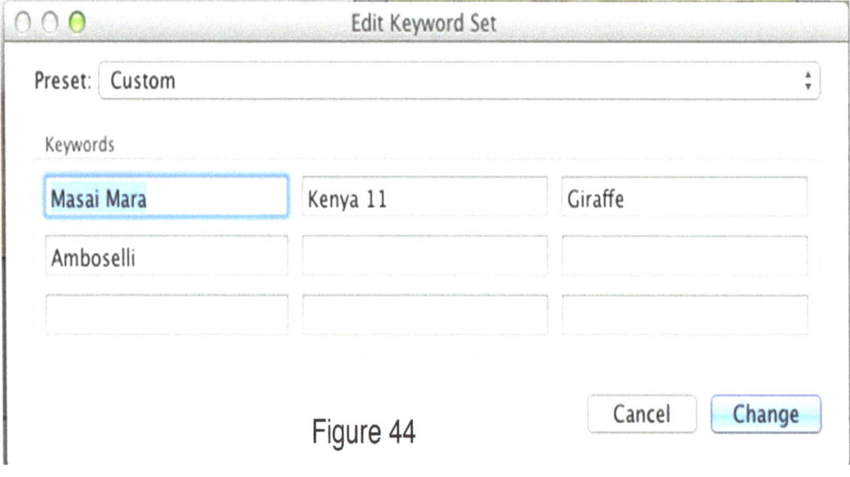

Figure 44

- You can go back and add keywords to the set in the future by selecting edit from the drop down menus in the Metadata keyword menu or the keyword set section of the Keywording panel.
- At the top of the dialog box click with the cursor on the double pointed arrow at the end of the box containing the name of the Lightroom® preset.
- From the drop down menu select "Save current settings as a new preset..".
- In the New Preset dialog box that appears, type a name for your new Keyword Set.

- Click with the cursor on the Create button at the bottom right of the New Preset dialog box.
- The name of the new Keyword Set will now be in the box at the top of the Keyword Set dialog box and the new keywords will be in the nine boxes.
- Click with the cursor on the Change button at the bottom right of the Keyword Set dialog box.
- The new Keyword set will be listed along with the Lightroom® Keyword Sets.

To use a Keyword Set do the following:

- Select an image or images
- Go to the keyword set and click with the cursor on any word in the keyword set
- The keyword will be added to the metadata of the image
- To remove a keyword from an image, highlight it and press the Delete key (Macintosh), Backspace key (PC)

TIP: Keywords can be imported into Lightroom® from another computer and exported to another computer from Lightroom. To Export Keywords from Lightroom, do the following:

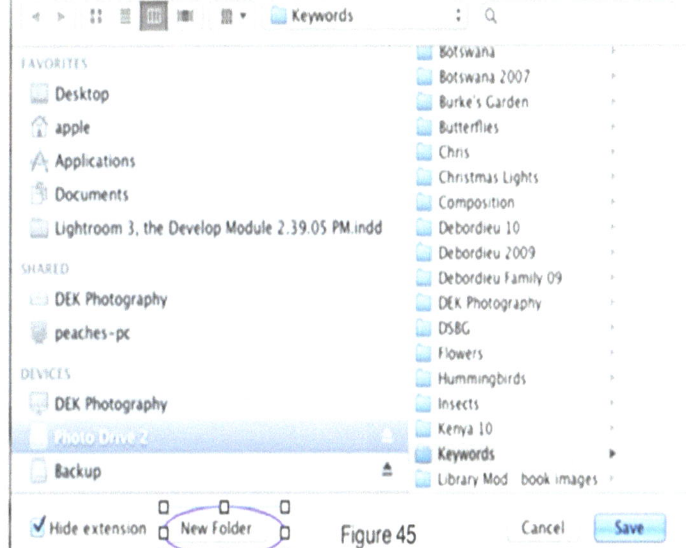

Figure 45

- Select the Keywords from the Keywords List.
- From the Metadata drop down menu at the top of the screen, choose "Export Keywords".
- In the Export Keywords popup menu that appears, Lightroom® will save the keywords as Lightroom® Keywords in the blank at the top of the Export keywords dialog box. (Figure 45) Note if you don't see this dialog box when you choose Export Keywords from the Metadata menu, click with the cursor on the arrow next to the top blank (Red Circle, figure 45) to expand the dialog box.
- Choose a location for the Keywords, your desktop for example or create a new folder by clicking with the cursor on the New Folder button at the bottom of the Export Keywords dialog box (Blue ellipse, figure 45).
- Click with the cursor on the Save button at the bottom right of the Export Keywords dialog box.
- The Keywords will be in a text file folder on your desktop.
- This folder can be copied to a flash drive and moved to another computer on which Lightroom® has been installed.
- To Import Keywords, connect a flash drive with the Keywords on it to your computer.
- From the Metadata drop down menu at the top of the screen, select Import Keywords.
- In the Import Keywords popup dialog box select the drive with the Keywords on it.
- Navigate to the Lightroom Keywords folder and select it.
- Click with the cursor on the Choose button at the bottom right of the Import Keywords dialog box.
- The Keywords will be imported into Lightroom and placed in the Keywords list.

## Finding Your Images

With your images flagged, rated, labeled, placed in collections and keyworded, the Library Filter bar becomes really powerful. You can find any of your images out of thousands very quickly by using a combination of the Text, Attribute and Metadata sections. With over 10,000 images in the Catalog, the following is an example of finding one image of a lion that was flagged as a pick, photographed at ISO 1000 with a 70-200mm lens in Kenya in September of 2010 with the keywords, Kenya, lion, stalking and huge:

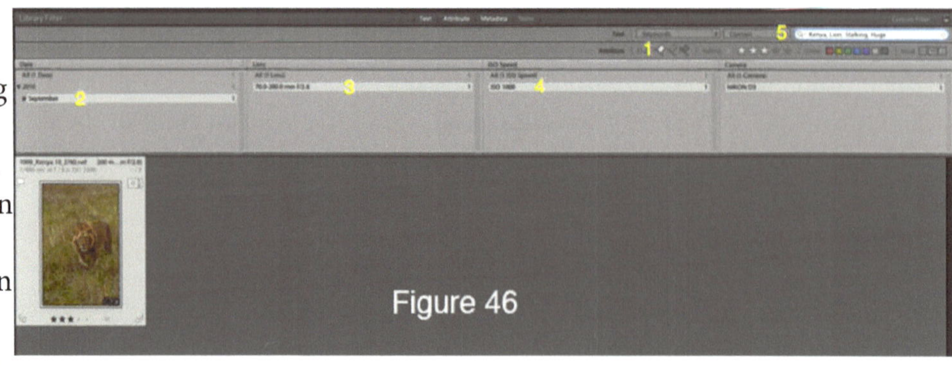
Figure 46

- Select the Collection lions.
- Open the Attributes section of the Library Filter bar and select the Pick flag icon to bring up only lions that have been flagged as picks (Number 1, Figure 46).
- Open the Metadata section of the Library Filter bar (Hold down the Shift key and click on the Metadata section.)
- In the first column of the metadata section, select Date and type in 2010 in the box that is present.
- Click with the cursor on the arrow to the left of 2010 and in the box that appears, type in September (Number 2, Figure 46).
- Only images of lions flagged as Picks and photographed in September of 2010 will be on the screen.
- In the second column drop down menu select lens.
- All the lenses used to photograph in September will appear in a list in the column.
- Select 70-200mm from this list (Number 3, Figure 46).
- Only images of lions flagged as Picks and photographed with the 70-200mm lens in September of 2010 will be on the screen.
- In the third column, select ISO speed.
- Select ISO 1000.
- Only images of lions photographed in September 2010 with the 70-200mm lens at ISO 1000 will be on the screen (Number 4, Figure 46).
- Open the Text section of the Library Filter bar. (Hold down the Shift key and click with the cursor on the Text section)
- In the first box, select Keywords
- In the second box select Contains All.
- In the third box type in the keywords, Kenya, lion, stalking and huge (Number 5, Figure 46).
- Only lions with those keywords, photographed in September, 2010 with a 70-200 mm lens at ISO 1000 will be on screen.

Usually, some where along the process of making selections or typing in keywords, the image you are looking for will appear on the screen. It is apparent that you have many tools in the Library Filter bar to find images if you take the time to organize your images by flagging, rating, labeling, keywording and placing them in collections in the Library module of Lightroom®.

## The Metadata Panel

Beneath the Keyword List panel is the Metadata panel. (Figure 47) This is a panel with a tremendous amount of information and options. It is also another way you can find images. In the header bar of the Metadata panel is a blank with a double pointed arrow on the right side of it. The first time you open the Metadata panel this bar will say "Default". If you click with the cursor on the double pointed arrow a menu will appear with different Metadata presets from which you can choose the metadata you want to see. Most of the time you are going to want to see the EXIF and IPTC metadata, so choose that one because it will show you the most metadata. If you have limited screen space, you might want to just select the EXIF metadata or the IPTC metadata to see them separately and avoid having to scroll up and down to find the information you want. There are blanks in all the Metadata sets except the EXIF metadata set for adding a title and/or caption to an image. You might want to do this in the IPTC metadata for an image you want to use in a book or slideshow, print or put up on the web or one you have sold to a client.

Below the Metadata header bar is a second bar labeled Preset. The first time you open the Metadata panel, the blank in this bar will say "None". If you click with the cursor on the double pointed arrow to the right of this blank you will see the Metadata Preset you created. Select your custom Metadata Preset and the IPTC Contact and Copyright sections will be filled in. Of course, if you applied your custom Metadata Preset to the images on import, these IPTC sections will already be filled out. Another option you have in the preset drop down menu is to edit the metadata presets. If you choose this option, the Edit Metadata Presets dialog box will appear on the screen. It is the same dialog box you filled in to create your Metadata preset before you imported your images. (Figure 20) You can edit your first Metadata Preset or you can create a new one with new information and save it.

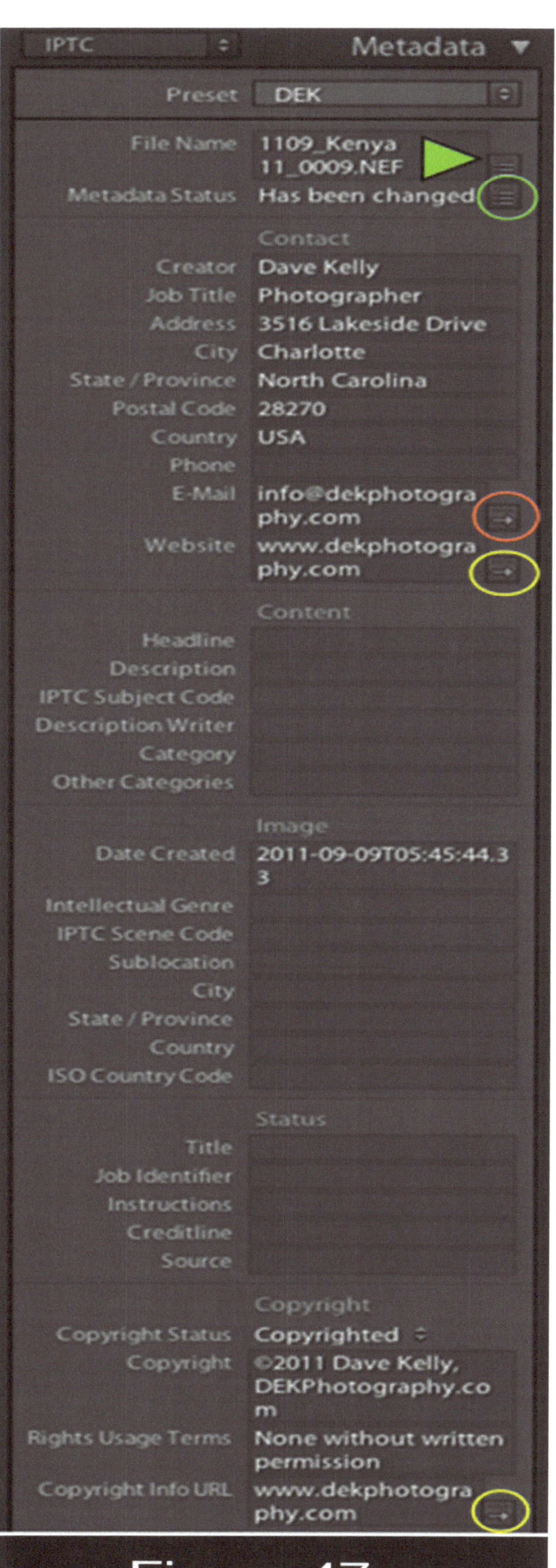

Figure 47

In both the EXIF and IPTC metadata sets, there are several menu options and filters that can be very useful. One of the options both the EXIF and IPTC metadata panels have in common is the ability to rename the image on screen or batch rename all the images in the current folder. Next to the file name blank on the right side is a menu icon (Green arrow, Figure 47). Clicking on this menu icon allows you to rename the image on your screen or batch rename all the images in the current folder. To rename one image or batch rename all the images in the current folder, do the following:

- Choose the file you want to rename OR,
- From the Edit menu at the top of the screen choose the "Select All" from the drop down menu, OR,
- Use the keyboard shortcut, hold down the Command (Macintosh), Control (PC) key and press the A key on the keyboard.
- In the Metadata panel click with the cursor on the menu icon to the right of the Filename blank.
- A file renaming dialog box will appear (Figure 16, Page 20).
- At the top of the file renaming dialog box it will tell you how many images you have chosen to rename.
- In the top blank of the file renaming dialog box will be the current filename template.
- To the right of the filename template is a double pointed arrow which when clicked on with the cursor will show you all the possible filename choices including any custom filename templates you created.

- Choose the filename template you want to use and type in any custom text in the box indicated.
- Click with the cursor on the OK button at the bottom right of the file renaming dialog box.
- All the selected images will be renamed.

TIP: The metadata panel is the third place you can rename your images. The first place is under the File Renaming panel in the import dialog screen, when you import them from a memory card or from a file on your computer. The second place is from the Library menu at the top of the screen. Select the images you want to rename and choose "Rename Photos" from the drop down menu. When choosing to rename images from the Library menu, the same file renaming dialog box will appear on the screen as the one from the Metadata panel (Figure 16, Page 20).

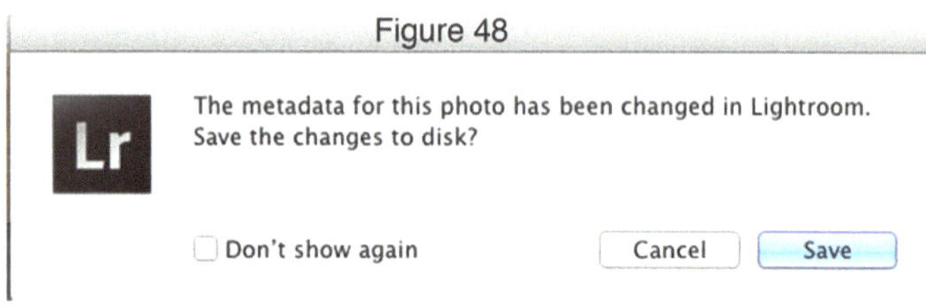


Looking at the IPTC Metadata first, there is one other menu icon below the Batch renaming menu, it is called Metadata Status (Green circle, Figure 47). It is to the right of the Metadata Status blank. If the metadata is up to date, then this icon will be blacked out and the blank will say "Up to date". If the metadata status has changed, the blank will indicate that the status has changed and the icon will be active. If you hover the cursor over the icon a message will appear that says "Resolve Conflict". Clicking with the cursor on the menu icon will bring up a dialog box that says "The metadata for this photo has been changed in Lightroom®. Save the changes to disk?"(Figure 48) This metadata status change can occur if you've added keywords or placed the image in a collection, rated, labeled or flagged the image. To resolve the conflict click with the cursor on the Save button at the bottom right of the dialog box.

Further down in the IPTC Metadata panel are three right pointing arrows. The first of these is next to a blank named "E-mail". The email listed in this blank is your own email if you placed it in the blank when you created your IPTC metadata preset. So, you can send a reminder email to yourself if you need to do that. However, you can type any email in this blank and if you then click with the cursor on the right pointing arrow (Red circle, Figure 47) it will bring up a New Message dialog box from your default email. You can then enter a subject, message, attach a file and send it. However, the file you attach must be one you have converted to a JPEG and properly resized. This is a much more complicated way to send an email from Lightroom® as you will see during the discussion on Exporting from Lightroom®

The last two right pointing arrows are next to blanks labeled "Website" and Copyright URL" (Yellow circles, Figure 47). Clicking with the cursor on either of these right pointing arrows will open the internet and take you to your website online.

Looking at the EXIF Metadata, the Batch Rename menu (Green Circle, Figure 50) is present here as in the IPTC Metadata panel. In addition to these two menu icons there are several right pointing arrows in the EXIF Metadata panel. These arrows act similarly to the selections in the Library Filter Bar. The following is what will happen if you click with the cursor on one of these right pointing arrows:

- The first of these arrows is by the blank labeled "File Path". (Blue circle, Figure 50). If you click with the cursor on this arrow it will show you where your image is located on your computer, either in the Finder on the Macintosh or in the Windows Explorer on the PC.
- The second arrow is beside the blank labeled "Cropped". (Red circle, Figure 50) Clicking with the cursor on this arrow will open the image in the Develop module with the Crop tool open.
- The third arrow down is by the blank labeled "Date Time Original" (Yellow circle, Figure 50) Clicking on this arrow will open the Metadata section of the Library Filter Bar and show you all the images cre-

ated on that date. The date will be highlighted in the Date column of the Library Filter Bar.

- The fourth arrow down is by the blank labeled "ISO Speed Rating" (White circle, Figure 50). Clicking with the cursor on this arrow will open the Library Filter Bar and show you all the images created using the indicated ISO Sensitivity rating.
- The fifth right pointing arrow is next to the blank labeled with the serial number of the camera used to create the image. (Purple circle, Figure 50). Clicking with the cursor on this arrow will open the Library Filter Bar and show you all the images taken with this camera. The camera serial number will be highlighted in the column labeled Camera Serial Number.
- The sixth arrow down is next to the blank for the lens you used to create an image you have selected. (Orange circle, Figure 50) Clicking with the cursor on this right pointing arrow will open the Library Filter Bar and bring up every image in your Catalog created with this lens. The lens will be highlighted in the Lens column of the Metadata section of the Library Filter Bar.
- The final right pointing arrow is by the blank labeled "GPS". (Black circle, Figure 50) Clicking with the cursor on this arrow, if you have a GPS enabled camera or you placed your images on a Google® map in the Map module of Lightroom® will show you the images placed on a Google® map.

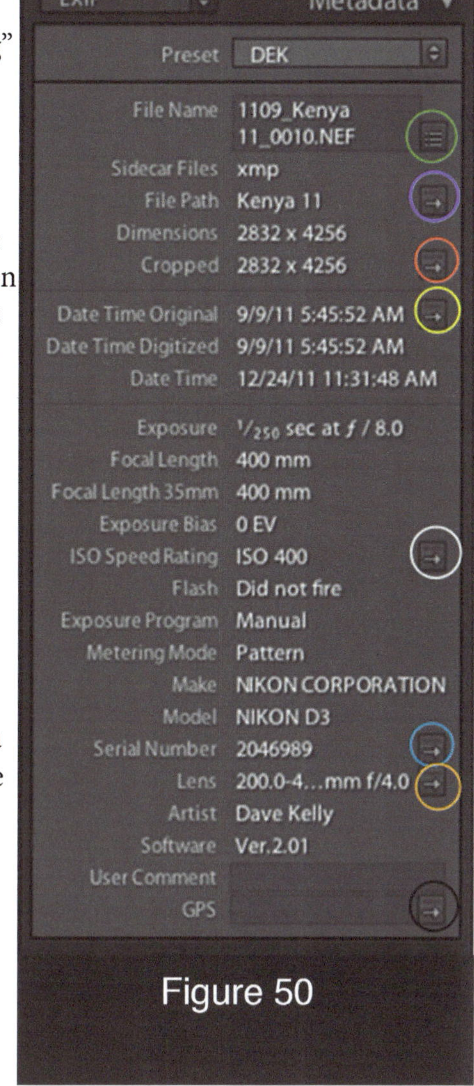

Figure 50

TIP: If you choose the IPTC and EXIF metadata section, the right pointing arrows will be in a slightly different order, but they will accomplish the same thing as they do when looking at just the IPTC or just the EXIF metadata. In addition, in the combined IPTC/EXIF metadata section you can also rate your images with stars and label them with colors. There are also blanks for placing a Title and Caption on an image or images. To apply stars, labels, titles and captions on one image or a group of images using the Metadata panel, do the following

- Choose the IPTC/EXIF metadata preset.
- Select an image or group of images in the Grid view.
- In the metadada rating section, click with the cursor on a number of stars and press the Enter/Return or Tab key.
- If you only selected one image the star rating will be applied to that image.
- If you selected more than one image, a pop up window will appear asking you if you want to apply the star rating to all the images selected. (Figure 51)
- In the blanks for Labels, Caption or Title, click with the cursor in the box and type the name of a color or type a title and/or caption in the appropriate blanks, press the Enter/Return or Tab key.
- If you only selected one image, the color label, title or caption will be applied to the image.
- If you selected a group of images a pop up menu will appear on screen

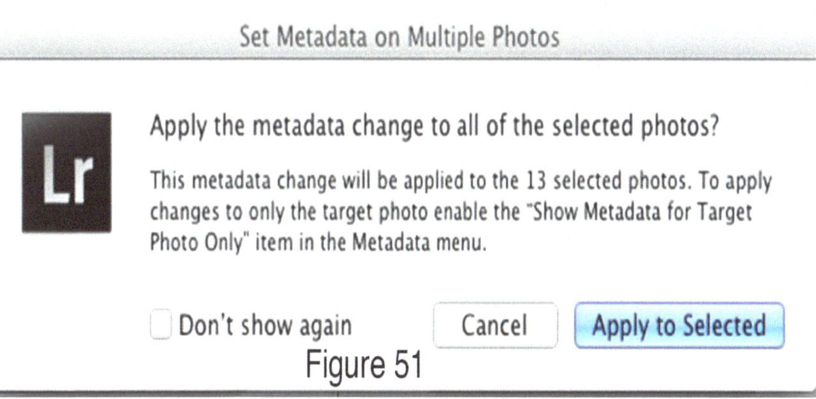

Figure 51

asking your if you want to apply the label, title or caption to all the selected images (Figure 51).

- Click with the cursor on the button at the bottom right of the dialog box labeled "Apply to Selected".
- The stars, color labels or title/caption will be applied to all the selected images.
- After applying the new metadata, the Metadata Status will have changed and the box next to Metadata Status will reflect the change, it will now say "Mixed" in the box.
- Click with the cursor on the menu next to Metadata Status, (Green circle, Figure 47).
- The same pop up dialog box will appear informing you the metadata has changed and asking you if you want to save the changes to Disk. (Figure 48)
- Click with the cursor on "Save" button at the bottom right of this box to bring the metadata up to date

The Metadata panel, which is often ignored can be very useful in finding images, but also in rating and labeling images and preparing them to go up on your website. Metadata is also useful to anyone viewing your images online such as advertising agencies or stock photography agencies in that they can find your images using keywords or captions and contact you via email or quickly go to your website.

## Publishing Services (in more detail)

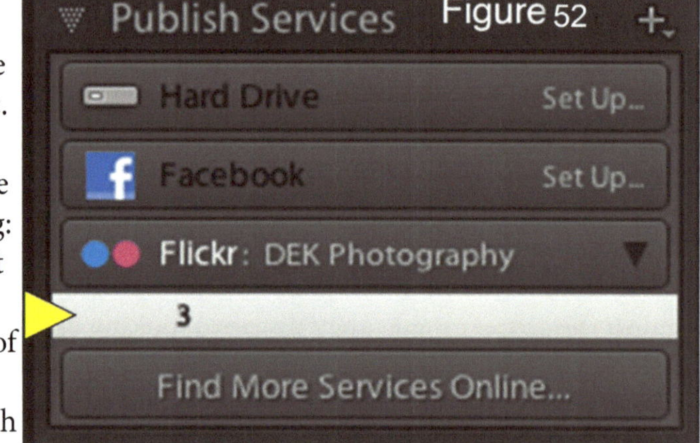


The last panel in both the left and right columns of panels is for Publishing services. Lightroom allows you to set up your account in one or more of the file sharing sites like Facebook®, Smugmug®, Flickr®, etc. and upload your images to those sites directly from Lightroom®. To set up to publish your images to the web on one of the file sharing sites, do the following:

- Create an account on the site to which you want to upload your images.
- Open the Publish Services panel at the bottom of the left column of panels. (Figure 52)
- Select the file sharing site to set up and click with the cursor on the words "setup" to the right of the name of the file sharing site.
- In the Lightroom® Publishing Manager dialog box that appears, (Figure 52A) fill in a description name for the account in the top blank titled "Publish Service".
- In the second blank down titled "Flickr® Account" in Figure 52A, you need to authorize the account, Click with the cursor on the "Log In" button to the right of the section.
- You will be taken to the file sharing site online to authorize your account.
- Back to Lightroom, in the Title section, set up how you want to title your images or leave the title blank.
- In the File Naming section, you can rename your images.
- In the video section you can choose to include video as well as the video format and quality.
- Set up the file settings, the format and resolution in the File Settings section.
- In the Image sizing section, set up the file size, width and height and how many pixels on the longest side.
- Select "Screen" for the type of output sharpening in the Output Sharpening section.
- Select what metadata you want included.
- Decide if you want to put a watermark on your images in the Watermarking section.
- Finally, in the last section, decide if the image should be public or private as well as the safety and type of file by placing a check mark in the appropriate box.

Once your account has been set up on the file sharing account, a bar will appear under the name of the file sharing site's name. This is the Photostream (Yellow arrow, Figure 52). All you need to do is select an image you want to publish and drag it to the Photostream. The image will be placed in the Photostream as a new photo ready to publish. The Photostream bar will also tell you how many images are waiting to be published. To see the images ready to be published as well as the photos already published and up in the photo sharing site, click with the cursor on the Photostream. There will be two sections in the Photostream, the images waiting to be published and the photos already published. (Figure 53) All you need to do to publish a photo to the file sharing site is select the photo and click with the cursor on the Publish button at the top right of the main screen (Yellow ellipse, Figure 53) or the Publish button at the bottom of the left column of panels in the Library module. If you want to remove a photo from your photo sharing site, select the photo in the Published photos section and press the delete (Macintosh), Backspace (PC) key and the image will be removed from the photo sharing site. The removed photo will show up in the Photostream under a heading called "Deleted Photos to Remove". You can re-publish the photo by clicking with the cursor on either one of the Publish buttons.

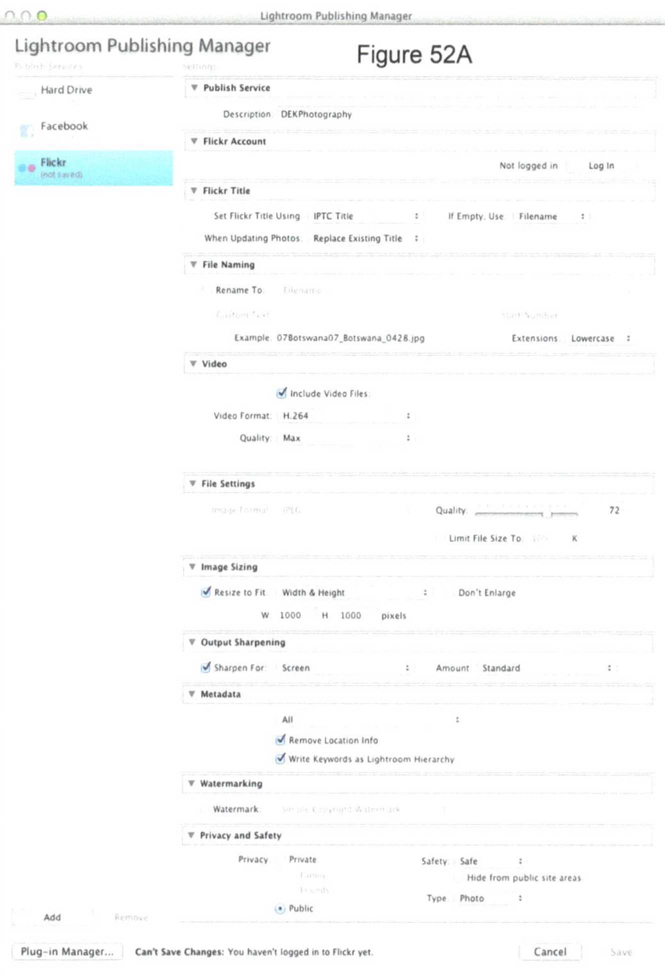


Lightroom® and file sharing sites like Flickr® work back and forth. So, if some one leaves a comment about one of your images, it will appear in the Comments panel a the bottom of the right side column of panels. You can also leave a comment about your image on the file sharing site by typing it in the Comments panel. The comment will be published along with the image online on the photo sharing site.

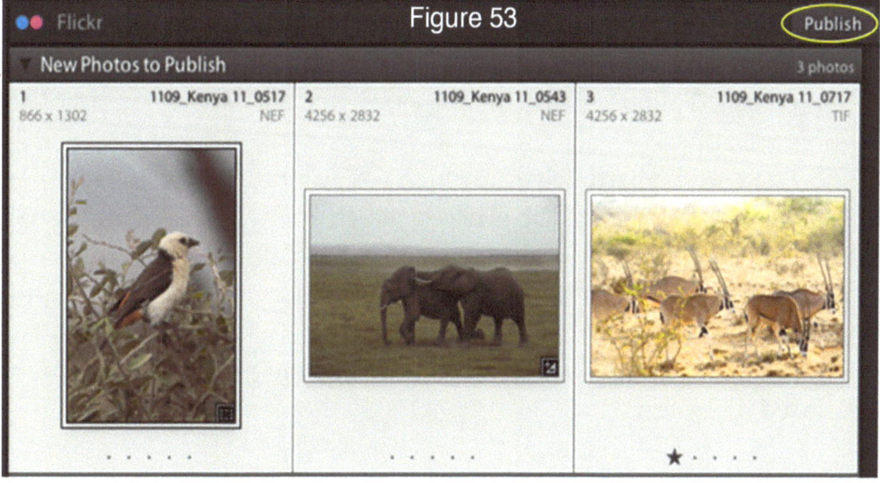


## Backing Up Your Catalog

In addition to your images being in your Catalog, all the instructions you have given Lightroom® for organizing and developing the images are there too. This makes backing up your Catalog extremely important. If your Catalog is on the computer hard drive or on an external hard drive and the drive fails and you haven't backed up the Catalog you will lose everything. Ideally, the Backup should be on an external hard drive, not the one where your Catalog is located. So, if you have your Catalog on an external hard drive you need a second external hard drive for backing up your Catalog. Hard drives are becoming smaller in size, larger in capacity and less expensive. It is worth getting a second one just to back up your Catalog, even if you have to plug it in every time you want to backup. To backup your Catalog, do the Following:

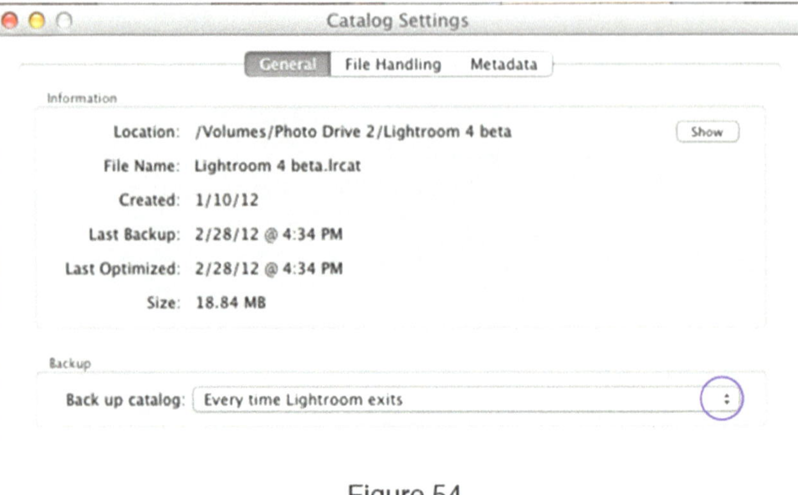

Figure 54

- The Catalog settings are found under the Lightroom® menu at the top left of the screen on the Macintosh or under the Edit menu on the PC. Open the Catalog settings dialog box (Figure 54) by clicking with the cursor on "Catalog Settings" in the menu.
- Select how often you want to backup your Catalog by clicking with the cursor on the double pointed arrow at the end of the blank in the second section. (Blue circle, Figure 54)
- After choosing how often you want to backup your catalog, (Figure 54A) close the Catalog Settings dialog box.
- When you close Lightroom, if it is time for a backup, a popup menu will appear. (Figure 55) This is where you can choose the hard drive on which to backup your catalog.
- Click with the cursor on the "Choose" button to the right of the location. (Blue ellipse, Figure 55)
- A "Choose Folder" dialog box will appear.

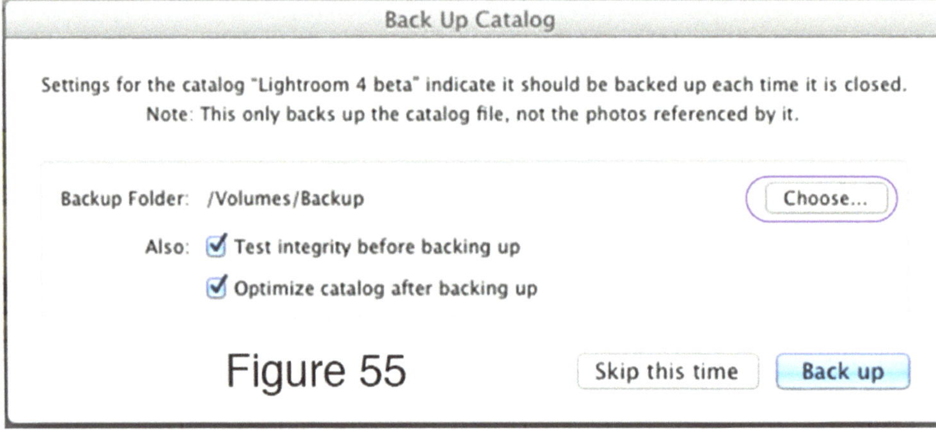

Figure 55

- Navigate to the hard drive on which you want the Catalog backup in the Choose Folder dialog box.
- After you have chosen the drive on which you want the Catalog backup, Click on the "New Folder" button at the bottom left of the Choose Folder dialog box.
- Name the new folder and click with the cursor on the Choose button at the bottom right of the dialog box
- Your Catalog will be backed up at the time you have indicated you would like it backed up when you close Lightroom®.

TIP: In the Backup Catalog dialog box you can also choose to test the integrity of the Catalog before backing up and optimize the Catalog after backing up. This will increase the amount of time it takes for the backup to take place, but both of these are valuable. Place a check mark in each of the boxes by clicking in them with the cursor.

Of course it is valuable to archive your images on DVDs or some other storage media after you have imported them and eliminated the rejects. Keep this storage media in a safe place and you will always be able to re-import the images to a new Catalog. However, you will not have the work you have done organizing the images into Collections or Stacks nor will you have the developing instructions, but you will have the images.

# Neat Lightroom Tricks

## Control/Right Clicking on a Folder

One way to save time with multiple tasks such as importing and exporting is to control click (Macintosh) right click (PC) on a folder in the Folders panel in the column on the left side of the screen. A pop up menu appears (Figure 56) that will let you do the following:

- Create a folder inside the folder on which you clicked. The folder on which you clicked is called the parent folder.
- Rename the folder.
- Remove the folder from Lightroom®.
- Hide the Parent folder or show the parent folder.
- Save metadata.
- Synchronize a folder.
- Update a folder location.
- Import images into the folder on which you clicked.
- Export the folder as a Catalog.
- Show the folder in the Macintosh Finder or the Windows Explorer.
- Get info about the folder.

Create Folder Inside "Kenya 11"...

Rename...
Remove...
Hide This Parent...
Show Parent Folder

Save Metadata
Synchronize Folder...
Update Folder Location...

Import to this Folder...
Export this Folder as a Catalog...

Show in Finder
Get Info

Figure 56

Of the choices in this menu, the most useful are Synchronize Folder, Import to this Folder and Export this Folder as a Catalog. (More on exporting as a Catalog shortly)

### Synchronize Folder

If you have added images to a folder outside of Lightroom®, they will not show in your Catalog. To update the folder, do the following:

- Control click (Macintosh), Right click (PC) on the folder to which you have added images or developed images outside of Lightroom® and from the pop up menu choose "Synchronize Folder," OR
- From the Library menu at the top of the screen, select "Synchronize Folder" from the drop down menu. (Figure 56)
- A pop up dialog box will appear on screen telling you the benefits of synchronizing. (Figure 56A)
- Click with the cursor on the Synchronize button at the bottom right of the Synchronize dialog box.

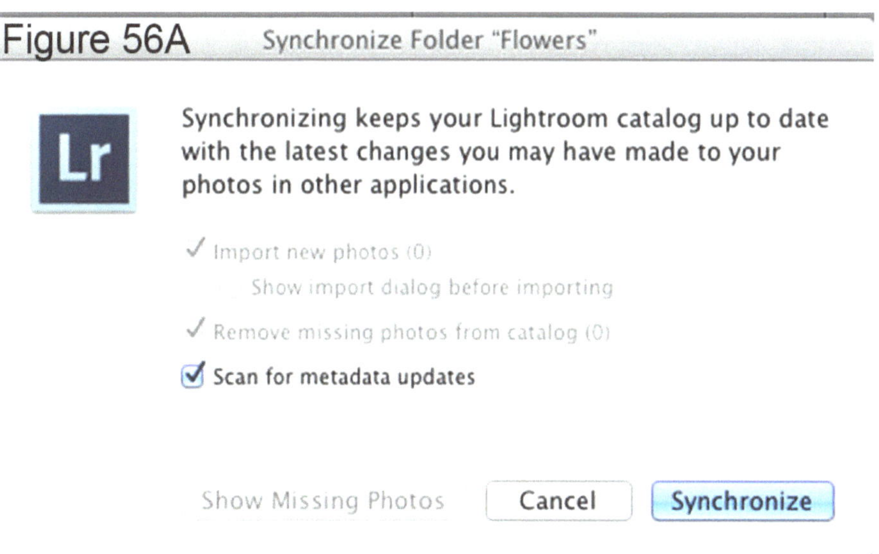

Figure 56A

- Lightroom® will scan the folder for any changes in metadata, new images, etc and make any changes or add any images to the folder.
- A progress bar will appear at the top left of the screen in place of the Identity Plate.

TIP: Synchronizing can also be helpful if you have an external hard drive that you use with both a laptop and desktop computer. If you import images into a folder while it is connected to the laptop and then re-connect it to the desktop, you will need to synchronize the folder so that the images are also in the folder on the desktop.

## Import into this Folder

Another handy shortcut from the pop up menu is to choose"Import into this Folder" when you Control (Macintosh), Right (PC) click on a folder. (Figure 56) The Import dialog box automatically opens. You will then need to choose a source from which Lightroom® will import the images, choose whether to Copy as DNG, Copy, Move or Add the images to the Lightroom® Catalog, choose to rename the images and whether to apply a metadata preset during the import. The destination folder is already chosen and highlighted in the Destination panel in the column of panels on the right side of the screen.

## Auto Importing

You can set up Lightroom® to import images automatically. In the process of setting up the Auto Import function of Lightroom® you will be creating a Watched Folder. Once your Watched Folder and Auto Import preferences are set up you will no longer need to use the Import dialog box. Whether you are importing a single image or a folder of images all you need to do is drag the image/folder to the Watched Folder and the import will take place automatically. To set up the Auto Import function, do the following:

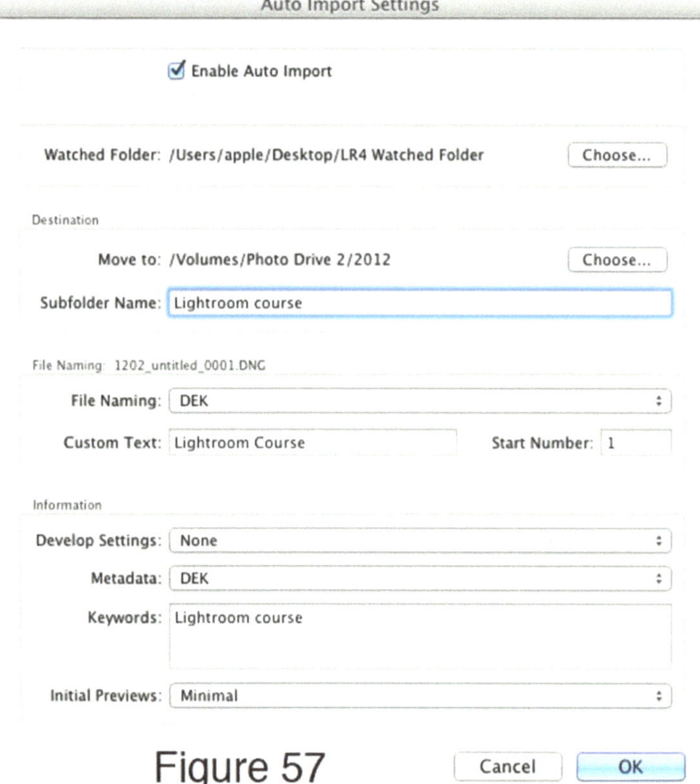


Figure 57

- From the File menu at the top of the page, select Auto Import and from the resulting drop down menu select Auto Import Settings
- The Auto Import Settings dialog box will appear on screen. (Figure 57)
- The first blank at the top of the Auto Import Settings dialog box has a check box to Enable Auto Import, this box will be grayed out until you fill in some of the other blanks.
- In the second section of the Auto Import Settings dialog box click with the cursor on the Choose button to set up your Watched Folder where you want it.
- Navigate to the drive or place you want the Watched Folder to be located. Make sure it is easy to find, the easiest place may be your desktop.
- The third section down is the Destination section, where you want your images to end up after they are auto-imported
- Click with the cursor on the "Choose" button and navigate to the drive and folder where you want the images to be moved after they are auto-imported.
- Either create a new folder and name it or select a folder already on the drive with images in it.

- Type a name for a sub folder in the blank in the Destination section.
- The fourth section down is for file renaming, choose your custom filename template, enter custom text if necessary and a start with a number.
- The last section is for applying a preset and metadata
- Select a preset if you have one you want applied.
- Choose your metadata preset with your copyright.
- Enter a keyword for the shoot in the Keyword blank.
- Make sure the initial preview is set to minimal so the images will be imported quickly.
- Click with the cursor on the OK button at the bottom right of the Auto Import dialog box.

Your Watched Folder is now set up in the location you chose and ready to auto-import your images. Now all you have to do is drag the images or a folder of images on to the watched folder and Lightroom will do the rest.

TIP: If you don't choose a destination folder, Lightroom® will automatically place the images in the Pictures folder (Macintosh), My Pictures folder (PC) and name the folder Auto Imported Photos. Remember, you need to check the Auto Import Settings frequently if you have designated a specific filename or keywords to be added as you may want to change them each time you import new images. You may also want to change the destination folder for importing a new group of images. It is probably a good idea to check the Auto Import Settings before dragging a file to the Watched Folder each time you want to import images using this function. Having a Watched Folder set up for Auto Imports does not preclude you from using the regular Import dialog box to import your images into Lightroom®

## Tethered Capture

Another way to import images into Lightroom® is to use the Tethered Capture function. This function allows you to bypass the memory card in your camera and import the image directly to your hard drive. To use the Tethered Capture function in Lightroom® do the following:

- Connect your camera to your computer using the USB cord that came with your camera (It's probably still in the box in which the camera came).
- Turn on your camera.
- Go to the File menu at the top left of the screen and from the drop down menu select "Tethered Capture"
- Select "Start Tethered Capture" from the pop up menu that appears to the right of "Tethered Capture".
- In the top section of the Tethered Capture Settings

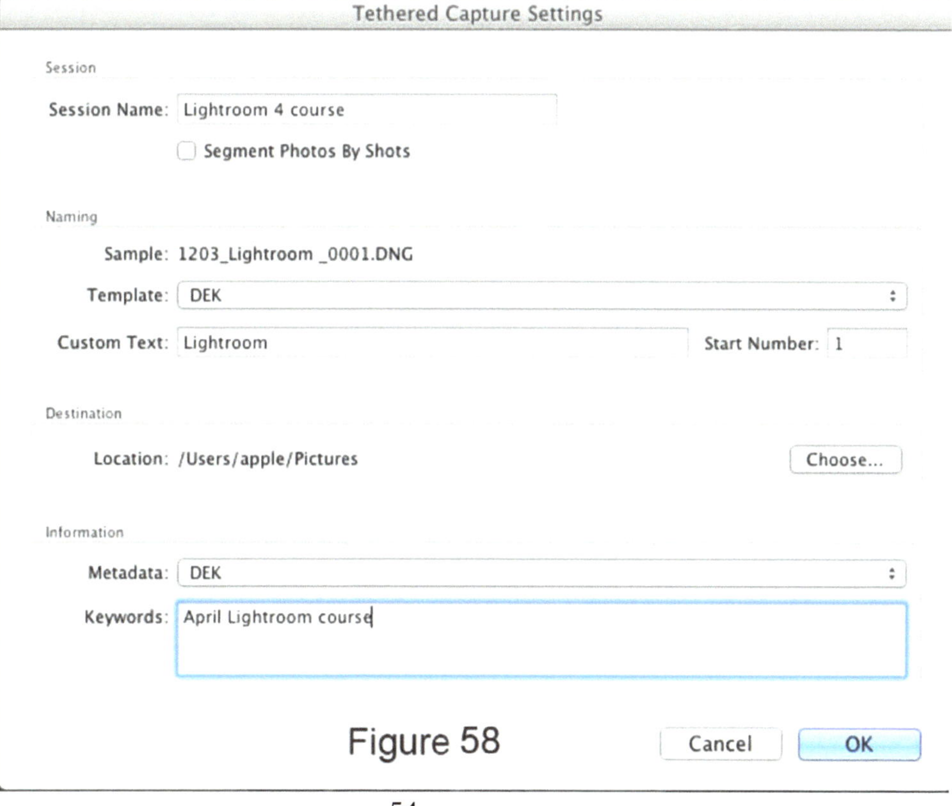

Figure 58

dialog box that appears (Figure 58)name the session in the top blank .

- Placing a check mark in the box labeled "Segment Photos By Shots" by clicking in the box with the cursor will allow Lightroom® to organize your images by shots.
- The second section down is for naming your images as they come in to Lightroom® (By default they will be named whatever you named the session plus a sequence).
- Click on the double pointed arrow at the end of the Template box and choose the custom filename template you have created.
- A Custom Text box will appear in which you can type the appropriate text.
- In the third section down, the Destination section, tell Lightroom® where you want the images to go on your computer.
- Click with the cursor on the "Choose" button in this section and navigate to the hard drive where you want the images to end up.
- Choose a folder on this hard drive or click with the cursor on the "New Folder" button at the bottom left
- Name the new folder if you created one.
- In the fourth section down, the Metadata section, select what metadata you want embedded in the images (Your metadata preset for example).
- Type in any keywords you want on the images in the last blank.
- Click with the cursor on the "OK" button at the bottom right of the Tethered Capture Settings dialog box.
- The Tethered Capture window will open on your screen, (Figure 59) it shows you the camera detected, your shutter speed, f-stop, ISO sensitivity setting and any develop preset if you have chosen one to be applied.

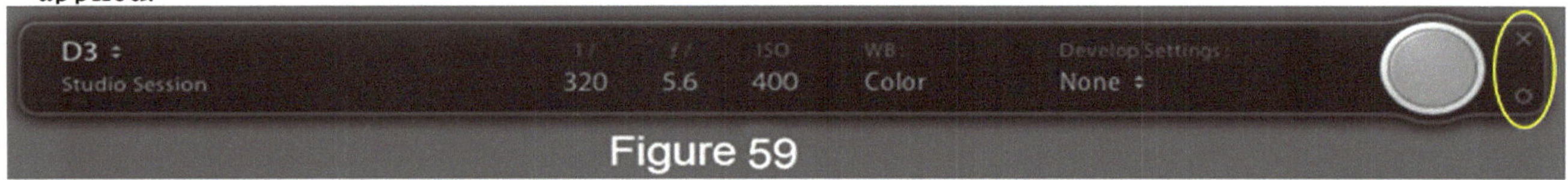

Figure 59

- To the right of the camera information is a large button that will fire your camera if you click on it with the cursor.
- To the right of the large button is an X on the top and an O on the bottom. (Yellow ellipse, Figure 59)
- Clicking with the cursor on the O will take you back to the Tethered Capture Settings dialog box.
- Clicking on the X will close the Tethered Capture function.
- You can also stop Tethered Capture by going to the File menu and selecting "Tethered Capture" from the drop down menu and then Stop Tethered Capture from the menu that appears.

TIP: To start Tethered Capture you must be in the Library module and by default Lightroom® will be in the Grid mode of the Library module. You can switch to the Loupe view if you want to see the images larger as they come in to Lightroom®. You can also switch to the Develop module where the images will be full screen. To do this, you must have started Tethered Capture, filled in the Tethered Capture Settings box and clicked with the cursor on the OK button at the bottom right of the Tethered Capture Settings dialog box. Either of these views will give you a chance to see the image in greater detail.

## Video

In Lightroom® 3 video could be imported into the Catalog, but there was very little that could be done with the video once it was imported. Lightroom®4 has several options for dealing with video in the Library module. Lightroom® 4 supports video from most digital SLR cameras, some of the higher end point and shoot cameras, some smart phones and some of the video cameras. First, video clips can be imported in the same way that still images are imported and they will appear in the Grid mode looking just like a still image with the first frame of the video showing in the cell. If you scrub across the cell in the Grid view with the cursor, the video will move across with the cursor giving you a preview of the video. In the bottom left corner of the video Lightroom® will also tell you the length of the video. As with a still image, you can bring the video into the Loupe view by double clicking with the cursor on the frame, choosing Loupe view from the View menu or using the keyboard shortcut, the E key. In the Loupe view a play bar will appear at the bottom of the video. (Figure 60)

Once in the Loupe view, the following can be accomplished in the Library module:

- Press the space bar to play the video or click with the cursor on the play arrow on the right side of the bar at the bottom of the video, (Yellow arrow, Figure 60).

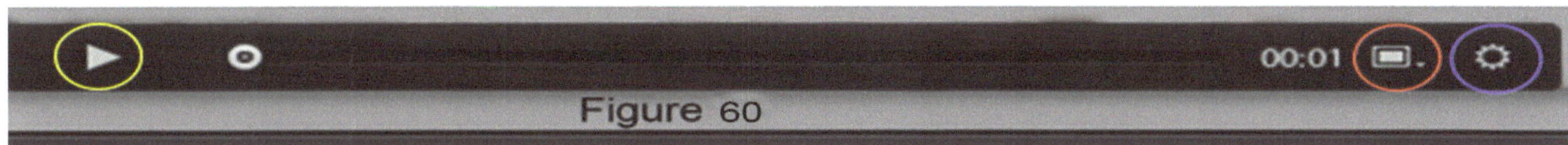

Figure 60

- Set a new in point at which the video will start playing.
- Set a new outpoint for the video to stop playing.
- Set a new Poster frame for the video to show in the Grid mode.
- Use the Quick Develop panel to make changes in the video.
- Capture a frame in the video, develop that frame as a still image in the Develop module.
- Create a preset of the develop settings on the captured frame
- Bring the developed captured frame back to the Library module and apply the develop settings Preset to the entire video clip.
- Export the video .

To set a new in point for your video, do the following:

- In the start and stop bar at the bottom of the video click with the cursor on the circular icon at the extreme right side of the bar (Blue circle, Figure 60).

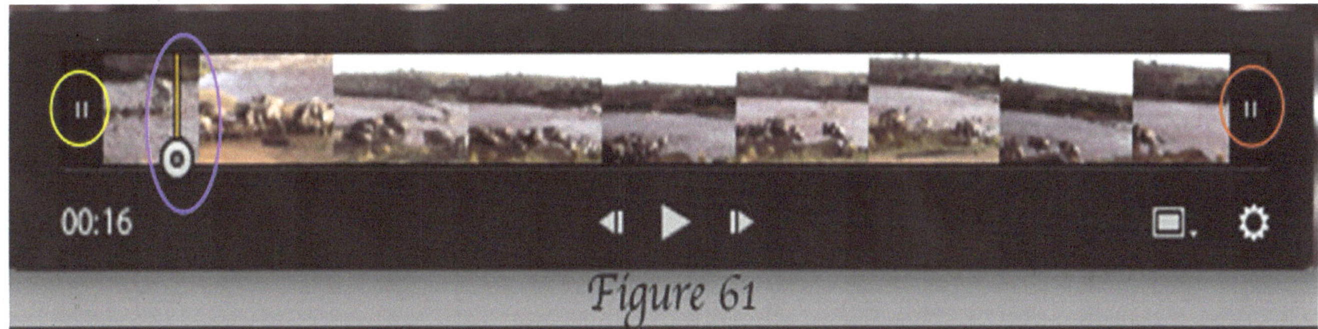

Figure 61

- A timeline will appear with thumbnails showing the frames in the video. (Figure 61)
- There will be a vertical line with a white circle at the bottom on one of the frames of the video frames. This is the video play head. (Blue ellipse, Figure 61)
- Play the video stopping when you reach the frame that will be the new starting point of the video.
- Click with the cursor on the two line icon on the left side of the timeline (Yellow circle, Figure 61) and drag to the new in point on the time line.
- Alternatively, play the video to the new in point and use the keyboard shortcut, hold down the shift key and press the I key on the keyboard to set the new in point.
- The video will snap to the new in point eliminating the previous frames.

To set a new outpoint, do the following:

- Play the video until it reaches the frame you want to be the new outpoint and stop it or drag to the new

outpoint.
- Drag the double line icon from the right side of the video (Red circle, Figure 61) back to the new outpoint.
- Alternatively, when the video reaches the new outpoint, use the keyboard shortcut, hold down the Shift key and press the O key on the keyboard to set the new outpoint.
- The video will snap to the new outpoint, eliminating the rest of the frames.

When you have multiple videos it is a good idea to set a Poster Frame (The image that shows in the Grid view)that lets you know what is in the video particularly if you have a certain content you want to see. Setting a Poster Frame makes it easier to find the video you want. To set a Poster Frame for the video, do the following:
- Scrub the Play Head in the timeline to the frame that either defines the video or has the content you want to use.
- Below the timeline click with the cursor on the second icon from the left end (it looks like a television screen, Red circle, Figure 60)
- From the drop down menu that appears select the second choice, "Set Poster Frame" (Figure 62).
- The frame you selected will now show in the Grid view.

You can also make changes to your video in the Library module using the Quick Develop panel. In the Quick Develop panel click with the cursor on the left and right arrows to change:
- The White Balance temperature and tint,
- Exposure,
- Contrast,
- Whites,
- Blacks,
- Vibrance.

If you try to move the video to the Develop module, you will get an error message in the Develop module telling you Video is not supported in the Develop module. However, there is a way to develop your video and take advantage of the tools in the Develop module from the Library module. What you need to do is Capture one of the video frames. This is also getting a little ahead of ourselves, but here's how you can do this:
- Scrub the Play Head over the clip or play the video clip until it reaches the frame you want to capture.
- Click with the cursor on the second icon from the right side of the timeline (the TV, Red circle,Figure 60).
- Select the first choice, "Capture Frame" in the pop up menu (Figure 62).
- The captured frame is a JPEG and will appear in the filmstrip at the bottom of the screen next to the video.
- Select the Frame.
- Move the single captured frame to the Develop module (Press the D Key on the keyboard) and make changes to that frame using the effects in the Develop module.
- Click with the cursor on the plus sign in the header bar of the presets panel in the column of panels on the left side of the Develop module to bring up the New Preset dialog box.
- Click with the cursor on the "Select All" button at the bottom left of the New Preset dialog box.
- Name the new preset, it will be stored with the other user Presets.
- Return to the Grid view in the Library module and select the video from which the captured frame was taken.
- In the Quick Develop panel, apply the user preset you created by developing the captured frame in the Develop module.

- The develop settings from the preset will be applied to the entire video clip.

This procedure will make more sense to you after you spend some time in the Develop module.

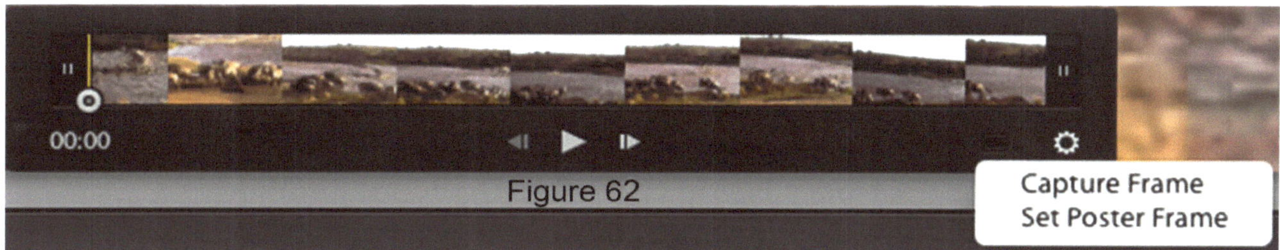


Figure 62

## Exporting video

To the Export dialog box in Lightroom®4, a section for exporting video has been added. (Red arrow, Figure 63) To export a video, do the following:

- Select the video to be exported in either the Grid view or the Loupe view.
- Click with the cursor on the Export button at the bottom of the left column of panels or use the keyboard short cut, hold down the Shift and Command, (Macintosh), Shift and Control (PC) keys and press the E key.
- In the popup export dialog box that appears on screen, at the top, select whether you want to export to a hard drive or burn the video to a CD/DVD.
- If you choose to export to a hard drive, in the top section of the export dialog box, "Export Location", select the location of the hard drive to which you want to export the video.
- In the second section, "File Renaming", choose to rename the file or not.
- In the third section, the "Video" section, check the box to include video files and choose a format and quality setting.
- In the metadata section choose the metadata you want embedded in the file.
- Click with the cursor on the Export button at the bottom right of the Export dialog box.

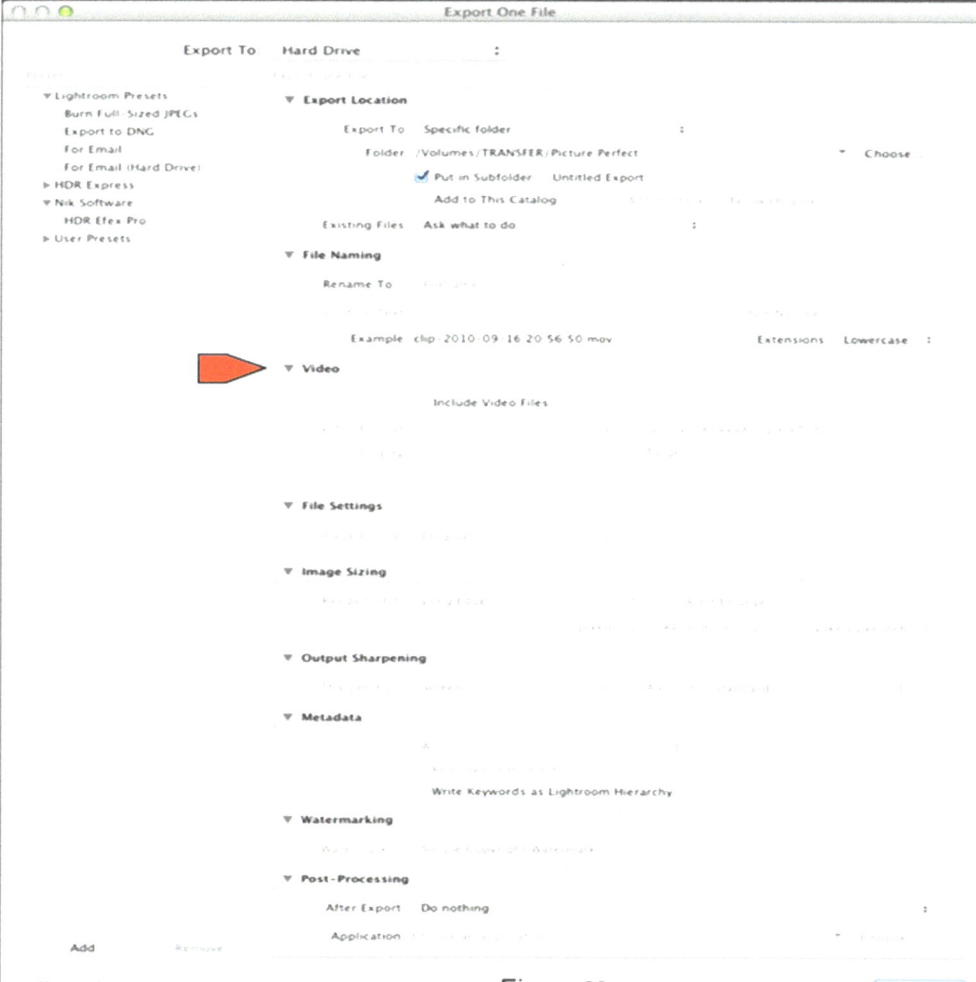


Figure 63

You can also use the Publish Services panel at the bottom of the left column of panels to upload your video to one of the supported file sharing sites. This is accomplished in exactly the same manner as uploading a still image to a file sharing site. Simply drag the video frame to the Photostream of the file sharing site you use. Click on the Photostream, select the video file and click with the cursor on the Publish button to upload the video to the file sharing site.

## Moving images from a laptop computer to a desktop computer

The Library Module enables you to make pretty impressive moves with your images. Not only can you put images in Folders and Collections, you can import and export images from one Catalog to another. Probably one of the most common procedures photographers do, is to take a Laptop computer into the field and import images into Lightroom® at the end of a days shoot. Upon returning home, the workflow first step is moving the images on the laptop computer to the larger desktop computer. This is especially valuable if you have worked on developing the images while your away from home. Lightroom® makes this step very easy. To move images from a laptop computer to a desktop computer, do the following:

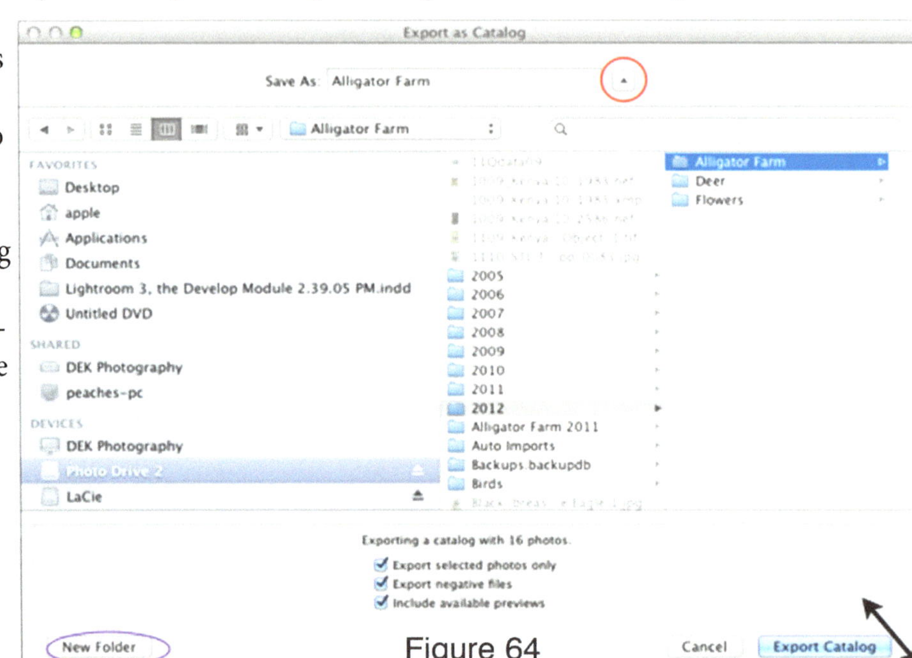


Figure 64

- ► On the laptop computer select the images you want to move to the desktop computer.
- ► From the File menu select "Export as a Catalog."
- ► If you don't see the expanded Export as Catalog pop up dialog box (Figure 64), click with the cursor on the arrow at the end of the "Save As" blank (Red circle, figure 64) to expand the dialog box.
- ► In the top blank of the Export as a Catalog dialog box give the new Catalog a name.
- ► In the second blank down, select where you want the Catalog saved.
- ► Click with the cursor on the bottom right corner of the dialog box (Black double pointed arrow, Figure 64) and drag the box out until you can see all of the devices connected to your computer and the folders in each device.
- ► Click on the "New Folder" button at the bottom left of the dialog box (Blue ellipse, figure 64.)
- ► Create the new folder and name it.
- ► Highlight the new folder to select it.
- ► If you have an external hard drive or big enough flash drive connected to your computer select it and place the new folder for the Catalog there.
- ► If you do not have an external hard drive connected put the Catalog in a folder on your desktop so it will be easy to find and then connect an external hard drive or flash drive and put the images on it.
- ► Disconnect the external hard drive from your laptop and connect it to your desktop computer.
- ► Open Lightroom® on the desktop computer.
- ► From the File drop down menu select "Import from another Catalog".
- ► In the Import from Lightroom Catalog dialog box that appears (Figure 65), navigate to the Catalog on

your external/flash drive and choose the Catalog.

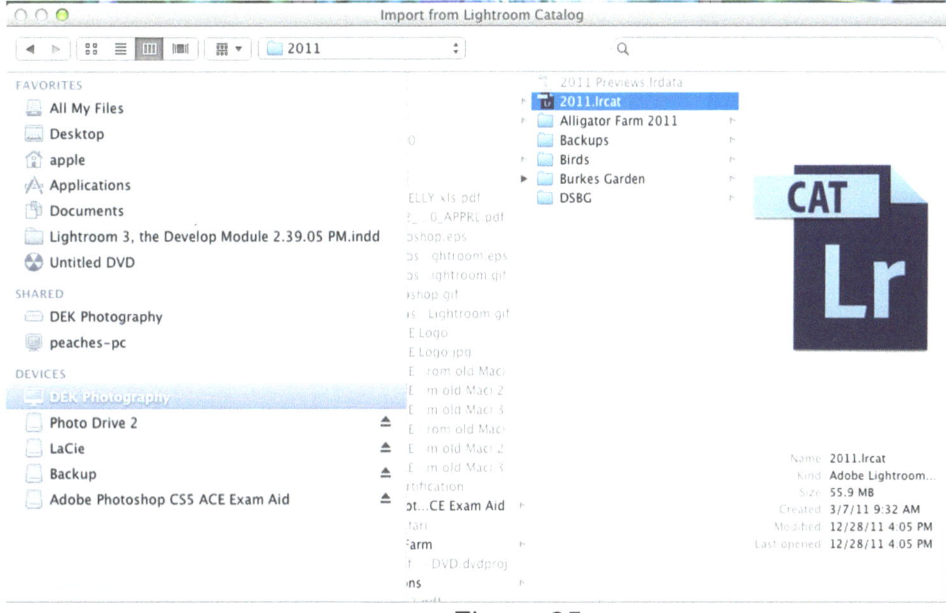

Figure 65

- The first Import from Catalog dialog box that will appear will check for duplicate or changed photos
- The second Import from Catalog dialog box that appears (Figure 66) will have all the folders in the Catalog listed in a column on the left side of the screen and the images to be imported on the right side of the screen.

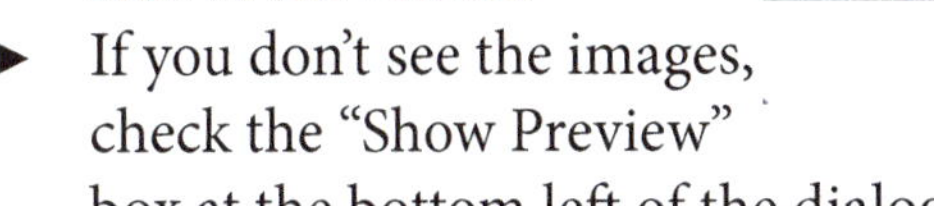

- If you don't see the images, check the "Show Preview" box at the bottom left of the dialog box (Figure 66).
- Expand the dialog box by clicking with the cursor on the bottom right hand corner and dragging to the right and down.
- Change the size of the thumbnail previews with the slider bar on the right beneath the images.
- Any duplicate images will be grayed out in the Import from Catalog dialog box.
- Choose whether to Add photos to catalog without moving or Copy photos to a new location and import from the File Handling drop down menu on the center left side of the dialog box.
- If you choose to copy the photos to a new location and import, a choose button will appear in the file handling section of the dialog box.
- Clicking with the cursor on the Choose button will bring up a new "Choose Folder" dialog box allowing you to navigate to the drive on your computer where you want the images and select it.
- If you want to create a a new folder for the photos, click with the cursor on the New Folder box at the bottom left of the "Choose Folder" dialog box.
- Name the new folder and click with the cursor on the Choose button at the bottom right of the Choose Folder dialog box.
- The "Choose Folder" Dialog box will disappear and the "Import from Catalog" dialog box will still be on the screen.
- Click with the cursor on the Import button at the bottom left of the "Import from Catalog" dialog box.
- The selected images/folders from the laptop computer Catalog will be imported to the desktop computer into your Catalog as a folder or folders.

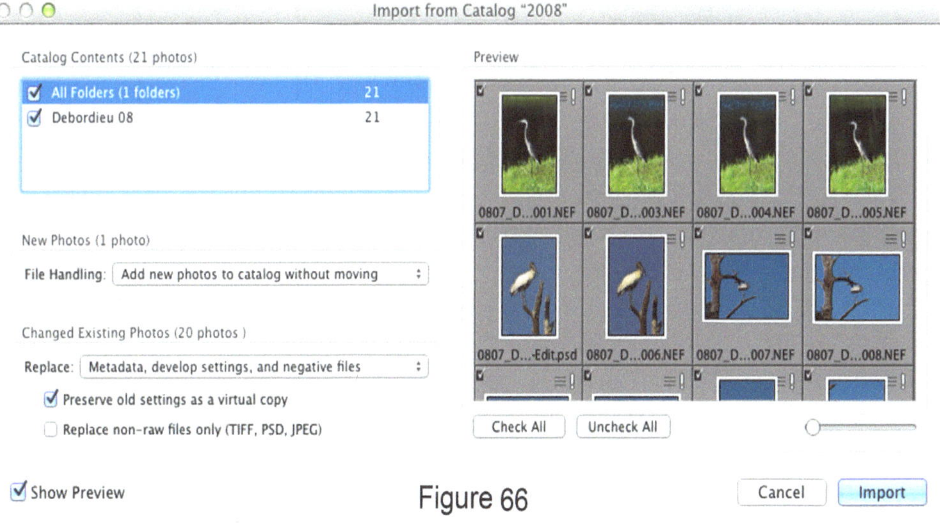

Figure 66

# Stacking Photos

One way to save room on your desktop is to Stack your images. If you have a number of images that were photographed with the same exposure settings or are of the same subject or have any kind of similarity, you can place them in a stack under one photo. Once in a stack, only the top image will show in the Grid view. That image will have the number of images in the stack in the top left corner. You can expand or collapse the Stack, move an image to the top of the stack, move an image up or down in the stack and split the stack. To place images in a Stack and work with the Stack, do the following:

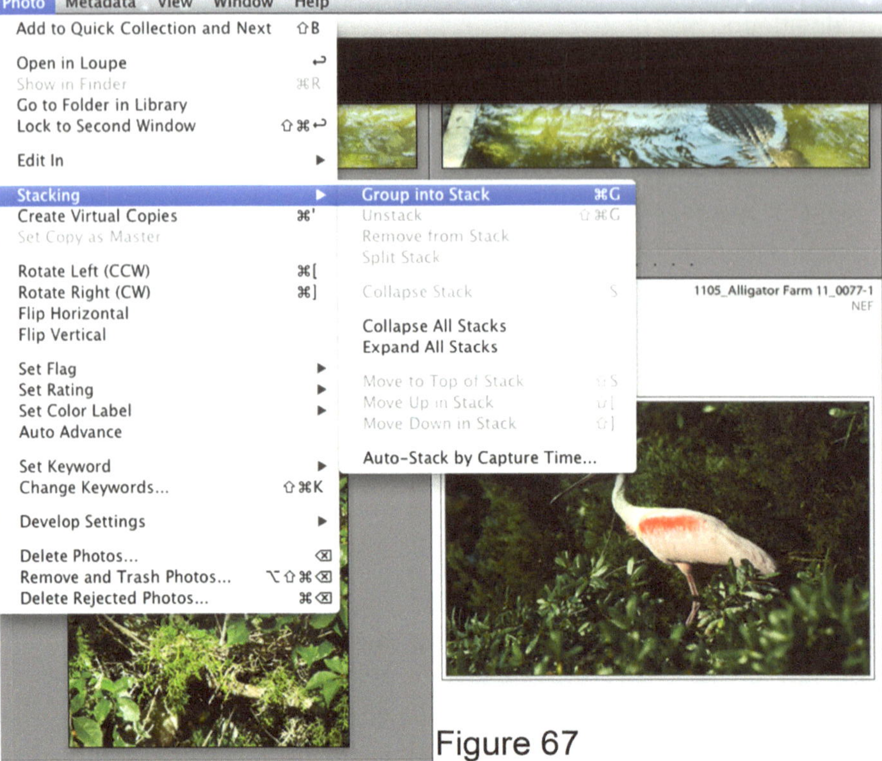

Figure 67

- ▶ Select the images you want in a Stack
- ▶ Go to the Photo menu at the top of the screen and from the drop down menu choose Stacking
- ▶ From the pop up menu that appears choose “Group into Stack”(Figure 67), OR:
- ▶ Save time by using the keyboard shortcut, hold down the Command (Macintosh), Control (PC) key and press the G key on the keyboard.
- ▶ The images will be in a Stack on the screen with only the first image chosen showing (Figure 68).
- ▶ To unstack the images, select “Stacking” and from the Photo drop down menu at the top of the screen .
- ▶ From the pop up menu that appears, choose “Unstack” (Figure 67)and the images will no longer be in a Stack.
- ▶ You can also use the keyboard shortcut to unstack the images, hold down the Shift and Command (Macintosh), Shift and Control (PC) keys and press the G key on the keyboard.
- ▶ To Expand the Stack and see the images in the Stack, go to the Photo menu at the top of the screen and from the drop down menu select Stacking.
- ▶ From the pop up menu that appears choose “Expand Stack” or use the keyboard shortcut, the S key.

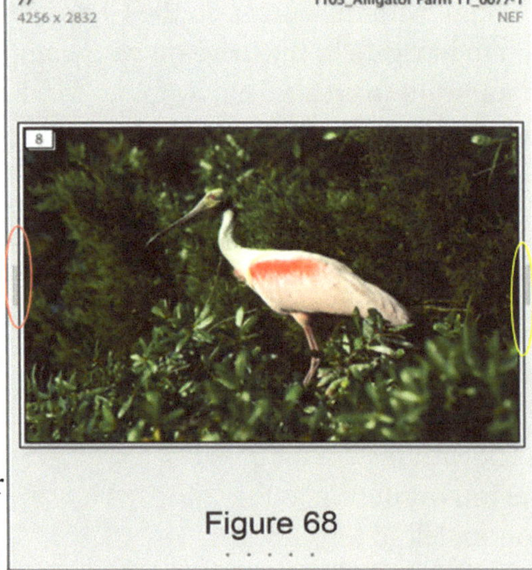

Figure 68

- ▶ Or, do it the easy way, click with the cursor on the two vertical lines on either side of the top image (Red and Yellow ellipse, Figure 68) and the Stack will open so you can see all the images in the Stack.
- ▶ To collapse the Stack again, follow the same procedure, except this time choose “Collapse Stack” from the menu or press the S key on the keyboard again.
- ▶ Or, do it the easy way, click with the cursor on either the two vertical lines on the left side of the first image (Red ellipse, Figure 68) and the Stack will collapse.
- ▶ If you want to add more images to the Stack, select the image and drag it to the Stack. The image will be

added to the Stack even if the Stack is collapsed.

- If you want to remove an image from the Stack, open the Stack, select the image you want to remove and from the Photo/Stacking menu select "Remove from Stack (Figure 67).
- You can also select which image appears at the top of the Stack by expanding the Stack, selecting the image you want on the top and from the Photo/Stacking menu choose "Move to top of Stack" (Figure 67) Or,
- Use the keyboard shortcut, hold down the Shift key and press the S key on the keyboard to move the selected image to the top of the Stack.
- You can move an image up in the Stack by expanding the Stack, selecting an image and from the Photo/Stacking menu select "Move up in Stack" (Figure 67) Or,
- Use the keyboard shortcut, hold down the Shift key on the keyboard and press the left bracket key ([) to move an image up one place in the Stack.
- To move an image down in the Stack, expand the Stack and from the Photo/Stacking menu select "Move Down in Stack" OR,
- Use the keyboard shortcut, hold down the Shift key on the keyboard and press the right bracket key(]) to move the image down one place in the Stack.

Another option you have with Stacks is to split the Stack. To Split the Stack, do the following:

- Expand the Stack .
- Select the image you want to be the top image in the second Stack.
- From the Photo/Stacking menu select "Split Stack" (Figure 67) and the Stack will be split into two Stacks with the selected image the top image on the second Stack.
- If you select "Split Stack" from the Photo/Stacking menu without expanding the Stack, the top image will be split off from the other images in the Stack.

TIP: Stacks can be pretty useful in organizing your images into groups. You can place all the star rated images or color labeled images into Stacks by the rating or the label instead of creating collections. Stacks are not available in Collections, only in Folders.

You can also expand or collapse all your Stacks at the same time by going to the Photo/Stacking menu and selecting "Expand All Stacks" or Collapse All Stacks". (Figure 67) All the Stacks you've created in the Library module will be expanded or collapsed.

Another option you have with Stacks is to place images in Stacks by Capture time. To stack your images by Capture Time, do the following:

- From the Photo/Stacking menu select the bottom choice, "Auto-Stack by Capture Time...".
- From the Auto Stack by Capture Time dialog box that appears, choose the amount of time you want between Stacks by sliding the slider on the slider bar (Figure 69).
- Sliding to the left will decrease the time between the Stacks and create more Stacks.

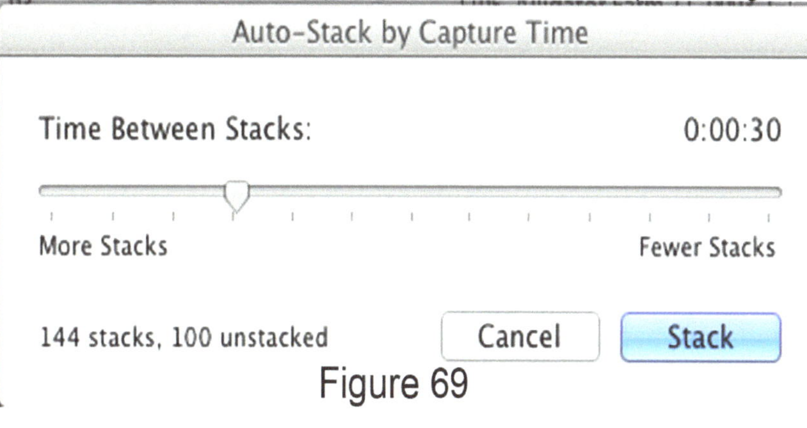

Figure 69

- Sliding to the right will increase the time between the Stacks and create fewer Stacks.
- As you slide the slider on the bar either way, Lightroom® will show you how many Stacks you will create and how many images will not be in a Stack at the bottom left of the Auto Stack by Capture Time dialog box.

- The interval you can set between Stacks can be up to one hour.

The Auto-Stacking could be very valuable for a photographer who works in a studio and has set appointments. There would be no need to change cards for each photo shoot, Lightroom® will stack the images for you by time intervals.

Stacking can be an alternative to placing your images in collections or a way to have the images on the screen in collections and still be in Stacks. After you have flagged, rated, labeled, keyworded and placed your images in Collections, you can easily place them in Stacks in their folders. To place your images in Stacks after you have classified them with flags, ratings, labels and keywords, do the following:

- Select a folder from the Folders panel.
- Use the Library Filter Bar to bring up all images rated with one of the star ratings or labeled with one of the colors, or keyworded with one keyword.
- These will now be the only images on the screen.
- Select all the images (Edit>Select All) or hold down the Command key on the Macintosh, Control Key on the PC and press the A key on the keyboard).
- Place the images in a Stack by going to the Photo menu and selecting Stacking and then "Group into a Stack" from the pop out menu (Figure 67) or use the keyboard shortcut, hold down the Command (Macintosh), Control (PC) key and press the G key on the keyboard.
- All of the similarly flagged, rated, labeled or keyworded images will now be in one stack.
- Go back to the Library Filter Bar and select "None" in the header bar
- All of the images in the folder will now be on screen with the images you placed in the Stack under one image with the number of the images in the Stack indicated at the top left of the top image.
- Repeat the process until all the images in the folder are in Stacks.

You will now, effectively have all your Collections on the screen in Stacks in the Folders panel. If you have flagged, rated and labeled your images but not placed them in Collections or keyworded them yet, you should put them in Collections first before you stack the images. If you put the images in Stacks and then select the Stack while it is collapsed to create a Collection, only the top image will end up in the Collection. If you have Stacked the images and want to put all the images in the Stack into a Collection, you must expand the Stack and select all the images in the Stack and then put them into a Collection. Other than saving room on the computer screen, which could be important with a small screen, there really is no advantage in having all your images in Collections and in Stacks.

## Copy Settings

While in the Library module, If you have images that have been developed in the Develop module, you can copy the develop settings from one image and paste them to another image without leaving the Library module. To copy develop settings from one image to another in the Library module, do the following:

- Select the image with the develop settings.
- From the Photo menu at the top of the screen, select "Develop Settings" from the drop down menu.
- From the menu that appears, select "Copy Settings" or use the keyboard shortcut, hold down the Shift and Command (Macintosh), Shift and Control (PC) keys and press the C key on the keyboard.
- Select the image to which you would like the develop settings applied.
- From the Photo menu at the top of the screen again select "Develop Settings" from the drop down menu.
- From the menu that appears, select "Paste Settings" or use the keyboard shortcut, hold down the Shift and Command (Macintosh), Shift and Control (PC) keys and press the V key on the keyboard.
- Lightroom® will paste the develop settings to the selected image.

For a faster way to apply develop settings from one image to the other in the Library module, do the following:

- Select the image with the develop settings and then select a separate image without the develop settings. (Only one image should be selected)
- From the Photo menu select "Develop Settings" and from the menu that appears, select "Paste Settings From Previous".
- Alternatively, use the keyboard shortcut, hold down the Option and Command (Macintosh), Alt and Control (PC) keys and press the V key on the keyboard.
- Develop settings from the first image selected will be applied to the second image selected.

A third way to apply settings from an image you have developed in the Develop module to another image without leaving the Library module is to do the following:

- Select the image with the develop settings.
- Select a second image without the develop settings by holding down the Shift key and clicking with the cursor on the second image if the image is adjacent to the image with the develop settings or hold down the Command key on the Macintosh, Control key on the PC and click with the cursor on the second image to select it if it is not adjacent to the image with the develop settings on it.
- There are two buttons at the bottom of the right column of panels that are grayed out until you click with the cursor on the second image to select it and then they become active.
- The Right button is for syncing settings from the developed image to the non-developed image.
- Click with the cursor on the "Sync Settings" button.
- A Sync Settings pop up box will appear on screen (Figure 70) This is the same Sync Settings dialog box you will find in the Develop module.

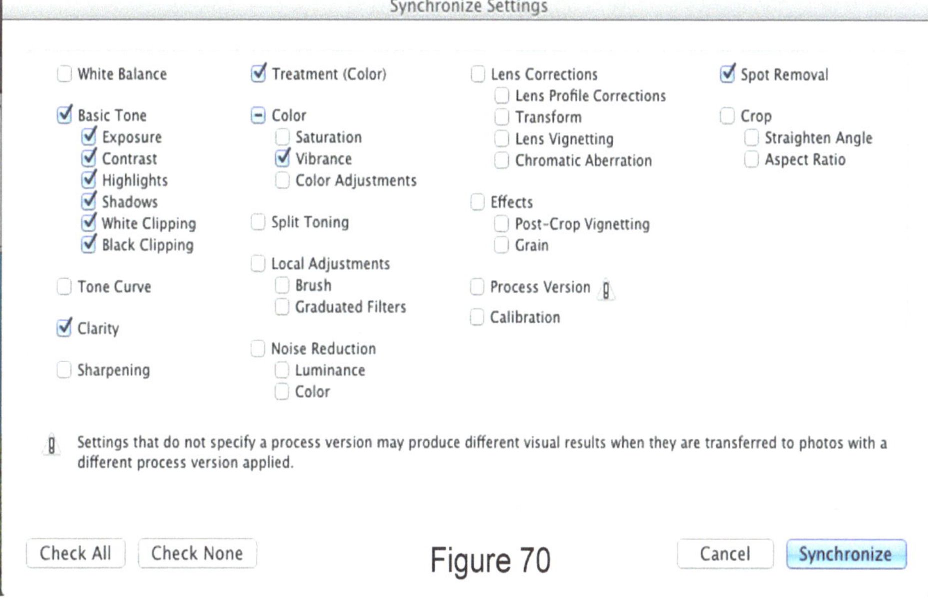

Figure 70

- You can check the boxes of the settings you changed in the Sync Settings dialog box or you can click with the cursor on the "Check All" button at the bottom left of the dialog box.
- The develop settings from the developed image will be applied to the selected non-developed image.
- If, in the future, if you want to know how you developed the image you should just check the boxes for the effects you changed when you developed the image in the Develop module.

TIP: To find out which effects were changed in the Develop module, select the image with the develop settings applied and in the Develop module click with the cursor on the History panel in the left column of panels in the Develop module. This will show you all the steps taken in developing the image.

## Virtual Copies

A Virtual Copy is an exact duplicate of an image. If the image has develop settings on it, the Virtual Copy will have the same develop settings. If the image has not yet had any develop settings applied to it the

Virtual Copy will have none also. What a Virtual Copy really is, is a set of duplicate instructions that Lightroom® saves with the image.

You can create a Virtual Copy of an image in the Library, Develop, Map, Book, Slide Show, Print and Web modules. To create a virtual copy, do the following:

- Select an image.
- From the Photo menu select "Create Virtual Copy"OR,
- Hold down the Control key on the Macintosh and click with the cursor on the image, for the PC, right click on the image.
- From the pop up menu that appears on screen, choose "Create Virtual Copy" OR;
- Use the keyboard shortcut, hold down the Command (Macintosh), Control (PC) key and press the apostrophe (') key on the keyboard.
- The newly created Virtual Copy will be placed in the Grid view and Filmstrip next to the original which is now called the Master Copy.
- The Virtual Copy is identified because the bottom left corner will appear to be folded up.
- You can then move the Virtual Copy to the Develop module for developing, leaving the Master Copy untouched.
- The Virtual Copy can be printed, included in a book, slide show or web gallery or moved to an external editing program like Photoshop®.
- You can create as many Virtual Copies of an image as you like and leave the original image untouched.

TIP: If you develop and image in the Develop module and then create a Virtual Copy of the image, you must go back to the original and reset it in the Develop module before you can develop it again. So, if you know you want to develop an image in several ways, for example, one color and one black and white, you can create two Virtual Copies in the Library module, go to the Develop module, find the virtual copies in the Filmstrip and develop one in color and then select the second Virtual copy and develop it in black and white. The original will be in the Filmstrip along with both virtual copies and you will not have to reset the original, just choose a Virtual Copy and develop it. The original image will still be in the Library module, but now the two Virtual Copies, each developed differently will be in the Grid view and Filmstrip right next to the Original.

## Color Label Sets

Under the Metadata menu at the top of the screen you will find a topic called "Color Label Set" as one of the choices. Clicking with the cursor on this choice will bring up a menu that lists three color label sets and the opportunity to edit one and create your own Color Label Set. (Figure 71) The first choice is "Bridge® Default", the second is "Lightroom® Default" and the third is "Review Status". If you also use Adobe Bridge® you may want to select this choice to keep the color labels consistent with the color labels you can use in Adobe Bridge®. In this case each color stands for a status of the image in Adobe Bridge® such as Selected or Approved. In the Review Status Color Label Set, each color stands for an activity that needs to be done, such as printing, color correction, etc. In the Lightroom® default Color Label Set, the colors are just labeled with the color. To see what each color in the different sets stands for, do the following:

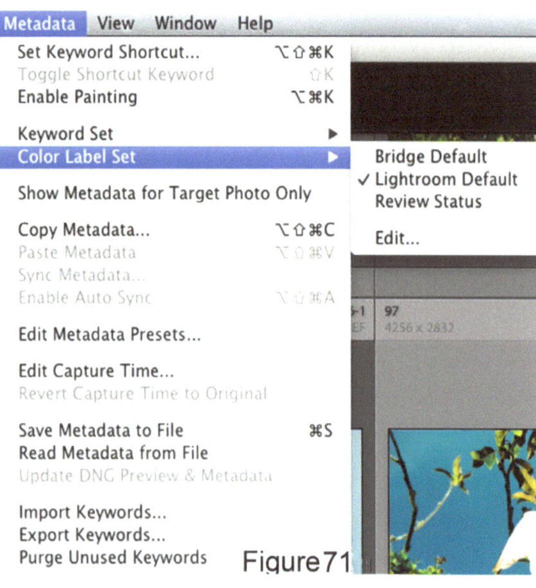

Figure71

- From the Metadata menu at the top of the screen, select Color Label Set.

- From the menu that appears select one of the Color Label Sets.
- After you select the Color Label Set, the menu will close.
- Go again to the Metadata menu and select Color Label Set.
- This time from the menu that appears select "Edit".
- The chosen Color Label Set will appear with an indication of what each color stands for.

By default, the Lightroom® Color Label Set will be active when you first open Lightroom® and when you place a color label on an image it will indicate that you have set the label to the color by showing you a message across the screen the says "Set Label to Red" or whatever color you chose. You can create your own Color Label Set and when you label an image it will tell you with what you labeled the image. For example if you are using a system where the color labels stand for an animal species, when you label the image with the color that stands for an animal, Lightroom® will flash a message across the screen telling you what animal is in the image. Creating your own Color Label Set is the easiest with the Lightroom® default Color Label Set. To create your own Color Label Set, do the following:

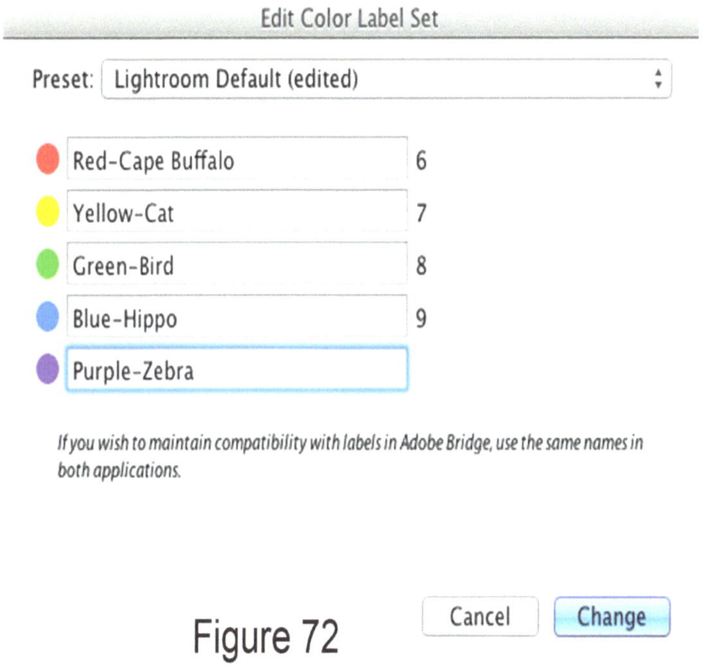

Edit Color Label Set

Preset: Lightroom Default (edited)

Red-Cape Buffalo 6
Yellow-Cat 7
Green-Bird 8
Blue-Hippo 9
Purple-Zebra

*If you wish to maintain compatibility with labels in Adobe Bridge, use the same names in both applications.*

Cancel Change

Figure 72

- From the Metadata menu at the top of the screen, select "Color Label Set".
- Make sure Lightroom® Default has a check mark in front of it indicating it is the selected Set.
- Select "Edit" from the Color Set menu (Figure 71).
- The Lightroom® "Edit Color Set" dialog box will appear with each color labeled with its name (Figure 72).
- Click in the box with the color name and type the new title (It's not a bad idea to keep the colors in the name).
- When you have changed all the names of the colors click with the cursor on the double pointed arrow at the end of the Preset blank at the top of the dialog box and choose "Save Current Settings as New Preset".
- In the popup box that appears name the new preset.
- Click with the cursor on the "Create" button at the bottom right of the popup box.
- Click with the cursor on the "Change" button at the bottom right of the Edit Color Label dialog box.

TIP: You can create as many Color Label Set presets as you need. So each time you import a different kind of image, you can create a new Color Label Set with which to label your images. It is also possible to restore the default presets, delete a preset and rename a preset. Any of these tasks are choices you can make when you click with the cursor on the double pointed arrow on the right side of the Preset blank at the top of the Edit Color Labels dialog box.

## Editing Capture Time

Embedded in the EXIF metadata is the Capture Time. Often when a photographer changes locations, he changes time zones. If the time set in the camera isn't changed then it will be wrong in the Metadata. Lightroom® has a way you can change the capture time in the EXIF Metadata. To change the capture time do the following:

- Select the group of images in the Grid view that have the wrong Capture Time.

- Go to the Metadata menu at the top of the screen and from the drop down menu choose "Edit Capture Time".
- The popup Edit Capture Time dialog box appears on screen (Figure 73).
- In the first section of the Edit Capture Time dialog box is for choosing the type of adjustment to be made.

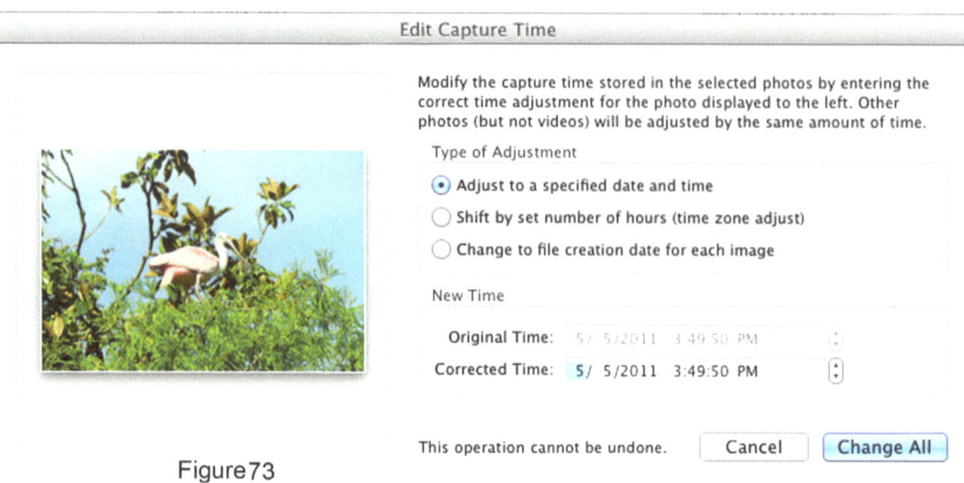

Figure73

- If the date and time are wrong, in the first section choose "Adjust to a specific date and time".
- The second section of the Edit Capture Time dialog box is for making the correction to the correct time.
- The original date and time will be indicated in the top blank of this section and will be grayed out.
- In the second blank, "New Time", you can click with the cursor on the day, month, year, hour, minute, second or AM or PM and type in the correction or you can use the up and down arrows at the end of the blank to move any of these parameters up or down to the correct time.
- If only the time is wrong, in the top section choose the second selection; "Shift by a set number of hours(time zone adjust)".
- In the second section both the Original Time and Corrected Time blanks will be grayed out and there will be a new blank with a zero in it to the right of the Original and Corrected Time blanks.
- Click with the cursor on the up or down arrows to the right of this new blank and select the number of hours to the plus or minus you want to change the time.
- When you select the hours to add or subtract the time in the Corrected Time blank will adjust and show the new time.

This is the only EXIF metadata you can change in Lightroom®

## Exporting Images

There are no Save or Save As commands in Lightroom. For the most part you do not need to save the work you've done in Lightroom®. What you are really doing when you develop an image, add metadata or make a virtual copy, etc., is giving Lightroom® a series of instructions and then Lightroom® is showing you what your image would look like if the instructions were applied to the image. The instructions are not applied until you either export the image to a folder outside Lightroom®, move the image to another program such as Photoshop® or you print the image in Lightroom®. Therefore, the Export command serves as the Save command. There are several ways to export images from Lightroom®. Exporting as a Catalog has already been discussed, but if you only want to export a few images to be edited in an external editing program or to be emailed Lightroom®, offers you several ways to do it. To export images to another folder do the following:

- Select the files you want to export in the Grid mode. If you don't select any, Lightroom® will assume you want to export all the files in the Grid mode on screen.
- Either click with the cursor on the Export button at the bottom left of the screen or from the File menu choose "Export" or use the keyboard shortcut, hold down the Shift and Command keys on the Macintosh, that would be Shift and Control on the PC and press the E key on the Keyboard
- The Export dialog box pops up and at the top tells you how many files you are exporting (Figure 74)
- In the top blank labeled "Export To:" choose where you want the files to go, to a hard drive or DVD/

CD or possibly to one of the plug-in programs you have installed on your computer.

- If you told Lightroom® you want the folders to go to a hard drive, in the next section down, labeled "Export Location", choose where you want the images to end up. Most of the time you will want the images to end up in a specific folder, so in the blank next to "Export To" choose "Specific Folder" from the drop down menu.
- If you click with the cursor on the "Choose" button to the left of the blank the Finder window on the Macintosh or the Explorer window on the PC will appear and you can navigate to the drive and folder where you want the images to be exported.
- You can also click with the cursor on the New Folder button at the bottom left of the Finder or Explorer window and create a new folder, name the new folder in the popup dialog box and click with the cursor on the Create button at the bottom right of the dialog box. Finally click on the Choose button at the bottom right of Finder or Explorer window.

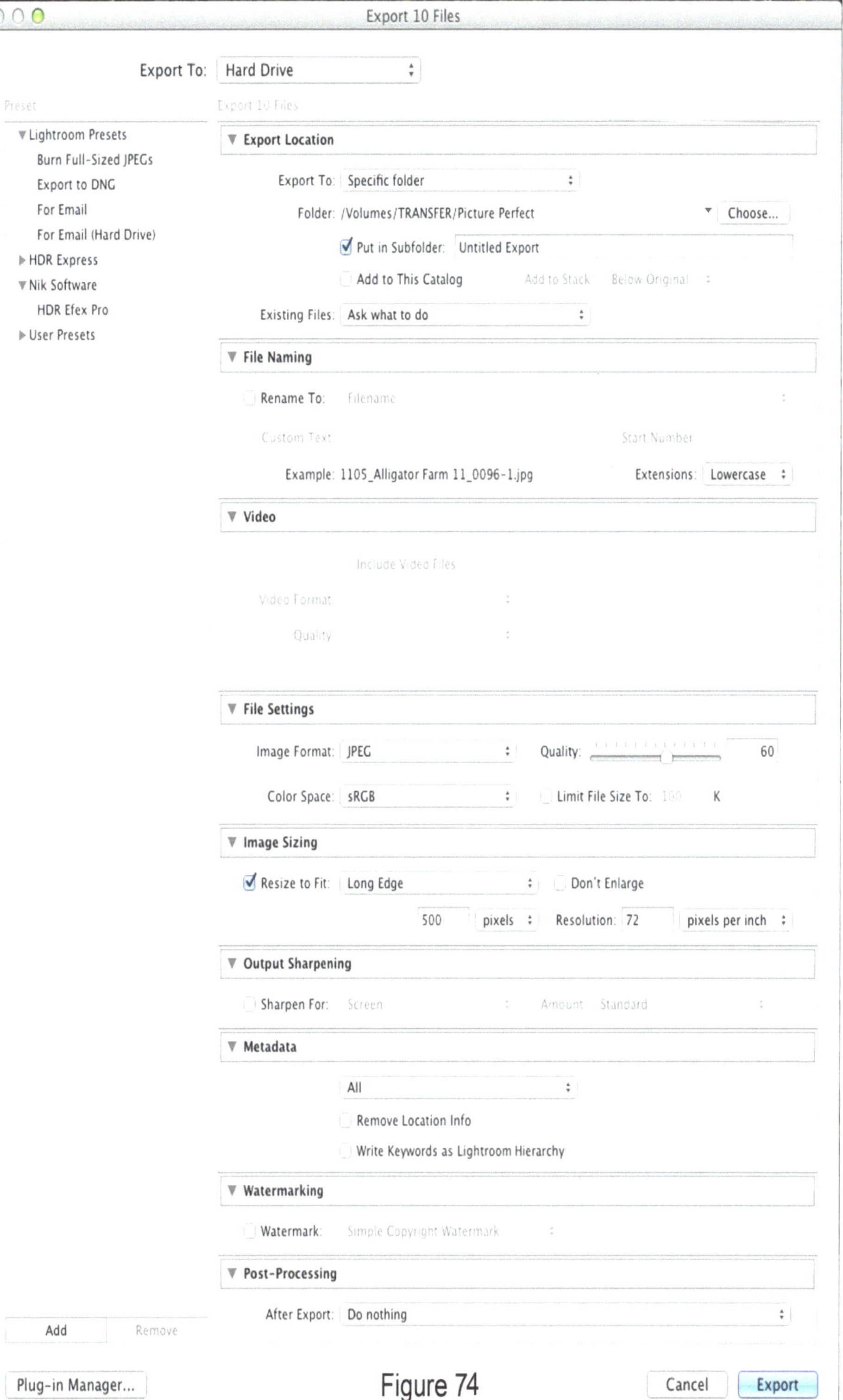


Figure 74

- Back to the Export Location section of the Export dialog box, if you want to place the images in a subfolder, place a check mark in the box next to "Put in Sub folder" and name the sub folder in the blank to the right.
- If you chose to export to a DVD/CD, the first section of the Export dialog box will not be present and in that case the File Naming section of the Export dialog box will be the first section.
- In the File Naming section of the Export dialog box, if you want to rename the images, place a check mark in the box in front of "Rename To:"
- Click with the cursor on the double pointed arrow at the end of the renaming blank and from the resulting menu choose a file naming template. You can choose your custom filename template or create a new

filename template by clicking with the cursor on "edit" at the bottom of the drop down menu.

- If you do not want to rename the images leave the check box blank.
- The third section down is for exporting video and you can choose to export any video you have in Lightroom®.
- Place a check mark in the "Include Video" box and choose the video format and quality from the menus that pop up when you click with the cursor on the double pointed arrows at the end of the respective blanks.
- The fourth section down is for File Settings. Click with the cursor on the double pointed arrow at the end of the blank and choose between JPEG, PSD, Tiff, DNG or Original.
- In the File Settings section you can also choose the color space, the quality using the slider bar and limit the file size to a certain number of kilobytes.
- The fifth section is for Image Sizing, here you can choose the resolution and the width and height in pixels, inches or centimeters. Note, if you selected "Original" you will not have any choices to make regarding file size, etc.
- The sixth section is for Output Sharpening, here you can choose to sharpen for a screen, glossy or matte paper and how much sharpening to do, low, standard or high or you can leave the box unchecked and do no output sharpening. Standard sharpening, which is the default, is usually adequate.
- The seventh section is for minimizing the metadata that accompanies the images or write keywords in Lightroom® hierarchy. If you minimize the metadata the history, snapshots, develop settings will not be exported with the image, it will be a smaller file. If you choose to write keywords as a Lightroom hierarchy and you move the images to another computer on which Lightroom® is installed you will preserve the hierarchy and in addition to Lightroom®, programs such as Adobe Bridge® will recognize that hierarchy.
- You can also place a Watermark on your images, more on this in a subsequent section.
- The last section, Post Processing, asks what you want to do after the images are imported. Your choices are to do nothing (The default), open in Photoshop® or in a plug-in program you have installed on your computer or another editing program or go to the Export Actions Folder (More on the Export Actions Folder in the next section).

## The Export Action Folder

In the Post Processing section at the bottom of the Export dialog box, by default the blank says "Do Nothing". (Figure 74) in the "After Export" blank. If you click with the cursor on the double pointed arrow at the end of this blank, in addition to doing nothing, you are given the choice of showing the image in the Finder (Macintosh), Explorer (PC), opening the image in Photoshop or another application or going to the Export Actions Folder Now. (Figure 75) The first three choices are self explanatory, however if you select the "Go to Export Actions Folder Now" choice from the this menu, Lightroom® will take you to the Export Actions Folder in the Finder on the Macintosh or in Explorer on the PC. If you use Photoshop® and you have created Actions in Photoshop® for things like placing your copyright or a watermark on your images, you can, in Photoshop®, create a droplet out of these Actions and place the droplets in the Export Actions Folder. With the droplet in the Export Actions Folder, it will be another choice in the "After Export" blank. What the droplet in the Export Actions

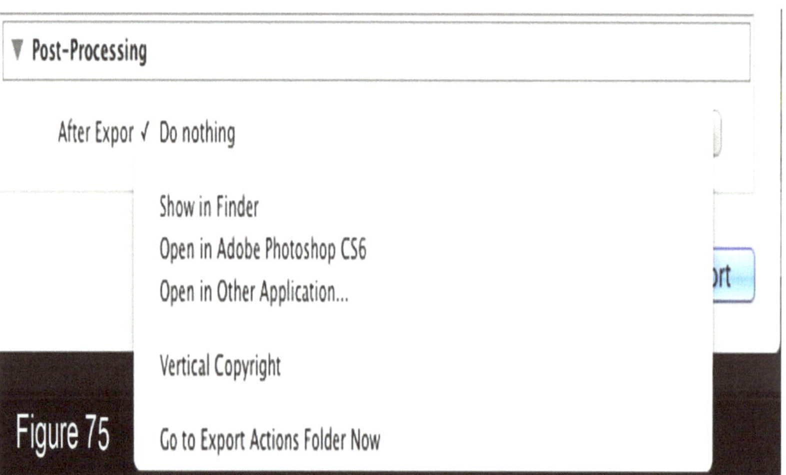

Figure 75

Folder does is point to the Action in Photoshop®. If you select the droplet from the drop down menu in the After Export blank, then after exporting the image or images to where you want them, Lightroom® will take the image or images back to Photoshop® and Photoshop® will run the Action on the images. For example, if you have created an actions in Photoshop® for preparing your images to go up on the web, that resizes the image, places your image on a new background layer, adds a drop shadow and your copyright and then converts the image to the sRGB color space, and finally flattens the image, you can convert that action to a droplet and copy and paste the droplet into the Export Actions Folder. The droplet will then be listed along with the other choices in the drop down menu of the Post Processing section of the Export dialog box.

TIP: Creating a droplet; To create a droplet do the following:

- Go to Photoshop and select one of your Actions from the Actions panel.
- From the File menu, choose "Automate".
- From the Automate menu choose "Create a Droplet.
- In the popup Create a Droplet dialog box top section choose where you want the droplet to go, the Desktop will probably be the easiest place to find it.
- In the second section of the Create a Droplet dialog box the Action set from which the action came and the name of the Action should already be in the Set and Action boxes.
- Place a check mark in both the "Suppress File Open Options Dialogs" and the Suppress Color Profile Warnings" boxes.
- In the third section, choose the destination folder by clicking with the cursor on the Choose button and navigating to where you want the droplet. I think creating a new folder on the desktop is a good place because it is easy to find.
- If you have a "Save As" step in your Action, place a check mark in the box in front of "Override Action 'Save As' Commands" so the droplet does not get saved somewhere other than where you want it.
- Rename the Action if you want to do that in the File Naming section.
- Click with the cursor on the OK button at the top right of the Create Droplet dialog box,
- The Droplet will now be in the folder on your desktop, open the Finder (Macintosh), Explorer (PC), navigate to the folder on your desktop, select the Action and then go to the Edit menu and select "Copy".
- Open the Export dialog box, select "Go to Export Actions Folder" and paste the droplet into the Export Actions Folder.

The next time you are exporting images, the droplet that points to the Action in Photoshop® will be available as one of your choices and if you select it, the images will be moved to Photoshop® and have the Action run on them. Just remember if the Action you want run is for vertical or horizontal images, only select the appropriate orientation for export.

TIP: If developing your images and then exporting them and using a droplet to take them to Photoshop to have the Action run is something you do all the time, then save it as a preset. For example, if when you finish developing the images you plan to put up on the web and then export them to a folder as RAW files so you will know where the images on the web are located on your computer, you can select the appropriate droplet (the one that re-sizes the image and puts your copyright on it) in the Post Processing section of the Export dialog box. Now after the export, the images will be in another folder re-sized, with your copyright and ready to go up on the web.

The other Export choices under the File menu are as follows:

- Export with Previous will Export the images with the previous settings you used the last time you exported images.
- Export with Preset allows you to select a preset from the Lightroom® Presets, from 3rd party plug-in Presets or from the User Presets you created and have the image exported with the preset applied.
- Export as a Catalog exports the files as a Catalog and is valuable in moving larger groups of images when

moving the images to a new computer or from a laptop to a desktop.

## Adding a Watermark

If you have created a Graphics Watermark in another editing program, Photoshop® for example, and saved it as a PNG file to preserve transparency, you can apply the Watermark to your images in Lightroom® before you export the images. You can also create a Text Watermark in Lightroom. Watermarks that have been imported into Lightroom® or ones created in Lightroom are available in all five modules. In the Library module the use will be mainly when you are exporting images. To create a Watermark in Lightroom®, do the following:

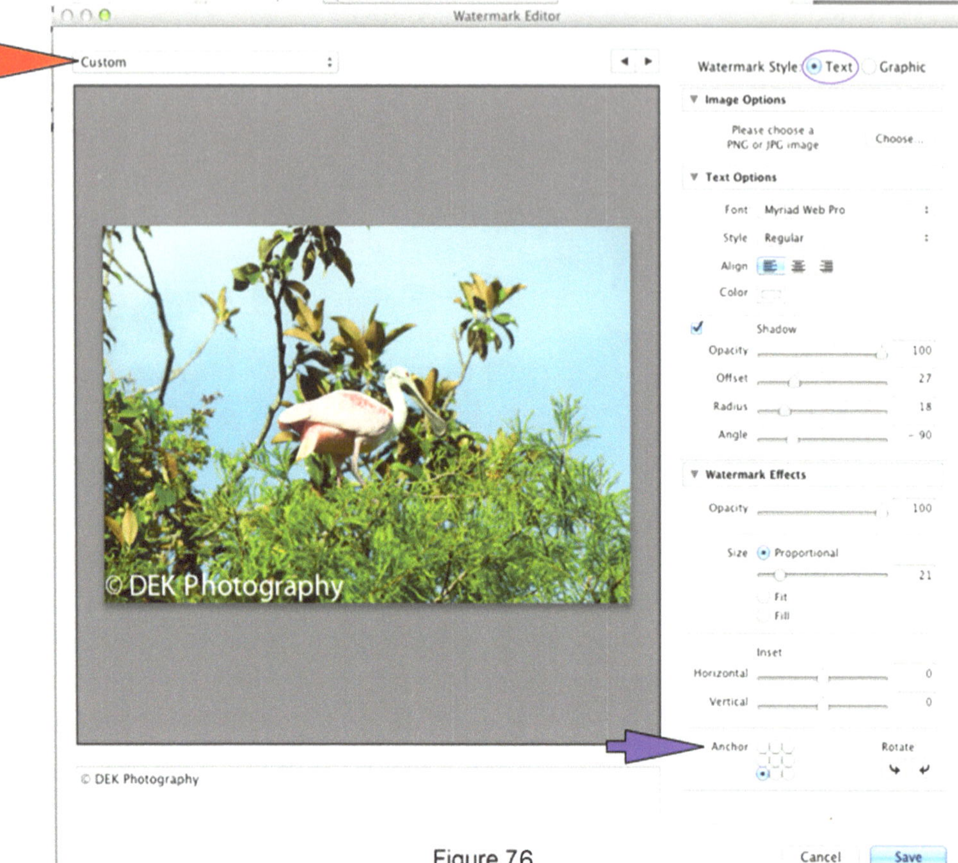

Figure 76

- ► On the Macintosh computer, click with the cursor on the word Lightroom at the top left of the screen, on the PC click with the cursor on the Edit menu at the top of the screen.
- ► From the drop down menu that appears, select "Edit Watermarks".
- ► In the Watermark Editor popup window that appears on screen, (Figure 76) select "Text" for the watermark style in the top line (Blue ellipse, Figure 76).
- ► If an image is selected in the Grid or Loupe view it will appear in a window on the left side of the Watermark editor box, if no image is selected the window will be empty and transparent.
- ► Select an image to show up in the window in order to see how the Watermark looks on an image.
- ► Click with the cursor on the box below the image window.
- ► Place the copyright symbol © by Holding down the Option (Macintosh), Alt (PC) and pressing the G key on the keyboard.
- ► Place some text next to the copyright symbol, the year, your name or company name, etc.
- ► Click with the cursor on the double pointed arrow at the right of the blank above the image window (Red arrow, Figure 76), this blank should say "Custom".
- ► From the drop down menu select "Save Current Settings as New Preset..."
- ► A "New Preset" dialog box will appear on screen.
- ► Name the New Preset and click with the cursor on the "Create" button at the bottom right of the New Preset dialog box. Your new Watermark will now be listed in the drop down menu in this blank along with any other Watermarks.
- ► You can edit the Watermark in the sections to the right of the image window in the Watermarks Editor dialog box.

- You can change the size, position and opacity of any Watermark and then save the changes.
- If you choose to use a graphic Watermark, Lightroom® will ask you to choose the Graphic.
- Navigate to where your PNG file is located on the computer and select Choose.
- Place the Watermark on the image and select the size, location and opacity.
- You can choose to anchor the watermark at any one of nine positions in your image (Blue arrow Figure 76)
- Save the current settings as a new Preset..

To add a Watermark to an image or images when exporting, do the following:

- In the Watermarking section of the Export dialog box (Figure 77), select the Watermark from the drop down menu by clicking with the cursor on the double pointed arrow at the end of the Watermark blank.

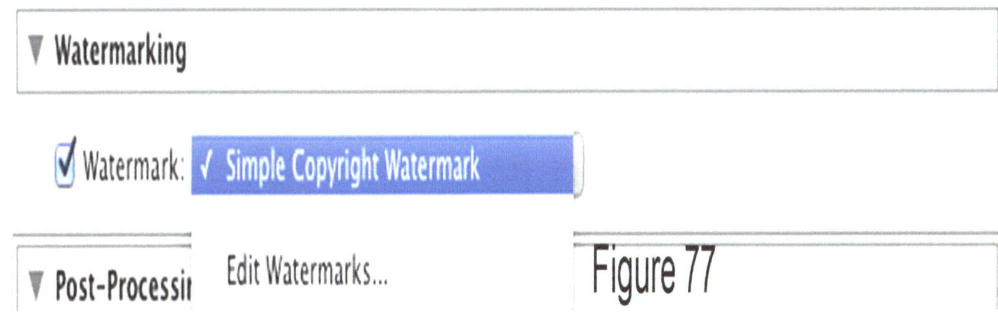

Figure 77

- Choose a Watermark if you have text Watermarks created and saved in Lightroom®.
- You can always go back to the Watermarks Editor window and make changes to any Watermark before you export the images.
- You can also create a new Watermark by choosing "Edit Watermarks from the drop down menu.
- Choosing "Edit Watermarks" will bring the Watermarks Editor dialog box up on the screen (Figure 76).
- Using the same procedure previously described you can create a new Watermark, save it as a preset and apply it to the images to be exported.
- If you have a graphics watermark saved on your computer you will need to select "Edit Watermarks" which brings up the Edit Watermarks dialog box on screen.
- In the Watermark Editor dialog box (Figure 76) select Graphic for the type of Watermark by placing a check mark in the circle in front of the word "Graphic" at the top right of the dialog box.
- Navigate to the Graphic Watermark on your computer and select it.
- The Watermark, text or graphic will be applied to the images selected for export when you click with the cursor on the Export button at the bottom right of the Export dialog box to export the images.

## Emailing From Lightroom

One of the new features in Lightroom 4® is the ability to email an image with a message directly from Lightroom®. You no longer have to develop your image, move it to Photoshop®, resize it and save it to a folder or the desktop to attach it to an email. All of the resizing, attaching to an email and sending can now be done from within Lightroom® in the Library module. First, you need to set up your email account in Lightroom®, to do this, do the following:

- From the File menu at the top of the screen, select "Email Photo" from the

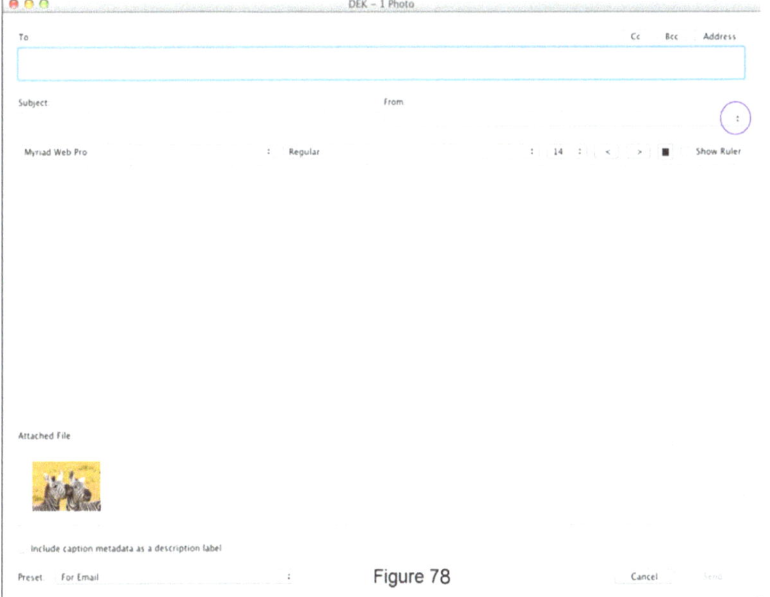

Figure 78

drop down menu or use the keyboard shortcut, hold down the Shift and Command (Macintosh), Shift and Control (PC) keys and press the M key on the keyboard.

- The Email Photo dialog box will pop up on screen (Figure 78).
- Before you can email from Lightroom ® you need to set up your email account.
- Click on the double pointed arrow at the end of the blank labeled "From" (Blue circle, Figure 78).
- Choose "Go to Email Account Manager..."
- The Email Account Manager Account dialog box will appear on Screen (Figure 79).
- Click with the cursor on the "Add" button at the bottom of the section on the left side of the Email Account Manager box (Blue circle, Figure 79).
- The New Account dialog box will appear on screen (Figure 80).

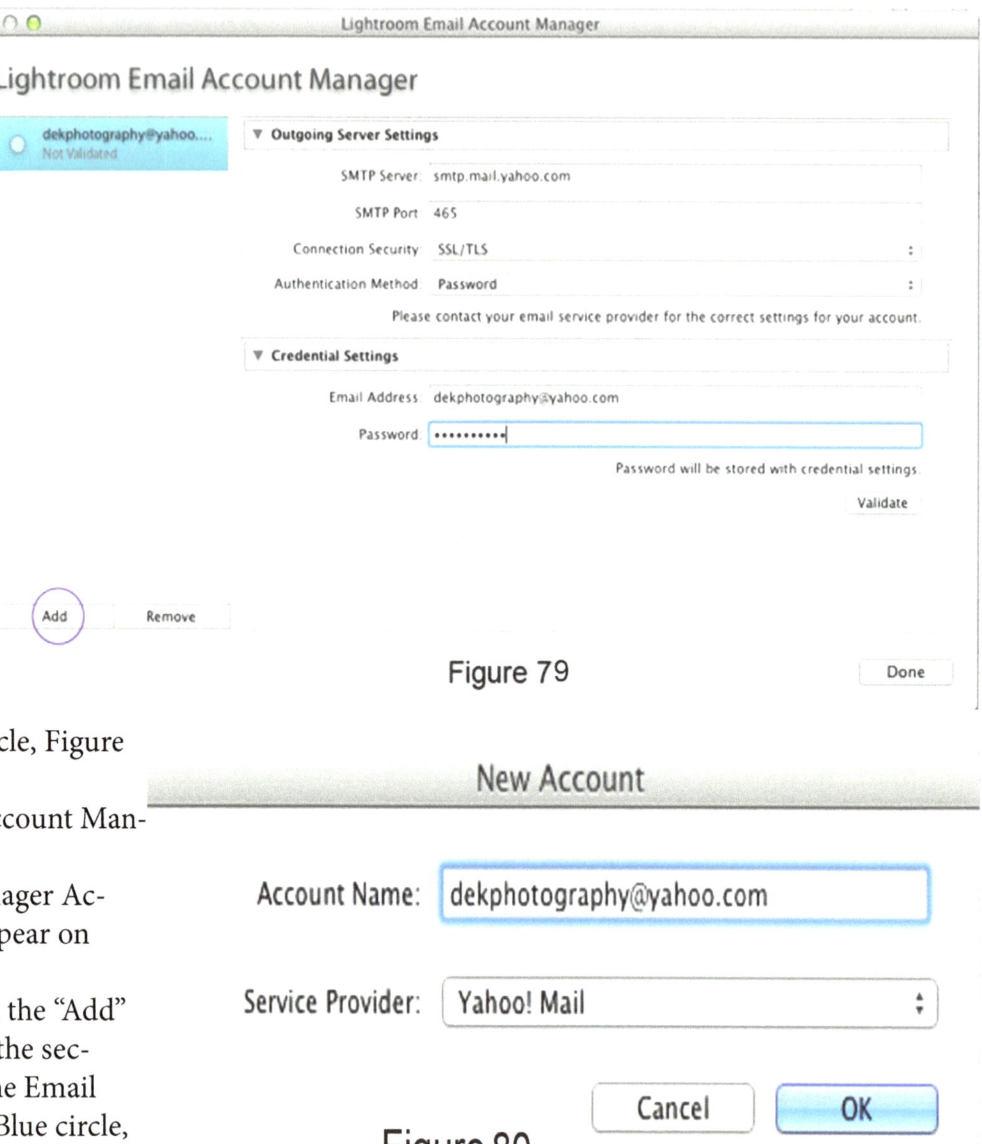


Figure 79

Figure 80

- Type the account name and service provider in the appropriate blanks.
- Click with the cursor on the OK button at the bottom right of the New Account dialog box.
- You will be returned to the Email Account Manager dialog box (Figure 79).
- In the Credential Settings section type your email address and password in the appropriate blanks.
- Click with the cursor on the Validate button at the bottom left of the Credential Settings section.
- After it has been validated, the email address will appear in the column on the left side of the Email Account Manager dialog box.
- You can add other email accounts or remove email accounts by clicking on the Add or Remove buttons at the bottom of the left section where the accounts are listed. (Blue circle, Figure 79)

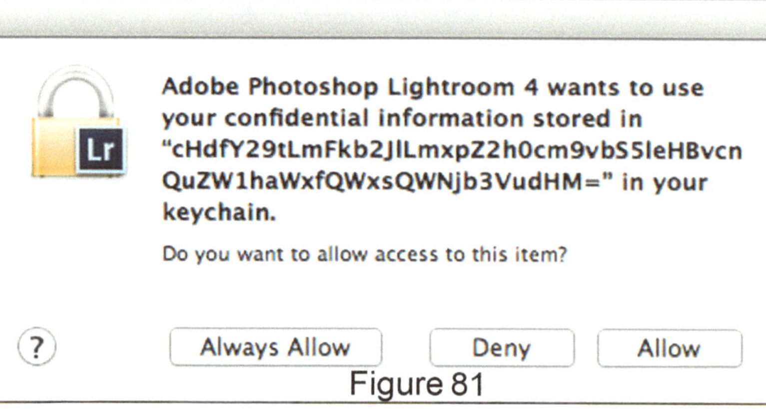


Figure 81

- Finally, click with the cursor on the Done button at the bottom right of the Email Account Manager dialog box.
- A dialog box will appear on screen asking you to allow Lightroom® to use your confidential information (Figure 81).
- Clicking with the cursor on the Allow button will return you to the Email dialog box (Figure 78).

To email from within Lightroom do the following:
- Develop your image in the Develop module and move back to the Library module.
- In either the Grid view or Loupe view, select the image or images you want to email.
- From the File menu at the top of the screen, select "Email Photo" or use the keyboard shortcut, hold down the Shift and Command keys (Macintosh), Shift and Control keys (PC) and press the M key on the keyboard.
- The Email dialog box will pop up on screen and your email account from which you are sending the email will be at the top of the dialog box(Figure 78).
- If you have several email addresses you can choose the one from which you want to send the email by clicking with the cursor on the double pointed arrow at the end of the "From" blank in the email dialog box(Blue ellipse Figure 78).
- Type the email address of the recipient in the "To" blank at the top of the dialog box or choose the email address from the Lightroom® Address Book (Figure 82).
- You can add email addresses of recipients to whom you frequently send emails to the Lightroom® Address Book by clicking with the cursor on the "Address" button at the top right of the Email dialog box. (Figure 78)
- The Lightroom® Address Book dialog box will appear on screen (Figure 82).
- Click with the cursor on the New Address button at the top left of the dialog box and add frequently used addresses in the New Address dialog box that pops up on the screen.

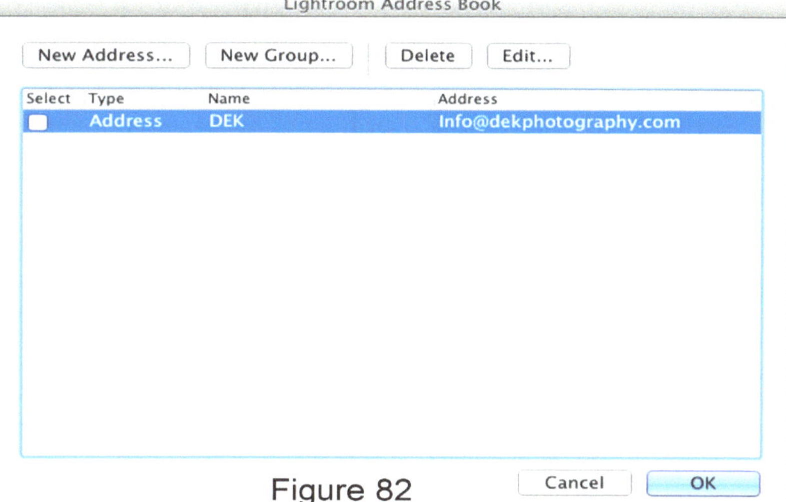

Figure 82

- With the Lightroom® Address Book open, you will be able to select the address of the recipient to whom you wish to send an email by clicking with the cursor in the box in front of each name.
- The address or addresses you choose will automatically be placed in the blank labeled "To" at the top of the Email dialog box. (Figure 78)
- You can also create groups, delete, add and edit addresses in the Lightroom® Address Book by clicking on the appropriate button at the top of the Lightroom Address Book dialog box.
- After selecting the recipient, type in a subject for the email in the Subject blank.
- Choose the email address from which you wish to send the email in the "From" box and a blank for your message will appear.
- Type your email message in the appropriate blank.
- The image you wish to send will already be in the "Attached File" blank at the bottom of the dialog box. (Figure 78)
- Choose whether to include Caption Metadata or not by placing a check mark in the box at the bottom of the Email dialog box.
- The last blank at the bottom left of the dialog box is for choosing the size of your image, you can choose from five presets, use the custom settings you have already defined in the Export dialog box or create

your own preset.

- To send the email click with the cursor on the "Send" button at the bottom right side of the Email dialog box.

## Getting Lightroom® to do the work (Automating)

There are a lot of ways to let Lightroom® do the work for you, especially in the Library module. What follows are suggestions for making Lightroom® easier to use as well as faster.

- Use only one Catalog.
- Set up your Catalog containing all your images on an external hard drive.
- Back up Lightroom® every time you close the program.
- Learn the keyboard shortcuts for the things you do the most often as well as for the tools you use the most often.
- Set up Presets for everything you can.

Automating importing your images can save you quite a bit of time.

- Set up a Watched Folder for auto-importing your images. Once set up, all you have to do is drag images to the Watched Folder and Lightroom® will import the images and place them in the folder you designated for you.
- If you want more control over the import process, set up Importing Presets, one for Copying the images to a new location and adding them to the Catalog and one for Adding the images to the Catalog without moving them. To set up these presets, do the following:
- In the Import dialog box, select the source for your images.
- Select to Copy to a new Location and Add to the Catalog or Add to the Catalog without Moving.
- Decide if you want to rename the images as they are imported with your custom filenaming template in the File Renaming section.
- Decide if you want to add a Metadata preset in the Apply During Import section.
- If you selected Copy to a New Location and Add, Select the destination folder, for example if you have your folders organized by years, and this is a new group of images, select the current year.
- Place a check mark in the box in front of "Into Sub folder" by clicking in the box with the cursor.
- Name the new Folder.
- Before you click on the Import button, there is, at the bottom center of the Import dialog screen a black box labeled "Import Presets", Click on the double pointed arrow at the right side of this box (Yellow circle, Figure 83).

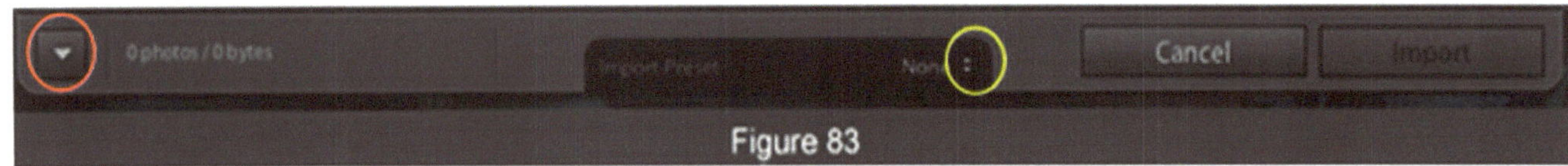

Figure 83

- From the resulting menu select "Save Current Settings as a New Preset".
- In the popup window, name the new preset and click with the cursor on the Create button at the bottom left of the New Preset dialog box.
- In the Import Preset dialog box of the Import screen, you can also delete or rename a preset.
- If you chose Add Without Moving, you only need to decide if you want to apply a Metadata preset during import.
- You can create Import Presets for adding images to the Catalog without moving them, copy and add to the Catalog, convert to DNG and add to the Catalog or Move and add to the Catalog for import of your images.

TIP: When you have created the Import presets, you will not have to use the expanded view of the import dialog box, all you will have to do if you are copying and adding is select one of the Import presets you created and fill in the blank for Metadata to add and a destination. If you are adding without moving, you only have to fill in the blank for Metadata. Clicking with the cursor on the arrow at the bottom left of the Import Screen (Red circle, Figure 83) will change the Import screen from the expanded view to the compact view. Of course, use the expanded view of the Import dialog box if you want to import only some of the images or want to import some of them to separate folders.

## Speeding Up Importing Images from Multiple cards

When you come back from a photo shoot with multiple cards to import into Lightroom® do the following:

- ► Make sure that "Order Added" is selected from the "Sort" order in the Toolbar. With "Order Added" selected, Lightroom® will not have to spend time figuring out where to place the images among the already imported images.
- ► Use a watched folder and set it up to import the images to a folder in Lightroom® but do not rename the images, OR,
- ► Set up the expanded Import dialog box with the first card.
- ► Select the subfolder destination in Lightroom®, add your Metadata Preset, but do not rename the images.
- ► When you have the import set up for the first card, create an Import Preset, name it and save it.
- ► Close the expanded view of the Import dialog box.
- ► Import the first card and check that the images are where you want them to be in the Folders panel.
- ► For each subsequent card, the Import Preset you set up should be on screen when the compressed Import dialog box opens.
- ► Click with the cursor on the Import button for each card.
- ► After all the images are imported, from the "Sort" menu in the Toolbar, select "Capture Time". Lightroom® will re-order the images so that the first one taken is first and the last one last.
- ► From the Library menu at the top of the screen, select "Rename Photos".
- ► In the Rename Photos dialog box select your custom Filename template and add the appropriate custom text.
- ► Your images will be in order and renamed.

**Speeding up the Organization of Images**

Unfortunately there is no way to get Lightroom® to decide which images should be Picks or Rejects or how many rating Stars or what Color label they should have. This is a task that cannot be automated, you will need to go through the images one by one, but you are going to do that anyway to find your best images aren't you? So you might as well organize them by a flag, rating or label or a combination of all three. Collections are one of the real strong points of Lightroom® and you want your images in collections anyway, don't you? Then why not create Smart Collections before you start the flagging, rating and labeling? That way, since Lightroom will place the images in the Smart Collections as you go through and apply flags, stars and labels, when you are all done, you will have your images placed in these Smart Collections. So, before you do the Flagging, Rating and Labeling, do the following:

- ► Decide how you want to use all the flags, star ratings and color labels. There are a possible seventy-one choices of the Flags, Stars and Labels by themselves or in combinations of flag as a Pick, Star ratings and Color labels.
- ► Write down for what each combination stands.

Before you start Flagging, Rating and Labeling, do the following:

- ► Create a Collection Set and name it.

- Create smart collections that will automatically organize the images as you flag, rate or label them.
- Place each Smart Collection in the Collection set you created.
- Start by creating a Smart Collection for images that are flagged as Picks.
- Next, depending on how you plan to use the Stars and Color Labels, create a Smart Collection for each of the classifications.
- For example, if you are using all the Stars and Color labels as I do when I classify the different species of animals on returning from an African photo safari, create a Smart Collection for the Picks and then create a separate Smart Collection for each Star rating, one through five and a Smart Collection for each one of the Color Labels.
- As you go through your images, decide first if the image is a Pick. As soon as you flag it a Pick it ends up in the Picks Smart Collection.
- Then, place the Star rating or Color Label or a combination of these on the image and it will end up also in the appropriate Star or Color label Smart Collection.
- In the Loupe view, place your flag, rating or label on the images as you move through them by using the keyboard shortcuts, P for a pick, the 1 key for one star, 2 key for two stars, 3 key for three stars, 4 key for four stars, 5 key for five stars, 6 key for the red label, 7 key for the yellow label, 8 key for the green label, 9 key for the blue label and the Painter tool for the Purple label.
- Use a combination of the P key, 1 through 5 keys for stars and 6 through 9 keys or the Painter tool for the color labels. For example, the P key plus the 3 key plus the 8 key would be an image that was a Pick with 3 stars and the Green label.
- After you have all the images in Smart Collections, chose a Smart Collection, select all the images in the Smart Collection and place the appropriate Keyword that identifies the collection on the images
- Follow through by placing identifying keywords on all the Smart Collections.

TIP: When you are working with only one Catalog, creating these Smart Collections will gather all the images in the Catalog. So, if you want to put just the images in the most recent Import or current folder in Smart Collections then add the keyword you embedded when you imported the images. That is why putting the location or other appropriate keyword on the images during import is important.

When you have finished classifying your images they will all be in Smart Collections and there will be no need to use the Library Filter Bar to find them and then put them in Collections, Lightroom® will have already done that for you. If you want to separate some of the images out of one of the Smart Collections into separate Collections you can select the images in the Smart Collection and create new Sub-Collections for each type of image. For example, if you photographed four different species of cats and labeled all of them with three stars, all the cats will be in one Smart Collection. Do the following:

- Go to the cats Smart Collection.
- Select all the lions in the collection.
- Click with the cursor on the plus (+) sign in the Collections header bar.
- Make sure the "Include selected photos" box is checked.
- Name the new collection and place it in the same Collection Set as the Smart Collections set but under the Cats collection.
- After you have created the lion collection, while the images are still selected, place the Keyword lion on them.
- Repeat the process with the cheetahs, leopards and serval cats.

TIP: Rather than have to go into one of the Collections or Smart Collections to separate out images, it is easier to just use a combination of Stars and Labels and create a Smart Collection before you start flagging, rating or labeling. For example, if all the cats are labeled with three stars, then create a Smart Collection for lions by putting a red label on them in addition to the three stars, put a yellow label on the Cheetahs and a green label on the leopards. Having created these Smart Collections, then as you flag, rate or label them you know that the 3 key and 6 key (36)will put a lion in a Smart Collection, 37 will do the same for a cheetah and 38 the same for a leopard. Also, then P-3-6 would be a lion flagged as a Pick, P-3-7 a cheetah flagged as a Pick and so on. There are enough combinations of flags, stars and labels to have all your images in Smart Collections when you finish.

When you are done, all your images will be in Collection Sets and Collections with Keywords on them. At this point it is time to turn your attention to the Picks Smart Collection. These are the images on which you want to put develop settings first. You will not have to search for them, they will already be there in the Picks Smart Collection ready to go to the Develop module.

What follows is a suggestion as to how to work on these images, especially if these are images that will end up on your website or going to a client when you are finished applying develop settings:

- Before you move them to the Develop module place as many Keywords on them as is appropriate to make them easily discoverable to stock photography agencies and advertising agencies.
- Move them to the Develop module and apply develop settings to bring out the best detail in the image.
- When you go back to the Library module, they will still be in the Picks Smart Collection in the Library module, but now they will have the develop settings and Keywords embedded in the metadata.
- Select the images for the website and export them to their own folder on an external hard drive keeping them in their original format, preferably RAW files.
- If you have created Actions in Photoshop for resizing and placing your copyright on the images in preparation for putting them up on the web, make droplets of those actions in Photoshop® and copy and paste them into the Export Actions folder.
- Select the appropriate droplet from the Export Actions folder in the Post Processing section of the Export dialog box.
- After you export the images, the originals, with develop settings and keywords will end up in their own folder (Lightroom® will know where it is) ready to be printed or shown to a client and in Photoshop will be the resized images with your copyright ready to go up on the website or emailed to a client.
- At this point, with all your images flagged, rated, labeled and keyworded you will be able to use the Library Filter Bar to quickly find any image in your Catalog.
- Finally, backup your Catalog when you close Lightroom®.

The Library module in Lightroom 4® is the most powerful asset management software program available to photographers today, take advantage of it.

# The Develop Module

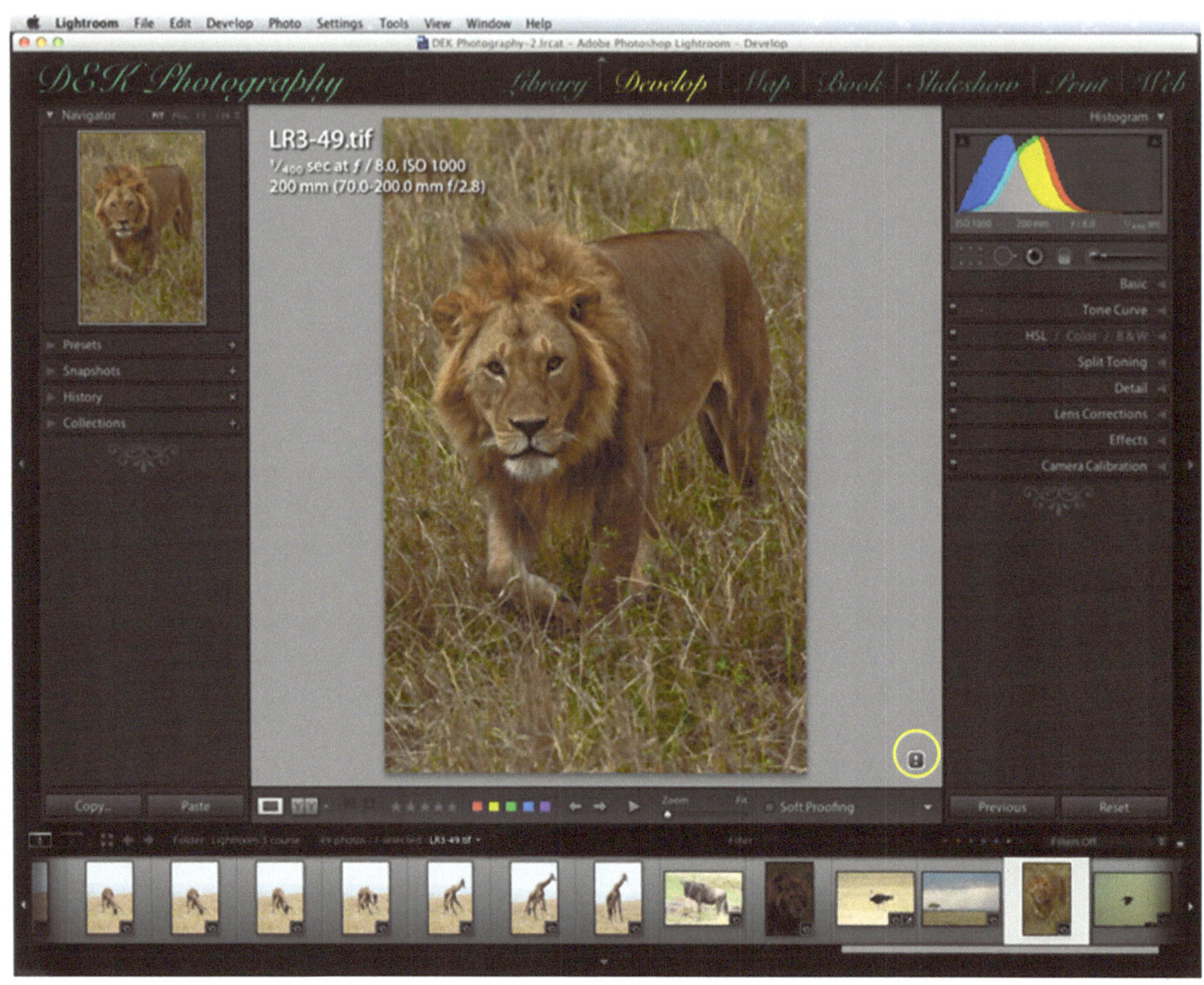


Figure 1

The first job of a photographer is to get exactly the correct quantity and quality of light to reach the camera's sensor. To be a complete photographer one must also have an understanding of how to use the digital darkroom on the computer to develop the images you create and that means knowing the software. When the camera is set to record RAW files, all the detail is captured in the image and it is up to the photographer to bring it out. The Develop module of Lightroom 4® offers photographers a full range of panels with which to develop a RAW file and bring out the best the image has to offer. The most obvious changes from Lightroom 3® is in the basic panel, where the Recovery, Fill Light and Brightness sliders are gone. Those three effects have been replaced by four sliders, a Highlights Slider and a Shadows slider and sliders with which the White Clipping and Black Clipping can be modified. The Exposure and Contrast sliders are still present and are more effective. The other not so obvious change is a very important one in the Camera Calibration panel. Where as the dynamic range of the camera profiles of the 2010 Process Version in Lightroom 3® were probably pretty close to the 5 to 6 stop dynamic range of the digital SLR camera. In Lightroom®4 the dynamic range of the camera profiles in the new 2012 Process Version appear to be much wider, probably closer to a nine stop dynamic range. All of the changes will be discussed with the individual panel discussions.

First, how do we get in to the Develop Module? There are several ways to get there, use any one of the following:

- Go to the module picker in the black bar at the top of the page and click with the cursor on "Develop".
- Press the D Key on the keyboard.
- Press and hold the Command and Option keys on the Macintosh or the Control and Alt keys on the PC and press the 2 key on the keyboard.
- When in any other module, using any of the keyboard shortcuts for the Develop module will open the Develop module with the tool or function for which the shortcut is used open.

Tip: You can switch to any module in Lightroom® by holding down the Command and Option keys (Macintosh) or the Control and Alt keys (PC)and pressing:

- The 1 key for the Library Module
- The 2 key for the Develop Module
- The 3 key for the Map Module
- The 4 key for the Book Module
- The 5 key for the Slideshow Module
- The 6 key for the Print module
- The 7 key for the Web module

Anytime a Develop Module keyboard shortcut (I'll get to those shortly) is pressed when in another module, you will automatically be taken to the Develop Module. For example if you press the R key, which is the keyboard shortcut in the Develop Module for the Crop and Straighten tool, you'll be transferred to the Develop Module and the Crop and Straighten tool will be open.

## Things to know:

- Pressing and holding the Command key on the Macintosh or Control key on the PC and then pressing the forward slash key (/) will bring up all the keyboard shortcuts for the module in which you are cur-

Figure 2

### Develop Shortcuts

**Edit Shortcuts**

| | |
|---|---|
| Command + U | Auto Tone |
| V | Convert to Black and White |
| Command + Shift + U | Auto White Balance |
| Command + E | Edit in Photoshop |
| Command + N | New Snapshot |
| Command + ' | Create Virtual Copy |
| Command + [ | Rotate left |
| Command + ] | Rotate right |
| 1-5 | Set Ratings |
| Shift + 1-5 | Set ratings and move to next photo |
| 6-9 | Set color labels |
| Shift + 6-9 | Set color labels and move to next photo |
| Command + Shift + C | Copy Develop Settings *A dialog will come up asking which settings to copy.* |
| Command + Shift + V | Paste Develop Settings |

**Output Shortcuts**

| | |
|---|---|
| Command + Return | Enter Impromptu Slideshow mode *Shows the current selected photos in a slideshow based on the current Slideshow module settings.* |
| Command + P | Print selected photos |
| Command + Shift + P | Page Setup |

**Navigation Shortcuts**

| | |
|---|---|
| Command + Left Arrow | Previous Photo |
| Command + Right Arrow | Next Photo |

**View Shortcuts**

| | |
|---|---|
| Tab | Hide side panels |
| Shift + Tab | Hide all panels |
| T | Hide/Show toolbar |
| F | Cycle screen modes |
| Command + Option + F | Go to normal screen mode |
| L | Cycle Lights Out modes |
| Command + Shift + L | Go to Lights Dim mode |
| Command + Option + Up Arrow | Go to previous module |
| Command + I | Show/Hide Info Overlay |
| I | Cycle Info Overlay |
| Command + J | Develop View Options |
| S | Show/Hide Soft Proofing Preview |

**Mode Shortcuts**

| | |
|---|---|
| R | Enter Crop Mode |
| Q | Enter Spot Removal Mode |
| M | Enter Graduated Filter Mode |
| K | Enter Adjustment Brush Mode |
| D | Loupe View |
| Y | View Before and After left and right |
| Option + Y | View Before and After up and down |

**Tool Shortcuts**

| | |
|---|---|
| X | Rotate Crop |
| O | Show/Hide Paint Overlay |
| H | Show/Hide Pins |

rently working (Figure 2)

- .

- Clicking on the background with the Control key (Macintosh) or Right clicking (Windows) on the background will give you the option of changing the background in LIghtroom®. You can change it from the default medium gray to white, light gray, dark gray or black. You are also able to add pinstripes from this menu.

There are changes in the interface of the Develop module in going from the Library Module to the Develop Module. The menu bar of the top of the page has some new menus.
The following are the differences between the menu bar of the Develop module and the menu bar of the Library module:

- The Library menu has been replace by a Develop menu.
- The Library Module Metadata menu has been replace by a Settings menu.
- A Tools menu has been added to the Develop module.

The following remain the same in the Develop module:

- The File, Edit, View and Window menus
- The Identity Plate below the menu bar
- The Module Picker

Other changes in the Develop module screen from the Library module screen are as follows:

- In the center of the screen is the work area containing the image on which you are going to work in the Loupe view.
- There is no Grid view in the Develop Module.
- Only one image at a time can be on the screen in the Develop module.
- If you select a second image from the film strip to compare with the first and go to Compare view (C key), Lightroom® automatically takes you into the Library Module and opens the Compare view.
- The main image screen is surrounded by the menu bar, the identity plate and module picker at the top, a column of panels on the left and right sides of the screen and the tool bar and film strip across the bottom.

Finally, as in the Library module, you can get more screen real estate for your image by hiding the right and left columns, toolbar, filmstrip, identity plate and module picker. The easiest way to do this is to hold down the shift key on the keyboard and press the Tab key on the keyboard to make all the columns, filmstrip, identity plate and module picker disappear. Also, press the T key to make the Toolbar disappear. Bring everything back by pressing the same keys on the Keyboard. On all four sides of the screen there are arrows pointing away from the center of the screen. Clicking with the cursor on any one of these arrows will cause the panel to disappear. The arrow will then point to the center of the screen and if you hover your cursor over the arrow, the panel will become visible again. Moving your cursor away from the arrow toward the center of the screen will cause the panel to disappear. Clicking with the cursor on the inward pointing arrow will bring the panel back.

## The Left Side Panels

The Column of panels on the left side of the screen (Figure 3) is also different from the Library Module. The Navigator Panel along with its choice of zoom sizes is still present. Now, the Catalog and Folders panels are gone and instead there are the Presets panel, Snapshot panel and History panel.

The Collections panel remains the same in all five Lightroom® modules. There are some changes to the Presets panel. In Lightroom 3® clicking with the cursor on the header bar or on the right pointing arrow in the header bar opened all the Lightroom® presets in a drop down menu. In Lightroom 4® clicking with the cursor on either the header bar of the Presets panel or the right pointing arrow to the left of the word Presets will open up eight sections of presets, each one containing different types of presets. These sections are as follows:

- Black and White Antique Creative Preset, containing one preset.
- Lightroom® Black and White filter presets, containing eight presets.
- Lightroom® Black and White Presets, containing seven presets.
- Lightroom® Black and White Toned presets, containing ten presets.
- Lightroom® Color presets, containing nine presets.
- Lightroom® Effect presets, containing seven presets.
- Lightroom® General presets, containing six presets.
- Lightroom® Video presets containing six presets.

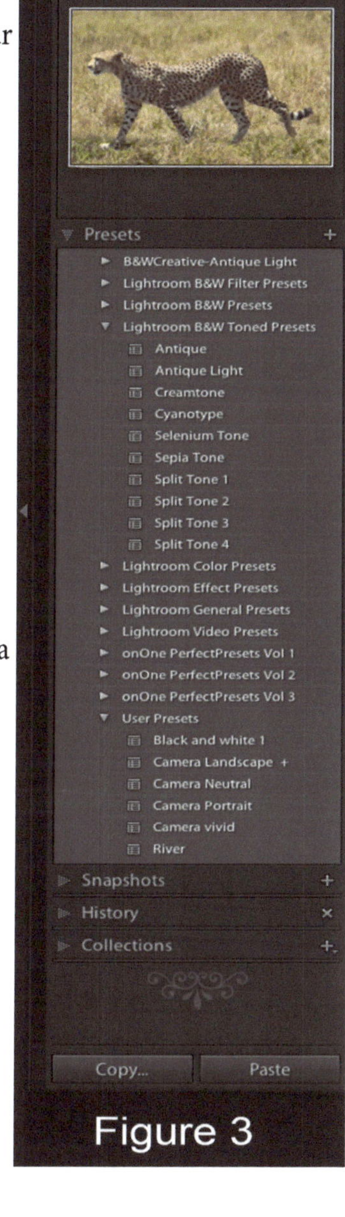

Figure 3

As in Lightroom 3 you can get a preview in the Navigator window of how any preset will look on your image by hovering the cursor over the name of a preset in the drop down menu.

Lightroom® comes with a large number of develop presets already installed. To these, you can add plug-in presets from another company and your own develop presets which will be listed at the bottom of the Presets panel under the heading "User Presets". To see all these presets, click with the cursor on the arrow to the left of the word Presets. Lightroom® will open up a drop down menu that shows you all the develop presets available to you.

## Creating your own develop preset

After you have developed your image, you can save the develop settings you used as a new preset. There are a couple of ways to do this. The easiest way is to click with the cursor on the Develop menu at the top of the page and from the drop down menu select "New Preset". Alternatively, click with the cursor on the plus (+) sign in the Preset's header bar. Either of these methods will open the "New Develop Preset" dialog box on screen. (Figure 4) Name your new preset something descriptive to indicate what the Preset will accomplish. If you do not need to know how the Preset was created then in the New Develop Preset dialog box click with the cursor on the "Check All" button at the bottom left of the dialog box. If, however, you think you might like to go back and see what the preset entails, do the following:

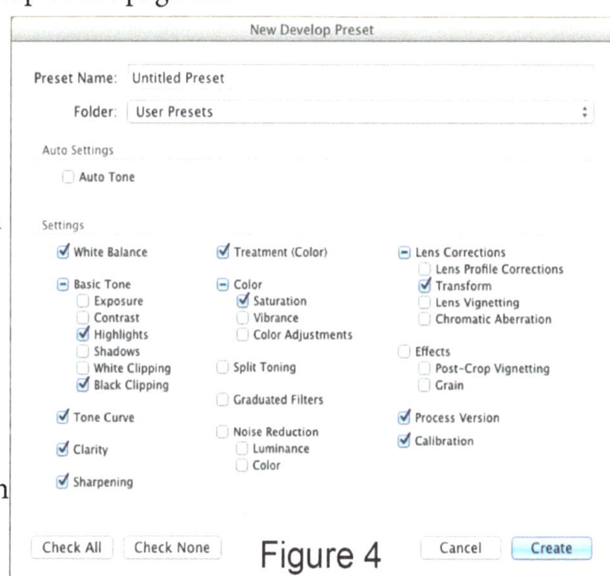

Figure 4

- Develop your image using the tools in the panels in the column on the right side of the screen.
- Open the Presets panel by clicking with the cursor

on header bar of the Presets panel on the left side of the screen.

- If you are in Solo mode, open the History panel by holding down the shift key on the keyboard and clicking with the cursor on the header bar of the History panel (This step is not necessary if you are not in Solo mode).
- Click with the cursor on the down pointing arrow at the top of the Lightroom® Presets panel to close the Lightroom® presets and leave the User Presets open.
- Make sure you can see the entire History panel with the changes you've made in the image.
- Click with the cursor on the Develop Menu at the top of the screen and select New Preset from the drop down menu.
- The New Develop Preset dialog box will open on the screen. (Figure 4)
- Give the new Preset a descriptive name in the top blank and include in that name the filename of the image from which the Preset was created.
- Using the History panel as a guide, place a check in the boxes of the effects you changed in editing the image by clicking with the cursor in the boxes
- Make sure to uncheck any boxes for effects you did not change
- Click with the cursor on the Create button.
- The new preset will be stored under User Presets at the bottom of the Presets Panel.

TIPS: First, depending on how large your screen is, if you click on the + sign in the header bar of the Presets panel to create a new develop preset and you cannot see the History panel you will not be able to scroll down to it once the New Develop Preset dialog box is open. Second, when the New Preset dialog box opens, it will have the boxes checked for the last preset you created. Third, Hovering your cursor over any one of the presets, default, plug-in or user presets, will show you in the Navigator window a preview of what the image would look like should that preset be applied to the image.

The following are the things you can do with presets:

- Any preset can be applied to images during import by selecting it in the "Apply During Import" section of the Import dialog box in the Library module.
- Lightroom® default Presets, third party plug-in Presets and User Presets can be exported.
- User presets and third party plug-in presets can be renamed or deleted
- User Presets can be updated with the develop settings from the current image on which you are working.
- User Presets can be shown in the Finder (Macintosh), Explorer (PC)

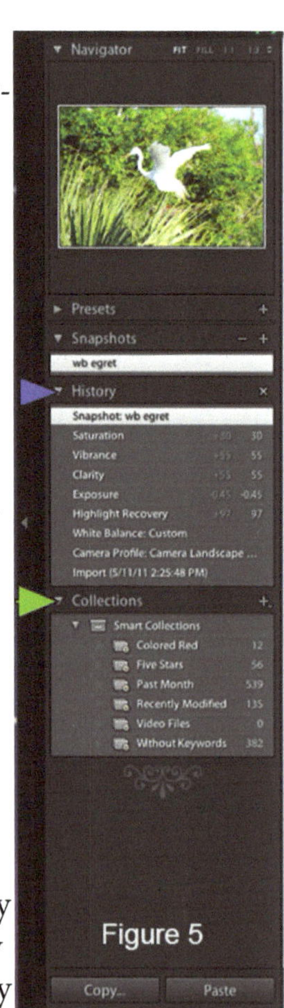

Figure 5

TIP: To delete a User Preset or third party Preset, highlight it by clicking on the name of the Preset with the cursor and then click with the cursor on the minus (-) sign in the header bar of the Presets panel. To apply a Preset to an image, export, rename, delete, update or show a Preset in the Finder/Explorer, Control (Macintosh) Right (PC) click on the name of the Preset and from the pop up menu select the appropriate choice.

## The History Panel

Below the Presets Panel are the Snapshot and History panels. Looking at the History Panel first, as you develop your image, every step you take is recorded in the History Panel (Blue arrow, figure 5). Unlike Photoshop, when you close Lightroom®, the history remains with the image. You can come back to the image at any time, open the History Panel and every step you've taken to develop the image will be right there in the History

Panel.

## The Snapshot Panel

You cannot change the order of the steps in the History Panel, but you can create a snapshot of any step you've taken in developing the image. To do this, select the step in the History Panel by clicking with the cursor on it and click with the cursor on the plus (+) sign to the right of the word Snapshots in the header bar of the Snapshot Panel just above the History panel. You'll be asked to give the snapshot a name and to create it in an on screen pop up box. If you click with the cursor on the arrow to the left of the word Snapshots in the Snapshots Panel, a drop down menu will appear and there you'll find the snapshot you just created. When you come back to the image later, you can open the snapshot and Lightroom® will open it at that history stage. You can then start editing it again with a different set of instructions if you wish.

## The Collections Panel

Finally, below the History Panel is the Collections Panel (Green arrow, figure 5). In the Develop Module the Collections Panel is exactly the same as it is in the Library Module. All of your collection sets, collections and Smart Collections are there. Although the Collections Panel is present in all five modules of Lightroom® 4, the following are the limitations to the Collections panel in all the modules:

- Collections can be created in all modules. Those created in the output modules are specific to those modules.
- The Library module is the only module in which you can add images from different folders to a collection.
- In the Develop Module, you can only add images to a collection from the current folder on which you're working. To add images from a different folder, you'll need to go back to the Library Module and change folders.
- The other five modules, Slideshow, Map, Book, Print and Web allow you to create a Collection that is specific to that module.

## Copy and Paste Buttons

At the bottom of the left panel are two buttons labeled "Copy" and "Paste". What these buttons allow you to do, is copy the develop settings from one image and paste those develop settings to another image. To copy develop settings from one image to another, do the following:

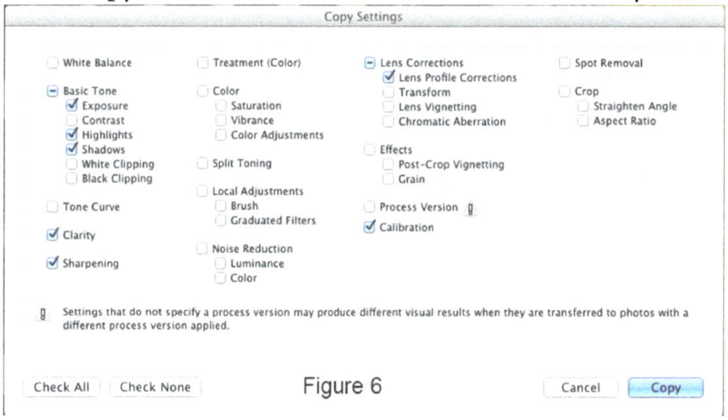

- Click with the cursor on the Copy button. This will bring up a Copy Settings dialog box(Figure 6).
- Check the boxes by the settings you changed in the original image.
- Click the Copy button at the bottom right of the Copy Settings dialog box.
- Select another image and click with the cursor on the Paste button at the bottom left of the screen.
- The settings you copied from the first image will be pasted onto the second image you selected.
- There are better ways to do this and these will be discussed a little later in this book.

Figure 6

## The Toolbar

Below the main image window you'll find the Tool Bar (Figure 7). In the Develop Module the Tool Bar is much the same as the Tool Bar in the Library Module. The keyboard shortcut to hide or show the Toolbar is

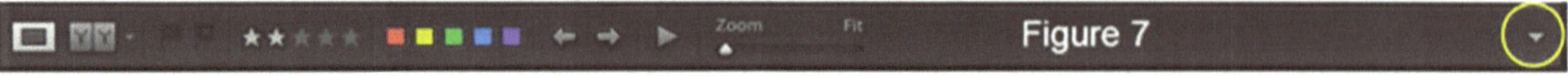


either the T key or the backslash key, both will do the job.
The following are the differences between the Toolbar in the Library Module and the Develop module. In the
Develop module Toolbar:

- There is no Grid view Icon.
- The icon for Loupe view is still there on the left side of the Toolbar.
- There is an icon for Before and After views (two squares with a Y in each square).
- Clicking on the Before and After icon clears the Tool Bar and leaves five icons, they are:
    - The Loupe view.
    - The before and after icon.
    - A split square with a right pointing arrow in the middle.
    - A split square with a left pointing arrow in the middle.
    - A split square with a top right pointing arrow and a bottom left pointing arrow.

The Keyboard shortcut for Before and After images is the Y key. However when you use the Y key to bring up the Before and After image it will take you to the default side by side images with Before on the left. Pressing the Y key again will take you back to the single After image. In order to bring up the four different Before and After views and cycle through them, you must click with the cursor on the Before and After Icon multiple times. The four different before and after views that you can cycle through by clicking with the cursor on the before and after icon are:

- Two side by side images with Before on the left (the default).
- A split image with Before on the left side.
- Two top and bottom images with Before on the top.
- A split image with Before on the top.

Looking at the Tool Bar with the three Before and after icons with arrows, these are icons that allow you to copy settings from the Before to the After images or from the After to the Before image. The first icon has a right pointing arrow and it allows you to copy the settings from the before image to the after image. The second icon has a left pointing arrow and allows you to copy the after image settings to the before image. The third icon has a top right pointing arrow and a bottom left pointing arrow. This choice lets you swap the settings between the before and after images. These last three icons are a little confusing and I'm not sure why you would do any of that. The rest of the Tool Bar is much the same as the Library Module tool bar. You can do the following just as you can in the Library Module:

- Flag an image as a Pick or Reject by clicking with the cursor on the appropriate Flag icon in the Toolbar.
- Rate the image between one and five Stars by clicking with the cursor on the appropriate Star icon in the Toolbar.
- Label the image with any of five different colors, red, yellow, green, blue, and purple by clicking with the cursor on the appropriate Color Label icon in the Toolbar.
- Navigate to the next or previous image by clicking with the cursor on the right or left pointing arrow in the Toolbar.
- Start an impromptu slide show by clicking with the cursor on the large right pointing arrowhead on the Toolbar.
- Zoom in or out on the image by clicking with the cursor on the slider bar and moving the slider left to

decrease the size of the image and to the right to increase the on screen size of the image.

- Set up an image for Soft Proofing (more on this later) by clicking with the cursor and placing a check mark in the box in front of the words "Soft Proofing".

If you don't see the Before and After icons (View Modes) flags, stars, labels, navigation arrow, impromptu slide show arrows, zoom slider, or Soft Proofing box, click on the down pointing arrow at the right side of the Tool Bar (Yellow circle, Figure 7) and from the drop down menu that appears, select which of these you'd like to show in the Tool Bar. The two things you won't be able to get in the Toolbar in the Develop module that were in the Toolbar in the Library Module are the Painter Tool and the Rotate icons.

## The Filmstrip

The Filmstrip at the bottom of the screen (Figure 8) contains all the images in the current folder or collection on which you're working as well as any images you've edited in an external editing program such as

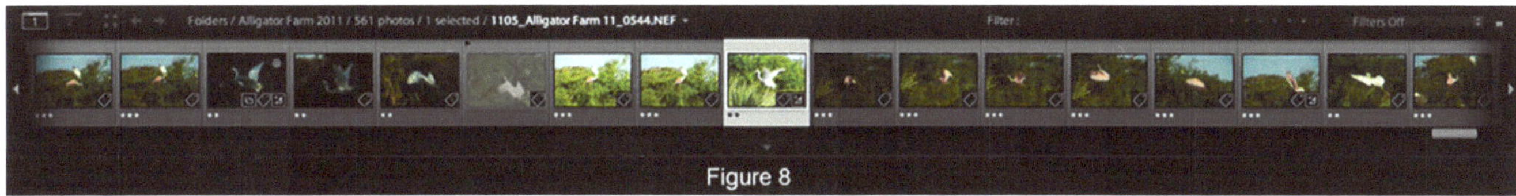

Figure 8

Photoshop and any virtual copies you have created. The following can be shown on images in the Filmstrip:

- Flags
- Rating stars
- Color labels
- Badges indicating the image has Keywords embedded in the metadata.
- Badges indicating the image has been edited in Lightroom®.
- Badges showing the image has GPS coordinates.
- Badges showing the image is part of a Collection.
- Virtual Copies.
- Images edited in an external editing program and saved back to Lightroom®.

In order to have Lightroom® show the above in the Filmstrip, it is necessary to go into Lightroom® preferences which is found by clicking with the cursor on the word Lightroom® at the top left of the screen on the Macintosh or the Edit menu on the PC. Choose the Interface preferences and make sure that the items you want to show on the images in the Filmstrip are checked.

The images edited in an external editing program and saved back to Lightroom® will, by default, have "-Edit.tiff" attached at the end of the file name and will be stacked next to the original. They will no longer be RAW files. In addition, any files of which you've made virtual copies (more on this later) will also be in the Filmstrip next to the original.

At the top of the Filmstrip, there is a black bar which has several useful items, they are as follows:

- Icons for using one or two screens.
- An icon, the clicking of which will take you to the Grid view in the Library Module.
- A left pointing arrow which when clicked on with the cursor will take you back to last panel, module or folder in which you were working.
- A right pointing arrow the clicking on of which will take you back to the panel, module or folder you left when you clicked on the left pointing arrow with the cursor.

- Text telling you the name of the folder currently in the Develop module.
- Text telling you the number of images in the current folder.
- Text telling you the filename of the image currently on the screen.

At the end of the filename of the image on which you are working you will find a down pointing arrow. Clicking on this arrow with the cursor will bring up a drop down menu that has four sections and allows you to do any of the following:

- In the first section, you can:
    1. See all the images in your catalog in the Grid mode of the Library module.
    2. See the images in the Quick Collection in the Library module
    3. See the images from the last import into Lightroom®.

- In the second section you can see your favorite sources, these would be Folders or Collections.
- In the third section you can see the folders on which you have recently worked in the Develop module. These are called "Recent Sources". Clicking on any one of your recent sources will bring up that folder in the Develop Module
- In the fourth section you can do the following:
    1. Add images to your Favorites
    2. Clear all your recent sources (Folders or Collections).

This feature makes it very easy to switch folders while remaining in the Develop module without having to go back into the Library Module, find the folder you want, click on it with the cursor to bring it up on screen, select an image and move it to the Develop module.

On the right side of this bar above the Filmstrip are the same icons as the ones in the Attribute section of the Library Filter Bar in the Grid view of the Library module. By clicking on the down pointing arrow you can choose what you want shown in the filmstrip. In addition to showing badges, you can choose to have Flags, Star ratings, and color labels shown beneath the images in the Filmstrip. You can use this section of the bar above the images in the Filmstrip much the same as you can use the Library Filter Bar in the Library module. When you choose any one of these selections by clicking on the attribute with the cursor, Lightroom® will show all the images in the filmstrip that meet the criteria you've selected. For example, if you click with the cursor on "equal to" and then click with the cursor on three Stars, Lightroom® will show you only those images rated with three Stars in the filmstrip. If you select "Filters Off" from the drop down menu all the images in the current folder or collection will appear in the filmstrip. Selecting camera info, default columns, or exposure info, will not make any visible change in the filmstrip. However, if you hover the cursor over an image in the filmstrip, the exposure info and camera info will appear on screen beneath the image.

## The Right Side Panels

Finally, you're ready for the column of panels on the right side of the screen. This is where the fun stuff is, you're ready to develop your images. There is the Histogram panel, one toolbar and eight panels for developing your images in the column on the right side of the main image. Each panel has sections in it for making changes in the image. For the most part, you'll be making changes in your image by moving a slider on a slider bar. Each slider bar has a distinctive name for the effect it will produce in the image. However, before you start making changes to your image, there are several things that will make your editing easier.

## MOVING BACKWARD

The first thing that will help you is to learn how to undo any and all changes you make in your image. So, the following are the ways you can step backward to undo any of the changes:

- Hold down the Command (Macintosh), Control (PC) and press the Z key on the keyboard to undo the last change you made.
- Each time you press the Z key on the keyboard while holding down the Command (Macintosh), Control (PC) key, Lightroom® will step you backward through the changes you've made in developing your image.
- Double clicking on the name of a slider bar after you make a change in the image will undo any change you made with the slider and return the slider to it's original position on the bar.
- Double clicking on a slider on a slider bar will return the slider to it's original position and undo the change you made with the slider.
- Double clicking on the name of a section in a panel will reset all the changes made on all the sliders in that section of the panel.
- Holding down the Option (Macintosh), Alt (PC) key will change the name of the section in which you are working to "Reset".
- Clicking on "Reset" while holding down the Option (Macintosh), Alt (PC) will reset all the sliders in the section and undo any changes you made in that section.
- Clicking on the word "Reset" at the bottom right of the screen will undo all the changes you made in all the panels and return the image to it's original state.

## BEFORE AND AFTER

A second thing that will make your editing easier is to know how to see a before and after of the image. The following will allow you to see Before and After views of your image as you edit it.

- Use the Before and After icon previously mentioned on the Tool Bar.
- Use the keyboard shortcut, the Y key to bring up a Before and After of the image.
- Pressing the Backslash (\) key on the keyboard will bring up the image full screen as it was before any changes were made and the word "Before" will appear at the top right of the screen.
- Pressing the Backslash (\) key a second time will return the image to the current editing stage.
- All the panels except the Basic panel have a light switch icon, usually at the top left of the panel, clicking with the cursor on this icon will turn off the changes you've made in that panel.
- Clicking with the cursor on the light switch icon a second time will turn the changes back on .

## MOVING THE SLIDERS ON THE SLIDER BAR

The third thing to know to make your editing faster and easier is to know how to move the sliders on the slider bars. The following are the different ways to move the sliders:

- Click on the slider with the cursor and drag it to a new position on the bar.
- Highlight the name of a slider by clicking with the cursor on it and use the plus (+) and minus (-) keys to move the slider on the bar.
- Hover the cursor over a slider bar and use the up and down arrow keys to move the slider on the bar.
- Clicking with the cursor in the scrubby slider box on the right side of a slider turns the cursor into a double pointed arrow and allows you to increase or decrease the effect by moving the cursor right or left.
- You can type a value into the scrubby slider box and it will move the slider on the bar.

In Lightroom 4, most of the sliders in the Basic panel, Tone Curve panel, HSL/Color/Black and White panel, Lens Correction panel, Effects panel and Camera Calibration start in the center of the slider bar. Usually these effects can be changed between plus 100 percent and minus 100 percent. Some of the slider bars have a starting position on the left side of the bar and the effect can be changed only from zero to plus 100. The exceptions are the Exposure effect slider which is has the same effect on an image as widening or narrowing the aperture on the camera, going to a higher or lower number f-stop or increasing or decreasing the shutter speed. You can make a change in the exposure to plus or minus five stops. This is a change from Lighroom®3 in which you could make a change of only plus or minus 4 stops. In the Basic panel, the Temperature and Tint sliders will be positioned at the Kelvin temperature at which the image was created. Other exceptions are in the Split Toning panel where the Hue and Saturation sliders for both the Highlights and Shadows start on the left side of the slider bar. The Balance slide in the Split Toning panel starts in the center of the slider bar. In the Detail panel, the sliders start in a default position on the slider bar for Sharpening and Luminance and Color Noise reduction. Finally, in the Effects panel, the slider for adding grain to an image starts at the left side of the slider bar. You can think of the changes you make with these sliders as percentage changes. For the sliders that start on the middle of the slider bar you, as you move the slider to the right, you will be increasing the effect by a certain percentage up to one hundred percent and when moving the slider to the left, you will be decreasing the effect up to minus one hundred percent. If you choose to highlight the name of an effect to use the plus and minus keys or hover the cursor over the slider bar and press the up and down arrow keys, the percentage of change in the effect will be a change of plus or minus 5 percent each time you press the plus or minus or up or down arrow keys. Holding down the Shift key on the keyboard and pressing the plus or minus or up and down arrow key on the keyboard will make a change of plus or minus twenty percent. Holding down the Option (Macintosh), Alt (PC) key as you press the plus or minus or up and down arrow keys gives you a little more accuracy by making a change of only plus or minus one percent. When highlighting the Exposure effect or hovering the cursor over the Exposure slider, each time you press the plus or minus or up and down arrow key the change in the exposure will be plus or minus one tenth of a stop. Holding down the Shift key while pressing the plus or minus or up and down arrow keys will make a change in the exposure of one third of a stop. As with the other sliders, holding down the Option key (Macintosh), Alt key (PC) will give you more accuracy as pressing the plus or minus or up or down arrow keys will make a change in the exposure of two hundredths of a stop.

Not all the other effects slider bars adhere to the percentage rule. The following sliders are the exception to the above rule:

- The Temperature slider in the White Balance section of the Basic panel is a Kelvin scale from 2000 to 50,000 degrees Kelvin.
- The Tint slider in the White Balance section of the Basic panel is for adding or removing a color tint in an image and goes from -150 to +150, however the color change is more important than the numbers change.
- The Hue sliders in the Split Toning panel goes from 0 to 360.
- The Sharpening amount slider in the Detail panel goes from 0 to +150 and starts at a default setting of 25.
- The Radius slider in the Detail panel goes from 0.5 to 3 and starts at a default setting of 1.0
- The Detail slider in the Detail panel goes from 0 to 100 and starts at a default setting of 25.
- The Masking slider in the Detail panel goes from 0 to 100 and starts at the left side of the slider bar at 0.
- It is not clear what the unit of measure is in the Detail panel.

## The Histogram

OK, now it's time to start developing your image. First, be aware that while Lightroom® treats RAW files, tiff files and JPEG files the same, there are some limitations to editing tiff and JPEG files in Lightroom®. These will be mentioned as we go along.

- Starting at the top of the right column, there is the Histogram. Like most histograms (Figure 9) there is much information here. By looking at the histogram, you can learn the following information.
- The distribution of tones in your image.
- The highlights, the brightest tones are on the right side.
- The darkest tones, the shadows, are on the left side.
- The mid-tones are in the middle.

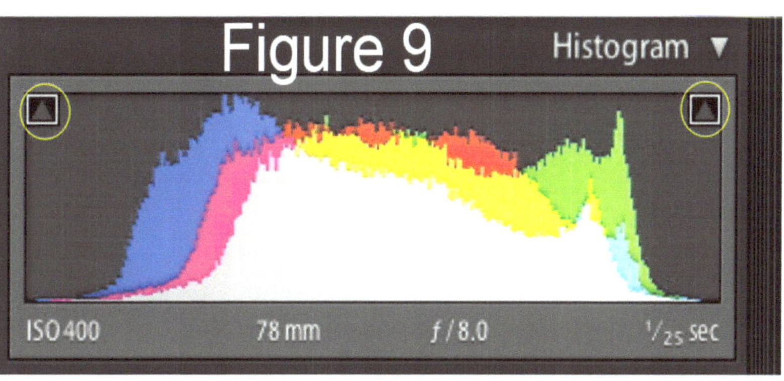


The histogram tells you if you have lost any details in the highlight area or shadow area of the image.

- If the histogram does not reach the wall on the right or left side, you have most of the detail in the highlights and shadows.
- If the histogram is climbing either the right or left wall as if it's trying to escape the frame, then you know you have lost some detail in the image, this is called clipping.

Lightroom® will also tell you where you have lost the detail in your image. There are two small square boxes on the top right and left of the histogram (Yellow circles, Figure 9). Hovering the cursor over either of these boxes will show you in the image where you have lost detail. Hovering over the box on the right will show lost detail in the highlights by turning the lost detail in the image Red. Hovering over the left box will show lost detail in the shadows by turning the lost shadow detail in the image Blue. If you click with the cursor on either one of these boxes, the clipped highlights and/or shadows will remain red or blue in the image. The keyboard shortcut to turn on both the highlight and shadow clipping warnings is to press the J key. To turn off the clipping warnings, you can press the J key a second time or click with the cursor on the boxes. What if you don't like those little boxes in the histogram? Then just Control (Macintosh) Right (PC) click with the cursor anywhere in the histogram and you'll get a menu that will let you hide the boxes so they don't show in the histogram. You can still turn on and off the clipping warnings in the image by pressing the J key. If you decide you do like those little clipping warning boxes, then Control (Macintosh) Right (PC) click in the histogram again and select show clipping indicators and they'll be back.

The histogram is divided into five sections and if you hover your cursor over any part of the histogram, the section that corresponds to that area of the Histogram will turn a lighter gray and the name of the area of the image affected will show up just below the histogram. Each area of the histogram corresponds to one of the Tone sliders in the Basic Panel (we'll get to those sliders shortly). So, by hovering the cursor over the histogram you can tell which slider will affect which area of the image. This is because in addition to the name of the tone slider to be affected showing up below the histogram, the name of the tone slider in the Basic panel will be highlighted. Another neat thing about the Histogram is that you can do some quick editing by clicking with your cursor in an area of the histogram and dragging it left or right to make corrections. As you drag the cursor right or left in the Histogram you will see the affected tone slider in the Basic panel move on it's slider bar. This last function is why I never use the Quick Develop panel in the Library module.

## The New Process Version 2012

Before you start developing your images, there is one important thing to know if you are moving your images from a previous version of Lightroom®. In Lightroom®4, the current Process Version is 2012 and it will make a significant difference in how you edit your images. When you bring up an image in the Develop module of Lightroom®4 you may see an exclamation point icon (!) in the gray area to the bottom right of the image(Yellow circle, Figure 10). This icon is letting you know there is a new Process Version available in Lightroom®4. There are several ways you can switch to the new Process Version.

- You can open the Camera Calibration panel, click on the double pointed arrow next to the words "Process Version" and from the drop down menu, choose 2012 (Current).
- A second way is to open the Settings menu at the top of the screen, choose "Process" from the drop down menu and then choose 2012(Current) from the pop up menu that appears.
- The easiest way is to simply click with the cursor on the exclamation point icon.

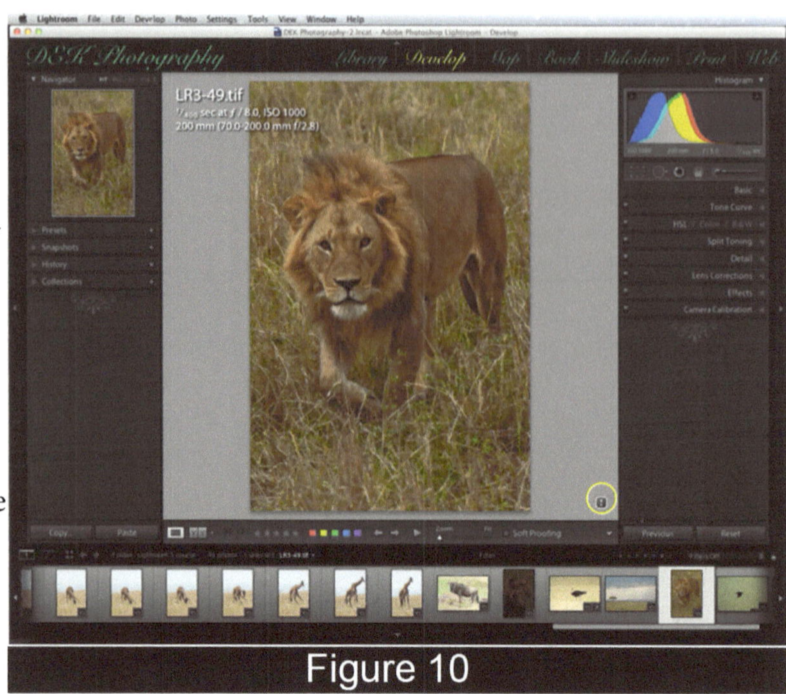

Figure 10

Clicking on the exclamation point icon will bring up a new pop up dialog box on screen telling you the following things:

- A new Process version is available.
- Converting to the new Process Version may cause significant visual changes in the image.
- Warning you to convert only one image until you are familiar with the new Process Version.

## The Camera Calibration Panel

Adobe recommends that the panels in the right side column be used in order from the top down. For the most part I think that's true. However, in my post-production workflow, I use the last panel, Camera Calibration first (I wish Adobe had made it the first panel). Here's the reason I like to use it first most of the time. What many people don't realize is that when you take a picture and look at it on the monitor on the back of the camera it looks (usually) pretty good. That's because you're looking at a JPEG image, even if you're shooting RAW files. That JPEG has had things like brightness and contrast added to it by the camera. When you bring the image up in Lightroom®, at first you are seeing the JPEG thumbnail as it is being imported, so it also looks good. However, when you bring the image up full screen, it doesn't look as good as it did on the back of the camera or when it was first imported. That's because you are looking at a RAW file when the image is brought up in the Loupe view in the Library module or in the Develop module. That RAW file which is just pure data, has had nothing added to it. Adobe probably realized that people liked the images they saw in the camera and so they added a series of camera profiles in the Camera Calibration panel. If you open the Camera Calibration panel when you're starting to edit your image, the first thing you should check is the Process version at the top of the panel (red arrow Figure 11). It should say 2012 (Current). If it doesn't, if it says 2003 or 2010, then click with the cursor on the double pointed arrow next

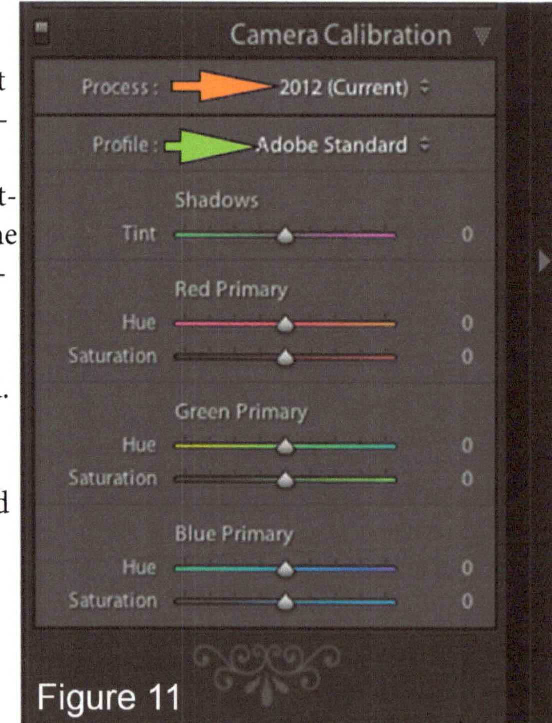

Figure 11

to 2003 or 2010 and select the 2012 (Current) process version. If you have images you developed in the 2003 or 2010 Process version, Lightroom may revert to that version. So, even if you are using Lightroom®4, if you bring an image into the Develop module that has been developed in the 2010 Process Version, the 2010 Process Version will be the one Lightroom® shows you. That's why you should always check the Process Version. Below the Process is the Profile (Green arrow, Figure 11), it will say Adobe Standard if your image is a RAW file. If the images is a JPEG, tiff, or HDR image, the profile will say Embedded and you will not be able to change the profile. This is another limitation to editing TIFF and JPEG files in Lightroom®, the Camera Calibration Profiles are not available for tiff and JPEG files. However, if it is a RAW file and you click with the cursor on the double pointed arrow to the right of "Adobe Standard", you'll get a drop down menu with multiple profiles. Depending on your camera there will be a different number of profiles. Figure 12 shows the available profiles for a Nikon camera. One of the purposes of these profiles is to match the in-camera profile style produced by the camera. Clicking on any one of the profiles will change the image slightly towards what you saw on the back of the camera when you took the picture. You will not use all the profiles. The profiles I use most often are Camera Landscape, Camera Portrait, Camera Neutral and Camera Vivid, but I recommend trying them all to find your favorites. By selecting a camera profile you can start developing the image from a stage you already like. However, my experience has been that the different camera profiles don't work very well with images shot under darker lighting conditions and/or at high ISO sensitivity settings.

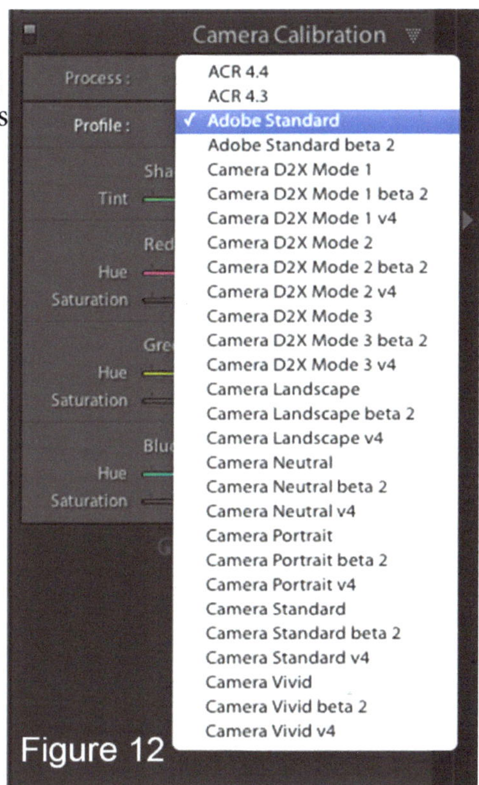

Figure 12

## The Crop and Straighten Tool

Right below the Histogram is a tool bar that has five very useful tools, the Crop and Straighten tool, the Spot Removal tool, the Red Eye Correction tool, the Graduated Filter tool and the Adjustment Brush tool. The last four will be covered a little later. In my workflow I use the Crop and Straighten tool right after I've picked a camera profile for my image in the Camera Calibration panel. Certainly I want to straighten my image if it needs it and sometimes I want to remove a portion of the image, burned out highlights in the sky for example. Also, cropping the image first may change the histogram and make using some of the tone sliders in the Basic panel unnecessary. Do one of the following to open the Crop and Straighten tool:

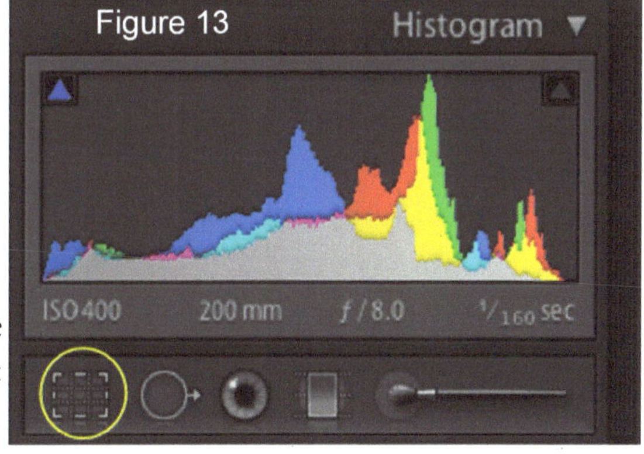

Figure 13

- Click with the cursor on the Crop tool icon (Yellow circle, Figure 13).
- Go to the Tools menu at the top of the screen and select Crop from the drop down menu.
- Use the keyboard shortcut, press the R key on the keyboard.

When you open the Crop and Straighten tool, a crop overlay will appear on the image. The default crop overlay is the rule of thirds, but there are five other crop overlays and pressing the O key on the keyboard will cycle through the different crop overlays on the image. If you do not want the crop overlay to appear on the image, there is a way to get rid of it. In the Toolbar at the bottom of the screen is a Tool Overlay menu. The default is Always, which means that the crop overlay will appear over the image when ever you bring up the Crop tool. Clicking with the cursor on the double pointed arrow for the Tool Overlay will give you a choice of never seeing the Crop Overlay, Always seeing it or Auto. With Auto, the Crop Overlay will not appear on the image until you click in the image to make a crop. Along with the crop preset on the image, a crop and straighten menu will appear between the tool bar and the Basic Panel. Hovering your cursor over any one of the icons will tell you what the tool will accomplish. The icons which appear In this menu enable you to do the following:

- You can crop to the original aspect ratio or select a custom aspect ratio from the Lightroom® presets.
- With the padlock icon locked, by default the aspect ratio is locked and your crop will remain the original aspect ratio as you crop the image
- Pressing the X key on the keyboard will change your crop from vertical to horizontal or the other way.
- Unlock the padlock icon by clicking on it with the cursor and you can select the aspect ratio for your crop from the presets in the drop down menu or crop to any aspect ratio you choose.
- Create your own crop dimensions by selecting "Enter Custom" from the drop down menu.
- Select the right angle ruler, called the Crop Frame tool and you can draw a crop in the image. With the padlock locked, the crop will be the locked aspect ratio. With the padlock open, you can draw any aspect ratio you choose.
- Select the Straighten tool which looks like a ruler and use the cursor to draw a line on anything in the image that should be straight, the horizon, for example, release the cursor and the image will be straightened and cropped.
- If you hold down the Command (Macintosh), Control (PC) key the cursor turns into the Straighten tool. Just drag the cursor across something that should be straight in the image and the image will rotate and straighten.
- Move the slider on the bar next to the word Angle and the angle of the image will rotate as it becomes straightened.
- Move your cursor outside the crop dimensions and it turns into a curved double pointed arrow. With this cursor you can rotate the image right or left
- Checking the box next to "Constrain Crop to Warp" keeps the crop to within the original image area.
- Reset the Crop tool by clicking with the cursor on the word Reset at the bottom of the panel.
- Pressing the Escape key on the keyboard will also reset the crop so you can start over.

The following are the ways to accept the crop you've made and close the Crop tool:

- Clicking with the cursor on the word "Close" at the bottom of the Crop panel.
- Click with the cursor on the Crop icon in the tool bar.
- Use the Keyboard shortcut, press the R key on the keyboard.
- Press the Return (Macintosh), Enter (PC) key.
- Click with the cursor on the word "Done" at the bottom of the image.
- Double click with the cursor in the image.

If you have selected "Enter Custom" from the drop down menu with the padlock open, Lightroom® will automatically save the crop size you enter. The next time you open the padlock and bring up the drop down menu, the custom aspect ratio you entered will be saved as a preset at the bottom of the drop down menu.

As with all of the develop settings you make in Lightroom®, the crop is nondestructive. When you accept the crop all you are doing is telling Lightroom® to display only the area of the image within the crop boundaries. After you accept the crop, if you again reopen the Crop tool, the entire image will still be there with your crop on it. You can then change the crop by moving the crop handles or change the aspect ratio, etc. and then accept the crop again.

## The Basic Panel

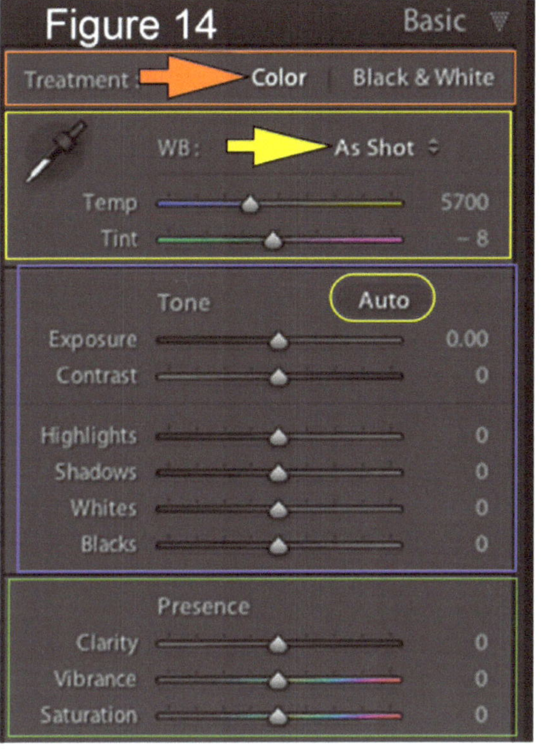


The top panel under the Histogram panel and tool bar is the Basic panel, one in which you'll spend much time (Figure 14). At the top of the panel is the Treatment section of the Basic panel (Red border section, Figure 14). Lightroom® recognizes whether the image is in color or black and white, but you can change the image from color to black and white or the other way simply by clicking with the cursor on black and white or color in the bar next to the word "Treatment"(Red arrow, Figure 14).

Below the Treatment section, the Basic panel has three sections in which you'll be working to correct and enhance the detail in your image, White Balance, Tone and Presence. There several keyboard shortcuts in the Basic panel for moving between the sliders, they are as follows:

- Move from one slider to another by clicking with the cursor on a slider.
- Pressing the period (.) key on the keyboard will jump the active slider to the next lower slider and the name of the now active slider will become highlighted.
- A message will appear in the main image window that will tell you which slider is now the active slider.
- With the name of the slider highlighted, you can use the plus (+) and minus (-) keys to move the slider left or right to achieve the effect you want.
- Pressing the comma (,) key on the keyboard will jump the active slider back to the one above the one you're currently using.
- Again, a message will appear in the main image window which will tell you which slider is now the active slider
- The name of the now active slider will highlight
- The plus (+) and minus (-) keys on the keyboard can now be used to make your adjustment

The Basic panel is the only panel in which you can press the period (.) and comma (,) keys on the keyboard to move from one slider to another. However, you can still highlight the name of a slider in another panel and press the plus (+) or minus (-) keys on the keyboard or hover the cursor on the slider bar and use the up and down arrow keys on the keyboard to move the slider left and right to achieve the effect you want.

### White Balance

Below the Treatment bar is the White Balance section of the Basic Panel(Yellow border section, Figure 14). The following are the different ways you can set the White Balance for your image:

- Select the White Balance Selector tool (it looks like an eyedropper) by clicking on the eyedropper icon or using the keyboard shortcut, press the W key on the keyboard
- Click with the eyedropper cursor on an area of the image that is supposed to be white or one that is neutral or suppose to be neutral, one with the values of the red, green and blue channels the same or

very close to the same.
- Go to the slider on the Temperature bar and move it left or right to select the degrees Kelvin and warm up or cool down the image.

When you first bring an image into Lightroom®, the White Balance selected will be "As Shot". (Yellow arrow, Figure 14) Clicking with the cursor on the double pointed arrow next to "As shot" will give you a drop down menu with the same choices your camera gives you as presets for white balance. These choices are:

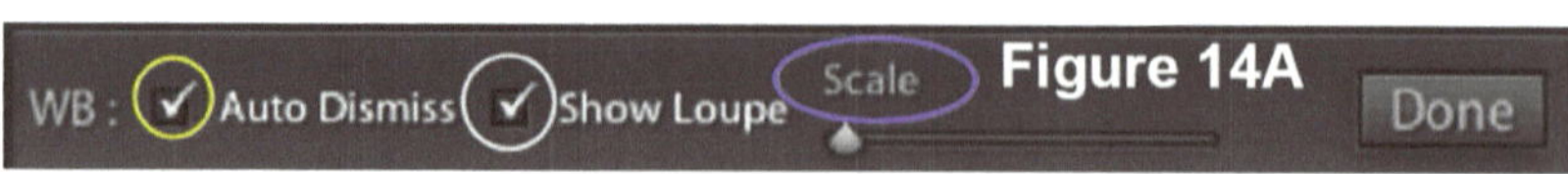

Figure 14A

- As shot
- Auto
- Daylight
- Cloudy
- Shade
- Tungsten/incandescent
- Florescent
- Flash
- Custom

Using the White Balance Selector tool or selecting a degrees Kelvin white balance from the Temperature bar will change the White Balance to Custom.

The White Balance Selector tool can be used as follows:
- On the image by itself to select an area that should be white or neutral.
- On the image with a loupe showing the values of the red, green and blue channels of any area over which the cursor is hovering.
- With the loupe showing the red, green and blue values you can find an area of the image that is neutral.

When the White Balance Selector tool is selected a new tool bar appears below the main image. There are two check boxes titled "Auto Dismiss" and "Show loupe". Placing a check mark by clicking with the cursor in the box marked "Auto Dismiss" (Yellow circle, Figure 14A) will cause the eyedropper cursor and White Balance Selector tool to disappear after you click on an area in the image. Leaving the box unchecked causes the White Balance Selector tool to remain active on the image and you can check another area to see if you can get a better White Balance.

The second check box (White circle, Figure 14A) is for turning on and off the loupe. Placing a check in the "Show Loupe"check box by clicking with the cursor will make the loupe visible. Leaving the box unchecked means the loupe will not appear with the eyedropper cursor in the image.

Next to the check box that makes the loupe visible or invisible there is a small slider bar titled "Scale" (Blue ellipse, Figure 14A)that allows you to magnify the squares in the loupe. Sliding the slider to the left will enlarge the squares in the loupe. I recommend making the loupe visible and sliding the slider bar to the left to make the loupe squares large. This can be a very valuable tool for getting the correct White Balance even If there is nothing in your image that should be white. You can use the White Balance Selector tool (eyedropper) to try to find an area of the image that has all three channels, red, green and blue values the same or very close to the same. This would be a neutral area and clicking on it with the cursor will give you a good White Balance. Enlarging the squares in the loupe allows you to sample a smaller area of the image and makes it easier to find a neutral area. At the end of the tool bar is the word "Done". Clicking on "Done" makes the White Balance Selector tool close.

White Balance in Lightroom® is the second section in which there is a limitation to editing JPEG and tiffs. The only White Balance choices available for JPEG and tiffs are As Shot, Auto and Custom.

White Balance is a personal preference. Some people like warm images, others like images a little cooler. Lightroom® gives you the opportunity to create a white balance you like with the two sliders called "Temp" and "Tint" at the bottom of the White Balance section of the Basic panel. The Temp and Tint sliders are used as follows:

- The Temp slider bar represents the temperature in degrees Kelvin and can be used to warm up the image by sliding the slider to the right or cool down the image by moving the slider to the left.
- You can fine tune the contrast in the image with the Temperature slider.
- The Tint slider bar can be used to remove or add a color tint to the image
- The box at the end of the slider bars is, as are all boxes to the right of sliders, a scrubby slider. Clicking in the box with the cursor will turn the cursor into a double pointed arrow. Moving the double pointed arrow either left or right will decrease or increase the degrees Kelvin. The slider will move on the bar and the image will become cooler or warmer or a color tint will be removed or added.

With both the Temperature and Tint sliders, you can highlight the name of the slider, use the plus and minus keys or hover your cursor over the slider bar and use the up and down arrow keys to make your White Balance changes. Each time you press the plus or minus key or the up or down arrow keys, the Kelvin temperature will change by a factor of 50 degrees. If you hold down the shift key it will change by a factor of 200 degrees. If you hold down the Option (Macintosh), Alt (PC) key and press the plus or minus key or up and down arrow keys, the Kelvin temperature will change only by five degrees. The Temperature slider has a limitation to editing TIFF and JPEG files. In the Temperature slider you are limited to moving the slider for TIFF and JPEG only plus or minus one hundred degrees Kelvin from the temperature at which the image was created, you don't have the entire Kelvin scale. Using the plus or minus keys or up or down arrow keys with a TIFF or JPEG will make a change of only 5 degrees and holding down the shift key makes a change of only 20 degrees. Holding down the Option (Macintosh), Alt (PC) key and using the plus or minus key or up or down arrow keys will make a change of only one degree on the Kelvin scale for a JPEG or tiff. So, with a tiff or JPEG file you don't have anywhere near the ability to change the White Balance.

**Tone**

Once you have tried the Camera Calibration presets, cropped and straightened your image (if it needs it) and gotten the White Balance the way you want it, it's time to move to the Tone sliders in the next section of the Basic panel (Blue border section, Figure 14). Probably the first thing you should try is the Auto button just to the right of the word Tone(Yellow ellipse, Figure 14). If you click on this button with your cursor or use the keyboard shortcut, hold down the Command (Macintosh), Control (PC )key and press the U key on the keyboard, Lightroom® will show you what it thinks the image should look like by moving some or all the sliders in the Tone section. So, try it and see if you like the results. If you don't like the results you can hold down the Command (Macintosh) or Control (PC) key and press the Z key to return the image to the previous state. However, it is possible the Auto Tone may give you a good place from which to start developing the image. Another option is to double click with the cursor on the sliders or the name of the tone sliders that have changed one at a time to return them to their beginning position. Doing this will give you a chance to see the difference each Tone slider made in the image and allow you to decide if you want more or less of the effect of that slider.

There is a big change in the sliders in the Tone section in the Basic panel. In Lightroom®3 only the Exposure slider started at zero on the middle of the slider bar. The other three tone sliders started at zero on the left side of the slider bar and could only be moved to plus 100%. In Lightroom®4 all of the tone sliders start at zero in the middle of the slider bar and can be moved to plus or minus 100%.

In Lightroom®3 there were four Tone effects sliders, in Lightroom®4 there are six Tone effects sliders. The Recovery, Fill Light and Brightness effects that were in Lightroom®3 are gone and have been replaced by Highlight, Shadows, Whites and Blacks effects in Lightroom®4. The Exposure and Contrast effects will have their effect on the entire image, each of the other effect sliders has its primary effect on one area of the image Five of the first Six tone effects sliders, Exposure, Highlights, Shadows, Whites and Blacks are the ones that correspond to the five areas in the histogram. If you click with the cursor on the slider of any of these five effect sliders, the area of the image that will be primarily affected by that slider will be highlighted in the Histogram. When you are moving one of the tone effect sliders, you will see the percentage of change you are making either positive or negative below the right side of the histogram. With the Exposure effect slider the change will be indicated as stops. Before moving any of the six tone effects sliders, I recommend turning on the clipping warnings in the histogram by pressing the J key on the keyboard or clicking with the cursor on the individual boxes in the top right and left of the histogram. This will show you the burned out highlights in red and the loss of detail in the shadow areas in blue on the image. In most cases, it will take a combination of the tone sliders to remove clipping and/or enhance the image. If you choose to highlight the name of the slider and use the plus or minus keys or hover the cursor over the slider bar and use the up and down arrow keys you will be able to make changes in equal increments. The following describes how these six Tone sliders affect your image:

- The Exposure slider, has the largest effect of all the tone sliders on the entire image, but with more emphasis on the highlights. Moving the exposure slider is similar to changing the shutter speed or aperture on your camera to let in more or less light. Moving the slider to the right is like slowing down the shutter speed or opening the aperture, going to a lower number f-stop and letting more light reach the camera's sensor. Moving the slider to the left is the opposite, letting less light reach the camera's sensor by changing to a faster shutter speed or narrower aperture, a higher number f-stop.
- Clicking with the cursor on the Exposure name to highlight it and pressing the plus or minus keys or hovering the cursor over the exposure slider bar and pressing the up and down arrow keys on the keyboard is equal to making a one-tenth of a stop change in the amount of light reaching the camera's sensor.
- After highlighting the Exposure slider by clicking with the cursor on the name or hovering the cursor over the Exposure slider bar, holding down the Option (Macintosh) Alt (PC) key while pressing the plus or minus keys or pressing the up and down arrow keys on the keyboard will make a change in the exposure equal to two hundreds of a stop on the image.
- After highlighting the Exposure effect or hovering the cursor over the Exposure slider, holding down the Shift key on the keyboard and pressing the plus or minus keys or the up and down arrow keys will make a change of one third of a stop on the image.
- Dragging the slider is faster, but not as accurate.
- To the right of all the sliders is a scrubby slider box that informs you how much of a change you've made.
- If you watch the histogram as you slide the Exposure slider to the right or left, which is equivalent to letting in more or less light, you'll see the histogram also moving to the right or left.

TIP: With Lightroom®3, the Exposure effect had a range of from minus four stops to plus four stops. In Lightroom®4 the Exposure slider has a range of from minus five stops to plus five stops, providing the ability to extract more data in a RAW image. Since a RAW image always has a greater latitude than the digital camera, more detail can be brought out of a RAW image in Lightroom®4. You might want to think of this as the image having a greater dynamic range.

TIP: Since the Exposure slider affects the highlights the most and moving the Exposure to the right will affect the highlights, one trick to knowing how far to the right you can move the exposure slider without clipping the highlights, is to hold down the Option (Macintosh), Alt (PC) key and click with the cursor on the exposure slider. The image will turn black and you'll start to see colors appear in the image when clipping of the highlights starts to occur as you move the slider with the cursor to the right. When one channel is clipped, that color, red, green or blue will appear on the screen. When the yellow colors appear, the red and green channels have been clipped, magenta means the red and blue channels have been clipped, cyan means the blue and green channels have been clipped, and when white or gray appears, all three channels have been clipped. So, when the first color starts to appear in the black screen as you move the slider with the cursor to the right on the bar, that tells you you're getting clipping and you should stop moving the slider to the right and move slightly back to the left to get rid of any clipping. You will have pushed the histogram as far to the right as you can without getting clipping of the highlights. You can also get rid of burned out highlights with the Exposure slider by sliding the slider to the left. However, this will also darken the entire image. Sometimes this can be good, especially if you need to add some contrast to your image.

- The Contrast slider, while not new to Lightroom®4, is much more efficient than it was in Lightroom®3. Sliding the Contrast slider to the right makes the shadows darker and deepens the blacks while making the highlights and whites lighter. The Contrast slider also increases color saturation in the image. It seems that the Contrast slider affects the blacks and shadows more than it affects the highlights and whites. What the Contrast slider does is spread out or expand the histogram when the slider is moved to the right adding contrast to the image. Moving the slider to the left will contract the histogram decreasing the contrast.
- The highlights slider affects mainly the brightest tones in the image. Sliding the Highlights slider to the right will make the brightest tones in the image lighter. Sliding the Highlights slider to the left decreases the brightness of the image without having much affect on the shadows or blacks. The effect produced by sliding the Highlights slider to the right or left is very subdued compared the effect produced by sliding the Exposure or Whites slider to the right or left. Sliding to the left does make the entire image look slightly darker however.
- When you click on the name of the Highlights slider to highlight it and use the plus or minus keys, or hover the cursor over the Highlights slider bar to use the up or down arrow keys on the keyboard, there will be a change of 5% each time you press the plus or minus or up or down arrow key on the keyboard.
- Holding down the Option (Macintosh) or Alt (PC) key while pressing the plus or minus keys on the keyboard or using the up and down arrow keys will give you more accuracy because each time you press one of these keys on the keyboard you will only be making a 1% change in the image.
- Holding down the Shift key on the keyboard and pressing the plus or minus or up or down arrow keys will make a change in the effect on the image of twenty percent to the positive or negative.

TIP: Holding down the Option (Macintosh) Alt (PC) key will do the same thing with the Highlights slider as it did with the Exposure slider. The entire screen will go black except for the burned out highlights which, depending on the channels that have been clipped, will exhibit the same colors as in the Exposure slider. Sliding the Highlights slider to the right with the cursor will let you know how far you can move the slider to the right before clipped highlights start to appear in the image. When the colors indicating clipped highlights start to appear, stop moving the slider. Moving the Highlights slider to the left will start to get rid of burned out highlights. Holding down the Option (Macintosh), Alt (PC) key while sliding the Highlights slider to the left will show you, as it did with the Exposure slider when all the clipped highlights are gone. It should be noted that it may take a combination of the Exposure and Highlights sliders moving to the left to get rid of all the burned out highlights.

The choice as to which slider, Exposure or Highlights you use to get rid of burned out highlights is an individual decision. If the overall image is too bright, then start with the Exposure slider and reduce the exposure by moving the slider to the left, watching to see the burned out highlights disappear. You can hold down the Option (Macintosh), Alt (PC) key to show just the burned out highlights, but you may want to periodically release the Option/Alt key or not use it at all so that you can see how dark the image is becoming. When the image starts to darken too much or whites seem to be turning gray, stop and back off the Exposure slider to the right to bring back some of the brightness. Then use the Highlights slider to get rid of the remaining burned out highlights by moving it to the left.

- The Shadows slider is another slider that will affect the entire image, but will have most of its effect on the shadows. This is a great slider to use when you have a backlit image because it will bring detail into the darker areas of the image. Unfortunately most of the noise hangs out in the darker areas of the image and by lightening the darkest area of the image you'll bring out any noise present in the image. Be careful when using the Shadows slider, it can make the image look a little or a lot washed out. You should think of this slider as slowing down your shutter speed to let in more light, which will make the image appear flat or washed out. Holding down the Option (Macintosh), Alt (PC) key on the keyboard and clicking on the Shadows slider will turn the screen white and any clipping in the shadows area will be seen as different colors against the white background, depending on which channels have been clipped.
- The Whites slider, which is really the White Clipping slider produces a much greater affect on the brightness of the image than the Highlights effect slider does and therefore on when highlight clipping will occur in the image. The Whites effect is similar, but not as strong as the Exposure Effect on the image. Almost any image will be brightened moving the Whites slider to the right. It has little effect on making the image darker. As with the previous tone sliders, holding down the Option key (Macintosh), Alt (PC) key will make the screen black and the different colors will show up on the screen when clipping in the highlights or whites occur.
- The Blacks effect slider when moved to the left, will have a much greater effect on the darkness of the image than the Shadows effect slider will. It's primarily effect will be to increase or decrease the density of the black tones in the image as its name implies. As with the Shadows slider, the Blacks slider will have only a small effect on the brightness of the image when moved to the right. The Blacks slider should be used sparingly as it will darken the whole image and cause loss of detail in the darkest areas of the image. However, the Blacks slider is one of the best sliders for adding contrast to your image. Holding down the Option (Macintosh), Alt (PC) and clicking on the Blacks slider with the cursor will turn the screen white, any lost detail in the darkest part of the image will be revealed. Moving the Blacks slider to the right can restore that lost detail. Moving the Blacks slider to the left will deepen the black tones and add contrast to the image. By holding down the Option (Macintosh), Alt (PC) key and turning the screen white, you will be able to recover clipping moving the slider to the right or tell how far you can move the Blacks slider to the left before loss of detail in the darkest part of the image occurs. When colors start to appear on the white screen, you have moved the Blacks slider too far to the left.
-

TIP: Don't get caught up in moving the Blacks slider to the left for more contrast and then trying to recover lost detail in the shadows by moving the Shadows slider to the right. This is almost always counter productive, causing you to lose the contrast you sought to produce while at the same time adding noise to the image. Lost shadows do not print, noise does.

So, to summarize the tone sliders, after you've tried the different profiles in Camera Calibration, cropped and straightened the image if need be and set the White Balance to your liking, then look at the Histogram to see if there is lost detail in either the highlights or shadows. Turning on the clipping warnings (J Key) will show you where the lost detail in the image is located. The lost detail will now show up as red in the lost highlights and blue in the shadow areas of the image. You can use a combination of the six tone sliders to recover burned out highlights, lost detail in the shadows, brighten or darken or add contrast to the image. If you get tired of moving sliders, remember, you can click with the cursor on one of the effects sliders, exposure for Example, to highlight it and hover the cursor over another slider, the Blacks slider, for example and if you have an image that has both burned out highlights and loss of detail in the shadows, press the - (minus) key and the up arrow key at the same time and you'll be correcting both lost highlights and lost detail in the shadows at the same time. There you have it, instant editing.

**Presence**

The final three sliders in the Basic Panel are in the section called the Presence effects sliders (Green border section, Figure 14). They are the Clarity, Vibrance and Saturation sliders. These three sliders will affect the image in the following way:

- The Clarity slider will add contrast and detail to the midtones when the slider is moved to the right with the cursor.
- To best see the effects of the Clarity slider, bring the image up to a 1:1 view in an area in which there are midtones. Moving the slider to the right will appear to sharpen the midtones.
- The Clarity slider will add more contrast to the midtones than the Contrast Tone slider
- Moving the Clarity slider to the left will soften or smooth out the midtones in the image.
- The Vibrance slider will make nonlinear changes in the colors in an image. Colors that are already strong will be left alone by the Vibrance slider and colors that are a little weaker will be boosted by the Vibrance slider.
- The Vibrance slider when moved to the right will expand the color palate and produce a wider variety of colors.
- The Saturation slider will make linear changes in all the colors in the image. Moving the Saturation slider to the right will boost all the colors by increasing the saturation of all the colors in the image. When moved to the left the Saturation slider will remove color in the image. Moving the Saturation slider to minus 100% will remove all the color in the image and it will appear as a grayscale image.

TIP: When working with skin tones, the Vibrance and Saturation sliders should be used in combination. Moving the Vibrance slider to the right will enhance the weaker colors and have little effect on skin tones. Sometimes adding some saturation to pale skin will make the skin tones more pleasing. Other times, especially with a ruddy complexion removing some saturation by moving the Saturation slider to the left will produce a more pleasing result.

Be careful of the Saturation slider, too much saturation will give any image an almost a garish appearance. However, if moved all the way to the left, it will give you a good preview of what the image may look like in black and white. There are better ways to create black and white images in Lightroom®, but sliding both the Vibrance and Saturation sliders all the way to the left can quickly give you a good idea of whether you want to create a black and white image from the current image.

Finally, if you would like to reset either the Tone section and/or the Presence section of the Basic panel, hold down the Option (Macintosh), Alt (PC) key. This will change the word "Tone" at the top of the section in the panel to "Reset Tone" and the word "Presence" to "Reset Presence". Clicking with the cursor on either will reset that section of the Basic panel.

## The Tone Curve Panel

Below the Basic panel is the Tone Curve panel. By default the Tone Curve panel opens with the Parametric curve (Figure 15). This is another place where you can increase the contrast in your image much better than you can using the Contrast slider in the Basic Panel. With the Contrast slider, the darks be come darker and the highlights become lighter. Often the shadows may need to be darkened but the highlights may not need to be made lighter or the other way around. With the Tone Curve panel you can selectively work on just the shadows or the highlights without affecting the other. The following are what is available in the Tone Curve panel:

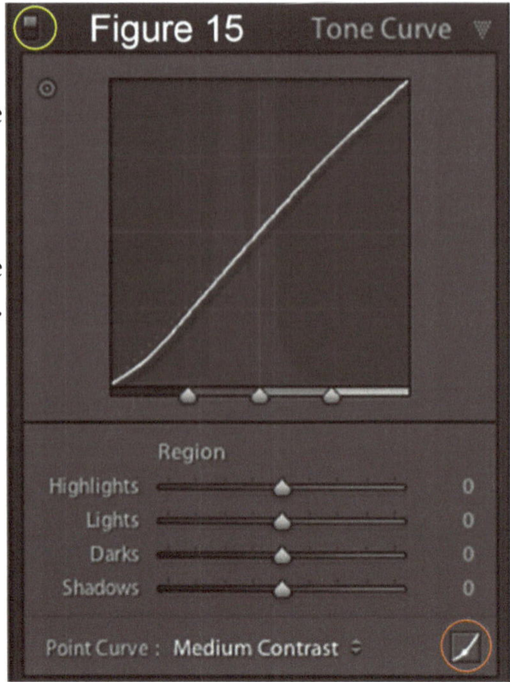


- At the top left side of the panel is an on/off switch (Yellow circle, Figure 15). After you've made a change in the image with the Tone Curve, you can turn the change off or back on by clicking this switch with the cursor. This switch will be found in every panel in the Develop Module from now on. The only panel that doesn't have an on/off switch is the Basic Panel. The Tone Curve panel can be set up two ways. The first is the default set up, the Parametric curve which makes global changes in the image. The second is the Point Curve set up which allows you to work on all three channels at once or on the individual red, green and blue channels.

The default Parametric Curve set up is as follows:

- Below the title bar with the on/off switch is the Parametric curve graph itself.
- Below the Parametric Curve graph is a section entitled "Region" that has four sliders, Highlights, Lights, Darks and Shadows. By default each slider is set to zero on the center of the slider bar.
- Below the four sliders are the words "Point Curve". If you are editing a RAW file it is set to Medium Contrast, if it is a tiff or JPEG you're editing, it will be set to Linear. That's because tiff and JPEG files have had some contrast added by the camera and a RAW file has no contrast added to it.
- If you click on the double pointed arrow after "Medium Contrast", you will get a drop down menu that gives you the choice of strong contrast or linear contrast in addition to medium contrast.

In the default Parametric Curve, you can add contrast to your image by choosing one of the following:

- The easiest way to add contrast is to click on the double pointed arrow next to Medium Contrast at the bottom right of the panel and select one of the other two choices, Linear or Strong Contrast to see if it adds the contrast you want.
- A second way to add contrast is to move up to the Region section and move the sliders in this section to obtain the contrast you want in the image. You can make the changes you want by moving the sliders the same ways you moved the sliders in the Basic panel:
    - ►By using the cursor to drag the slider on the slider bar,
    - ►By highlighting the name of the slider and using the +/- keys,
    - ►By hovering the cursor over the slider bar and using the up and down arrow keys,
    - ►By using the scrubby slider at the end of the slider bar,
    - ►By typing in a value in the scrubby slider box.

You can also reset any of the sliders or the entire panel by doing any of the following:

►By double clicking on the name of the adjustment or on the slider on the bar,

►To reset the whole section, hold down the Option (Macintosh) or Alt (PC) key and the word "Region" will change to "Reset Region", just click on "Reset Region" to reset all the sliders at the same time.

- A third way to add contrast is to move up to the graph and hover your cursor over any part of the Parametric curve. Two things will happen, first a dot will appear on the curve in the area over which you're hovering and second, as in the histogram, the area over which you're hovering will be identified in the graph by the name of the area appearing in the graph. The four areas of the graph identified correspond to the four sliders in the Region section of the Tone Curve panel.

To change the contrast in the image, do the following:

- Move the cursor left or right until the dot on the Parametric curve is over the area you want to change.
- Change the contrast, by simply dragging the cursor down on the left side of the Parametric curve to darken the shadows or darks and up on the right side of the Parametric curve to lighten the highlights or lights areas.

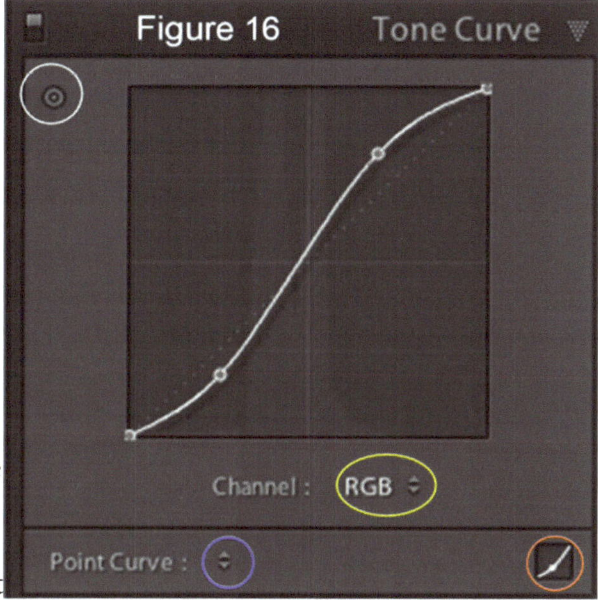


This procedure will give you the classic "S" shaped curve and increase the contrast in the image. You will also notice a shaded area on either side of the Parametric curve. Lightroom® will not let you move the Parametric curve outside the shaded area. If you would like to override these restrictions you will need to change to the Point Curve set up of the Tone Curve panel. To do this, click with the cursor on the icon of the point curve next to Medium Contrast (Red Circle, Figure 15). Doing this will cause the Region section to disappear along with the restrictions on either side of the graph.

The Point Curve set up of the Tone Curve panel is similar to the Curves adjustment in Photoshop®. (Figure 16) You can place points on the curve and drag them up or down without any restrictions. If you don't like the result you get, you can click with the cursor on a point and drag it off the curve. The Point Curve contains one of the big changes from Lightroom®3 to Lightroom®4. Below the graph will be a Channels section that allows you to target all three channels or the individual red, green or blue channels separately. (Yellow ellipse, Figure 16) By default, all three channels, RGB will appear next to the word "Channel", but you can click on the double pointed arrow next to RGB and select either the red, green or blue channel on which to work. What this allows you to do is increase or decrease the intensity of any of the individual channels or change the colors of the individual channels. You can also place as many points on the curve any where you want them by just clicking with the cursor on the curve in the graph. Also, there will not be any restrictions on how far up or down you drag the points so you can create any type of curve you like. As in the Parametric Curve, you can place points on the Point Curve and then drag all three channels down in the shadows area on the bottom left side to darken the shadows and Blacks. Dragging the Point curve up on the top right side will brighten the highlights and whites. As in the Parametric Curve, this will produce the classic S-shaped curve and increase the contrast in the image. If you choose one of the red, green or blue channels, once you place points anywhere on the graph you can drag up or down to increase or decrease the color of the channel as follows:

- In the red channel, moving any point on the graph down will move the reds toward cyan. On the left side the darker shades of reds will be affected, on the right side the lighter shades will be affected.
- Moving any point on the curve up in the red channel will intensify the red tones in the image.
- In the Green channel, moving any point on the graph down will move the greens towards magenta, with the darker shades affected on the left side of the graph and the lighter shades affected at the top on the right side of the graph.
- Moving any point on the curve up in the green channel will intensify the green tones in the image.
- In the Blue channel, moving any point on the graph down will move the shades of blue toward yellow, with the darker shades affected on the left side of the graph and the lighter shades affected at the top right side of the graph.
- Moving any point on the curve up in the blue channel will intensify the blue tones in the image.

The Point Curve section of the Tone Curve panel is the second place in Lightroom®4 that you can remove a color cast and/or change the temperature of an image. The first place being the White Balance section of the Basic panel.

TIP: Once you have created a curve that creates a contrast you like with the Point Curve, you can save the new Point Curve to be applied to other images. To do this, do the following:

- Click on the double arrow by Point Curve(Blue circle Figure 16) at the bottom of the panel.
- You'll see that besides Linear, Medium and Strong Contrast selections, "Custom" and "Save" options have been added to the drop down menu.
- Select save from this menu.
- A pop up Save Point Curve dialog box will appear on screen.
- Name the new Point Curve in the top blank of this dialog box.
- Select the drive in the dialog box where your Catalog is located.
- With the drive selected, click with the cursor on the "New Folder" button at the bottom left of the dialog box
- Name the new folder "Curves".
- Click with the cursor on the "Save" button at the bottom right of the New Point Curve dialog box. The new Point curve preset will be added and will be another choice along with Linear, Medium and Strong Contrast in the drop down menu.

The last way, and my favorite way to add contrast to an image is with the Targeted Adjustment Tool. It will work with either the Parametric Curve or the Point Curve. The Tone Curve panel is the first panel to have this tool, it's located just to the top left of the graph and looks like a little target (White circle, Figure 16). Clicking on this tool icon turns the cursor in to crosshairs and the target with the up and down pointing arrows is located just to the right of the crosshairs. The up and down pointing arrows on the target remind you that you can only drag up or down with the cross hairs cursor. If you place the cross hairs over a tone in the image and drag up that tone and any similar tones in the image will be lightened. Dragging down will darken the same tones. So, you can accurately increase the contrast by dragging dark tones down and light tones up. The selected areas of both the Parametric curve and the Point curve will move up or down in the graph as you drag with the Targeted Adjustment Cursor. Be aware that when you click with the Targeted Adjustment cursor on a tone, the cursor disappears. As you drag down or up you will see the tones on which you click darken or lighten and the Parametric or Point curve will change in the graph. You will not be able to see the Targeted Adjustment cursor again until you release the cursor. If you have the Parametric curve with the Region section open, the grayed out area will be present in the graph and you'll be limited by how much you can drag up or down. However, if you've changed from the Parametric curve to the Point curve, you can drag up and down as much as you want. When you get the contrast the way you want it, with either the Parametric curve or Point curve, you can save the new Tone Curve as another preset. If you have the point curve open you can use the targeted adjustment tool on the individual red, green and blue channels to increase the channel color or change it to the opposite color.

## The HSL/Color/Black and White Panel

The next panel down is the HSL/Color/Black&White panel. (Figure 17) This is where you can really boost colors in an image or convert an image to black and white. Remember, when working with a RAW file, there is no color space, just raw data. It's up to you to bring out the colors. There are two choices for working with the colors in your images. With both, you can work on the hue, saturation or luminance of each color. Across the top of the panel the three choices for working with colors are: HSL,(which stands for Hue, Saturation and Luminance), Color and B&W (Black and White). Moving the Hue slider you can actually change a color. However, you should know that the color change will be towards the colors on either side of the color you want to change. For example, if you want to change the hue of the blue color, moving the slider to the right will make it more purple and moving it to the left will make the blue more aqua so you are limited by the colors on either side of the blue. You cannot change the blue all the way to red with the Hue sliders. The saturation slider will increase the intensity of the color when the slider is moved to the right. Moving the slider to the left will fade the color until there is none of the color left at minus 100 Saturation. The Luminance slider will increase or decrease the brightness of the individual colors.

**Hue/Saturation/Luminance (HSL) Section**

Working with the first choice on the header bar, the HSL configuration, I think is an easier and faster way to work with colors. This configuration has all the colors listed in three different sections. The first is the section for hue, the second for saturation and the third for luminance (Figure 17). In addition, the Targeted Adjustment tool is available for all three sections (Yellow circles, Figure 17). When you choose the HSL section by clicking on it with the cursor in the header bar at the top of the panel (White ellipse, Figure 17), a second bar will appear with a choice of "Hue", "Saturation", "Luminance" or "All" in it. The following are your choices for viewing the three sections of the HSL section:

- If you want to see all three sections click with the cursor on "All" in the bar below the header bar of the panel.
- If you only want to see only one section, then just click with the cursor on that one section in the bar below the header bar.
- If you want to see two sections, click with the cursor in the bar below the header bar on one section and hold down either the Shift key or the Command (Macintosh) or Control (PC) and click with the cursor on the second section you wish to have open.
- If you selected All and only want to see one section, then in the bar below the header bar, click with the cursor on the one section you want open and the other two will close.

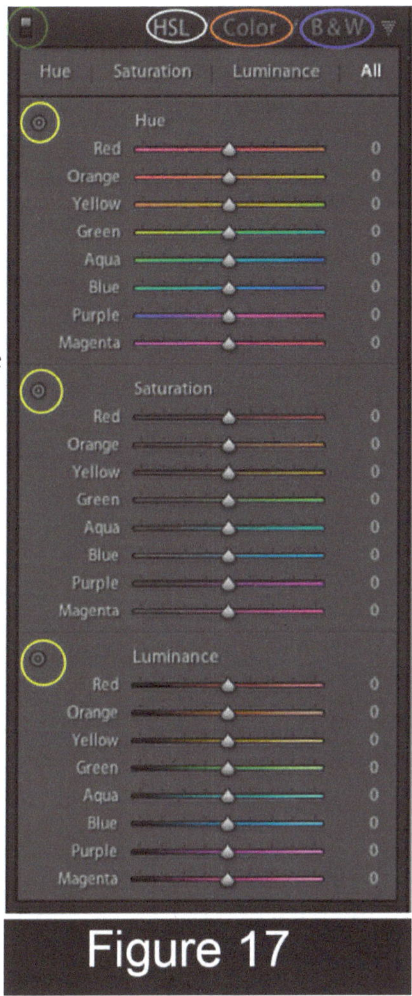

Figure 17

You can change the hue, saturation or luminance of any of the colors by doing one of the following:

- Clicking with the cursor on the slider on the slider bar and moving it left or right.
- Clicking on the name of the color to highlight it and using the + or - keys on the keyboard.
- Hovering the cursor on the cursor over the slider bar and using the up and down arrow keys on the keyboard.
- Clicking with the cursor on the Targeted Adjustment icon and placing the Targeted Adjustment cursor on a color in the image and moving the cursor up and down.

As in the Tone Curve panel, when you click on the Targeted Adjustment icon (Yellow circles, Figure 17) in one of the sections, the cursor turns into the cross hairs with the target and up and down arrows. By placing the cross hairs of the new cursor over a color in the image you can change the hue, saturation or luminance (which ever Targeted Adjustment tool you chose) of that color by dragging up or down in the image. Dragging the cursor up in the Hue section moves the slider on the bar to the right but there is a sort of paradox here, because dragging the cursor up changes the selected color toward the color of the slider below the selected color and dragging the cursor down moves the slider on the bar to the left and the selected color more toward the color above the selected color. For example, selecting a blue tone in the image and dragging the cursor up will move the blue toward purple, the color slider below the blue slider and dragging down will move the blue toward aqua, the color slider above the blue color slider. In the case of the color red, dragging the cursor up moves the slider to the right and moves the color red toward orange, the color of the slider below the red color slider. Moving the cursor down moves the slider on the red color bar to the left and the red color moves toward magenta. In the Saturation section of the HSL panel, dragging up increases the saturation of the selected color and dragging down decreases the saturation of the selected color. As you would expect, in the Luminance section of the HSL panel, dragging the Targeted Adjustment cursor up brightens the selected color and dragging down darkens the selected color. If you watch the slider bars in the section on which you're working, you'll see them start moving and you can tell you which colors are being changed. Because of this, you have accurate control over the colors you want changed. For example, if you want to increase the saturation of the red color in your image, you place the cross hairs over what appears to be red in the image and drag it up. When you look at the slider bars, both the red and the orange slider are moving to the right. If you only want the red color changed, then all you have to do is double click on the orange name or slider on the bar and it will return to zero, where it started, only the red color in the image will be changed. Very neat and very fast too. Try it on a pale blue sky and you'll get an image that looks like it was shot with a polarizing filter.

To reset the colors in the Hue, Saturation or Luminance sections, double click on the title of the section. To reset all of the colors in the HSL section of this panel, hold down the Option (Macintosh), Alt (PC) key. This will turn the names of the sections, Hue, Saturation and Luminance to "Reset Hue, Saturation and Luminance". Click with the cursor on each of the sections while holding down the modifier key to reset the section. So, it will take three clicks with the cursor to reset all the effects in the HSL section.

**Color Section**

The middle choice in the header bar at the top of the panel, Color (Figure 18) is probably better for working on an individual color. Open the Color section by clicking with the cursor on the word "Color" (Red ellipse, Figure 17). The following are the ways in which you can work with individual colors:

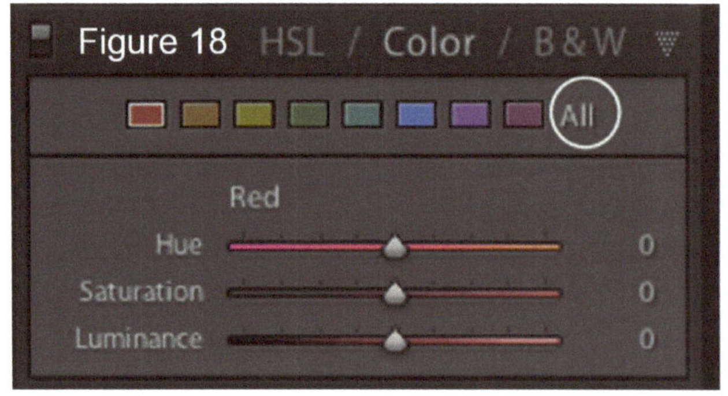


- When you select "Color" a color bar opens across the top of the panel below the header bar of the panel, from which you can select a color on which you want to work.
- Select a color and a panel opens the color with three slider bars, one for hue, one for saturation and one for luminance.
- The sliders start at 0 on the center of the bar and can be moved to a value of +100 or -100 to change the hue, saturation or luminance.
- You can move these sliders using the same methods as used in the other panels.
- You can select just one color on which to work or you can open other colors by either holding down the Shift key and clicking with the cursor on the other colors you would like open or hold down the Command (Macintosh), Control (PC) key and clicking with the cursor on any other colors you want open at the same time.
- To close a color when you have multiple colors open click with the cursor on the color you want to close in the color block at the top of the panel.
- If you want all the colors open at the same time, click with the cursor on All at the top right of the color bar at the top of the panel (White circle, Figure 18).
- You can also open all of the colors by double clicking with the cursor on any one of the color blocks at the top of the panel.
- As you move the slider on the bar, all the areas in the image of that one color will be changed.

To reset colors do the following:

- With one color open you can double click on the Hue, Saturation or Luminance sliders to reset that effect.
- To reset all three effects, Hue, Saturation and Luminance double click on the name of the color, Or,
- Hold down the Option (Macintosh), Alt (PC) Key on the keyboard. This turns the name of the color into "Reset Color". Click with the cursor on reset color to reset all three effects at the same time.

TIP: You cannot reset all the colors at the same time in the Color section of this panel. To reset all the colors, rather than holding down the Option/Alt key and clicking with the cursor on the individual colors which now say "Reset Color", it is easier to do it in the HSL section of the panel. So if you want to reset all the colors easily, move to the HSL section of this panel where you only have to hold down the Option/Alt key and click on Reset Hue, Saturation, Luminance, three clicks to reset all the colors as opposed to eight clicks in the Color section. Any changes you made in the Color section will be the same in the HSL section when you move to that section.

You will be able to see the changes you are making in the color of your image. So for example, if you want to work on only the Reds, Greens and Blues, click with the cursor on the Red color and Shift or Command (Macintosh), Control (PC) click with the cursor on the green and blue color blocks. This method seems to be the more difficult way to work on the colors compared to using the HSL method. Using the Color section has more value if you only want to work on one Color.

**Black and White Section**

The final choice in the header bar of this panel is Black and White. In addition to clicking with the cursor on B&W in the header bar (Blue ellipse Figure 17), the following are other ways to turn your image into a Black and White image:

- Click with the cursor on Black and White in the Treatment bar at the top of the Basic panel.
- Remove all the color saturation from the image by moving the Saturation slider in the Presence section of the Basic panel to -100.
- Select one of the twenty-five Black and White presets in the Presets panel to the left of the main screen.
- Use the keyboard shortcut, press the V key on the keyboard to turn a color image into a black and white image.

TIP: If you want to start with one of the black and white presets, you can get a preview of what your image will look like by hovering your cursor over the name of a preset. LIghtroom® will show you in the Navigator window a preview of the image with the preset applied.

Any one of these methods may give you a black and white image you like or at least a good starting point from which to work. If there are none you like, you can always reset the image to its original state by clicking with the cursor on Reset at the bottom right of the screen. Then, click with the cursor on B&W in the header bar of the HSL/Color/B&W panel.

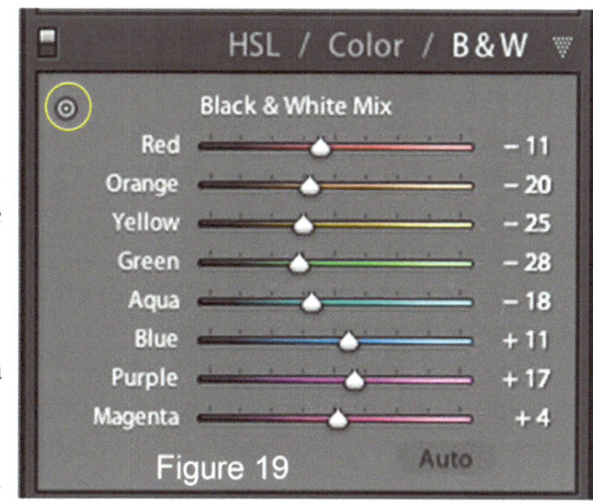

Figure 19

TIP: One of the things you may want to try before you turn your image to black and white, is to go back to the Basic Panel and drag the Clarity, Vibrance and Saturation sliders all the way to the right. This will boost the colors in the image. They won't look good in color and it may not work for black and white either, but sometimes it makes a good start for a black and white image.

When you turn your image into a black and white image in the HSL/Color/B&W panel, only one section will be visible on screen with all the color effects sliders moved to new positions on the slider bars to indicate what changes have been made in each color when the image was converted to black and white (Figure 19). The Targeted Adjustment Tool (Yellow circle, Figure 19) is also present in this section of the panel. The following are available to you For creating a black and white image:

- Move the sliders on the slider bar in the black and white section to see if you want to brighten or darken a particular color.
- Use the Targeted Adjustment tool to make changes in the contrast in the image.
- Use the Targeted Adjustment tool to brighten or darken an area of the image.
- The Targeted Adjustment tool works particularly well on skin tones in a black and white image.
- Turn on the clipping warnings (J key), go back to the Basic panel and use the tone sliders to get rid of lost detail in the highlights or shadows. If you have an effect highlighted in the Basic panel, you don't have to go back and open the Basic panel, just use the plus (+) and minus (-) keys to increase or decrease an effect and use the period (.) and comma (,) keys to switch between effects.
- Go to the Tone Curve panel and change the Point Curve to Strong Contrast.
- Use the Targeted Adjustment tool in the Tone Curve panel to change the contrast in the image.

You can use the Targeted Adjustment Tool in either the Black and White section of the HSL/Color/ B&W panel or in the Tone Curve panel to increase the contrast in the image. By clicking with the cursor on a dark tone in the image and dragging down or on the lightest tones and dragging up you'll increase the contrast in the image.

Other options for working with a black and white image that you might want to try are to use the Temperature and Tint sliders in the White Balance section of the Basic panel or use the Hue and Saturation sliders in the highlight and shadows sections in the Split Toning panel. You can also use the Targeted Adjustment tool in the Point Curve section of the Tone Curve panel to create some very nice black and white images.

TIP: Once you have created a black and white image you like, it's a good idea to save the settings as a new preset.

### Creating a Black and White Preset

Creating a black and white preset is no different than creating any other develop settings preset. To create a new Black and White preset, do the following:

- Open the Presets panel by clicking on it with the cursor.
- If you are in Solo mode, also open the History panel by holding down the shift key on the keyboard and clicking on the header bar of the History panel (this step is unnecessary if you are not in Solo mode).
- Close the Lightroom® presets by clicking on the down pointing arrow next to Lightroom® presets in the Presets panel on the left side of

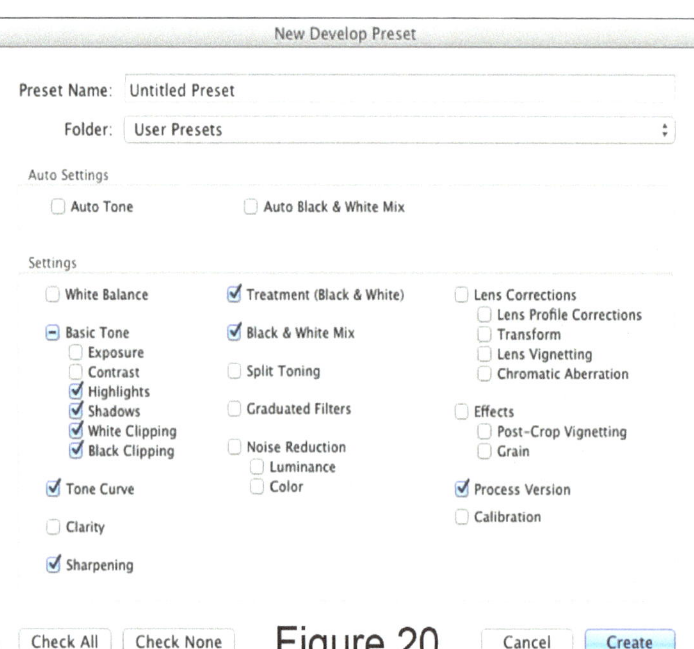

Figure 20

the screen. Keep the User Presets open.

- Make sure you can see the entire History panel and all the steps you've taken for changes you've made in the image.
- Click with the cursor on the Develop menu at the top of Lightroom® and from the drop down menu select New Preset or click with the cursor on the + sign next to Presets.
- In the New Preset dialog box that appears on screen (Figure 20), give the new preset a name and include the filename of the image you used to create the preset along with B&W.
- When the New Preset dialog box opens, the effects you changed the last time you created a preset will still be checked, so, at the bottom of the New Preset dialog box click with the cursor on "Check None" to clear the effects changed in the last preset
- Using the History panel as a guide, click with the cursor in the check boxes of the effects you changed in creating the black and white image.
- Click with the cursor on Create at the bottom right of the dialog box.
- The new Black and White preset will be placed under the User Presets section of the Presets panel

TIP: Open both the Presets and History panels before you select New Preset because once you have selected New Preset from the Develop menu or clicked on the plus (+) sign in the Presets header bar, you will not be able to open the History panel. Make sure you can see the entire History panel before you select New Preset because once the New Preset dialog box opens you will not be able to scroll down to see the History panel.

TIP: You can just place a check mark in the box labeled "Check All" at the bottom of the New Preset dialog box, which is easier than checking the effects you changed, but then you will not know how the preset was created. You can apply the preset and then go through each of the panels in the Develop module to see how the effects have changed, which would be time consuming. If you want to go back to see how the preset was created then when you name the preset, include all or part of the filename of the image on which the preset was created. You can then go back to the image and in the History panel see the steps taken to create the preset.

Next time you want to convert an image to black and white, all you have to do is bring up the image in the Develop Module, go to User Presets and click with the cursor on the black and white preset you created. You can also apply the new Black and White preset during import of an image by selecting this preset from the User Presets under the Apply during Import section in the Import dialog box.

## The Split Toning Panel

The Split Toning panel (Figure 21 allows you to do some pretty neat things to the color in your images. Using the Split Toning panel you can add color to the highlights or shadows. For example, adding color to a black and white image lets you create a duotone image. With the highlights sliders you can add vibrant colors to things such as a sunrise or sunset. The Split toning panel has five sliders, hue and saturation sliders at the top of the panel for the highlights and hue and saturation sliders for the shadows at the bottom of the panel. Between the sliders for the highlights and shadows is a balance slider. The following are the different ways you can use the sliders in the Split Toning panel:

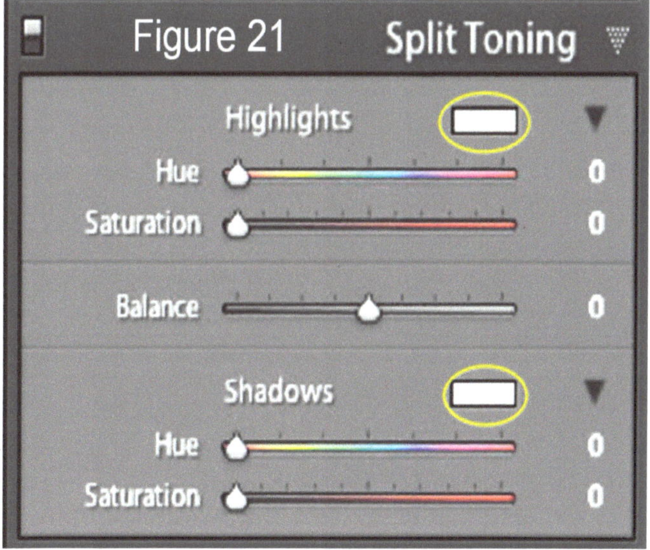


- By sliding the highlights or Shadows Hue slider to the right you can choose a color to add to the highlights or to the shadows. However you will not be able to see the color change in the image.

- Hold down the Option (Macintosh), ALT (PC) key on the keyboard and move the Hue slider to the right until the slider is over the color you want to add to the image. Lightroom® will show you the color over which you are sliding at one hundred percent saturation in the image.
- When you let go of the cursor, the image will return to its original state.
- Move the highlights or shadows Saturation slider to the right until you reach the saturation of the color you want in the color you chose with the Hue slider.
- The higher you boost the Saturation, the larger the area of the image that is affected.
- When the color in the image has the desired saturation stop sliding the slider to the right.
- Sliding the highlights or Shadows slider all the way to the right will saturate the highlights or shadows one hundred percent with the chosen color.
- The Balance slider moved to the left gives a priority to the colors in the shadows, moved to the right gives a priority to colors in the highlights.

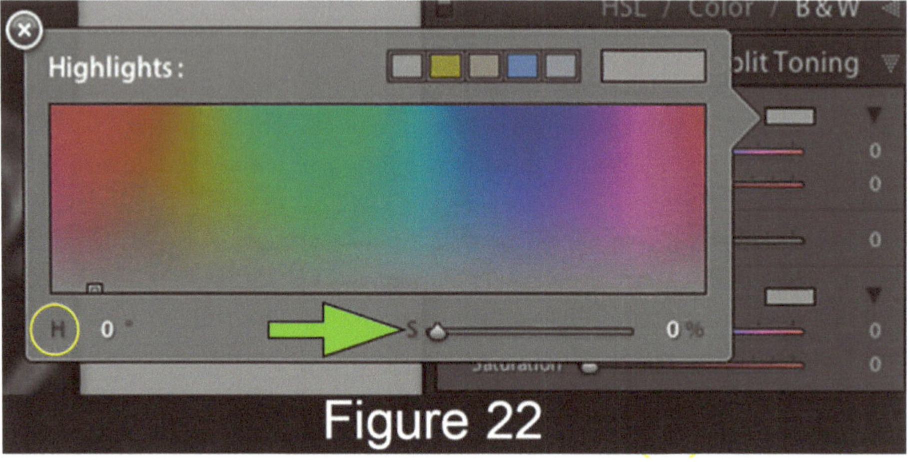

Figure 22

A second way to add colors or change colors in an image, and I think is an easier way, is to use the Color Picker box which is located to the right of the word "Highlights" at the top of the panel and to the right of the word "Shadows" in the bottom of the panel. (Yellow ellipse, Figure 21) Clicking with the cursor on either of these boxes brings up a color picker box for the highlights or shadows with the entire gamut of colors from which you can choose. (Figure 22) To add or change a color in either the highlights or shadows, do the following:

- When you place your cursor over the Color Picker box it changes into an eye dropper cursor.
- Clicking in the color picker box with this eye dropper cursor will add/change the colors of the highlights or shadows depending on which Color Picker box you clicked.
- Click with the cursor at the top of the box and slide to the left or right. As the cursor is moved right to left or left to right you will see a preview of what the colors in the highlights or shadows will look like at one hundred percent saturation as they change.
- Select a color you want to add to the image and slide the cursor up and down in the Color Picker box. Sliding up and down increases or decreases the saturation of the color you selected.
- There is also a Saturation slider (Green arrow, Figure 22) at the bottom right of the Color Picker box which moves left and right as you move the cursor up and down in the Color Picker box. You can also use this saturation slider to change the saturation of the color of the Highlights or Shadows in the image.
- On the bottom left side of the Color Picker box is the letter H (Yellow circle, Figure 22) with a scrubby slider box to the right of it. This H stands for Hue. If you hover your cursor over the scrubby slider box to the right of the H, the cursor turns into a hand. Moving the hand left or right changes the hue in the image.
- Clicking with the cursor on the X at the top left corner of the Color Picker box or clicking with the cursor anywhere outside the Color Picker box will make it disappear.

TIP: When working with a color image in the Split Toning panel, you might try boosting the colors in the highlights and adding a slight blue hue to the shadows. You can create some really outstanding sunrise and sunset images using the Split Toning panel Color Picker box.

After creating a black and white image, you can add a color cast to the image in the Split Toning panel. Once you have developed your black and white image the way you like it, you can create a duotone image in the Split Toning panel. It might be a good idea to try out some of the twenty six black and white presets in the Presets Panel. They will allow you to put a color cast like sepia, or a color filter on your image to create a duotone image. You can make a duotone image out of a color image, but it really works best on a black and white image. If you do want to do it on a color image, it's a good idea to go back to the Basic panel and decrease the Saturation just a little, it will give you better results in the Split Toning panel. Try it with images of colorful flowers or sun rise and sunset images.

## The Detail Panel

After you have done most of the developing of your image, you should go to the Detail panel to remove any noise and sharpen the image. When you open the Detail Panel, the first thing you'll see is a preview, zoom window containing part of the image. If you move the cursor over this window, the cursor will change into a hand cursor. You can click with the hand cursor in the image, the hand will grab the image (yes it will) and you can move the image around in the window until the area you want to see is in the window. However, Lightroom® has a tool that will quickly let you get the part of the image you want to see into that preview window. It's the little square icon to the left of the zoom window (Yellow circle, Figure 23). To get the area of the image you want in the preview, zoom window, do the following:

- Click with the cursor on this icon and the cursor turns into a cross hair.
- Go to the on screen image and place the cross hair cursor over the area of the image you want to see in the preview, zoom window, an eye for example.
- Click with the cursor on that area and it will show up in the zoom window.

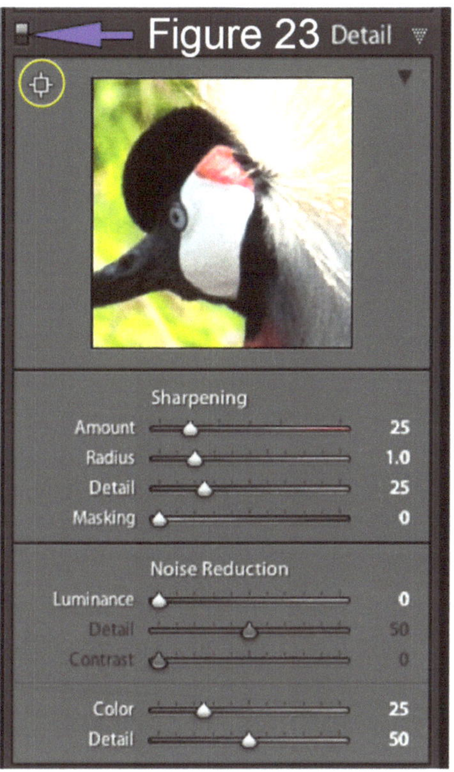


All the sliders in the Detail panel start at zero on the left side of the slider bar. The first section in the Detail panel is Sharpening. However, before you think about sharpening the image you need to evaluate the image for digital noise. If it is an image with a lot of noise in it, you should take care of that noise first. You don't want to sharpen the noise, so, start with the Noise Reduction section, which is below the Sharpening section. There are two types of noise that can occur in an image, Color noise and Luminance noise. Digital noise gets into an image in one of two ways. Noise in an image is produced by electrical disturbances that are present in any sequence of electrical activity, which is what creating an image in the digital camera is, a sequence of electrical activity. So, in low light situations, using slow shutter speeds, there is more time for the electrical disturbances to be recorded. If we ramp up the ISO setting to make the camera more sensitive to light, we are magnifying the electrical disturbances in the image. Either way, we get the digital noise usually in the darkest areas of the image.

### Removing Color Noise

Color noise is the red, green and blue artifacts you see in the image. To remove the color noise, do the following:

- Magnify the image to 3:1 or greater so you can see the color noise better.
- Move the Color slider to the right, watching the image to see the noise disappear.
- Removing digital noise almost always causes loss of detail in the image.
- If you start to lose detail in the image, move the Detail slider to the right to get the detail back.

The Color noise reduction slider does a good job of removing color noise without losing too much detail in the image. The default setting for the color noise reduction slider is 25 and in most cases that will be enough to remove the color noise when the image is brought into the Detail panel. The Color slider is a percentage type slider and usually you only have to move it to between 25 to 35 to remove the color noise. Anytime you remove noise from an image there is a chance of losing detail. That is why you have a Detail slider in case you do lose some detail. Moving the detail slider to the right will bring back some lost detail. Be careful with the Detail Color slider, moving it too far to the right in an effort to bring back detail can also bring back some of the color noise.

**Removing Luminance Noise**

After you get rid of the Color noise, the Luminance noise is what's left. Luminance noise presents a different problem. As you move the Luminance slider to the right, you'll see the image becoming softer, the edges start to blur, so, you're losing detail in the image. To remove Luminance noise, do the following:
- Magnify the image to 2:1 or greater.
- Move the luminance slider only until you start to lose detail in the edges in the image.
- Use the Luminance Detail slider to bring back that detail.
- The Detail slider tries to bring back detail at the edges.
- The Luminance Contrast slider will try to bring back edge detail around the light and/or dark edges.

TIP: When you are trying to find the right balance between the Luminance smoothing and the Luminance detail, highlight the Luminance Noise Reduction slider by clicking on it with the cursor and hover the cursor over the Luminance detail slider. Hold down the Option (Macintosh), Alt (PC) key on the keyboard and use the +/- keys for the Luminance Noise reduction slider and the up and down arrow keys for the Luminance Detail slider. This will give you the ability to fine tune the Luminance noise reduction. The reason for holding down the Option (Macintosh), Alt, (PC) key is that each time you press the plus or minus key or up and down arrow key the change will only be one percent in the image. Without holding down the Option/Alt key, the change will be five percent each time you press the plus/minus or up/down key. So you can make very small changes in the image with this method. You can also highlight the Luminance Contrast slider and use the plus/minus keys with the Option (Macintosh), Alt (PC) key on the keyboard to make very fine changes in the Luminance contrast.

**Sharpening the Image**

Once you've taken care of the noise problem, you're ready to move on to sharpening the image. While Adobe has placed the panels in the column on the right side of the develop module in the order in which Adobe thinks you should use them, you can do sharpening at any time in your workflow. In fact, it might be a good idea to do sharpening on an image you are not quite sure is in sharp focus before you do anything else to that image. This way, if you can't get the image sharp, you won't waste your time with the other panels. What sharpening is really doing is looking for the areas of contrast, whether they are dark/light or color contrasts. These areas are really the edges and Lightroom® makes these edges in the image stand out by increasing the contrast. There are four slider bars in the sharpening panel, Amount, Radius, Detail and Masking. The first slider is the Amount slider. Until you move the Amount slider to the right to add some sharpening, the other three sliders are grayed out. The default settings for the sharpening sliders are :
- 25 for the Amount

- 1.0 for the Radius
- 25 for the Detail
- 0 for Masking

The functions of the sliders in the Sharpening section of the Detail panel are as follows:

- The Amount slider is just what it's name implies, it tells Lightroom® how much sharpening or increase in contrast at the edges to do.
- The Radius slider determines how far out from the edges the sharpening will occur.
- The Detail slider determines to how many edges the sharpening is applied, in other words how much contrast it should look for to sharpen the edges.
- The Masking slider allows you to mask the sharpening in areas where you don't want the sharpening.

TIP: Hold down the Option (Macintosh), Alt (PC) and click with the cursor on any one of the sliders. The image will become a grayscale image and you might be able to better see the sharpening. The Masking slider is the most useful. When you hold down the Option (Macintosh), Alt (PC), and click with the cursor on the Masking slider, the entire image will turn white because you have sharpened the entire image. As you move the Masking slider to the right, areas of the image turn black. These black areas are no longer sharpened, they have been masked. Using the Masking slider you can limit your sharpening to just the most important edges.

The one thing you don't want to do is to over sharpen the image. So, what follows is a suggested workflow for sharpening your image:

- Bring the image up to at least a 1:1 magnification so you can see the sharpening that is occurring..
- Move the Amount slider to the right to about 85.
- Leave the Radius slider at the default value of 1.0.
- Leave the Detail slider at the default value of 25.
- Hold down the Option (Macintosh), Alt (PC) and click with the cursor on the Masking slider (the entire image turns white) and move it to the right to mask the sharpening in areas where you don't want it.
- Use the on/off switch at the top left of the panel (Blue arrow, Figure 23) to monitor how much sharpening you are doing.

There really isn't a set number for how much sharpening to do, you'll have to eyeball it to get what you like. I usually start by taking the sharpening amount slider to 85 and then increase or decrease from there until I get what I want. With the radius slider, the smaller the radius setting, the more sharp the edges will appear. The larger the radius setting the more the sharpening will appear blurred because it is spread out over a larger area. Usually a Radius setting of about 1.0 is a good place to start. The third slider is the Detail slider. This slider has to do with how many edges do you want Lightroom® to find and sharpen. With a low Detail setting, only the highest contrast edges will be sharpened. The higher you set the Detail setting the more edges Lightroom® will find and sharpen. This is the slider that can make the image appear over sharpened quickly. The over sharpened look created by taking the Detail slider up too high can be corrected by the next slider down, the Masking slider. You can mask the sharpening you've done to the image by using this slider. The best way to use it is to hold down the Option (Macintosh), Alt, (PC) key and click with the cursor on the Masking slider. This will turn the entire image white (actually, if you hold down the Option/Alt key and click on any other slider in the Sharpening section of the Detail Panel, it will turn the image to grayscale). As you move the Masking slider to the right, the areas being masked will turn black. Depending on how much masking you do, you can confine the sharpening to just the high contrast edges if you want to do that. Don't forget about the light switch icon at the top left of the Detail Panel (Blue arrow, Figure 23), it allows you to see the before and after of the image in this panel so you can see the sharpening effects. In fact, it's a good idea to turn the switch on and off as you make changes with the sliders in the Detail panel. Very often, increasing the sharpening may bring some noise back into the image and it may be necessary to go back and forth between the Sharpening section and the Noise Reduction section until you get the image the way you like it.

## The Lens Correction Panel

The Lens Correction panel was a new panel in Lightroom®3 and it has changed significantly in Lightroom®4. There are three sections to the Lens Correction panel, Profile, Color and Manual. In this panel you can correct distortion, both horizontal and vertical, vignetting, chromatic aberration and rotation.

### Profile Lens Correction

Profile is the auto mode and probably where you should start in the Lens Correction panel. (Figure 24) When you select Profile, and place a check mark in the box labeled "Enable Profile Correction", (Yellow circle, Figure 24) the following is what will happen:

- Lightroom® will search the large database of over six hundred lenses that it contains and will recognize the lens with which you took the picture. The make, model and lens profile will appear in the three blanks in the center of the section.
- The Distortion and Vignetting sliders at the bottom of the panel will become active.
- Lightroom® will automatically correct the image and remove any vignetting caused by the lens to the lens profile and you might see a slight change in the image.

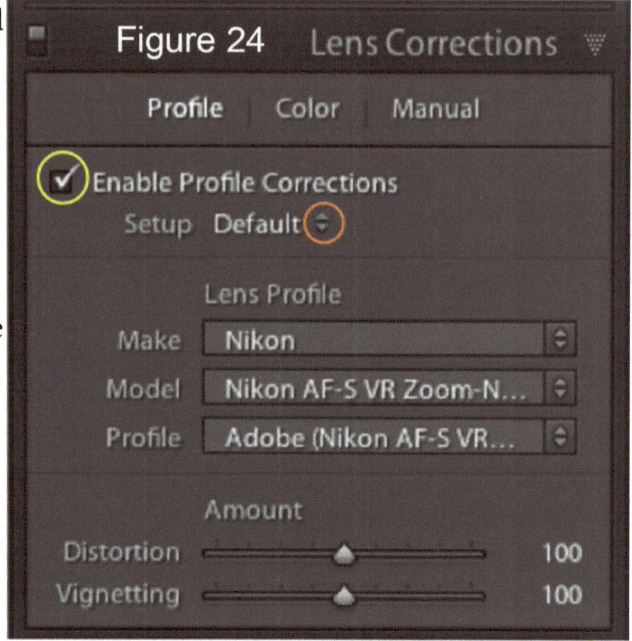


It's not a bad idea to try this Profile auto mode on all your images to see if there is an improvement in the image. If you think there is still some distortion, there is a blank below the Enable Lens Correction blank labeled "Setup". By default, this blank says "Auto" If further lens correction is needed, click with the cursor on the double pointed arrow to the right of the word "Auto" and you will have a choice of "Default or Custom". You can also make further changes to the profile with the Distortion and/or Vignetting sliders at the bottom of this section and store them as the new lens profile default. To do this:

- Click with the cursor on the double pointed arrow next to Setup (Red circle, figure 24).
- Select "Custom" from the drop down menu.
- Make the changes to the Distortion, and Vignetting sliders you think are necessary.
- Again, click with the cursor on the double arrow next to Setup.
- From the menu that appears, select "Save New Lens Profile Defaults".
- The new lens profile will be saved using the same name for the lens that is already in the lens profiles

There are a lot of lens profiles already in Lightroom®, but if you can't find yours, you can set up your own in the Manual section of the Lens Correction panel.

- Pick the closest lens to the one you used.
- Make the changes in the image with the sliders at the bottom of this section.
- When you're done, again click with the cursor on the double pointed arrow next to setup and select "Save new lens profile defaults" from the drop down menu.
- Just remember which lens profile you changed to match your lens, because it will still have the same name already in the lens profiles. A second way to set up the less common camera/lens combination profiles is to go to http://labs.adobe.com/ and download the free Adobe Lens Profile Creator Tool.

**Manual Lens Correction**

The Profile section of the Lens Correction panel will correct the distortion in the image, but there may still be some perspective correction needed. The Manual section of the Lens Correction Panel will allow you to make those perspective corrections using the five sliders in the section labeled "Transform". (Figure 25) These five sliders will allow you to do the following:

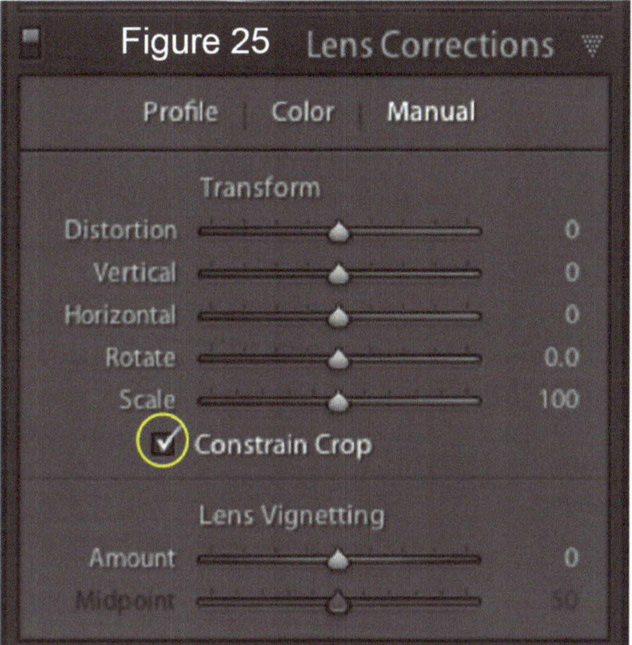


- With the first slider, labeled "Distortion", moving the slider to the left appears to suck the borders of the image in and moving to the right appears to bloat the image.
- The second slider, labeled "Vertical" allows you to change the image vertically. Moving the slider to the left appears to tip the top of the image forward. Moving the slider to the right appears to bring the bottom of the image forward.
- The third slider, labeled "Horizontal", will change the image horizontally. This slider appears to move the right side of the image back when moved to the left. Moving the slider to the right appears to make the left side of the image move back.
- The fourth slider, labeled "Rotate" is probably the most useful of the five sliders in that it allows you to rotate the image. Moving the slider to the left rotates the image clockwise, to the right rotates the image counter clockwise.
- The last slider, the Scale slider has to do with the size of the image. Moving the slider to the right expands the image and moves it closer, moving to the left contracts the image.

When you hover your cursor over the slider on any one of the slider bars, a grid will appear on the image. You can use this grid to help you get rid of the distortion. In addition to removing distortion from an image caused by the lens, you can make some subtle creative changes in an image using the sliders in the Manual section of the Lens Correction panel. For example, the Rotate slider will allow you to correct a horizon that is off. You can also use the Rotate slider to tilt a head in a portrait. This can be useful if the subject has one eye slightly higher than the other eye. The Scale slider will allow you to bring in a subject so that it looks closer to the camera. With portraits the Horizontal slider will allow you to make one side appear farther from the camera. If your subject has one eye that appears larger than the other, this can make the larger eye look slightly smaller. So there all kinds of advantages to using the Lens Correction panel, it has more uses than just removing distortion from an image.

TIP: Often in the process of changing the image, especially with the Rotate slider, a gray area will appear at one of the borders. To get rid of this gray area, click with the cursor to place a check in the box by Constrain Crop (Yellow circle, Figure 25) and Lightroom® will then crop out any areas that contain no information.

**Removing Chromatic Aberration**

Between the Profile and Manual sections in the header bar at the top of the Lens Correction panel is a new section labeled "Color". This new section is so new it was not in the public beta version of Lightroom®4 and it has to do with removing Chromatic Aberration. (Figure 26) Chromatic aberration is a phenomenon that sometimes appears in high contrast areas of an image photographed with a wide angle lens. It appears as a color fringe in the high contrast ares. Chromatic aberration is difficult to see unless you zoom the image in to a three to one or four to one magnification. In the public beta version, there was a box at the bottom of the panel in which you could place a check mark and Lightroom® would automatically remove the chromatic aberration. In this new section of the Lens Correction panel the check box is at the top of the section. Now in addition to this auto mode for removing chromatic aberration there is a Defringe tool and section containing four sliders. They are there just in case Lightroom®s auto mode doesn't work. There are two ways to work in this panel. The first is with the Defringe tool, it looks like an eye dropper. (Yellow circle, Figure 26) To use this tool, do the following:

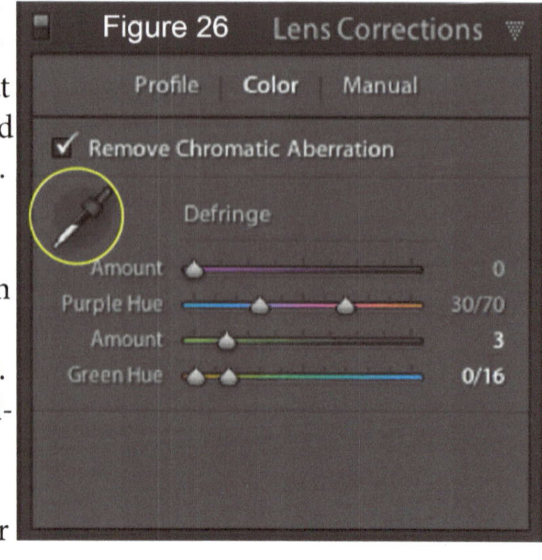


- Click with the cursor on the eye dropper icon.
- Take the eye dropper tool over the image and click on the color of the chromatic aberration you want to remove.
- The chromatic aberration colors should disappear.

In most cases, just checking the "Remove Chromatic Aberration" box will be all that is necessary.

The second way to manually get rid of chromatic aberration is to move the sliders on the four slider bars. There are two Amount sliders and one slider for a purple hue and one for a green hue in the Defringe section. Identify the color of the chromatic aberration and move the appropriate amount slider. Move the slider away from the color of the Chromatic Aberration to watch the chromatic aberration disappear.

### Adding or Removing Vignetting

Finally, at the bottom of both the Profile and Manual sections of the Lens Correction panel are two sliders for removing or adding vignetting. (Figures 24 &25) The effect will be more evident using the Manual section of the Lens Correction panel. Moving the Amount slider to the right will remove vignetting or add a white vignetting to the image. A lot of people like to add a vignetting effect to their images, so moving the Amount slider to the left will add a black vignetting to the corners of the image. How close the vignetting gets to the center of the image is controlled by the Midpoint slider. Moving this slider to the left brings the vignetting closer to the center of the image, moving it to the right moves the vignetting out towards the corner of the image. The vignetting in the Lens Correction panel only works on images that have not been cropped. If an image has been cropped, the vignetting will be applied to the uncropped image and you will not be able to see it after cropping the image.

## The Effects Panel

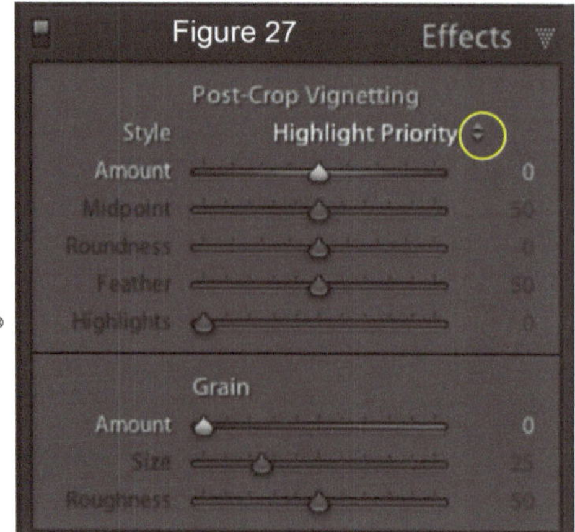


The Effects panel (Figure 27) is where you can undo all the hard work you put in to remove vignetting and noise (just kidding). In this panel you can add vignetting and grain to your image, if you would like to do that. Remember I said some people like a vignetting effect in their images? Well, in the top section of the Effects panel you can create whatever vignetting your heart desires. The vignetting you add to an image in the Effects panel, will go with the image if you crop it, Adobe® calls this Post Crop Vignetting. Also, if you crop the image first, in the Effects panel you will be able to add vignetting to the image after you have cropped it. Remember, you can add vignetting in the Lens Correction panel, but if you crop the image after adding the vignetting, you'll lose it, whereas if you add the vignetting in the Effects panel and then crop the image the vignetting will still be there in the image. You have three choices for adding the vignetting. By default, Highlight Priority will show in the panel next to the word "Style". You will find the other two choices by clicking with the cursor on the double pointed arrow to the right of "Highlight Priority". (Yellow circle, Figure 27) The three different styles are:

- Highlight priority, which is the one you'll probably use the most. The Highlight priority tries to maintain the brightest areas of the image in the vignette and gives you a kind of burned-in look, not completely black around the edges while not darkening the highlights.
- Color priority which tries to keep the colors in the vignette on the image and not darken them too much.
- Paint Overlay, just adds black or white around the edges of the image depending on which way you move the slider.

There are five sliders in the Post Crop Vignetting section of the Effects panel, Amount, Midpoint, Roundness, Feather and Highlights. The last four sliders are grayed out until you add some vignetting to the image with the Amount slider. The last slider, highlights will remain grayed out unless you move the Amount slider to the left to add the dark vignetting to the corners of the image. The default position of the Amount, Midpoint, Roundness and Feather sliders is on the center of the slider bar and they can be move to +100 or -100. The Highlight slider's default position is at 0 on the left side of the slider bar and it can be moved to +100. The functions of the vignetting sliders are as follows:

- Moving the Amount slider to the right gives you a white vignetting around the edges of the image.
- Moving the Amount slider to the left gives you a black vignetting around the edges of the image.
- Moving the Midpoint slider to the right will move the vignetting out toward the edges of the image, decreasing the vignetting effect.
- Moving the Midpoint slider to the left will move the vignetting toward the center of the image increasing the vignetting effect.
- Moving the Roundness slider to the right will move the vignetting towards the center of the image from oval to a more circular effect.
- Moving the Roundness slider to the left will move the vignetting out toward the edges of the image taking it from circular through oval to a more rectangular effect.
- Moving the Feather slider to the right will soften the effect and make the vignetting effect a more gradual transition as it moves away from the center of the image.
- Moving the Feathering slider to the left will harden the edges of the vignetting effect taking away the gradual feathering effect.
- The Highlight slider is only available when the Amount slider has been moved to the left, adding a dark vignetting to the image.
- Moving the Highlight slider to the right will help maintain the highlights in the darkened corners of the image.

The bottom section of the Effects panel is for adding grain to your image. So, if you worked hard to get rid of the grain of digital noise, you can undo it here. If you like grainy images then you can add it here in the Effects panel. Why would you want to do that? Whatever, it's a choice you have in Lightroom® 4. What it really is, is an attempt to get the appearance of a film based type image that many people apparently like, so Adobe added it to Lightroom® 4. Adding grain works best for black and white images. You have three sliders with which to add grain, Amount, Size and Roughness. Until you add some grain to the image by moving the Amount slider to the right, the Size and Roughness sliders are grayed out. The Grain sliders produce their effect as follows:

- Adding grain by moving the Amount slider makes the other sliders active.
- The default position on the slider bar for the Amount slider is 0.
- Moving the Amount slider to the right adds more grain to the image.
- The default position for the Size slider on the slider bar is 25.

- Moving the Size slider to the right increases the size of the grain.
- Moving the Size slider to the left decreases the size of the grain.
- The default position on the slider bar for the Roughness slider is 50.
- Moving the Roughness slider to the right spreads out the grain, blurring the edges.
- Moving the Roughness slider to the left makes the edges of the grain sharper.

The amount of grain you add would be a personal preference, so you have to slide until you like the amount you added. The second slider is the size slider, so you have to decide if you want little tiny pebbles or big rocks. The last slider is the Roughness slider. I think of the roughness slider as spreading out the grain and blurring it. The more you slide to the right, the more the size of the grain seems to spread out and look blurred. The more you slide the Roughness slider to the left, the sharper the edges of the grain become. I don't like the effect that moving the sliders to either the extreme right or left give me, but, if I liked images with grain, I would like images better with the grain sliders moved to some where between 35 to 45 on each slider. However, just like White Balance it's your preference.

## Back to Camera Calibration

We started developing an image by using the camera profiles in the Camera Calibration panel at the bottom of the right side panels. Below the camera profiles are some sliders that allow you to change how the colors look when the images are imported from the camera. Not everyone will use this panel, but if you feel the colors you're getting from your camera are a little bit off, you can change the way they look here. There are several ways to do this in Lightroom®, the first is done with White Balance, the second is done here in the Camera Calibration panel. To review the use of the White Balance section of the Basic panel to change the way colors look, do the following:

- Go to the White Balance section of the basic panel.
- Use the White Balance eyedropper tool and click on something that should be white or move the slider on the slider bar to warm up or cool down the image.
- Use the Tint slider to change the colors or remove a color cast in the image.
- Go to the Develop menu at the top of the screen and select New Preset from the Drop down menu to bring up the New Preset dialog box (Figure 29), or,
- Click with the cursor on the + sign next to Presets in the Presets panel header to bring up the New Presets dialog box.
- Name the new preset something like WB colors.
- Click with the cursor on Check None at the bottom of the panel.
- Click with the cursor in the box next to White Balance.
- Click with the cursor on the Create button at the bottom right of the box.
- The new colors preset will be stored with the User presets.

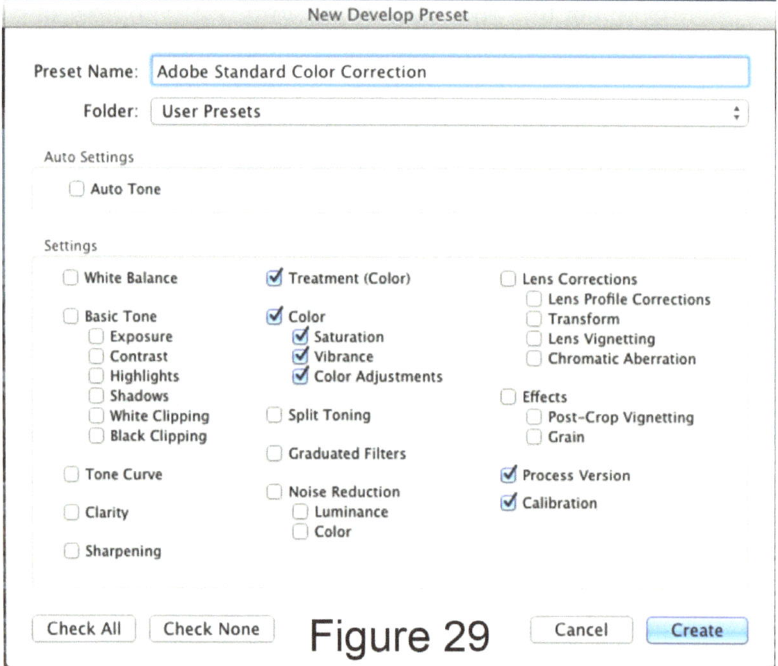

Figure 29

The second way to change the way colors in an image look coming from the camera is to use the Camera Profiles in the Camera Calibration panel. You can use the Adobe® Standard or select one of the other Camera Profiles from the drop down menu. With the profile selected, you can use the Tint slider which is also present in the Camera Calibration panel or the primary red, green and blue sliders to change the hue and/or saturation of the three primary colors to adjust them to what you feel they should be. Changing the primary colors in the profiles in the Camera Calibration panel will have no effect on the sliders in the other panels. Once you have the colors the way you want them, you can create a preset that can be applied to other images. To create the preset, do the following;

- Click with the cursor on the plus sign (+) in the header bar of the Presets panel on the left side of the screen or from the Develop menu at the top of the screen, select "New Preset".
- In the New Develop Preset dialog box (Figure 29) that appears, name the new preset, include the name of the Camera Profile you changed.
- Click with the cursor on the "Check None" button at the bottom left side of the dialog box.
- All of the check marks in the boxes should clear except the Process Version box which should still be checked.
- Click with the cursor to place a check mark in the box in front of the word "Calibration".
- Also place a check in the boxes in front of "Treatment" and "Color". This will also place check marks in the boxes labeled, "Saturation", "Vibrance" and "Color Adjustments".
- Click with the cursor on the "Create" button at the bottom right of the dialog box.

If you feel the colors coming from your camera are consistently too green, red or blue, or not red, green or blue enough, you can create a new preset for the default Adobe® Standard camera profile. To create a new Adobe® Standard camera profile, do the following:

- Take a picture of someone holding up a color chart.
- Observe the primary colors, red, green and blue in the image.
- Use the hue and/or saturation sliders of the three primary colors in the Camera Calibration panel to correct the colors in your image.
- Open the New Develop Preset dialog box. (Figure 29)
- Name the new preset something like "Adobe® Standard Corrected".
- Click with the cursor on the "Check None" button at the bottom left of the dialog box.
- Make sure there is still a check mark in the box in front of Process Version
- Click with the cursor in the box in front of Calibration (last one on the bottom right).
- Click with the cursor on the Create button at the bottom right of the dialog box.
- The new preset will be stored with User Presets.

Once you have your new color presets, they can be applied to an image during your editing or applied when the images are imported by applying the preset under the "Apply During Import" section in the Import dialog box. While the new Camera Calibration color presets will not change the tone sliders in the image, they probably will change the Temperature and Tint sliders in the White Balance section of the Basic panel.

## What Now?

So, you've been through all the panels on the right side of the Develop Module and there are some other tools still to go over, but first, I've got a couple of suggestions for you.

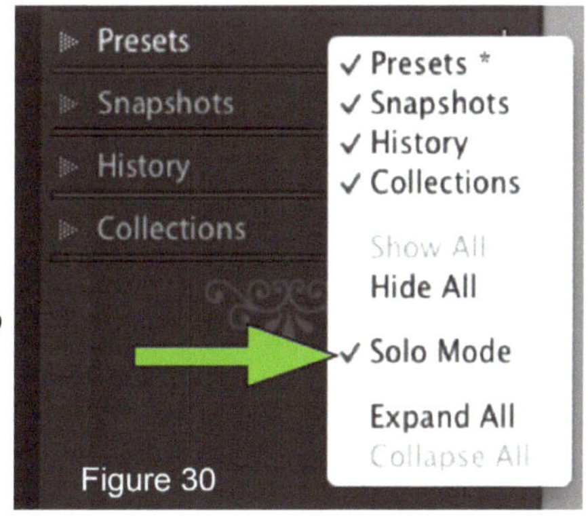

Figure 30

- Use Solo Mode: When you go to edit your images, first make sure you're in Solo Mode, you get there by Control (Macintosh), Right (PC) clicking with the cursor on any panel header or the blank space below all the panels on both the left and right sides and selecting Solo Mode from the drop down menu that appears. (Green arrow, Figure 30) What this does is close one panel when you open another. This way you will not have to scroll through all the panels to find the one you want. If you want a second panel open, hold down the Shift key on the keyboard and click with the cursor on the second panel you want open.

- Use the Clipping Warnings: Turn on the clipping warnings by pressing the J key on the keyboard.
- Keep the Basic panel active: After you are done with the effects in the Basic panel and move to another panel and make changes with the sliders in those panels, often the changes you make in the other panels will cause changes such as burned out highlights or loss of detail in the shadows. For example, if you are working with the Targeted Adjustment Cursor in the Luminance section of the HSL panel and you increase the brightness (luminance) of a bright color such as yellow or decrease the luminance of a dark color such as purple, some of the highlights might burn out or there may be a loss of detail in the shadows. This loss of detail will show up in the image as red or blue colors. To keep the basic panel active, click with the cursor on one of the effects to highlight it before you leave the Basic panel.
- If you prefer to have the basic panel open when you're working in another panel in Solo mode, you can hold down the shift key on the keyboard and click with the cursor on the Basic panel header bar and it will open along with the panel in which you're working. However, when you select another panel in which to work, both the Basic panel and the one in which you were working will close and you'll have to shift click on the Basic panel again to open it.
- Use the Targeted Adjustment tool in the Tone Curve and HSL/Color/Black and White panels. It's faster and you can place the effect exactly where you want it.
- In the HSL/Color/Black and White panel, you can tell which colors are being affected by the movement of the sliders on their bars as you move the Targeted Adjustment cursor up or down.
- If there is a color you don't want to change you can simply double click with the cursor on the name of that color or the slider on the bar of that color and that will return the color to it's original level. For example, if you're using the Targeted Adjustment tool to change the saturation of the yellow color and the orange slider also is moving, just double click on the orange slider name or the slider on the orange bar to return the orange color to its original position on the slider bar and then only the yellow color will be affected by the Targeted Adjustment tool.
- Use the light switch icon, available in all panels except the basic panel, to check the adjustments you made with each panel. Do it after you've made the adjustments in each panel. When you are finished developing the image, if you decide you don't like the resulting image it's hard to go back and check each panel to find which panel caused the adjustment you don't like.
- Learn the keyboard short cuts so you don't have to go to the tools menu at the top of the screen to get the tools you need. It saves a lot of time. To see all the keyboard shortcuts for the panel in which you are working, hold down the Command (Macintosh), Control (PC) key and press the forward slash key (/) on the keyboard.

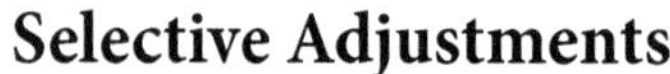

## Selective Adjustments

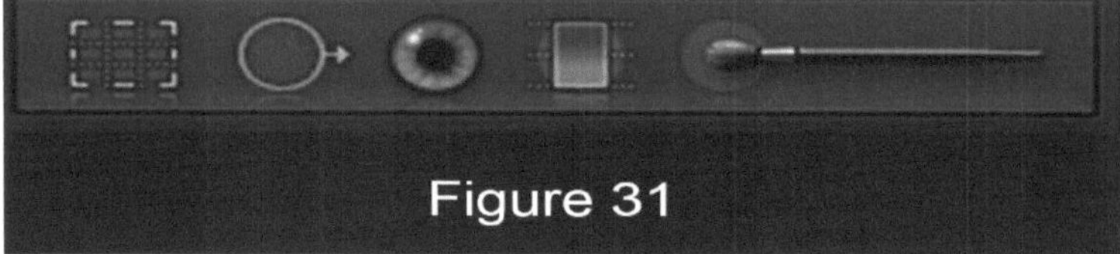

Figure 31

Below the Histogram is a toolbar (Figure 31) containing five tools, the Crop Overlay tool, the Spot Removal tool, the Red Eye Correction tool, the Graduated Filter tool and The Adjustment Brush. Hovering the cursor over the tool icon will identify what each tool is. All of these tools can be very helpful in developing an image. The Crop Overlay tool has already been discussed as it is the second step in my workflow Now for the other tools, All of these tools were new in Lightroom® 2 and they're the same in Lightroom® 3 and 4.

**The Spot Removal Tool**

The second tool in the tool bar under the Histogram is the Spot Removal Tool (Yellow circle, Figure 32) and it does just what its name implies, it removes spots in the image. To get to the spot removal tool, do one of the following:

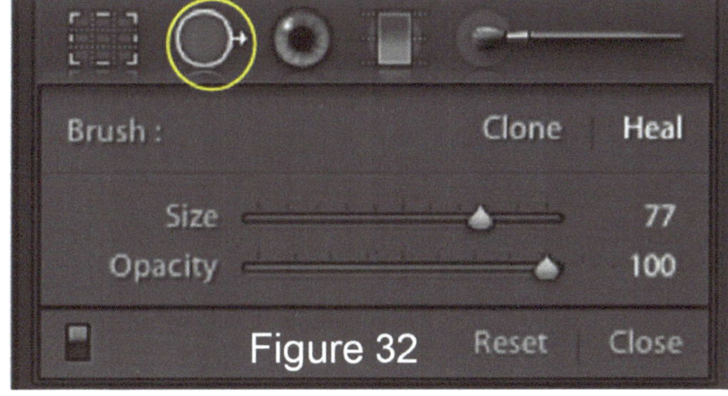

Figure 32

- Click with the cursor on the icon in the tool bar under the histogram.
- Go to the Tools menu in the menu bar at the top of the screen and select Spot Removal in the drop down menu.
- Use the keyboard shortcut, press the Q key on the keyboard.

When you activate the Spot Removal tool, the cursor turns into a circle with cross hairs in the Center. There are two methods of using this tool, two different types of tools, Clone and Heal. The clone method is similar to the Clone Stamp tool in Photoshop®, except you don't need to select a target area from which to clone, it takes detail from one area of the image and moves it on top of another area of the image. The Heal method on the other hand is more like blending or merging the data from one area of the image to another. If there is a lot of variety of detail in the area from which you are trying to remove a spot you will be better off using the Heal tool. You can adjust both the size of the tool and the opacity. It's best to leave the opacity at 100% unless, for some reason, you want to just minimize the spot you're trying to remove. The size of the Spot Removal tool can be adjusted in the following ways:

- Clicking with the cursor on the slider on the Size slider bar in the panel and moving the slider left or right.
- Hovering the cursor over the Size slider bar in the panel and using the up and down arrow keys. The up arrow key enlarges the Spot Removal tool, the down arrow key makes it smaller.
- Using the scrubby slider at the end of the slider bar in the panel.
- Typing in a value in the scrubby slider box .
- With the Spot Removal tool over the image, use the scroll wheel on the mouse.
- When over the image, if you hold down the Command (Macintosh), Control (PC), the Spot Removal cursor turns into cross hairs (+) by themselves, without the circle. Place the cross hairs on a spot, click with the cursor and drag the brush out to the size you need to remove the spot. When you let go of the cursor the spot will disappear.

TIP: If you click with the cursor to remove a spot and find that your brush is not large enough to remove the entire spot, you can hover your cursor over the edge of the circle of the Spot Removal tool and the cursor will change into a double pointed arrow. Click with the cursor and drag outward to make the tool larger and remove the rest of the spot.

I think the scroll wheel is the easiest way to adjust the size of the Spot Removal tool. To use the Spot Removal tool, all you have to do is:

- Adjust the Spot Removal tool diameter to just slightly larger than the size of the spot you want to remove.
- The Spot Removal tool has cross hairs (+) in the center of it, place the cross hairs of the Spot Removal tool over the spot.
- Click with the cursor and the spot will disappear.

When you place the cross hairs of the Spot Removal tool over a spot to be removed and click on it with the cursor a second circle appears somewhere near the Spot Removal tool and the spot disappears. This second circle is the sample area from which the Spot Removal tool is taking the details to replace the spot in the case of the Clone method or trying to blend the details from the two circles with the Heal tool. If you don't like the result, you can simply click with the cursor on the second, sample area circle and drag it around to an area that gives you a better healing or cloning.

In the toolbar at the bottom of the screen, there is a Tool Overlay menu that gives you several choices as to how you view the screen when the Spot Removal tool is active (Figure 33), in other words which circles you can see on the image with the Spot removal tool active. The default choice is "Auto", but if you click with the cursor on the double pointed arrow next to Auto (Yellow circle, Figure 33), the other three choices will appear in a drop down menu. The following are the choices for viewing the circles when the Spot Removal tool is active:

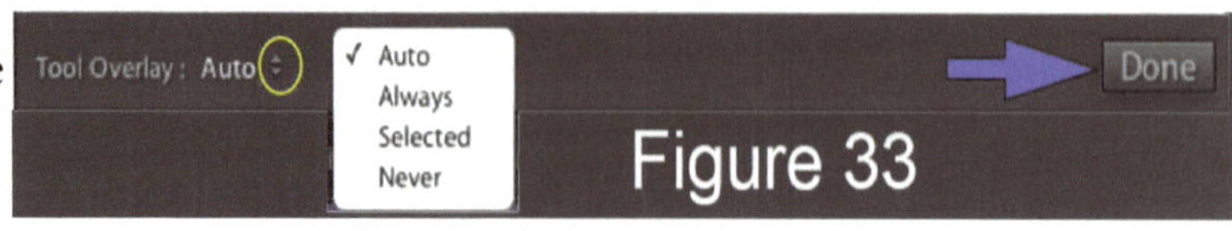

Figure 33

- Auto, the circles will be visible when the Spot Removal tool is over the image. However, if you move the Spot Removal tool off the image at the top or bottom of the image, all the circles will disappear.
- Always, the circles will be visible when the Spot Removal tool is active regardless of whether the tool is over the image or not.
- Selected, you can select the circles that will be visible by double clicking on the circle you want visible and only the selected circles will be visible. However, after you choose "Selected", any spot you remove after that selection will have the circle visible.
- Never, none of the circles will be visible on the image.

If you want to hide all the circles when the Spot Removal tool is active, just press the H key on the keyboard and they'll all disappear. Press the H key on the keyboard again and the circles will reappear. With the Spot Removal tool active, but the circles hidden, you can still hover your cursor over a spot and move the sample area circle to another area or enlarge the circle. Hovering the cursor over the spot with the circles hidden will turn the cursor into the hand tool to move the sample area circle or a double pointed arrow to enlarge the Spot removal tool. If you'd like to remove a circle, click on it with the cursor and press the Delete (Macintosh),Backspace, (PC) key on the keyboard. You'll see a little puff of smoke and hear a mini explosion sound, the circle will disappear and the spot will be back.

TIP: One thing that can be helpful when you have light spots against a lighter background, such as the sky, is to move the Blacks slider in the Basic panel to the right. This will make the spots easier to see and remove. It will also make some faint spots more obvious. When you're done removing the spots, move the Blacks slider back to where it was. There is a bar at the bottom of the Spot Removal tool panel that contains the light switch to allow you to see the before and after of the work you've done with the Spot Removal tool. (White circle, Figure 32) Over to the right side of this bar there is also a reset button and a close button. The reset button (Blue Ellipse, Figure 32) lets you start over with the Spot Removal tool. You can turn off the Spot Removal tool by doing one of the following:

- Click with the cursor on the Close button at the bottom right of the Spot Removal tool panel. (Red ellipse, Figure 32)
- Click with the cursor on the Spot Removal tool icon in the toolbar under the Navigation panel. (Yellow circle, Figure 32)
- Click with the cursor on the Done button on the right side of the tool bar below the image.(Blue arrow, Figure 33)
- Use the keyboard shortcut, press the Q key on the keyboard, or
- Go to the Tools menu and deselect the Spot Removal tool.

**The Red Eye Correction Tool**

Next to the Spot Removal tool on the tool bar beneath the Histogram is the Red Eye Correction Tool (Yellow circle, Figure 34). This tool is self explanatory. To open the tool, you need to click with the cursor on the icon in the bar or go to the Tools menu at the top of the screen and select Red Eye in the drop down menu.

There is no keyboard shortcut for the Red Eye Correction tool. To use the Red Eye Correction tool, do the following:

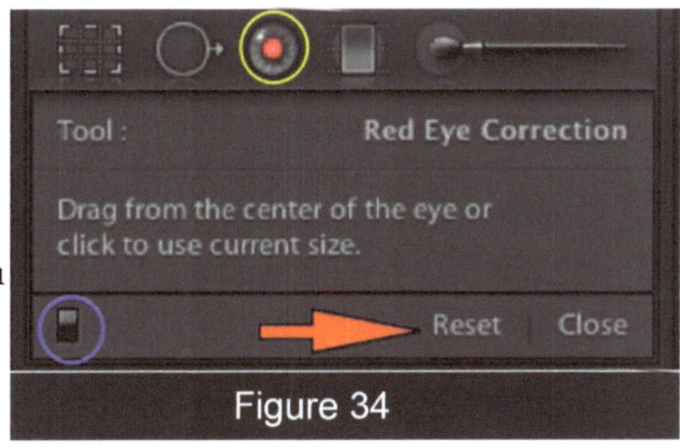

Figure 34

- Select the Red Eye Correction tool, the cursor turns into a crosshairs cursor (+).
- Place the crosshairs over the eye needing correction.
- Hold down the mouse button and drag the Red Eye Correction tool out to match the pupil size.
- Alternatively, use the scroll wheel on the mouse to match the pupil size.
- Click with the crosshairs in the cursor on the eye to be corrected.
- The Red Eye Correction will take place.

If you find you did not drag far enough to eliminate all the red eye, you can increase the size of the Red Eye Correction tool. The light switch icon is also present in the bar at the bottom of the panel (Blue circle, Figure 34) as are the reset and close buttons.(Red arrow, Figure 34)

To close the tool:

- Click with the cursor on the close button
- Click with the cursor on the Red Eye Correction tool icon in the tool bar beneath the Histogram, or
- If you have a lot of time to kill during your editing, you can go to the Tools Menu at the top of the screen and click on Red Eye in the drop down menu to turn it off.

**The Graduated Filter Tool**

This tool simulates a graduated neutral density filter used on a camera lens. However, it does a lot more than allow you to darken or lighten a portion of the image. To Open the Graduated Filter tool, you can:

- Click on the Graduated Filter tool icon in the bar underneath the histogram panel (Yellow circle, Figure 35),
- Use the keyboard shortcut, press the M key, or
- Go to the Tools menu at the top of the frame and click on Graduated Filter from the drop down menu.

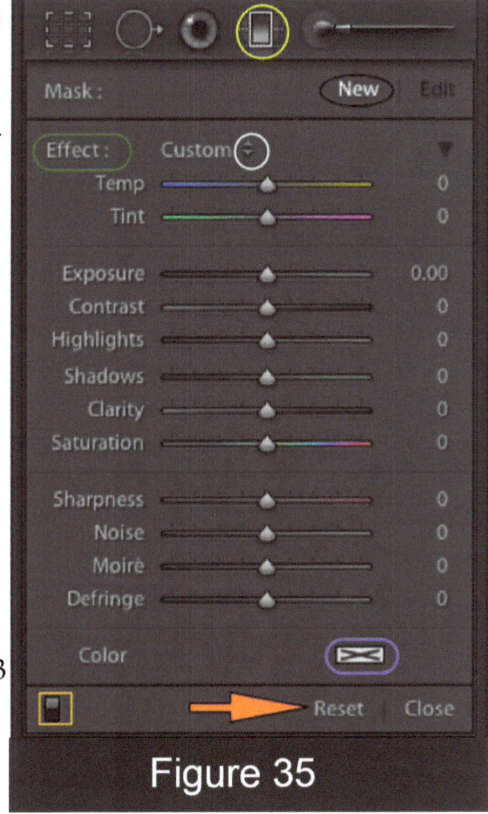

Figure 35

Once selected, the Graduated Filter menu opens up beneath the tool bar. There are twelve sliders for different effects, twice as many as were in the Graduated Filter tool in Lightroom®3. These are the effects that the Graduated Filter tool can apply to selected areas of your image. Starting at the top of the Graduated Filter tool and in descending order, the first two sliders, Temp and Tint are the same sliders as are in the White Balance section of the Basic panel. The next four sliders, Exposure, Contrast, Highlights and Shadows, are the same as the sliders in the Tone section of the basic panel. The next two sliders, Clarity and Saturation are the same as the Clarity and Saturation sliders in the Presence section of the Basic panel. Of the last four sliders, Sharpness is still present as it was in Lightroom®3 and three new sliders, Noise, Moire and Defringe have been added. Moving a slider to the right increases the effect, moving a slider to the left decreases the effect.

Above the sliders on the left side of the menu is the word Effect, (Red ellipse, Figure 35) and to the right of the word Effect is the name of one of the twelve Effects with a double pointed arrow to the right of the name of the effect. (White circle, Figure 35) By clicking on the double pointed arrow a pop up menu will appear with the names of the twelve effects and five new special effects you can apply to the image. (Figure 36) First, dealing with the top twelve effects in this pop up menu, when you click on the name of one of these first twelve effects, the following will happen:

- The name of the effect you clicked on with the cursor will appear next to the double arrow.
- Lightroom® will move the slider for that chosen effect to where it thinks it should be.
- All of the other effects will remain at the default zero position on their slider bars.
- If you then click on another effect, Lightroom® will return the previous effect slider to 0 and move the slider of the newly chosen effect to the position on the slider bar that Lightroom® thinks is the correct position for the image.
- These settings are really presets that Lightroom® has included to make things easier for you.

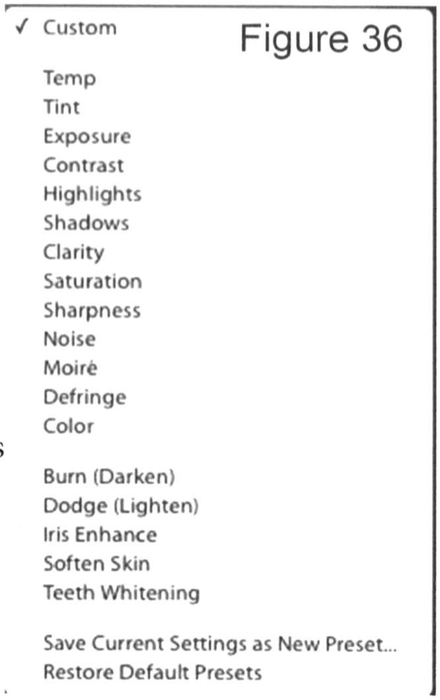

Figure 36

✓ Custom

Temp
Tint
Exposure
Contrast
Highlights
Shadows
Clarity
Saturation
Sharpness
Noise
Moiré
Defringe
Color

Burn (Darken)
Dodge (Lighten)
Iris Enhance
Soften Skin
Teeth Whitening

Save Current Settings as New Preset...
Restore Default Presets

So, you can get Lightroom®'s opinion of where the sliders should be for each of the twelve effects of the Graduated Filter. You can also move each of the effects on the slider bars manually. When you make a change in any of the effects by moving a slider on the bar, the name of the effect at the top next to the double pointed arrow will change to Custom. What these effects are in this drop down menu are presets that Lightroom® has installed. For example, if you click on Highlights in this drop down menu. Lighroom® sets up the Graduated Filter to work on only the highlights in the image.

Below the sliders is a color selection box from which you can chose a color and add a color cast to the Graduated Filter. (Blue ellipse, Figure 35) Clicking on the box brings up the color picker dialog box which is the same as it was in the Split Toning panel.

TIP: When editing sunrise or sunset images, using the color picker tool from the color selection box to select a hue and saturation to add to the image can make your image spectacular.

When you activate the Graduated Filter tool, the cursor changes into crosshairs (+) when placed over the image. To apply the Graduated Filter effects to the image, place the cursor over the image where you want the effect to start tapering off. For example if you want to darken a sky by decreasing the exposure, then place the cursor over the image where the sky meets the land and click with the cursor on that point. The darkening effect will go from the top of the image to the point where you clicked with the cursor. As you drag down with the cursor, three lines will appear on the image. The middle line will be where you want the effect to start tapering off. From that point on down, the effect will taper off and in the case of exposure, become lighter. The following are the ways that you can use the Graduated Filter:

- You can start anywhere in the image and drag in any direction. If you start at the top, which is where most people start and drag down, the greatest effect will be at the top of the image and will gradually decrease as you drag down through the image.
- Start at the bottom and drag up, The greatest effect will be at the bottom of the image and decrease as you drag up.
- Start at one side and drag toward the other side.
- Start at a corner and drag toward the opposite corner
- Hold down the Option/Alt key and start in the center, the effects will spread out from the center and taper off as it moves toward the top and bottom of the image, if you drag down the greatest effect will be at the top, drag up and the greatest effect will be at the bottom of the image

- If you'd like to change the direction of the effect of the Graduated Filter, hold down the Option/Alt key and press the apostrophe (') key on the keyboard, the effect will be reversed.

Another good thing to know is that if you hold down the shift key, you'll be able to drag in a straight line. This is a good idea if you've had six cups of coffee or over served yourself at cocktails last night and have a little bit of a tremor. As you drag in any direction, the following will occur:

- Three lines will appear in the image and they will separate further apart the farther you drag in the image .
- The first line will be where you started (unless it was the center) and it will stay there.
- The second line will be the midpoint of the effects and will have a white circle with a black center on the middle of the line.
- The third line will be the bottom of the effect
- When you're finished dragging, let go of the mouse button

TIP: If you're holding down the Shift key to drag in a straight line, let go of the mouse button first, not the Shift key or else you may get a skewed effect that you didn't want.

Once the Graduated Filter effects are on the image you can go back to the other sliders and move them to add the different effects until you have them the way you like them.

TIP: It's a good idea to start with only one effect on the Graduated Filter. Starting with only one effect lets you know where the effect will be in the image. After you have placed the Graduated Filter on the image, then go back and add effects from the other sliders. That way you'll know if you like the effect of each slider. If you place the Graduated Filter on the image with multiple effects and you don't like what it gives you, then you will not know which effect caused the poor result on the image.

To get out of the Graduated Filter tool, do one of the following:

- Click with the cursor on the Graduated Filter icon in the tool bar underneath the Histogram panel. (Yellow circle, Figure 35)
- Press the keyboard shortcut, the M key on the keyboard.
- Go to the tools menu and click the Graduated Filter check mark off in the drop down menu (who would do this?)
- Click with the cursor on the word close at the right of the bar on the bottom of the panel
- Press the Return (Macintosh),Enter (PC) key on the keyboard.

After you stop applying the Graduated Filter, a white dot with a black center will appear in the image at the center of the Graduated Filter effect. Lightroom® calls these dots pins. Want to get rid of this pin, but keep the Graduated Filter tool active? Press the H key on the keyboard to hide the pin. Also, when you leave the Graduated Filter for another tool or panel, the pin or pins will disappear and reappear the next time you open the Graduated Filter on the image.

There are several ways you can reset the Graduated Filter tool and start over. Before you close the Graduated Filter tool, notice that the word Reset is just to the left of the word close. If you want to start over, do one of the following:

- Click with the cursor on the word Reset. (Red arrow, Figure 35)
- Hold down the Option (Macintosh), Alt (PC) key and the word Effect(Green ellipse, Figure 35) at the top left of the panel will turn into the word Reset.
- Click with the cursor on the word Reset to reset the settings and start over with the Graduated Filter.

If you want to add second or third Graduated Filter effect to the image, maybe from a different angle, do one

of the following:
- Go back into the Graduated Filter Tool panel and click with the cursor on "New" (Black ellipse, Figure 35) if it isn't already selected.
- When you bring up a second Graduated Filter tool, the sliders on the effects slider bars will be where you left them on the first Graduated filter.
- Hold down the Option (Macintosh), ALT (PC) which changes the word "Effect" into "Reset", to reset the Graduated filter tool click on the word "Reset" when it appears. Make your changes on the sliders for the new Graduated Filter.
- Apply the new Graduated Filter effect to the image from a different angle or direction.
- After you close the Graduated Filter tool, there will be a white pin on the image for each of the Graduated Filters you applied to the image.
- To hide or show the white pins while the Graduated Filter tool is active, press the H key on the keyboard.

Once a Graduated Filter effect has been applied to an image and you've gone on to another tool or panel, you can go back into the Graduated Filter tool and edit the effects of any of the previously applied Graduated filters. To do this do the following:
- Open the Graduated Filter tool (use the keyboard shortcut, the M key).
- Find the white pin of the Graduated Filter you want to edit and click on it with the cursor (This is the white pin that is on the center line of the Graduated Filter).
- The white pin will turn black indicating it is now active.
- The Graduated Filter tool will reopen, the three lines will reappear in the image and the sliders will be on the slider bars where you left them.
- Make the changes in the Graduated Filter you want.
- Close the Graduated Filter tool.

The choices you have for making changes to the effects when editing a Graduated Filter are as follows:
- You can move the sliders on the Effects slider bars to new positions.
- You can tilt or skew the Graduated Filter effect by placing the cursor close to the center dot. The cursor will change into a double pointed, curved arrow allowing you to move the Graduated Filter effect in a circular pattern.
- You can move any of the three lines in the Graduated Filter effect by placing the cursor over one of the lines. The cursor will change into a hand cursor. Clicking with the hand cursor on any one of the three lines will cause the hand to grab the line (really) and you can drag it to a new position, changing the distribution of the Graduated Filter effect.

The Graduated Filter tool is very versatile. For example, if you've photographed a Sunset and want to Sharpen and brighten just the sky and clouds, you can leave all the sliders at zero and just change the Highlights and Sharpen sliders to create the effect you want. At the same time, you can add an orange or red color cast to the image by selecting one of those colors from the Color Picker Box. I find the Graduated Filter tool especially useful in landscape images where I want to bring out more detail in the clouds or in sunrise and sunset images where I can add a color hue to the clouds and sky.

With the Graduated Filter tool, the light switch icon is located at the bottom left of the panel and you can use it to turn off and on the effects you applied with the Graduated Filter tool. (Orange square, Figure 35)

To close the Graduated Filter tool, do one of the following:
- Click with the cursor on the Graduated Filter tool icon in the toolbar underneath the histogram.
- Click with the cursor on the "Close" button at the bottom right of the panel.
- Use the keyboard shortcut, press the M key.

- Go to the Tools menu at the top of the screen and from the drop down menu uncheck Graduated Filter tool.

**The Adjustment Brush**

Unlike Photoshop, where you can select an area of pixels and apply an effect on just those pixels, Lightroom® doesn't have the ability to work on pixels. However, with the adjustment brush, you can paint in an effect or adjustment to specific areas of the image. To open the Adjustment Brush do one of the following:

- Click on the Adjustment Brush Icon in the toolbar underneath the Histogram (Yellow ellipse, Figure 37).
- Use the keyboard shortcut, press the K key on the keyboard.
- From the Tools menu at the top of the Lightroom® screen, select Adjustment Brush.

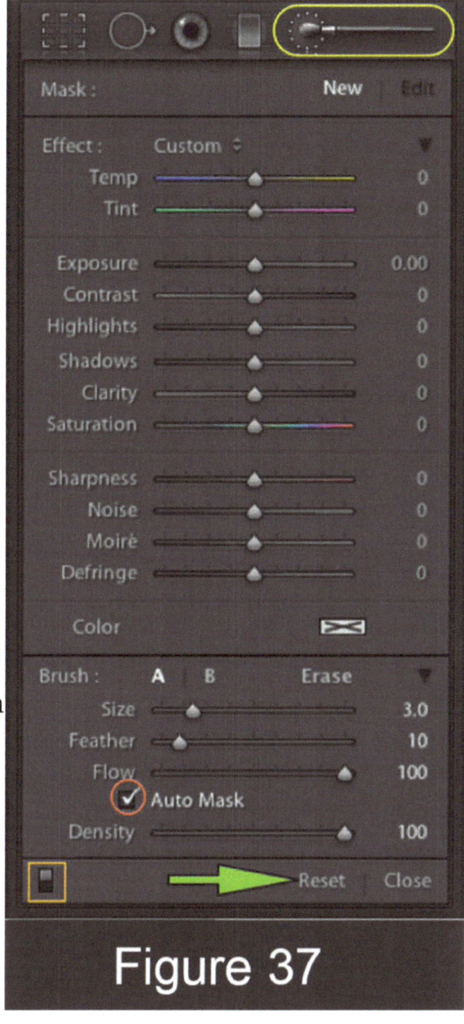

Figure 37

Once opened, the same twelve effects sliders and color box for adjusting the image that were in the Graduated Filter tool will appear in the top section of the Adjustment Brush and they will work exactly the same way. In fact, if you've used the Graduated Filter tool first, the twelve sliders and color box settings from the Graduated Filter tool will still be set for the adjustments they were set to for the Graduated Filter. So, make sure you check the effects settings out, especially the color box, so you don't apply an effect you don't want. It is probably a good idea to reset the Adjustment brush each time you open it. To reset the Adjustment Brush, hold down the Option (Macintosh), Alt (PC) key which will turn the word "Effect"at the top of the panel into the word "Reset". Click with the cursor on the word "Reset" to return the Adjustment brush to its default settings. This will bring all the effects sliders back to the default zero position on the slider bars and change the color box to transparent. There is a Reset button at the bottom right of the Adjustment Brush panel (Green arrow, Figure 37), but if you just opened the Adjustment brush and the settings are from the Graduated Filter, clicking on this Reset button will not reset the Adjustment brush. This Reset button only works to reset the Adjustment Brush after you have applied some effects to the image. The same presets that are present in the Graduated Filter tool are present in the Adjustment Brush tool, so, you can find out what Lightroom® thinks each effect setting should be, just as you did in the Graduated Filter tool. Just select an effect from the drop down menu which is exactly the same as the menu in the Graduated Filter tool, (Figure 36) and look where Lightroom® places the slider on the bar for each effect. The last five of these presets, Burn, Dodge, Iris Enhancement, Soften Skin and Teeth Whitening are presets for editing mostly portraits.

The bottom section of the Adjustment Brush tool, is for brush settings. You can have three different brushes ready to go. They are labeled A, B and Erase. You can use the sliders in this section to set the size of the brush, feather the brush and set the flow and density which have to do with opacity. You can use the keyboard short cut, the forward slash key (/), to switch between brushes A and B. You can change either brush, A or B into the eraser brush by holding down the Option (Macintosh), Alt (PC) key on the keyboard.

Below the flow slider is an important check box that will save you much time when using the Adjustment brush. It is called the Auto Mask (Red Circle, Figure 37) and you can turn Auto mask on by clicking in this box with the cursor or use the keyboard shortcut, the A key, to put a check mark inside the box. With the Auto mask turned on, the Adjustment brush looks for edges or contrast and tries not to let the effect cross this edge. The Adjustment Brush has a crosshairs in the center and as long as you keep the cross hairs from crossing over an edge or contrast area, the effect will only be applied to the original area where you started with the adjustment brush.

The actual brushes have four settings you can change to create the type of brush you want. You can increase the size, feathering, flow or density of the brush. Size is just how large or small you want to make the brush. Feathering has to do with the brush making a transition from hard to soft. The more feathering you set, the more the brush gradually transitions or becomes softer or decreases the effect out toward the edge of the brush The flow has to do with how much effect the brush puts on the image with each stroke. You can think of the Flow setting as loading a paint brush. The more paint you put on the brush, the heavier the stroke and the more it covers the underlying surface. The less paint you put on the brush the more brush strokes you need to cover the underlying surface. Low Flow settings require that you go over the area of the image multiple times to gradually build up the effect until you have it the way you want it. A high flow settings lays down the effect quickly and usually doesn't require a build up. To set the size and feathering of the brush you can:

- Use the Size slider bar in the panel. Moving to the right enlarges the brush, moving to the left decreases the size of the brush.
- Use the Feather slider bar in the panel. Moving to the right increases the feathering to create a softer brush edge, moving to the left decreases the feathering to create a harder brush edge.
- Use the right and left bracket keys on the keyboard to increase or decrease the size of the Adjustment Brush.
- Hold down the Shift Key and use the right and left bracket keys on the keyboard to increase or decrease the feathering of the Adjustment Brush. The right bracket key with the Shift key as a modifier increases the amount of feathering creating a softer edged brush, the left bracket key with the Shift key as a modifier decreases the amount of feathering creating a harder edged brush.
- With the brush over the image, use the scroll wheel on your mouse to increase or decrease the size of the Adjustment Brush.
- With the brush over the image, hold down the Shift key and use the scroll wheel on the mouse to increase or decrease the feathering of the Adjustment Brush.

If you use the Size slider in the panel, when you place your cursor on the slider on the bar, the brush will appear just to the left of the right column of panels and you will be able to see the size change as you move the slider left or right. Sliding to the right makes the brush larger, to the left makes it smaller. If you are working in the image with the Adjustment brush, it makes more sense to use either the right and left bracket keys on the keyboard or the scroll wheel on the mouse. You will be able to place the Adjustment Brush over the area on which you want to work and make it the size you want it to be as you work. For example, if you are working with a large brush to apply an effect and come to a small area of the image where you want the effect it will be quicker to resize the brush with the bracket keys or scroll wheel on the mouse to get the brush to match the size of the area to which you want to apply the effect.

With the Flow slider in the panel, you can change the amount of Flow in two ways. The first way is to move the slider on the slider bar to set the Flow low by moving the slider to the left and high by moving the slider to the right. The second way to change the Flow is to use the Zero through the nine keys on the keyboard. Zero sets the Flow to on hundred percent, the one key sets the flow to ten percent, the two key sets the Flow to twenty percent and so on up to on hundred percent with the zero key. It is often smart to set a low Flow setting and build up the effect gradually. However, if you know you want the full effect then set the Flow setting to one hundred percent.

The Density slider affects all the effects in the Adjustment Brush and has to do with intensity. With the Density slider set to one hundred percent, all the effects will be as intense as their individual settings and the Flow setting allow. Both the flow and density sliders seem to accomplish the same thing, increasing the opacity of the brush. If you move Density slider to the right, the effect becomes more opaque or intense on the image. Therefore, you can control the build up of the effects on your image with the Adjustment brush by using a combination of the Flow and Density settings.

To use the Adjustment Brush tool, do the following:

- Set up brush A and brush B to be two different sizes and set the feathering to your preference.
- Set the Eraser brush to be about half the size of the A brush.
- Place a check mark in the Auto Mask box by clicking on it with the cursor.
- Select an effect you would like to apply to an area of the image, start with only one effect.
- Set the slider of the effect you want to apply to a setting that will allow you to see the effect taking place on the image (you'll be able to change it).
- Set the Flow and Density sliders depending on whether you want the full effect right away or want to gradually build up the effect in the area of the image on which you are working.
- Paint with the brush on the image where you want the effect to be applied.
- Increase or decrease the size of the brush to match the area on which you are working.
- A dot with a black center will appear in the image when you stop painting. This dot is called a pin.
- Hover your cursor over the pin and a mask will appear showing you all the areas on which you applied the effect, the keyboard shortcut to turn the mask on and off is the O Key
- Evaluate the effect to make sure you have covered all the areas on which you wanted to apply the effect and none where you don't want the effect.
- Use the Eraser brush to remove the effect from any unwanted area. The keyboard shortcut for turning your brush into the eraser brush is to hold down the Option (Macintosh), Alt (PC) key.
- Go back to the effects and choose a second effect you would like to add to the area.
- Decide if the second effect is what you want and then go to another effect and add it.
- Repeat the process of adding effects until the area of the image is the way you want it.
- Use the before and after light switch at the bottom left of the panel (Orange square, Figure 37) after each effect you apply to see how the individual effects change your results in the image.

TIP: Start out applying just one effect to your image and apply that effect to the entire area on which you want the effect. Once you have applied this one effect, you can go to the other effects sliders and move their sliders on the slider bars, this will apply their effect on the same area of the image that you applied the first effect. The second effect applied will be added on to the first effect. This way you can evaluate each individual effect as you place it on the image. If you apply multiple effects at the same time with the Adjustment Brush and you don't like the effect, you will not know which effect produced the result you do not like.

TIP: When working with the Adjustment Brush in the image, the brush has crosshairs (+) in the cursor. By placing a check mark in the Auto Mask checkbox just below the Flow slider in the second section of the Adjustment Brush panel (Red circle, Figure 37), you can paint outside the area on which you want the effect and not have the effect applied to the outside area. As long as you keep the crosshairs inside the area on which you want the effect, the effect will not be applied to the outside area. For example, if you're painting with the Adjustment Brush on some mountains against a blue sky, as long as you keep the crosshairs (+) sign over the mountains, no effect will be applied to the blue sky even if some to the brush goes over the blue sky. If you do not have a check mark in the Auto Mask box, then the effect will be applied to the blue sky if your brush goes over an area of the blue sky.

TIP: You can paint with the Adjustment Brush in a straight line by holding down the Shift key on the keyboard.

When you are finished applying effects with the adjustment brush, a pin will appear on the image. If the pin is black it indicates that Adjustment Brush effect is active and can be edited. If the pin is white, that indicates the Adjustment Brush used to create that effect is inactive. If you close the adjustment brush to go to another panel, the pins will disappear. When you return to the Adjustment Brush, the pins will reappear and will all be white. To edit the effect of any Adjustment Brush, you must click with the cursor on the white pin of the effect you wish to edit to activate it. After activating an Adjustment Brush to edit it, hover your cursor over the pin and a red mask will appear on the image showing you where the effect of that Adjustment Brush was applied on the image and your cursor will change into a right and left pointing arrow. To change the color of the mask, go to the Tools menu at the top of the screen and from the drop down menu select "Adjustment Brush Overlay". Your choices besides red are green, white and black. If you would like to see the mask as you are applying the effect, there is a checkbox at the bottom left of the tool bar below the main screen that says "Show Selected Mask Overlay". (Yellow circle, Figure 38) Placing a check mark in that box by clicking in it with the cursor will show the mask in the area where the effect is being applied. However, be aware that if you check this box, you will only see the mask being applied, you will not be able to see the effect and the difference it is making in the image. It is not a bad idea to periodically turn the mask on as

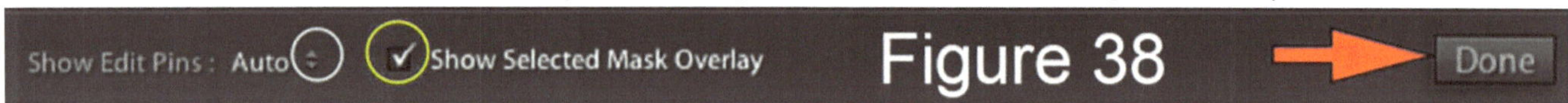

Figure 38

you are working, to make sure you cover the whole area on which you want the effect.

If you click with the right and left arrow cursor that appears when you hover your cursor over an Adjustment Brush pin and drag to the left, you will see the effects return toward their initial position on the slider bars. Drag back to the right and the effects will return to the position on the slider bars that you placed them in creating the effect. Once you have reached that position, dragging further to the right will not increase the effect on the image. This function allows you to soften or scale back the adjustment on the image.

As in the Graduated Filter tool, you have a choice in the Toolbar of when and how the white edit pins show on the image. The default setting for showing the pins is "Auto" Clicking on the double pointed arrow next to "Auto" (White circle, Figure 38) will give you the same choices as in the Graduated Filter tool. In addition to Auto you can choose between Always, Selected and Never. The pins can also be hidden by using the keyboard shortcut, pressing the H key on the keyboard.

The Adjustment Brush is a versatile tool that allows you to get exactly what you want in your image. If you look at the twelve sliders, you can apply any one of the adjustments to any area of your image by sliding the Adjustment Brush sliders to the right or left. For example, if you wanted to apply sharpening to just one area, slide the Sharpening slider to the right. Add detail to the mid-tones by increasing the Clarity effect and applying that effect to just the area of the image with the mid-tones. Selecting the Contrast slider may be a good way to add contrast, because the Adjustment Brush, set to increase contrast, will make the dark shades darker and the bright shades brighter only in the area where you applied the contrast effect. Applying negative clarity to just the skin tones in a portrait can smooth out the skin. So, there are many ways you can use the Adjustment Brush. However, my recommendation would be to work with just one slider at a time, make the change you want on a slider, leave the other sliders at zero and then apply the effect with the Adjustment Brush. That way you can see exactly the changes you're making in the image as you make them. To do this, do the following:

- Set all the effects sliders to zero.
- Paint with the Adjustment brush over the area where you want the effects.
- Select one effect and move the slider to place the effect on the image
- Write down the position of the slider on the bar from the number in the scrubby slider box to the right

of the slider bar.
- Move the slider for the first effect back to zero (double click with the cursor on the name of the effect).
- Select another effect and move the slider to see what that effect looks like on the image.
- Continue changing the effects until you know which ones you want on the selected area.

Once you know which effects give you the best results on the image and you have written down their positions on the slider bars, go back and move the sliders of those effects to the desired position on the slider bar.

If you set multiple sliders to new values and then apply the multiple effects with the Adjustment Brush, it might be hard to see what you're really doing to the image and if you don't like the result, it's hard to figure out which effect to change. There are times when you need to use a combination of sliders, for example, you can whiten teeth by decreasing the saturation and then increasing the White sliders (there's a better way to whiten teeth coming up). It might be more time consuming, but I think you'll get better control of the changes you're making in the image. My advice is, play with all the sliders in the Adjustment Brush, both individually and in combinations to see what effects you can produce. Also, don't forget about the on/off light switch at the bottom left of the panel.

To close the Adjustment Brush tool, do one of the following:
- Click with the cursor on the "Done" button at the right side of the toolbar (Red arrow, Figure 38)
- Click with the cursor on the Adjustment Brush icon in the toolbar underneath the histogram.
- Use the keyboard shortcut, press the K key on the keyboard.
- Go to the Tools menu and from the drop down menu click with the cursor on Adjustment Brush to uncheck it.

## Neat Lightroom® Tricks

Now that you've been through all the right side panels and tools and learned how you can use them to develop your images, there are a couple of other things you ought to know. First, you really haven't done anything to your images yet. You haven't changed one pixel, either darkened or lightened or changed the color, nothing. In fact, your images aren't really in Lightroom® like they are when you open them in Photoshop®. However, you really haven't been wasting your time. First, Lightroom® knows where your images are on your computer and second, Lightroom® is not a pixel based editing program. All you've been doing is giving Lightroom® a series of instructions and Lightroom® has been showing you what your image would look like if those instructions were applied to the image. They won't be applied to your image until you either export the image to another program like Photoshop® or until you print the image from Lightroom®.

### Using the History Panel

Another interesting thing is that Lightroom® keeps all the instructions with the image in the History Panel on the left side of the Develop Module. Unlike Photoshop®, which, when you close the image, the history of what you did to the image is lost, Lightroom® keeps the history (instructions) with the image. There is no "Save" or "Save As" under the File menu in Lightroom®, because you don't have to save anything, Lightroom® does it for you. You can close Lightroom® and not open it for months or open Lightroom® and develop other images and the instructions you gave Lightroom® for any image you developed will still be there in the History panel on the left side of the screen. You can reset the image as often as you like and all the instructions including the resets will be in the History panel. There is a way to delete all the history. There is an X on the right side of the History panel header bar and if you hover your cursor over this X, the words "Clear All" will appear in the header bar. Clicking with the cursor on this X will delete all the history steps you have taken in developing the image. Pretty slick, yes?

Here are some other neat tricks you can do with Lightroom®:

- You can drag any state in the History panel to a before image in the Before/After view to compare the stages of development.
- You can Control (Macintosh) Right (PC) click with the cursor on a Snapshot and drag it to the before preview in the Before/After view.

Either of these steps will allow you to compare a stage of developing with the current stage.

**Creating Virtual Copies**

Here's another neat thing about Lightroom®. You already know you can create a snapshot of any step in your editing process by highlighting a step in the History Panel and clicking on the + sign next to Snapshots on the left side of the Develop Module. You can also create a Virtual Copy of any image. To create a Virtual Copy, do one of the following:

- Go to the Photo menu at the top of the screen in the Develop Module and in the drop-down menu select "Create Virtual Copy".
- Alternatively, Control Click (Macintosh) Right Click (PC) with the cursor anywhere in the image and you'll get a pop up menu, (Figure 39)one of the selections of which is "Create Virtual Copy," (Red arrow, figure 39) select this option.
- Another alternative is to use the keyboard shortcut, hold down the Command(Macintosh), Control (PC) key and press the Apostrophe (') on the keyboard.

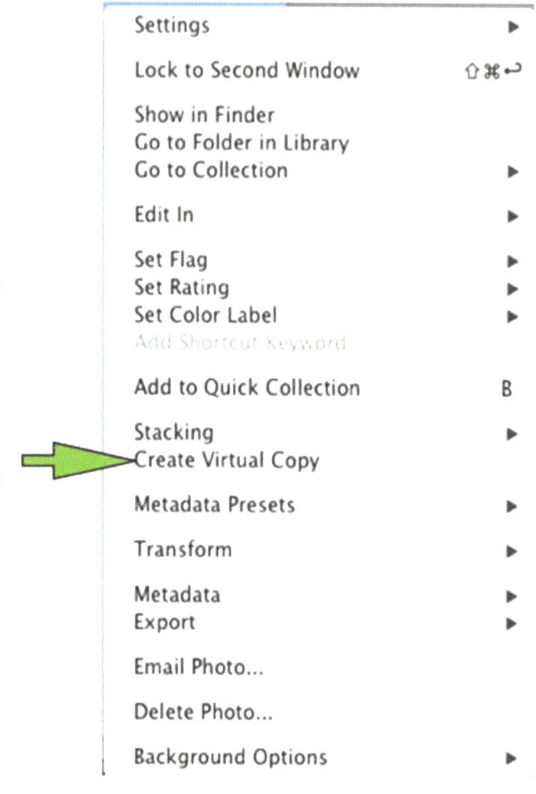

Figure 39

Either way when you create a Virtual Copy, Lightroom® creates an identical copy of the image as you developed it and places it right next to the original in the Filmstrip or in the Grid view in the Library Module. What's the advantage to this you ask? Well, if, for example, you created black and white image from a color image, you can do the following:

- If you create a virtual copy of the black and white image you can go back to the original which is now called the Master Photo and at this point will also be black and white and click with the cursor on the Reset button at the bottom right of the screen to reset the Master Photo back to the original color image.
- You can then edit it a different way, maybe in color this time and then create a virtual copy of the new color image and then again reset the Master Photo to its original state.
- You can have as many virtual copies of an image as you want and still have the Master Photo as it was before you started developing it.

Here is the most important thing to know about Master Photos and Virtual Copies. When you create a Collection, all the images in the Collection should be Virtual Copies. Why is that, you want to know. It's pretty simple, if you use a Master Photo in a collection in any module and then you go back to the Master Photoin a folder or another Colleciton and change it in any way, rename it, put new develop settings on it, anything, then every where that Master Copy is, in any collection in any module, those changes will show up on the Master Photo in those Collections or Folders. For example, if you create a slideshow and use a Master Photo in the slideshow and then go back to the Develop module and create a black and white image of the Master Photo, the image in the slideshow will now be black and white. If you use a Virtual Copy in the slideshow then any changes made on the Master Photo will not show up in the slideshow. However, if you rename a Master Photo or a Virtual Copy, all the images will be renamed. It gets even worse. If you use a Virtual Copy in a collection and then put that Virtual Copy in another collection, if you edit the Virtual Copy in the first collection then the changes will show up in the second collection. But, Lightroom® solves this problem for you, because if you look at a New Collection dialog box in any module, there is a check box that says "Make new virtual copies". Click with the cursor in this box when ever you make a new collection in any module and you avoid the problem. True, you'll have a lot of Virtual Copies, one for each module, but you can have as many as you want.

You'll know which are the virtual copies, because they will all have the bottom left corner turned up in the Filmstrip at the bottom of the page and in the Grid view in the Library module. But, here's the really neat thing, no matter how many virtual copies you make, you won't be taking up any significant space on your hard drive with all these virtual copies, because all they are is a set of instructions, they are not new images. If you're coming over from Photoshop® this idea takes some getting used to, doesn't it?

## Working in the Basic panel from another panel

How about some more neat things in the Develop Module. As you move throughout the Develop module panels and make changes with the different effects, the previous changes you've made can be affected. For example, if you got rid of all the clipping using the tone sliders in the Basic panel and then you use the Targeted Adjustment cursor in the Luminance section of the HSL panel to brighten a color, some clipping may occur in the image. For most people that would require that you scroll back up, open the Basic panel and work with the tone sliders again to get rid of the clipping. But, you're not most people now, you can work in the Basic panel while still being in another panel. Here's how to do it:

- Start by turning on the clipping warnings (J key).
- Before you leave the Basic panel, click with the cursor on the name of any effect in the Basic panel to highlight it.
- When you are working in another panel, you can still make changes to any slider in the Basic panel without going back and opening up the Basic panel.
- Because you left one of the effects in the Basic panel highlighted, you can use the plus (+) and minus (-) keys on the keyboard to make changes in any effect in the basic panel.
- You can navigate to any effect slider in the Basic panel and make it the active slider by using the period (.) or comma (,) keys on the keyboard.
- Pressing the period key (.) will move the active slider in the Basic panel down to the next slider.
- Pressing the comma (,) key on the keyboard will move the active slider up to the next higher slider in the Basic panel.
- You will know which effect you are working with because when you use the period or comma key to go to the next higher or lower effect, the name of that effect will appear for a few seconds in the bottom center of the work area.
- After you have navigated to the slider you want, use the plus and minus (+/-) keys to make changes with the active slider.
- So you can make changes in the Basic panel when working in another panel without having to go back and open the Basic panel again.

In the example, if you highlight the Exposure slider name, then you go to the Targeted Adjustment Tool in the Luminance section of the HSL Panel and by increasing the Luminance too high you start to get some burned out highlights in the image (they show up because you turned on the clipping warnings, remember?), but you like the brightness of the rest of the image. At this point, all you have to do is press the minus key on the keyboard a couple of times and the burned out highlights will start to disappear. That's because by pressing the minus key you're moving the Exposure slider to the left. If instead the image starts to darken too much using the Exposure slider, you can press the period (.) key on the keyboard twice and the Highlights slider will be come the active slider. Pressing the minus key will move the Highlights slider to the left, darkening the highlights. You could then press the comma (,) key on the keyboard twice and go back to the Exposure slider and press the plus key to brighten the image or you could press the period key twice and make the Whites slider the active slider and then press the minus key to decrease the whites in the image. All this will happen without leaving the Luminance section of the HSL/Color/Black and White Panel.

Each time you move from one effect slider to another in the Basic panel, a message will appear in the bottom of the image indicating which effect it is with which you can use the plus and minus keys on the keyboard to make changes in the image. You will also get a message in the image each time you press either the plus or minus key telling you how much of a change you made with the plus or minus key on the slider. Holding down the shift key while pressing either the plus or minus key will make a change of one third of a stop with the exposure slider or a twenty percent change in the other tone sliders. Holding down the Option (Macintosh), Alt (PC) key when pressing the plus or minus key will make a two hundredths of a stop change with the Exposure slider or a one percent change with the other tone sliders. So, you can make some very accurate develop changes in an image using the Basic panel at the same time you are working in another panel. Try it, you'll like it.

**Getting Rid of Clipping**

Most people get rid of clipping in an image using the Tone sliders in the Basic panel, or at least they think they do. Often after working with the Tone sliders to remove clipping, with the clipping warnings turned on (J key), there does not appear to be any clipping in the image, no red or blue indicating lost detail and neither side of the histogram is climbing the wall as if it's trying to escape. However, there may still be some lost detail in the image. I believe that all three channels in an area have to be clipped for the red or blue clipping to appear on screen in the image or for the Histogram to climb the wall. If only one or two channels have been clipped then there will appear to be no clipping in the image with the clipping warnings turned on or in the histogram. The easy way to find out is to hold down the Option (Macintosh), Alt (PC) key and click with the cursor on the Highlights, Shadows, Whites and Blacks sliders one at a time. Doing this will cause the screen to turn black with the Highlights and Whites sliders and white with the Shadows and Blacks sliders. The lost detail will show up as different colors on the screen depending on which of the red, green or blue channels are clipped. You can try to get rid of this clipping when holding down the Option/Alt key and moving which ever slider you are currently using and you may be able to get rid of the colors on the screen. Often you will not be able to get rid of the lost detail and if you can, it may make the image too dark or too light. You can then go to the Exposure slider, hold down the Option/Alt key and try to brighten or darken the image by moving the Exposure slider right or left until colors start to appear on the screen and then back off. The problem is that with the Option/Alt key held down you cannot see how much you are brightening or darkening the image until you let go of the Option/Alt key. So, what should you do? Of course, you should use another of the neat Lightroom® tricks. Here's the neat part of this trick, in the highlights, you already know which channels have been clipped by to colors in the black screen. If only the red, green or blue channels are clipped, that color will appear on the screen. If the red and green channels have been clipped, yellow will appear on the screen. Magenta will appear on screen if the red and blue channels have been clipped and cyan will appear if the green and blue channels have been clipped. To get rid of the lost detail in the highlights, do the following:

- Open the Point Curve section of the Tone Curve panel.
- Hold down the Shift key and click on the Basic panel to open it.
- Start with the Highlights slider, in the Basic panel and hold down the Option/Alt key and click on the slider.

- If there is an area where only red, green or blue shows on the screen, choose that channel in the point curve section of the Tone curve panel.
- Place your cursor at the top of the curve on the right side of the graph, the cursor will change into a double pointed up and down arrow (Yellow Circle, figure 40). Move the curve slightly down the right side of the graph with this cursor.
- Go back to the Highlight slider and holding down the Option/Alt key click on the slider.
- The lost detail in the color of the channel in the image should be gone.
- If yellow shows on the black screen then follow the same process with the green channel in the Point Curve.
- When you go back to the basic panel and hold down the Option/Alt key and click on the Highlight slider the yellow color should be gone and only red should be visible on the screen.
- Follow the same procedure with the red channel in the Point Curve section of the basic panel.
- When you go back to the Highlight slider in the Basic panel and hold down the Option/Alt key and then click on the slider, all colors should be gone and the screen should be black.
- All the clipping in the highlights will be gone.

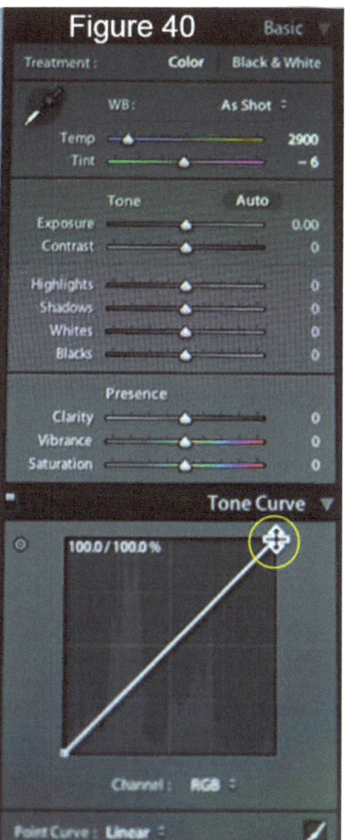


Things are a little different with the Shadows and Blacks sliders. Holding down the Option/Alt key and clicking on the Shadows or Blacks slider will turn the screen white. If there is lost detail in the channels here the colors will be different. The channel most often clipped in the shadows is the blue channel. If the blue channel is clipped yellow will show on the white screen. Cyan will show up if the red channel is clipped and magenta will show up if the green channel is clipped. If you remember that moving the red, green or blue channels down on the curve in the Tone Curve panel takes the colors more toward cyan, magenta or yellow respectively, this makes sense. So, the thing to do with the clipping in the shadows and/or blacks is the following:

- Again, open the Point Curve section of the Tone Curve panel and shift click on the Basic panel to open it.
- Hold down the Option/Alt key on the keyboard and click on either the Shadows or Blacks slider to turn the screen white.
- If yellow shows on the white screen, select the blue channel in the Point Curve section of the Tone Curve Panel.
- Click with the cursor on the bottom left of the curve to get the double pointed up and down arrow cursor and drag the curve up along the left side of the graph.
- Again hold down the Option/Alt key on the keyboard and click with the cursor on the Shadows or Blacks slider.
- If there are still colors on the white screen do the same thing with the red or green channels in the Point Curve section of the Tone Curve panel.

TIP: If the cursor is placed over the Point curve on the graph, it will turn into a crosshairs cursor and will move the curve up or down inside the graph. If the cursor is on the edge of the graph at the top right or bottom left, it will be the double pointed up and down arrow you want to slide the top of the curve down the right side of the graph or the bottom of the curve up on the left side of the graph.

TIP: You can also use this technique when you have burned out the highlights in all three channels, red, green and blue. In this case, when you hold down the Option/Alt key and click on either the Highlights slider or the Whites slider, there will be no colors, only white in the area of the burned out highlights. If you cannot bring back the lost detail with the Tone sliders in the Basic panel, you can in the Tone Curve panel using the RGB channel instead of the individual channels

Often when using the Point Curve to get rid of clipping, the image can start to get washed out. If that happens you can go to the Contrast effect slider and move it to the right or you can hold down the Option/ Alt key and click with the cursor on the Exposure slider to turn the screen black. Next, move the Exposure slider to the left just a small amount and you will get rid of the washed out appearance of the image.

So, now you're asking is there an easy way to determine if there is clipping in the image if none is visible with the clipping warnings turned on and the histogram looks OK? Is the only way to hold down the Option/Alt key and click on the slider of the Highlights, Shadows, Whites or Blacks? As a matter of fact there is an easy way to tell if there is still clipping in the image, and that's the next neat Lightroom® trick.

The Clipping Warnings

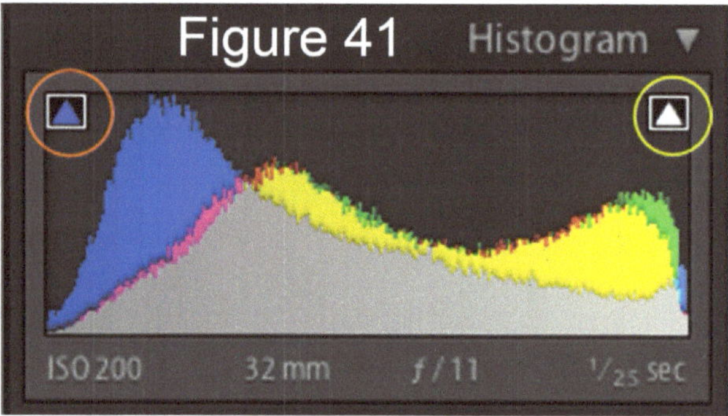


The square boxes with the triangles inside them at the top right and left of the Histogram are the clipping warning indicators. As previously mentioned, they can be turned off and on by hovering the cursor over them, clicking on them with the cursor or using the keyboard shortcut, pressing the J key. When the clipping warnings are turned on there will be a white box around the triangles. If there is no clipping in any channel in the image the triangles will be grayed out, but if there is some clipping in the image, even if you cannot see it with the clipping warnings turned on and the Histogram is not climbing the walls on either side, the triangles will be white in the white square boxes. (Yellow circle, Figure 41) This is when you need to hold down the Option/Alt key on the keyboard and click with the cursor on the Highlights, Shadows, Whites and Blacks sliders to find out where the loss of detail is and correct it using the sliders in the Basic panel or the Point Curve section of the Tone Curve panel.

The Clipping Warnings can give you another indication of a problem in your image. If you notice that the shadow triangle is blue (Red circle, Figure 41) or the highlight triangle is red, it can mean you have a color cast in your image in addition to loss of detail in the highlights or shadows. Most of the time getting rid of the lost detail will correct the color cast, but occasionally, especially in the shadows, you may need to move the Tint slider, usually to the right to get the Shadows Clipping Warning triangle to gray out.

**Moving Develop Settings From One Image To Another**

More neat stuff. You've developed an image and it's just the way you want it. Now you would like to use those Develop Settings on another image. There are several ways this can be accomplished.

**Copy and Paste**

One of the ways of moving develop settings from one image to another, Copy and Paste, has already been discussed (Page 79), however, just to review, do the following:

- After you develop an image, you can click with the cursor on the Copy button at the bottom left of the screen in the Develop module.
- Copy and Paste selections are also available in the Edit menu at the top of the screen.
- A Copy Settings dialog box will appear on screen. (Figure 6, page 79)

- You can place check marks in the boxes in front of the effects you changed by clicking in the boxes with the cursor, OR
- You can just click with the cursor in the "Check All" box at the bottom left of the dialog box.
- Do not click on the "Check All" box if you cropped the first image and do not want to crop the second image or make sure you uncheck "Crop" in the Copy Settings dialog box.
- Next, select another image and click with the cursor on the Paste box at the bottom left of the screen.
- The Develop Settings from the first image will be applied to the second image.

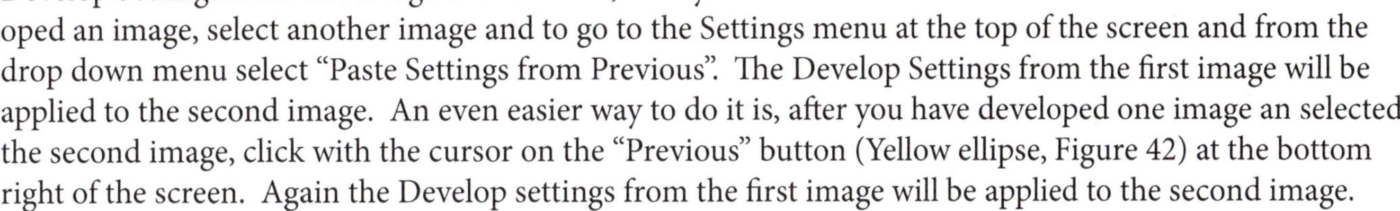

Figure 42

This seems to me to be the hard way to do it. A second way to paste Develop Settings from one image to another is, after you have developed an image, select another image and to go to the Settings menu at the top of the screen and from the drop down menu select "Paste Settings from Previous". The Develop Settings from the first image will be applied to the second image. An even easier way to do it is, after you have developed one image an selected the second image, click with the cursor on the "Previous" button (Yellow ellipse, Figure 42) at the bottom right of the screen. Again the Develop settings from the first image will be applied to the second image.

**Synchronize Develop Settings**

How about this, if the original image you developed is one of a series you shot with the same exposure in the same lighting conditions you can do the following:

- First, select the image you developed in the Filmstrip, it will show up on the main screen in the Develop module.
- Then select all the others in the series by holding down the Shift key on the keyboard and clicking with the cursor on the last one in the series if they're consecutive in the filmstrip or hold down the Command (Macintosh) Control (PC) key and click with the cursor on each of the others in the series if they're not consecutive in the Filmstrip.
- As soon as you select another image in the filmstrip, the Previous button next to the Reset button at the bottom right of the screen will change to one that says "Sync".

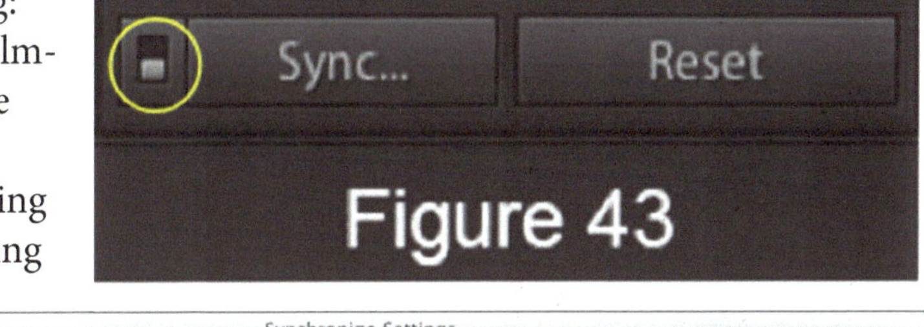

Figure 43

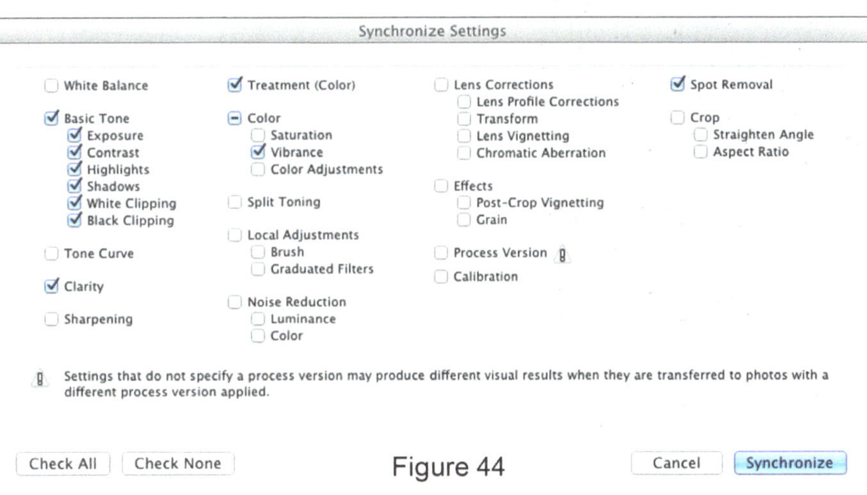

Figure 44

- If you then click with the cursor on the button that says Sync (Yellow circle, Figure 43) you'll bring up a Synchronize Settings dialog box (Figure 44) with all the possible settings changes you can make in an image.

When the synchronize settings dialog box comes up, it will have the settings that were used the last time you synchronized settings between two images. The Synchronize Settings dialog box is the same dialog box as the Copy Settings dialog box, it's just named different here. So, here's the sequence to follow to make sure you synchronize the settings you want:

- Make sure you have the History panel open on the left side of the image.
- Click with the cursor on the Check None button at the bottom left of the Synchronize Settings dialog box,
- To be accurate, you can use the History panel as a guide and place a check in the check boxes of the effects you changed in developing the image by clicking with the cursor in the boxes.
- Of course, if you are in a hurry or just lazy, you can also just click with the cursor on the "Check All" button at the bottom left of the Synchronize Settings dialog box.
- Click with the cursor on the Synchronize button at the bottom right of the Synchronize Settings box.

TIP: You can skip the Synchronize Settings dialog box by having all the boxes checked and then when you are ready to sync the effects, hold down the Option (Macintosh), Alt (PC) key and click with the cursor on the Sync button. All of the develop settings will sync to the selected images.

All the settings changes in the effects you made in developing the original image will now be applied to all the selected images. There is an even easier way to move develop settings from one image to another or to multiple images and it is even easier and faster than using the Sync button to synchronize settings. So if you are in a hurry or just lazy this next trick is for you.

**Auto-Sync Develop Settings**

If the Sync Settings method is not fast enough for you, then here's an even slicker way to do it:

- Select an image to be developed.
- Before you edit the selected image, select the images from the same series with the same exposure and same lighting conditions in the Filmstrip by Shift or Command (Macintosh), Shift or Control(PC) clicking on them with the cursor.
- Next, notice the light switch icon next to the word Sync (Yellow circle, figure 43) (the same icon that's on all the panels except the basic panel, the one that shows you the before and after for each panel, the one you already forgot about).
- Click with the cursor on that light switch and the Sync button will change to say "Auto Sync" (Yellow ellipse, Figure 45).
- Once Auto Sync is selected, from that point on any change you make on the selected image in the work area on the main screen will be applied to all the selected images in the Filmstrip.

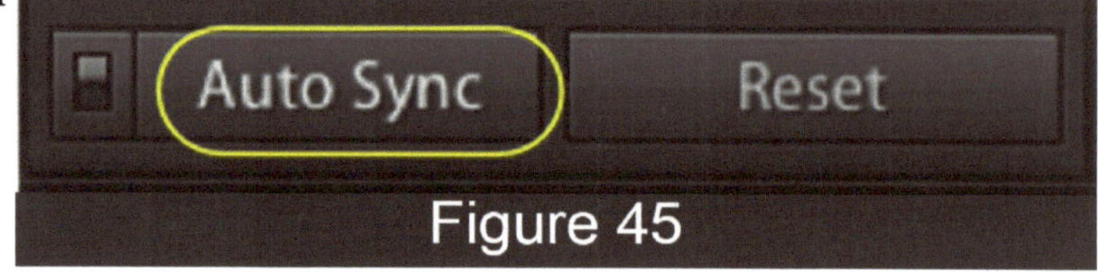

Figure 45

It's kind of like batch processing in Photoshop® only better, simpler and faster.

Here's another very useful neat Lightroom® trick. The Auto Sync feature will come in very handy if you find you have used a lens with a spot on it or a camera with a spot on the sensor. If that occurs, here is all you have to do:

- Go to the Library Filter bar in the Library module and select the Metadata section.
- Select the lens or serial number of the camera that has the spot and bring up all the images taken with that lens or camera.
- Select all the images and move to the Develop module by pressing the D key on the keyboard.
- You will see one of the images on the main screen and all the selected images highlighted in the filmstrip at the bottom of the screen.
- Bring up the Spot Removal tool by pressing the Q key on the keyboard.
- Select the Heal Spot Removal tool.
- Adjust the size of the Spot removal tool to the size of the spot you want to remove.

- Place the Spot Removal tool over the spot and click with the cursor.
- The spot will be removed from all the selected images whether they are in portrait or landscape mode.

How about another neat trick, only it has to do with the Library Module, but it relates to the Develop Module. If you edit an image in the Develop Module and then go back to the Library Module, you can sync the develop settings from the recently edited image to other images in the Library module without going back to the Develop module. There are several ways to sync develop settings to other images in the Library module. The first way is to sync the settings by bringing up the Sync Settings dialog box (Figure 44) and checking the boxes of the effects you changed in developing the image. To bring up the Sync Settings dialog box in the Library module, do the following:

- Select the image you edited in the Develop Module (it's probably already selected) in the Grid view or the Filmstrip at the bottom of the page by clicking on it with the Cursor.
- Hold down either the Shift key to select consecutive images or the Command key (Macintosh), Control key(PC) to select images that are not consecutive images in the Grid view or Filmstrip.
- As soon as you select a second image, the two buttons at the bottom right of the screen in the Library Module, which were grayed out until you selected the second image will now be active and say Sync Metadata and Sync Settings. (Figure 46)
- Clicking with the cursor on the Sync Settings button will bring up the same Sync Settings dialog box as in the Develop module. (Figure 44)
- Check the boxes for the effects you changed on the image in the Develop module and those effects will be applied to the selected image or images right in the Library Module.

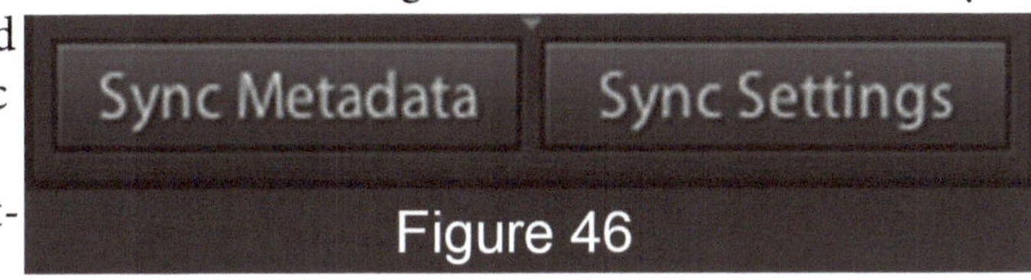

Figure 46

A second and easier way to move develop settings from one image to another in the Library module is to do the following:

- Select the image with the develop settings.
- Select a second image or images on which you want to place the develop settings from the first image.
- Go to the Photo menu at the top of the page and from the Photo menu select "Develop Settings".
- From the pop up menu that appears select "Paste Settings from Previous". (Figure 47)
- The develop settings from the first image will be applied to the second image.

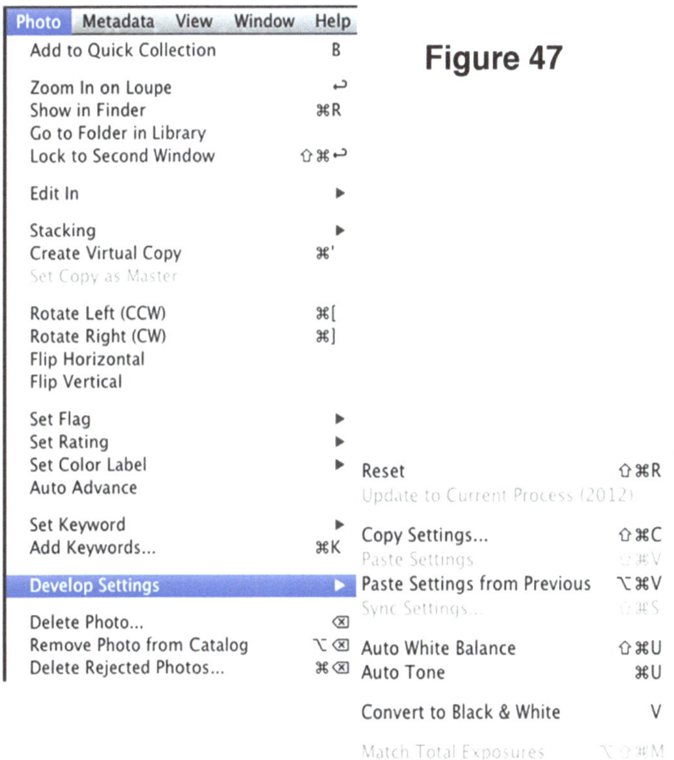

Figure 47

Copy and Paste settings are also available from the Develop Settings in the Photo drop down menu. Any of these methods can be a big time saver, especially if you missed selecting an image in the Filmstrip of the Develop Module to which you would like to apply develop settings from another image.

## Matching Tonal Exposure

There is another neat trick you can use in the Develop module with under exposed or over exposed images or with images where you like the exposure of one image and want the same exposure on another image. It's easy to apply the exposure from one image to another, just do the following:

- Select the image that has the exposure you like.
- Select another image by Command (Macintosh), Control (PC) clicking with the cursor on an image that is either under exposed over exposed or one for which you would like the exposure of the first image you selected.
- With both images selected, go to the settings menu at the top of the screen and from the Settings menu select "Match Total Exposure". (Blue highlight, Figure 48)
- Lightroom® will evaluate the exposure of the first selected image and change the exposure of the over/under exposed images to match the first image.

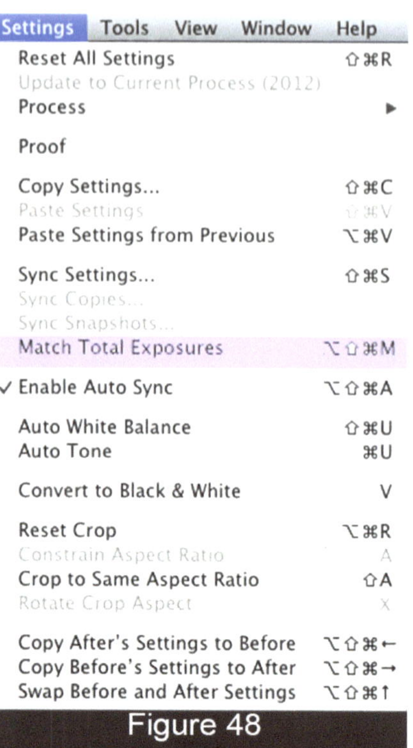

Figure 48

### Adding color to a Black and White image

One of the effects that a lot of people like is to add color to just one portion of a black and white image. With this trick you are really taking away all the color saturation except for the one you want to remain in the image. To do this, do the following:

- In an image with lots of colors, an image with red roses for example, in the HSL section of the HSL/Color/Black and White panel, move all the saturation sliders, except the red saturation slider, to the left to get a grayscale image.
- Move the red saturation slider to the right to increase the red color saturation of the red roses.
- You should end up with a grayscale image with red roses being the only color in the image.
- You can then go to the basic panel and move the Tone effects sliders and the presence effects sliders to get a very nice half grayscale, half color image.

### Adjustment Brush Tricks

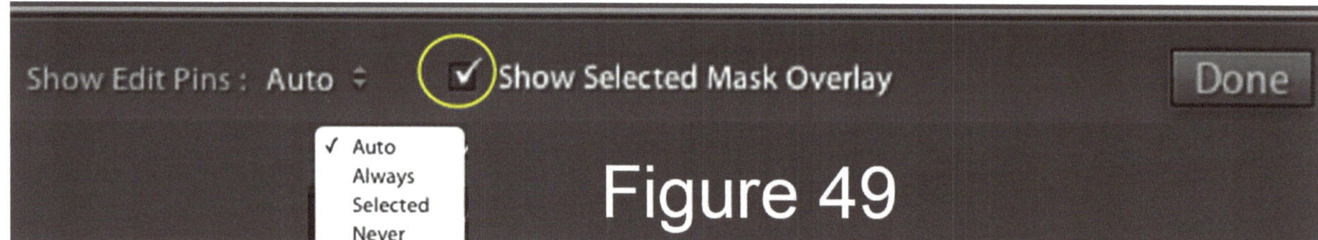

Figure 49

There are a couple of ways you can apply the Adjustment Brush. One way has already been discussed. Start with just one effect and set the slider so the effect can be seen on the image as you apply it. Once you have the effect where you want it, then add different effects to the area with the different effects sliders. This way you will know how each of the different effects change the image. The second way to use the Adjustment Brush is as follows:

- Turn on the Adjustment Brush mask overlay by clicking with the cursor in the box in the toolbar at the bottom of the screen that says "Show Selected Mask Overlay." (Yellow circle, Figure 49)
- Either select one of the effects you know you want to apply to an area of the image, although it is not necessary to place an effect on the image with this method because with the overlay mask turned on you will not be able to see the effect on the image.
- Set the brush size, feathering, flow and density and make sure Auto Mask is turned on.
- Paint on the area where you want the effect(s) to be on the image.
- You can zoom in on the image by holding down the space bar and clicking with the cursor on the area to be magnified.

- After zooming in, keep holding down the space bar and the cursor turns into a hand cursor with which you can move around the image.
- By zooming in and moving around the image you can place the adjustment accurately in the image.
- When you have the overlay mask placed exactly where you want it, turn off the overlay mask by again clicking with the cursor in the "Show Mask Overlay" box on the toolbar.
- You can now go to the effects sliders in the Adjustment Brush and move them watching the effect as it is placed on the image.
- Effects can be added, increased or decrease until you have the selected area of the image as you want it.
- This method may eliminate having to use multiple brushes to achieve the effect you want.

TIP: Once you have placed an effect on an area of the image, it does not preclude you from using a new brush to place an effect on part of the area where the first brush has its effect.

The Adjustment Brush is one of the most versatile tools in Lightroom®. There are presets in the Adjustment Brush panel. As previously mentioned, you can find these presets by clicking with the cursor on the double pointed arrow at the very top of the panel. There will be either the name of an effect or the word "Custom" to the left of the double pointed arrow. Clicking with the cursor on this double pointed arrow will bring up a menu with all of the different effects available to you with the Adjustment Brush. These are all presets for the different effects. Lightroom® will evaluate the image and set the slider on the effect's bar where it feels it should be. For example, if you choose the Exposure effect and have an image that is light, Lightroom® will move the Exposure slider to the left to decrease the exposure. If the image is too dark, Lightroom® will place the slider to the right on the bar to lighten the exposure in the selected area. The last five of these presets can come in pretty handy. The Burn and Dodge presets are pretty much self explanatory, they darken or lighten a selected area of the image. The last three, Iris Enhance, Skin Softening and Teeth Whitening are for developing portraits and they do a great job. With the Iris Enhance effect you can also add a more vibrant color using the Color Picker box at the bottom of the Adjustment Brush panel. I've found that with the Teeth Whitening preset, after applying it, the exposure needs to backed off a little to make it more realistic. So, they are not perfect, but with all the available effects in the Adjustment Brush, you can make them perfect. To use any of the presets, all you have to do is select the task you want to accomplish with the portrait and select the effect. As with all the effects in the Adjustment Brush, once you have the effect applied to the area of the image where you want it, you can move the sliders on the effects slider bars to increase or decrease the effect on the image.

\

Finally, here is where the Adjustment Brush really comes in handy. You do not have to use the presets to accomplish the tasks you want, but you will be amazed at what you can do just setting the sliders on the effects slider bars. The following are just some of the things that can accomplished with the Adjustment Brush:

**Blurring the background**

- Set the Sharpness slider to minus one hundred percent and paint the background all around your subject
- You can also paint over the entire image with the Adjustment Brush at minus one hundred percent and then hold down the Option (Macintosh), Alt (PC) key and paint out the blur effect on your subject. Sometimes this is the faster way to do it.
- The background can be blurred even more by adding a negative Clarity effect to the Adjustment Brush.

## Increase the depth of field

- The Exposure slider in the Adjustment Brush will allow you to make a plus or minus four stop change in the image.
- Setting the Exposure slider to one or two stops to the negative will bring back some detail in the distant background of the image by darkening it slightly.

**Bring back burned out highlights in the background**

- Images with backlit subjects often have the background burned out, especially pictures taken against the sky.
- Painting with the Adjustment Brush Highlights effects slider set to a negative value can get rid of the burned out highlights.
- Adding a color, such as blue for the sky, from the Color Picker box in the Adjustment Brush panel can not only eliminate the burn out but make the image look more natural.

**Change colors**

- You can remove the color of an object in an image by painting over it with the Adjustment Brush Saturation effect set to minus one hundred percent.
- Then with a new Adjustment Brush pick a color from the Color Picker box and paint the new color over the desaturated area.
- The new color can be lightened or darkened with the Exposure slider

**Adding contrast or Dodging and Burning:**

- You can lighten just one area of your image by moving the Exposure slider to the right and applying the brighter effect to an area that you feel needs to be brighter
- Select a new brush and move the Exposure slider to the left and apply the darker effect to another area of the image
- You can choose the Dodge or Burn preset from the effects presets and darken or lighten one area of the image.

**Smoothing out skin tones:**

- Set the Clarity slider to a minus position on the slider bar and use it to smooth out skin in a portrait.
- You can also choose the Soften Skin preset from the effects presets menu, place the effects of the Adjustment Brush where you want them and move the Clarity and Sharpness effects sliders to perfect the effect.

**Removing Moire**

One of the little noticed effects in the Adjustment Brush is Moire. This is an undesired artifact of digital capture. It is a ripple type effect that shows up on some types of fabrics. It can be removed by moving the Moire slider to the right and turning of Auto Mask and then painting over the area of the image containing Moire

These are just a few of the effects that can be accomplished with the Adjustment Brush, and I'm sure with experimentation many more can be discovered.

**Soft Proofing**

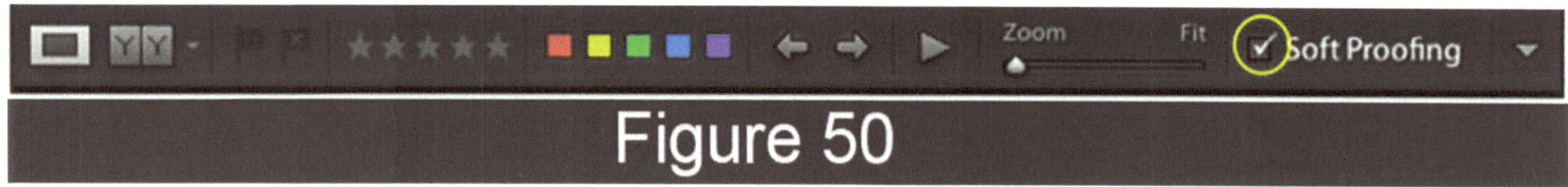


Figure 50

Adobe has added Soft Proofing to Lightroom® 4, probably because they had so many requests for it. It is found in the Develop module, allowing you to see a soft proof preview of the image before taking it into the Print module for printing. What Soft Proofing allows you to do is push out of gamut colors into a smaller color space, such as sRGB for the web or Adobe RGB or ProPhoto RGB for your printer. You now have control over the way your colors are converted for an output device, a screen or printer. There are two ways to turn on Soft Proofing. The first way is to place a check mark in the box in front of the words "Soft Proofing" on the toolbar. (Yellow circle, Figure 50) The second way is to press the S key on the keyboard.

The first thing you will probably;y notice is that the background behind your image has changed. The default background for soft proofing is called Paper White. You can change the background by control (Macintosh), Right (PC) clicking on it. A pop up menu will give you several choices for changing the background from 100 % white through black. Also, the words "Proof Preview" will appear in the top right corner of the work area on screen. Another thing you'll notice is that the Histogram has changed. In the regular Histogram when you hover your cursor over the image, the numbers for the red, green and blue channels that appear under the Histogram are percentages. In the Soft Proofing Histogram they are actual numerical values for each channel that appear under the Histogram when you hover your cursor over the image.

Another thing you'll probably notice about the Soft Proofing Histogram is that the icons at the top right and left of the Histogram have changed. They are no longer clipping warnings, the left icon is for soft proofing an image for a computer screen. (Blue circle, Figure 51) When turned on the colors that are out of gamut for a screen will show up on the screen as red or blue depending on whether they are highlights or shadows. The icon on the top right of the Histogram is for showing out of gamut colors for a destination such as a printer. (Red circle, Figure 51) When this icon is turned on, the out of gamut colors for the profile you have chosen will show up on the screen.

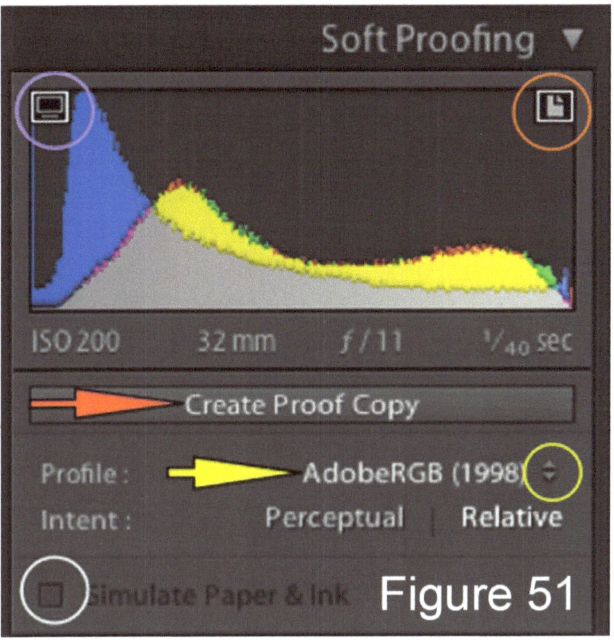

Figure 51

The profile for the monitor should be sRGB, but the destination profile for other devices (Yellow arrow, Figure 51), such as a printer, can be chosen by clicking with the cursor on the double pointed arrow to the right of the current profile (Yellow circle, Figure 51). A drop down menu will appear giving you the choice of profiles that are installed on your computer. (Figure 52) For example, all the ICC profiles for your printer will be listed in the drop down menu. All you have to do is choose the one on which you want to print and click with the cursor on it. The printer ICC profile will show up in the profile blank. You also have the choice of "Other" at the bottom of the drop down menu. (Figure 52) Selecting the "Other" choice allows you to navigate to other printer profiles installed on your computer and choose them.

sRGB
AdobeRGB (1998)

SPR2400 PremiumGlossy
SPR2400 PremiumLuster
✓ SPR2400 PremLuster BstPhoto.icc
SPR2400 PremLuster PhotoRPM.icc
SPR2400 PremSmgls BstPhoto.icc

Other...

Figure 52

Once you know where the out of gamut colors are in an image for either the monitor or for printing the image you can correct them. However, you probably don't want to do this on your original image and Adobe realized this so they have given you the opportunity to Create a Proof Copy (Red arrow, Figure 51). What this proof copy really is, is a Virtual copy. You can make the changes in the Proof (Virtual) Copy for the printer or monitor. One of the easy ways for correcting out of gamut colors for either the monitor or printer, is to go to the HSL panel select the Target Adjustment tool and decrease the saturation of the out of gamut colors. However, this may not work well for all the different profiles, so another option is to use the Target Adjustment tool to change the hue of the image just slightly to bring the colors back into the gamut. You also can use the Adjustment Brush tool to change the saturation of out of gamut colors in specific areas of the image. Finally, you can use the Tone and Presence effects sliders to bring highlights and shadows back to in gamut colors.

Also, remember that if you are working on a Master Copy and you don't create a Proof (Virtual) Copy, any changes you make in an image in the develop module will be applied to all the other copies of this Master Copy in all your collections. That includes renaming an image. So, you might want to consider creating a Virtual Copy to add to a Collection instead of just dragging the original image to a Collection.

## Moving to Photoshop®

Once you've developed your image and are satisfied with it, you may want to move it to Photoshop for final editing or to merge several images to HDR Pro or Photomerge to create a panorama. Before you do that you need to make sure the Lightroom® Preferences are set the way you want them. To do that, you need to go into the External Editing Preferences. You get to Lightroom® preferences by clicking on Lightroom® at the top left of the screen on the Macintosh and by clicking on the Edit menu on the PC. Select "Preferences" from the drop down menu and then select External Editing in the preferences menu. You're given the choice of opening the file as either a PSD or Tiff file. The PSD file is the native Photoshop file and the one with which Photoshop® is probably the most happy. However, I like to open files as TIFF files in Photoshop® just to make sure I don't drop down menu and then select External Editing in the preferences menu. You're given the choice of opening the file as either a PSD or Tiff file. The PSD file is the native Photoshop file and the one with which Photoshop® is probably the most happy. However, I like to open files as TIFF files in Photoshop® just to make sure I don't lose any detail in exporting the file to Photoshop®. Actually, I rarely open a file as a TIFF file in Photoshop® when I'm going to work on just the one file and then save it back to Lightroom®. When I move a file to Photoshop, I click on the Photo menu and under "Edit in," I select "Open as a smart object in Photoshop". There are two reasons for this. First, I'm opening a RAW file and I know I don't lose any detail and second, when I save it back to Lightroom® it is saved as a TIFF file, but since I do my printing from Lightroom®, I know I haven't lost any detail in all the opening and saving of the file. If you're going to merge the images to HDR or Photomerge for a panorama, you won't be able to open them as smart objects, you only have a choice of opening them as TIFFs or PSDs.

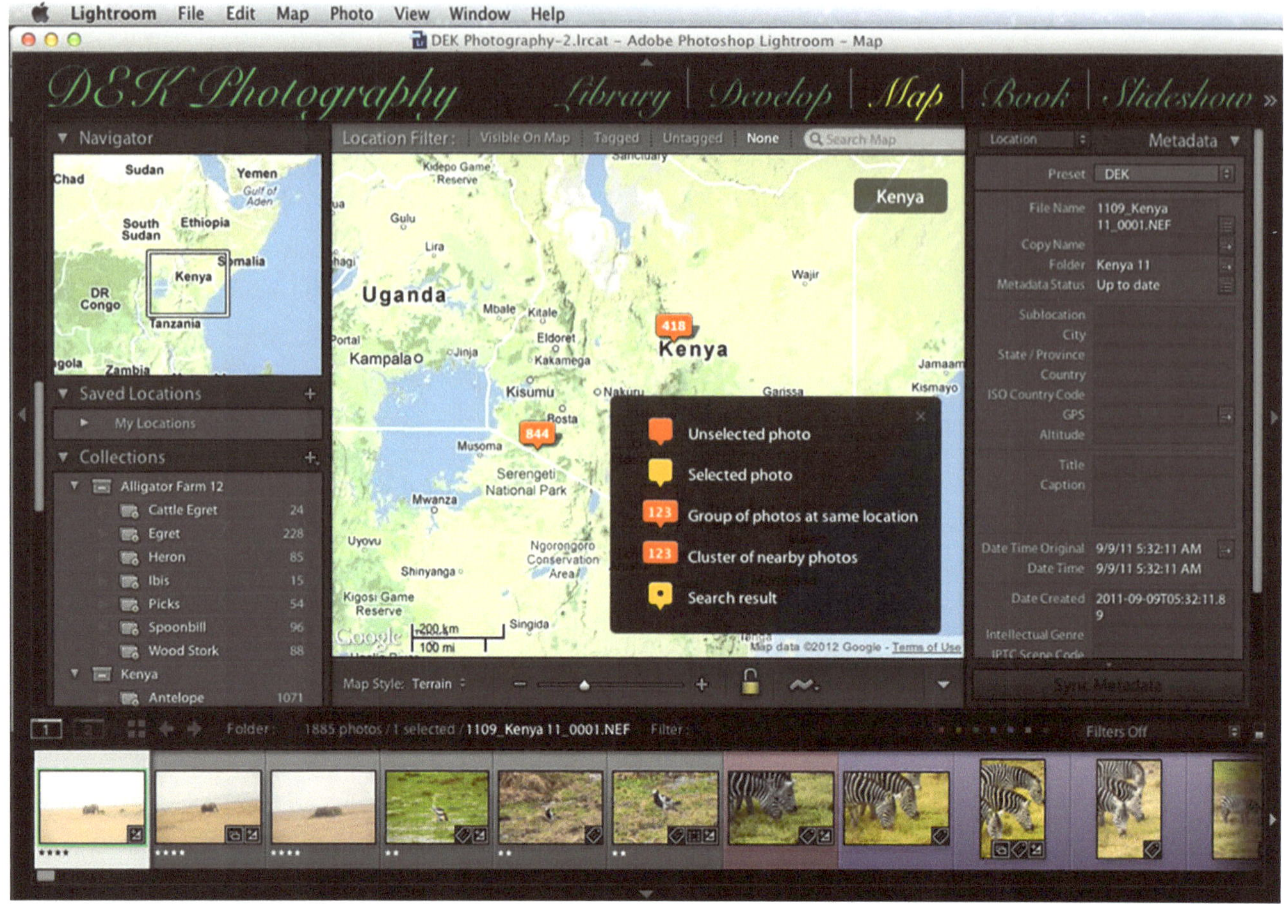


# The Map Module

Photographers group their images together based on a lot of different parameters, people, time, date, year, etc. Now Lightroom®4 makes it easy to organize images based on location in the new Map module. What the Map module really is, is a combining of GPS data embedded in the metadata of an image and Google maps. If your camera automatically embeds GPS data in the image, then when you import your images into Lightroom®4 they will automatically be placed on a Google map at the location they were photographed, but that is only if your computer has internet access. There is a way to organize your images on Google maps if they do not have the GPS coordinates embedded in the metadata and that will be discussed shortly.

### The Screen Setup

To start, the screen in the Map module is quite a bit different from the screen in the other modules. Starting with the menus across the top of the screen, the File, Edit, Photo, View, Window and Help menus are still present and to them a Map menu has been added. The Identity Plate and Module Picker are still across the top of the screen. In the left column of panels, the Navigator window is present, but the magnification levels are gone. Below the Navigator window there are only two panels, Saved Locations and Collections. The Toolbar is present across the bottom of the image, but with fewer choices and the Filmstrip across the bottom of the screen is unchanged. In the right column, only the Metadata panel is still present.

## Viewing the Map

If your images have the GPS data recorded and are placed on the map when you import them you have several views of the map on which you can see your images. There are also a couple of ways to zoom in and out on the map. First, the different map views are Hybrid, Road Map, Satellite, Terrain, Light and Dark. There are three ways you can move between the different map views, they are as follows:

- From the View menu at the top of the screen select the map view from the drop down menu.
- Click with the cursor on the double pointed arrow next to the Map view on the Tool bar (Yellow circle, Figure 53) and choose the Map view from the menu that appears.
- Use the Keyboard shortcut, hold down the Command (Macintosh), Control (PC) key and press the 1 key for the Hybrid map, 2 key for the Road Map, 3 key for the Satellite map, 4 key for the Terrain map, 5 key for the Light map and 6 key for the Dark map.

Figure 53

The cursor in the Map module is not the same magnifying cursor of the Develop module, but you can zoom in and out on the map by doing the following:

- Move the slider bar on the toolbar to the right to zoom in on the map. (Blue ellipse, Figure 53)
- Move the slider bar on the toolbar to the left to zoom out.
- Press the plus (+) key on the keyboard to zoom in on the map.
- Press the minus (-) key on the keyboard to zoom out on the map.
- No modifier key is necessary to zoom in or out with the plus and minus key in the Map module.
- Hold down the Option (Macintosh), Alt (PC) key and drag a square around an area on the map to zoom into that area.
- Use the scroll wheel on your mouse to zoom in and out.

When you zoom in on the map, the places where the images were photographed will spread out showing you exactly where the image was created.

## Placing Images on the Map

If your camera does not embed GPS data into the image there is still a way to place your images on the Google map. To place images that do not have GPS data embedded, do the following:

- In the Search Map blank at the top right of the work area (Blue arrow, Figure 54), type in the location where the images were taken. If you do not have an exact address, Lightroom® will show you several possible locations from which to choose.
- Choose the closest location from the list and Lightroom will place a marker at that location on the map.(Yellow marker, Figure 55)
- If you have the exact address, Lightroom®

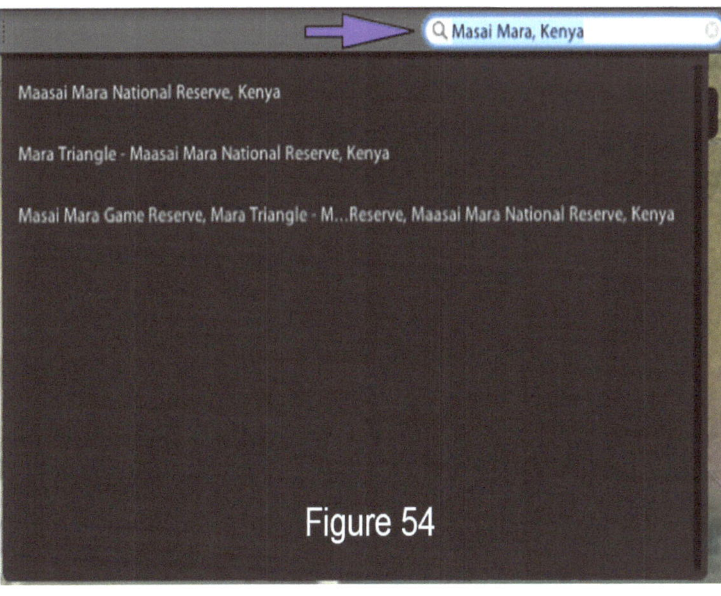


Figure 54

will place the marker on the map at that location.

- Select the images in the Filmstrip at the bottom of the screen that were taken at that location and drag them to the marker on the map.
- When the images are placed on the map, the number of images at that location will be indicated in the marker.
- You can also select images in the Filmstrip and just drag them to a position on the map. Lighroom® will add the GPS location data to the image in the Metadata panel as well as adding the name of the location to the Metadata.
- Another way to pair the images to a location on the map is if you know the GPS location, you can select the images and type the GPS data into the GPS Field in the metadata either in the Library module or the Map module.

Figure 55

- You can also select an image in the Filmstrip and then Control (Macintosh) Right (PC) click a position on the map and Lightroom® will add the GPS coordinates to the metadata of the image.

## The Track Log

- A final way to map your images in the Map module is if you have software that records a Track Log. The file format that Lightroom supports is GPS and there is software available which will convert the data for you.
- Some smart phones and many GPS devices have the ability to record a Track Log.
- To load the Track Log, it will be a GPX file, click with the cursor on the GPS Track Logs icon (Blue circle, Figure 53) and select "Load Track Log" from the menu that appears on screen.
- Load the Track Log into the same folder where your images are stored.
- Click with the cursor on the Track Log and the Track Log will be displayed on the map as a blue trail according to where you walked or drove to take your photos.
- If your camera was not set to the correct time you can select "Set Time Zone Offset" from the GPS Track Logs menu.
- With the Track Log loaded, select the images taken at this location and again click on the Track Log icon and from the menu that appears on screen, select "Auto Tag Photos".
- The photos will then be mapped.

## Scrolling through Images on the Map

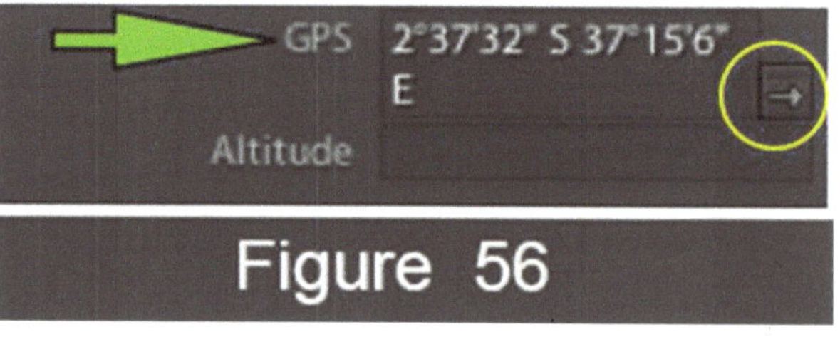

Figure 56

Once you have your images on the map, you can lock the markers in place by clicking with the cursor on the Lock icon on the toolbar (Red circle, Figure 53) or use the keyboard shortcut, hold down the Command (Macintosh), Control (PC) key and press the K key on the keyboard.

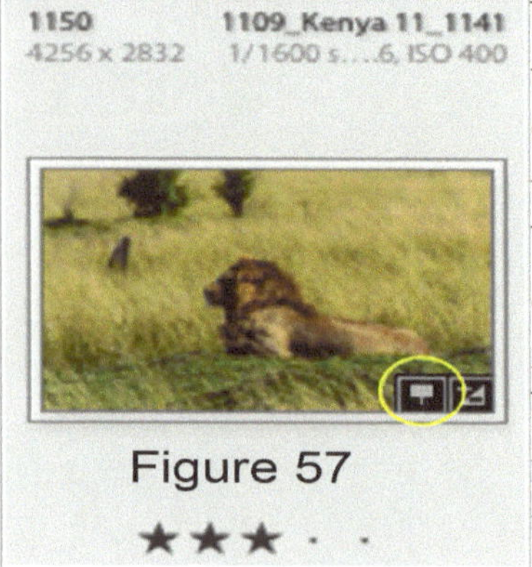

Figure 57

With the images mapped, you'll find that Lightroom® has added the GPS data to the metadata in the Metadata panel. (Green arrow, Figure 56) Also a new badge has been added to the images in both the Grid view of the Library module and in the Filmstrip. (Yellow circle, Figure 57) Clicking with the cursor on either the badge in the Grid view of the Library module or on the badge in the Filmstrip from any module in Lightroom® will bring you to the Map module with the location of the marker on the map on screen. If you click with the cursor on the marker on the map, Lightroom® will show you the first image and allow you to scroll through the images by clicking with the cursor on the right or left pointing arrows on either side of the image. (Yellow circles, Figure 58) The view will be the Loupe view and at the top of the screen will be the info you selected to show in the Loupe view from the View menu in the Library module, either Info 1 or Info 2.

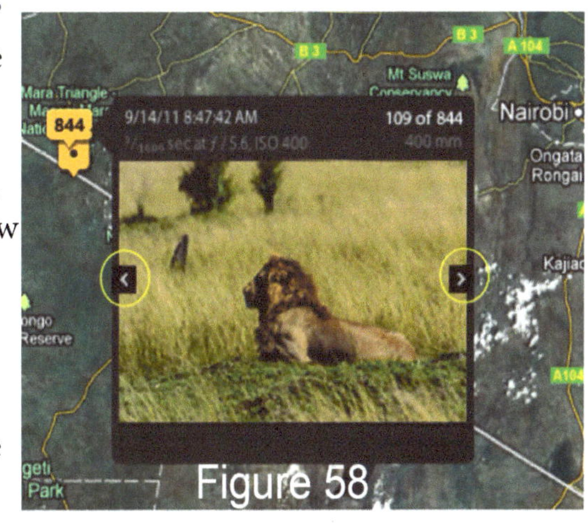

Figure 58

## Saving Locations

If there are areas where you photograph frequently, you can save the locations. To save a location, do the following:

- Open the Map module to one of your locations on which you have mapped images.
- Click with the cursor on the plus (+) sign in the header bar of the Saved Locations panel at the top of the left column.
- A New Location dialog box along with a white circle, which is really a location overlay icon, will appear on screen on the map behind the dialog box. (Figure 59)
- Lightroom® will place a name for the location in the top blank, but you can change it to whatever you want.
- There is a Radius slider bar in the Options section with which you can increase or decrease the size of the location overlay circle.
- To the right of the slider bar is the diameter of the circle and you can choose the unit of measure (Kilometers, Meters, Miles or Feet) by clicking with the cursor on the double pointed arrow in the box to the right of the diameter.
- You can remove the location information from the Metadata when the images are to be exported by placing a check mark in the box labeled "Private". (Blue Ellipse, Figure 59)
- Click with the cursor on the Create button at the bottom right of the dialog box.
- The Location will be in a folder labeled "My Locations" in the Saved Locations panel at the top of the left column of panels.
- After you have created a location, the location overlay white circle will still be on the map. Often the location overlay white circle is too big or not big enough, so, the second way you can change the diameter of the white overlay circle is to click with the cursor on the white circle at the top of the big circle (Yellow circle, Figure 60) and drag it down to make location overlay radius smaller or up to enlarge the location overlay radius.

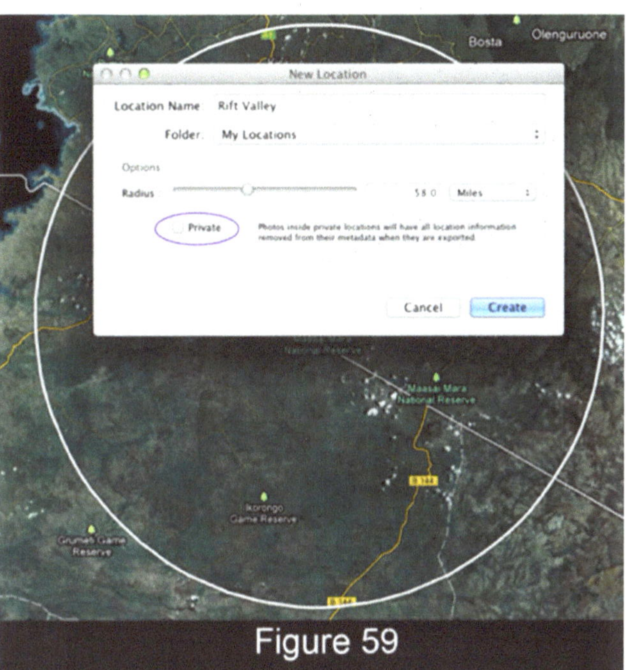

Figure 59

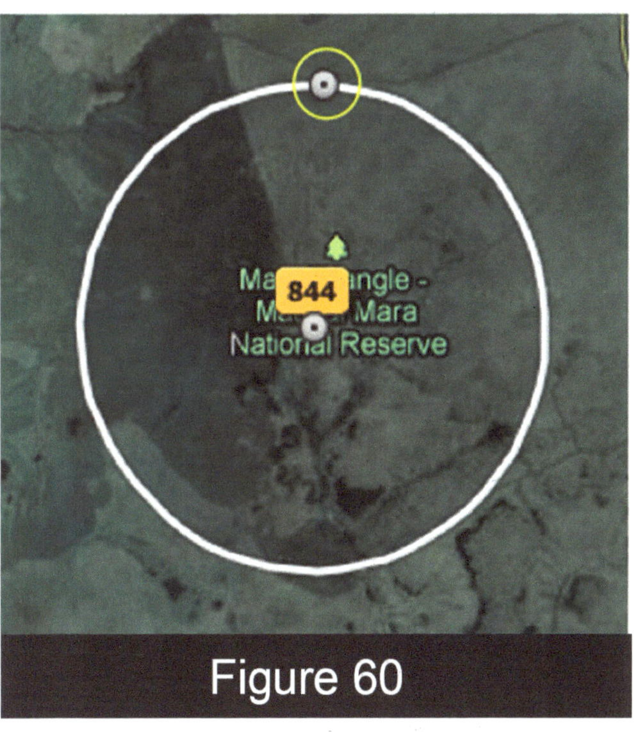

Figure 60

- The location overlay circle can also be moved by clicking with the cursor on the white dot in the center of the circle and moving it to where you want it to be on the map.
- You can toggle the visibility of the location overlay white circle by pressing the O key on the keyboard.

## Viewing all Images

When in the Map module the only images in one of your saved locations you will be able to see will be the ones in the Folder or Collection on which you are currently working. All of the other saved locations will be listed in the Save Locations panel at the top of the left column of panels, but they will indicate that there are no images present. (Figure 61) The Folder or Collection on which you are currently working will have the number of images at the location indicated to the left of the name of the Folder or Collection. To see all of your markers with the numbers of images there are at each location you must go to the Library module, open the Catalog panel and select "All Photographs. With "All Photographs" selected, when you return to the Map module all the saved locations will indicate the number of images at each location. If you want to see all the markers you have placed on the Google maps, you must zoom the map out as far as you need to in order to see where all your markers are placed.

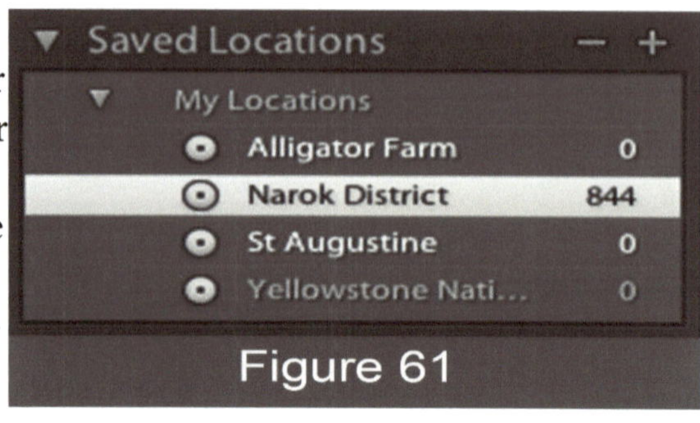

Figure 61

## More Option with the Map Markers

Other options you have with the marker for the images are found by Control (Macintosh), Right (PC) clicking with the cursor on the marker. A pop up menu from which you choose to do the following will appear on screen.

- Zoom in on the images.
- Select images.
- Set all GPS coordinates the same.
- Delete the GPS coordinates from the images.

## Removing GPS and Location Metadata

On occasion you might want to delete the GPS coordinates or all the location metadata from an image, especially one that is to be exported. As previously discussed, you can remove the location information for images to be exported by placing a check mark in the Private box (Blue ellipse, Figure 59) in the New Location dialog box. The second way, mentioned above, is to Control (Macintosh), Right (PC) click on a marker on the map and select "Delete GPS Coordinates" from the pop up menu. The third way is to select the images in the Filmstrip and press the Delete (Macintosh), Backspace (PC) key on the keyboard. A pop up menu will appear on screen asking you if you want to delete the GPS coordinates from all the selected photos or just the active one. (Figure 62) With the images selected in the Filmstrip, you can also remove all the location metadata from the images by holding down the Command (Macintosh), Control (PC) key and pressing the Delete (Macintosh), Backspace(PC) key on the keyboard. The same pop up menu will appear on screen asking you if you want to delete all the location metadata from the selected images or just from the active image. (Figure 62)

Figure 62

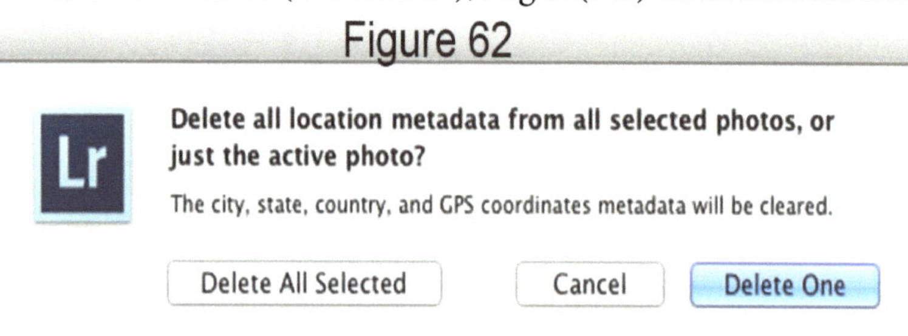

## The Location Filter Bar

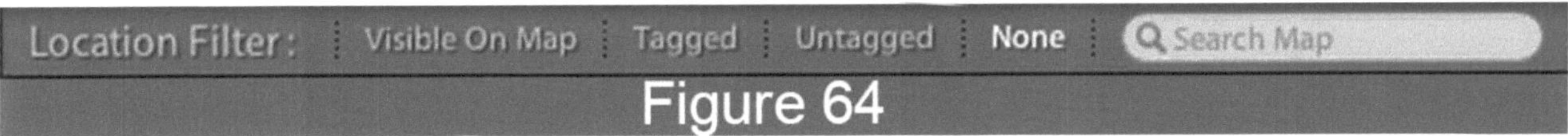


Figure 64

At the top of the screen in the Map module is a Location filter bar that depending on which selection you make in the filter bar will highlight images in the Filmstrip. The following are the choices you have in this filter bar:

- Images that are visible on the map.
- Images that are tagged.
- Images that are not tagged
- All the images in the filmstrip.

For example, if you select "Visible on the Map" the images that are visible on the map will be highlighted in the Filmstrip. Selecting "None" from this filter bar will show you all the images in the Filmstrip with none of them highlighted. You can select "Tagged" to see images that are tagged, usually the same as those visible on the map

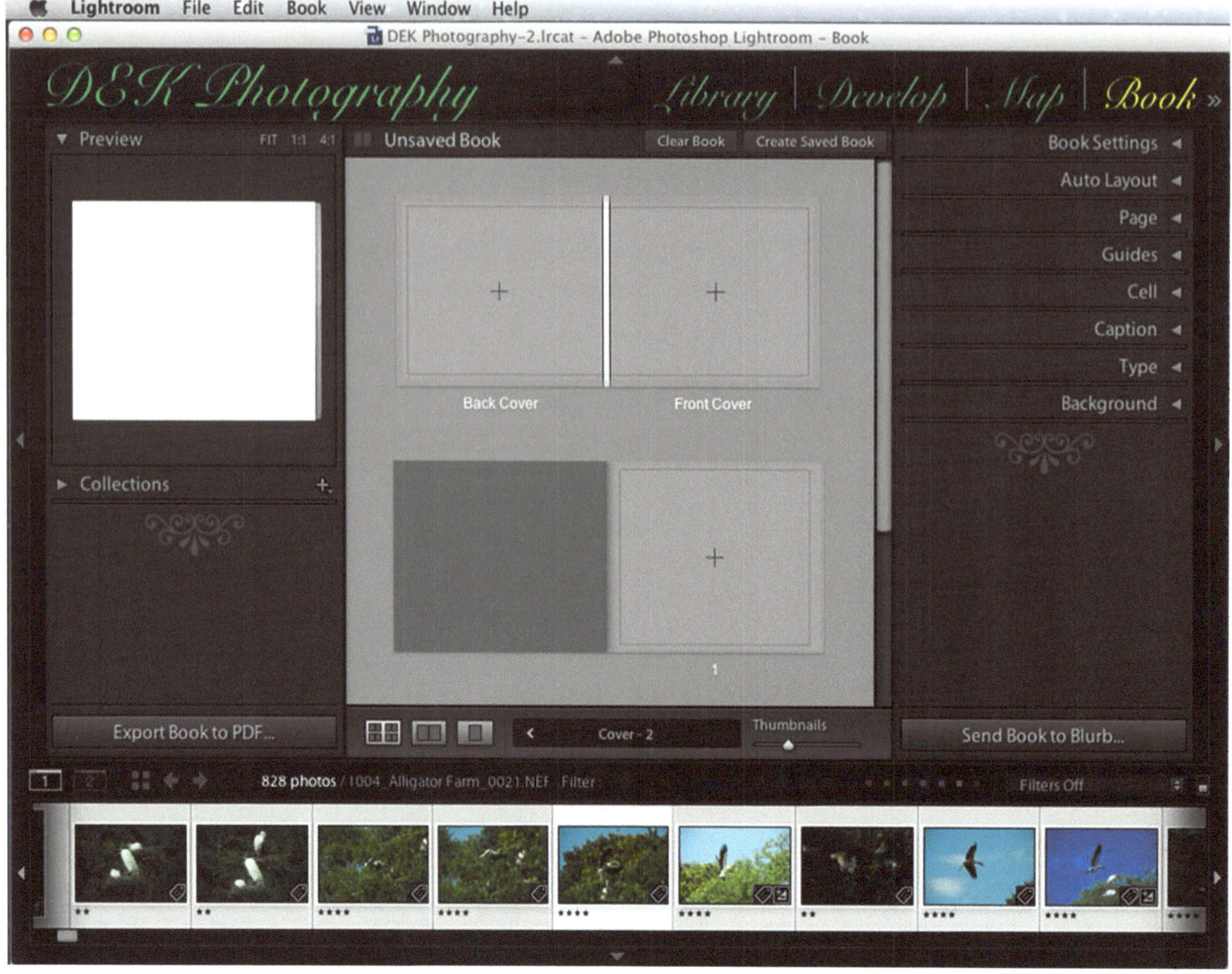


# The Book Module

New to Lightroom®4 is the Book module. You now have the ability to publish your own book of images directly from Lightroom® and it's easy. Before you start creating your book, it's a good idea to think about why you want to do it. Just like creating an image with your camera, you want to have an idea of what you want to convey to the viewer or what attracted you to the scene. When creating a book of your images, you want to have an idea of what you want to show the reader. It might be something as simple as showcasing your images as in a portfolio that will get you more jobs or clients or you have a series of personal images or images of your family you want to collect together and share with them as a keepsake or you want to show images from a trip. There are many good reasons to create a book.

### The Screen Setup

In the Book module the menus at the top of the screen have changed. Now in addition to the File, Edit, View, Window and Help menus there is the Book menu. The Lighroom® menu, Identity Plate and Module Picker are still there. However, in the left column of panels, there is only a preview window at the top, with three choices of magnification levels, Fit, 1:1 and 4:1, the Collections panel and a button that allows you to export your book to a PDF. The work area on the center of the screen now contains thumbnails in which you will find the Back and Front cover at the top and below the covers you will find left and right page layouts, called Spreads. The Filmstrip is unchanged, but the toolbar has changed. In the Book module there are three icons on the left side of the toolbar that allow you to see multi-pages, a single spread and an individual page. In the center of the toolbar is a blank that will let you scroll through the pages in your book when you are in either the spread view or the page view. On the right side of the toolbar is a thumbnail slider which allows you to increase or decrease the size of the thumbnails of the spreads or the pages.

## Preparing the images

Before taking the images into the Book module, there are several tasks to accomplish. Starting in the Library module, you will need to make a couple of decisions. First, decide what the title of the book will be and second, decide which images you want in the book. The best way to organize the images is to put them in a Collection. For organization, if you feel you are going to create more than one book, it would be a good idea to create a Collection Set and then create a Collection for each book you plan to create, inside the Collection Set. Once you have the images for one book in a Collection there are a couple of things that will make things easier for you in the future especially if the images are from different folders. Here is what you should do next:

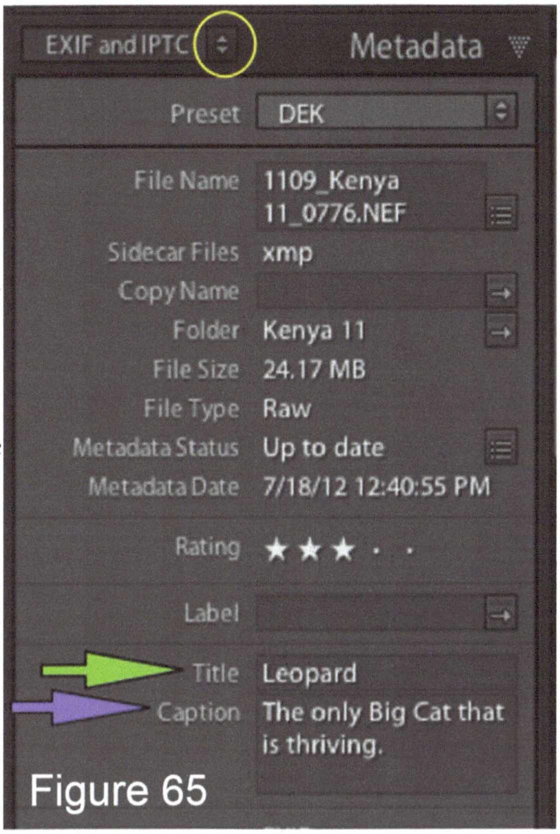

- From the Edit menu at the top of the screen click with the cursor on "Select All", OR
- Use the keyboard shortcut, hold down the Command (Macintosh), Control (PC) key and press the A key on the keyboard.
- Go to the Keywording panel and type in a keyword that has part or all of the title of your book.
- While still in the Metadata panel, click with the cursor on the double pointed arrow next to the Metadata Set blank at the top of the Metadata panel (Yellow circle, Figure 65) and choose "Large Caption".
- In the Large Caption blank, (Blue arrow, Figure 65) type in descriptive information you want to show along with the image in your book.
- Type in a title for the image in the Title blank (Green arrow, Figure 65)
- If there are images on which you would like to place a develop preset or convert to black and white, select those images and open them in the Develop module to place those develop settings on them.
- When finished with the captions and placing develop settings on the images, move the Collection to the Book module by either clicking with the cursor on the Book module in the module picker at the top of the screen or use the keyboard shortcut, hold down the Command and Option (Macintosh), Control and Alt (PC) keys and press the 4 key on the keyboard.

Figure 65

TIP: You can add or change captions to the images in the book after creating it, but you will need to go back to the Metadata panel in the Library module to change the captions and then from the Book menu at the top of the screen, select "Update Metadata Captions". Now you are ready to go to the Book module.

## Book Settings

The top panel in the right side column of panels is where you will find the Book Settings. (Figure 66) Adobe has partnered with Blurb® allowing you to upload your book directly to the Blurb® website from Lightroom® and have it printed. There is a double pointed arrow next to Blurb® that will give you a choice of having your book printed to a PDF or JPEG. You would want to do this if you were going to have some one other than Blurb® print your book. The advantage of having Blurb® print your book is that you can choose the size and layout of the book, the type of cover and the paper quality. To make your choice of the size, layout, cover and paper quality click on the double pointed arrow to the right of each of the choices. You will get an idea of what Blurb® will charge you to print the book when you make selections for each of the choices. The cost will be shown at the bottom of the Book Settings panel and will automatically change as you make your choices. The last choice to make in the Book Settings panel is whether or not you want the Blurb® logo on the last page of your book. Letting Blurb® place their logo on the last page will significantly reduce the cost of the book.

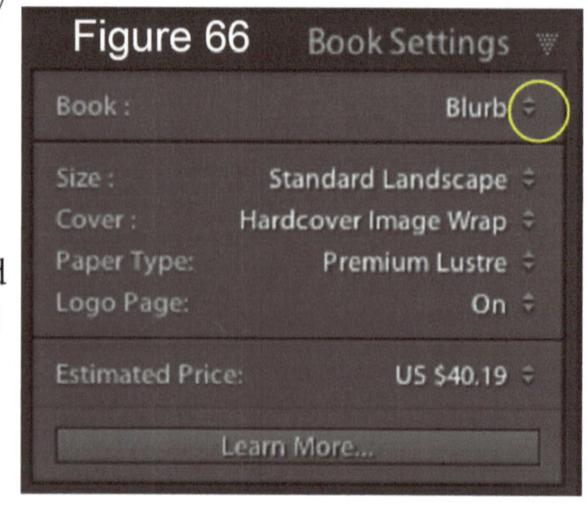


## Book Preferences

To find the book preferences, go to the Book menu at the top of the screen and from the drop down menu select "Book Preferences". A pop up Book Preferences dialog box will appear on screen. (Figure 67) In the top section, you get to choose whether the image fills the page or fits on the page. (Blue arrow, Figure 67) If you choose "Zoom to Fill", the image will take up the whole page and probably be cropped. Choosing "Zoom to Fit", the image will fit in the frame on the page and will not be cropped.

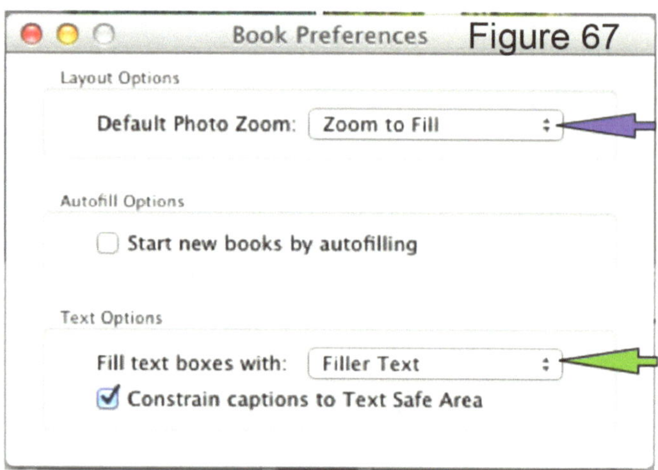


In the second section of the Book Preferences dialog box you can have Lightroom® automatically place the images in the spaces on the page. If you want Lightroom® to do this then place a check mark in the box in front of "Start new books by auto filling". If you would rather manually place the images on the pages then leave the box in this section unchecked.

The third section you can choose to have Lightroom® place filler text in the text boxes or place title or caption metadata in the text boxes. (Green arrow, Figure 67)

## The Auto Layout Panel

The Second panel in the right column of panels is the Auto Layout panel. (Figure 68) In the top section of the Auto Layout panel are the Presets. The default preset is One Photo Per Page. Clicking with the cursor on the double pointed arrow next to the default preset will show you three other presets from which you can choose. They are as follows:

- Left Blank, Right One Photo, Caption
- Left Blank, Right One Photo
- One Photo Per Page (default)

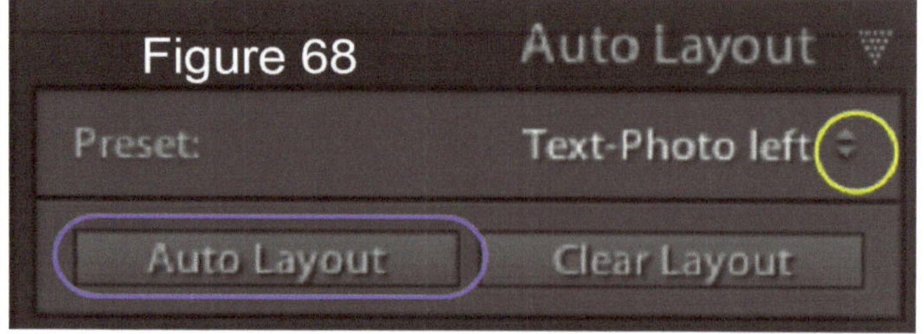

## Editing the Auto Layout Presets

The final choice in the Auto Layout drop down menu is "Edit Auto Layout Preset". (Figure 69) Choosing the Edit option will bring up the Auto Layout Preset Editor. (Figure 70) In the blank at the top of the dialog box is the One Photo Per Page default preset with a double pointed arrow to the right. (Black circle, Figure 70) Clicking with the cursor on the double pointed arrow shows you the other available presets. In the dialog box, both the left and right pages are shown. At the top of the left side is a blank that by default says "Same as Right Side" with a double pointed arrow to the right of this choice. (Red circle, Figure 70) Clicking with the cursor on this double pointed arrow will, in addition to the default, give you the choice of leaving the page blank or two other choices, "Random from Favorites" and "Fixed Layout". Initially, leave the default as "Same as Right Side" for which the default is Fixed Layout. To edit the Auto layout presets, do the following:

Left Blank, Right One Photo, Caption
Left Blank, Right One Photo
One Photo Per Page
✓ Text-Photo left

Edit Auto Layout Preset...

Figure 69

- The second blank under Fixed Layout on the right pages says "1 Photo" with a double pointed arrow to the right. Clicking with the cursor on this double pointed arrow (Blue circle, Figure 70) will present you with eleven different choices for arranging pictures on a page, everything from 1 photo per Page to multiple photos per page.
- Each of the choices has a different number of choices. For example, 1 Photo has forty-seven different page layouts, 2 photos has thirty-six different page layouts, 3 photos has 28 different page layouts, etc.
- Many of the page layouts have text boxes included.
- Some of the page layouts at the bottom of the Modify Page menu are identical to the one, two, three and four page layouts, but with some additions such as vignetting or frames.
- Scroll through the different layouts and choose the one that best suits your needs.
- After choosing the layout, choose whether to have the images zoom to fit or fill the space on the chosen page and whether to match the long edges.
- Finally choose whether you want the metadata captions to show on the page and align with the photo. Also choose the font for the captions by checking the appropriate boxes.
- When your choices for the layout are made click with the cursor on the double pointed arrow to the right of the Preset blank at the top of the dialog box (Black circle, Figure 70) and choose "Save Current Settings as New Preset" from the pop up menu that appears on screen.
- A New Preset dialog box will pop up on screen in which you can name the new preset and create it by clicking with the cursor on the Create button at the bottom right of the dialog box.

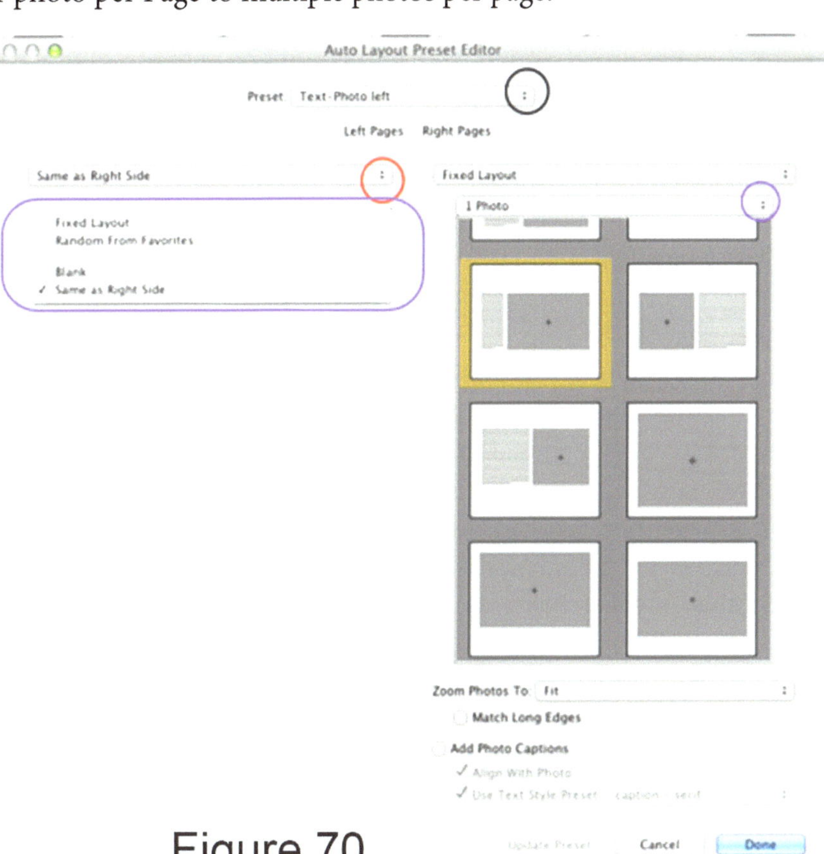


Figure 70

TIP: You can edit your preset later by selecting it in the Presets box at the top of the Auto Layout Preset Editor dialog box. All you have to do is make the changes in the layout and then either click with the cursor on the "Update Preset" button at the bottom left of the dialog box or choose "Update Preset" from the Preset drop down menu at the top of the dialog box. You can also delete the preset from this same Preset drop down menu at the top of the Auto Layout Preset Editor dialog box.

## Placing, Organizing and Removing the Images on a Page

Once you have prepared you images, moved them into a Collection and into the Book module, selected your book settings, preferences and decided on the page layout all you need to do in the Auto Layout panel is click with the Cursor on the Auto Layout button in the panel. (Blue ellipse, Figure 68) Lightroom® will determine how many pages it needs and populate all the spaces on each page with the images. If you have chosen a page layout with multiple images, Lightroom® will populate the spaces with the images in your collection starting with the first one. For example, if you have chosen a page layout with four images, the first four images in the image collection will be placed on the first page, the second four images in the image collection will be placed on the second page and so on. To add the images manually, select the image and drag it to a blank page or a frame on a multi-image page. The page will have a yellow highlight around the frame when you hover the image over the page and when you release the cursor the image will be placed on the page. If you change your mind about the image you want on a page simply select another image and drag it to the same page. The page will again be highlighted in yellow when you hover the image over it and when you release the cursor the new image will replace the previous image on the page. In addition to changing the image on a page the following are what you can do with the images placed on the pages:

- Move any image to a new page by clicking on it with the cursor and dragging it to a new position.
- Swap an image in a spread or with another image in another spread. Simply select the image and move it to the image with which you want to swap it. When you release the cursor, the images will be swapped.
- Move a page or spread to a new position in the book by, in the Multi-page view, click with the cursor on a page or in a spread, click on one image in the spread and then hold down the Shift key and click on the other page in the spread. You can then click with the cursor in the yellow bar at the bottom of an image or spread and drag the page or spread to a new position in the Multi-Page view. When you get the page or spread to the new position, a vertical yellow line will appear in the new position, indicating it is OK to move the page or spread to that position. Release the image and it will be in the new position.
- Move multiple spreads by clicking with the cursor on one page of a spread and then Shift click on the other page in the spread. Then continue to hold down the Shift Key and click on other images in other spreads if the spreads are consecutive or Command/Control click on other spreads if they are not consecutive. You can select as many spreads to move as you want, even if they are not consecutive spreads.
- To move the spreads to a new position, click with the cursor in the yellow tab area underneath one of the spreads and drag the spreads to a new position. A vertical yellow line will appear telling you it is OK to move the Spreads to that position. Release the cursor and the spreads will be in their new positions.
- The Spreads will be placed in the new positions in the order in which you Shift or Command/Control clicked on them.
- Delete an image from a page by clicking with the cursor on the image to select it and then pressing the Delete (Macintosh), Backspace (PC) key.
- Remove an image from a page by Control (Macintosh), Right (PC) clicking on the image and from the resulting on screen menu select "Remove Photo".
- Remove a page on which there is an image by Control (Macintosh), Right (PC) clicking on the page and selecting "Remove Page" from the resulting menu.
- Zoom in on an image, which is really cropping the image on the page, by clicking with the cursor on the image and moving the zoom slider bar that appears above the page to the right. (Figure 71)
- Move the zoomed in image around on the page by clicking with the cursor on the image, holding down the cursor and moving the image around on the page until the portion you want to see is visible.

TIP: You can set the zoom rate for multiple images or all the images in the book by doing the following:

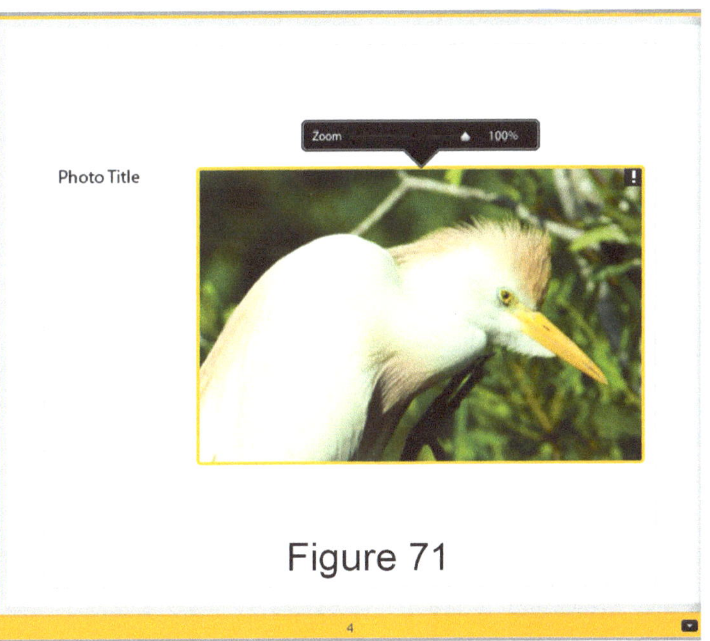

Figure 71

- In the Multi-page view, click with the cursor on one page in a spread and then hold down the Command (Macintosh), Control (PC) key on the keyboard and click with the cursor on other images to select them. Select as many as you like.
- Next, click with the cursor on one image to bring up the zoom slider on top of the image.
- Move the zoom slider at the top of one of the images to the right and all the images will zoom to the same zoom setting.
- Set the zoom rate for all the images in your book by going to the Edit Menu and from that menu choosing "Select All Photo Cells"
- Alternatively, use the keyboard shortcut, hold down the Shift, Command and Option (Macintosh), Shift, Control and Alt (PC) keys and press the A key on the keyboard.
- Next, click with the cursor on one image to bring up the Zoom slider.
- Move the zoom slider to the right and all the images will zoom to the same level.
- After setting the zoom level, especially for multiple images, check all the images to make sure you don't need to move some of them to get what you want to show on the page.
- When you are finished setting the zoom rate for all the images click with the cursor on the background to deselect all the images.

## Viewing One Spread or One Image

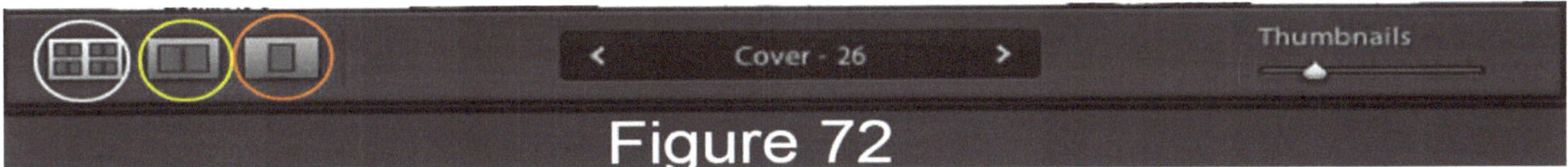

Figure 72

With the images placed on the pages there are several ways you can view individual pages or right and left pages, called Spreads together. In the Toolbar of the Book module, there are three icons on the left side that are used to show you all the pages, a spread or one page. By default, when you populate the pages in the Auto Layout panel you will be looking at the multi-page view, the back and front covers at the top and all the spreads. The multi-page icon in the toolbar (White circle, Figure 72) will be active. You can increase or decrease the size of the thumbnails in the Multi-page view by pressing the plus (+) or minus (-) key on the keyboard. Clicking on the second icon will bring up on screen the selected spread. (Yellow circle, Figure 72) If no spread is selected, Lightroom® will bring up the first spread on screen. With the spread on screen, you can click with the cursor on either the left or right page and the zoom slider bar will appear at the top of the page. You can zoom in on the image by moving the zoom slider to the right and move the image around on the page by clicking with the cursor on the image and dragging it. Clicking with the cursor on the third icon will bring up a selected page on screen. (Red circle, Figure 72) If no page is selected Lightroom® will bring up the first page. Again, the zoom slider will appear on screen at the top of the page and you will be able to zoom in on the image and move it around on the page. A second way to bring up just one page is to double click with the cursor on a page. When dealing with the back and front cover spread at the top of the page, you can only bring up both images, not one at a time. Even double clicking with the cursor on either the back or front cover brings up both images. You can click with the cursor on one cover and the zoom slider will appear above the image allowing you to zoom in on the image and then click with the cursor on it and move the image around on the cover. Another way to cycle through the views from multi-page view to spread view to page view is to hold down the Command (Macintosh), control (PC) key and press the plus (+) or minus (-) key on the keyboard. Starting from the multi page view, the first time you press the plus key on the keyboard while holding down the modifier Command or Control key, the multi-page view will become the spread view. The second time you press the plus key when holding down the Command/Control key the spread view will become the page view. The third time you press the plus key, the image on the page will be magnified. Holding down the modifier Command/Control key and pressing the minus (-) key on the keyboard will cycle the images back from magnified to page view to spread view to multi-page view. Of course, there are also keyboard shortcuts to cycle through the different views. Holding down the Command (Macintosh), Control (PC) key and pressing the E key on the keyboard will take you to the multi-page view, pressing the R key on the keyboard while holding down the modifier Command/Control key will take you to the spread view and pressing the T key on the keyboard while holding down the modifier Command/Control key will show you the single page view.

## The Page Panel

Below the Auto Layout panel is the Page panel. It has some of the same information as the Auto Layout panel regarding page Layouts, but in the Page panel you can change all of the page layouts or only one page layout. You can also add a page, add a page with a different layout or a blank page. To change the page layout for all of the pages in your book, do the following:

- Click with the cursor on the Multi-image icon in the toolbar. (White circle, Figure 72)
- From the Edit menu at the top of the screen choose "Select All".
- Click with the cursor on the down pointing arrow on the right side of the Page panel. (Yellow circle, Figure 73)
- Choose a new page layout from the resulting on screen Modify Page menu that appears. (Figure 73A)
- Click with the cursor on the selected new page layout in the Modify Page menu.
- All of the pages will now have the new page layout.

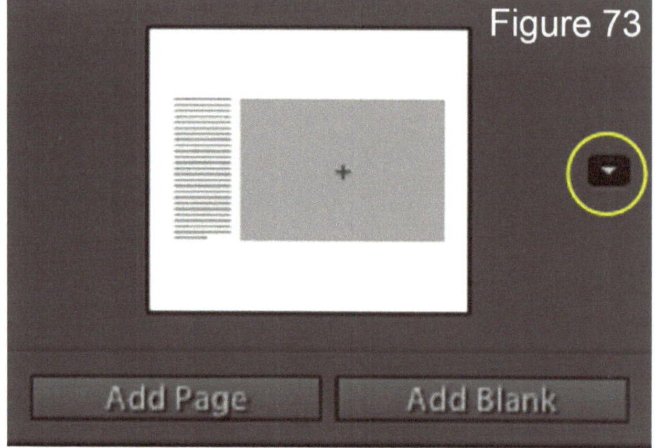


To change the layout of both images in a spread or just one page of a spread, do the following:

- Highlight the spread by clicking with the cursor on one page and then hold down the Shift key on the keyboard and click with the cursor on the other page in the spread.
- To change only one page in the spread, click with the cursor on the page with the layout you want to change.
- Click with the cursor on the down pointing arrow on the right side of the Page panel (Yellow circle, Figure 73) to bring up the Modify Page menu. (Figure 73A)
- From the Modify Page menu that appears choose the new page layout.
- Click with the cursor on the new page layout in the Modify Page menu.
- Both images in the spread or the highlighted page in the spread will change to the new page layout.

To add a page, either a page for a picture or a blank page, do the following:

- Click with the cursor on the Multi-page view icon in the toolbar.
- Select the page after which you want the new page to show up.

- To add a page with a layout for a picture and/or text, click with the cursor on the "Add a Page" button at the bottom left of the Page panel.(Figure 73)
- To add a blank page, click with the cursor on the "Add Blank" button at the bottom right of the Page panel. (Figure 73)
- The new page will be placed after the selected page in the book.
- If you selected a left page, the new page will be the right page in that spread.
- If you selected the right page of a spread, the new page will be the left page in the following spread.

Figure 73A

Modify Page:
Favorites
1 Photo
2 Photos
3 Photos
4 Photos
Multiple Photos
Two-Page Spreads
Text Pages
Clean
Creative
Portfolio
Travel
Wedding

TIP: By default, the new page will have the same layout as the selected page after which you added the new page, unless you clicked with the cursor on the "Add Blank" button. You can change the layout to any layout you wish by choosing the new layout from the Modify Page menu (Figure 73A)that appears when you click with the cursor on the down pointing arrow on the right side of the Page panel. (Yellow circle, Figure 73)

One or more of the page layouts will probably turn out to be your favorites. In that case, you should save those layouts as your favorites. All you have to do is click with the cursor on the disclosure arrow at the bottom of one of the pages that has your favorite layout (Blue circle, Figure 74) or in the Page panel, click on the disclosure arrow to the right of the template in the panel to bring up the Modify Page menu (Figure 73A) with all the templates. Scroll to your favorite page layout and Control (Macintosh), Right (PC) click with the cursor on the layout. The words "Add Layout to Favorites" will appear on screen. When you move your cursor over these words, a blue band will appear over the words. Click with the cursor on the blue band and the layout will be added to your favorites. The next time you bring up the Modify Page menu of layouts, clicking on "Favorites" at the top will show you all the layouts you have indicated to Lightroom® are your favorites and you will not have to scroll through all the layouts to find the one you want. If you want to remove a layout from your favorites, all you have to do is bring up your favorites in the Modify Page menu and Control (Macintosh), Right (PC) click on the layout you want to remove and the words "Remove Layout from Favorites" will appear with a blue band across them. Click with the cursor on the blue band and the layout will be removed from your favorites.

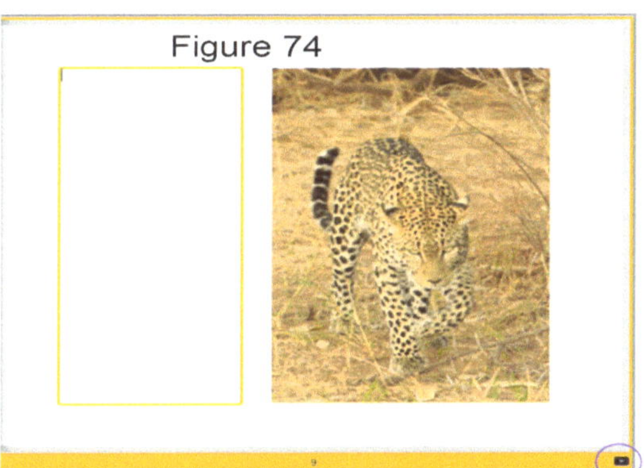
Figure 74

## The Guide Panel

The Guide panel (Figure 76) gives you some very useful information about how your final book will look when printed. Placing a check mark in the different boxes in this panel will show you how the pages will be affected by printing. You can activate the Guide panel by placing a check mark in the "Show Guides" box at the top left of the Guides panel. The following are what placing a check mark in the individual boxes will show you:

- Placing a check mark in the top box, Page Bleed" will gray out the edges of the page and show you an area that may be cropped out when the book is printed. This can be important if you have selected a page layout where the image fills the entire page.
- Placing a check mark in the second box, Text Safe Area, will show you a gray box on the image. All of your text captions, titles and information must be inside that gray box for them to be printed.
- The Third box, Photo Cells, is important if you have a page layout containing multiple cells. By placing a check mark in the box in front of Photo Cells, you will be able to see all of the cells whether

they have images in them or not. By default the main cell on the page will have an image in it and you just have to drag an image to the other cells. If the box is turned off, you will not be able to see the cells. You can still select an image and drag it to the other cells, because when you drag an image over the cell, the cell outline will become visible. It is just easier to drag the images to the cells when they are visible.

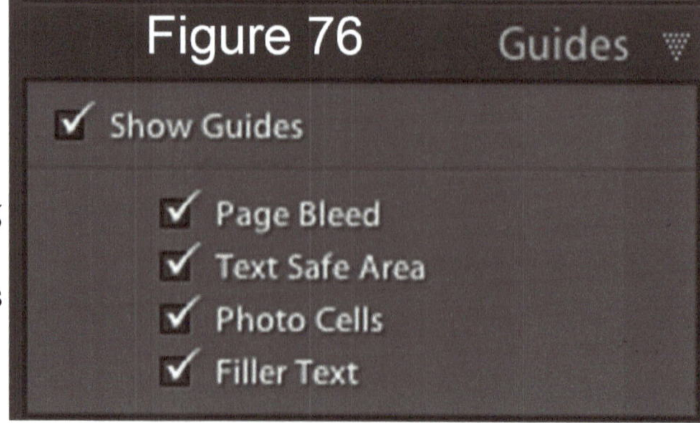


- The last check box is for Filler Text. If in the Book Preferences you chose to fill text boxes with Filler Text, then that text will show up anywhere you have a text box in your book. If you did select to fill the text boxes with Filler Text, it is a good idea to turn this checkbox on because it will remind you where you need to add text in your final product. Even if you forget to add text to a text box, the Filler Text will not print in the final product.

## Cells and Padding

The next panel down is the Cell panel. (Figure 77) Here you can change the size of the image on a page and move it right or left or up and down. Be default, when you first open the Cell panel the top of the panel will say “Padding” and there will be one Amount slider bar in the panel. The Cell panel will be available in any of the views, Multi-page, Spread or Single Page views, but unless you have a page chosen the slider will be grayed out. Once you choose a page by clicking on it with the cursor, you can move the slider on the bar to the right and all four sides of the page will move toward the center of the page producing a smaller image in the center with an increasingly larger white border. If you click with the cursor on the black down pointing disclosure arrow (Yellow circle, Figure 77) to the right of the slider, the panel will be enlarged and you will now have four slider bars, one for all four sides. (Figure 77) By default, the four sliders will be linked and moving one slider to the right will move all sliders to the right, producing the same effect as the single Amount slider. Unlink the sliders by clicking with the cursor on the box to the left of “Link All”. (Red circle, Figure 77) You will then be able to move one slider by itself. For example, moving the Left slider to the right will move the image to the right side of the page and decrease its size while making the white border on the left side of the page larger. Moving any one of the sliders to the right will make the white border on that side larger and move the image. In this way you can make room for a text box or another image on any of the four sides of the image. Another use for the Padding is to place a gutter between images on the same page. For example, if you have chosen a page layout with four images and then selected zoom to fill, the images will be right next to each other without a gutter between them. In the Cell panel, you can select one of the four images, unlink the sliders and place a gutter between the left and right images by moving the right and left sliders the same amount for each image. Next, move the top and bottom sliders the same amount to create a gutter between the top and bottom images. You must unlink the sliders each time you switch images and move each slider the same amount to create four equal size images. Rather than moving the sliders, the easy way to create an equal size gutter is to click with the cursor in the scrubby slider box to the right of each slider and type an equal value into each of the boxes.

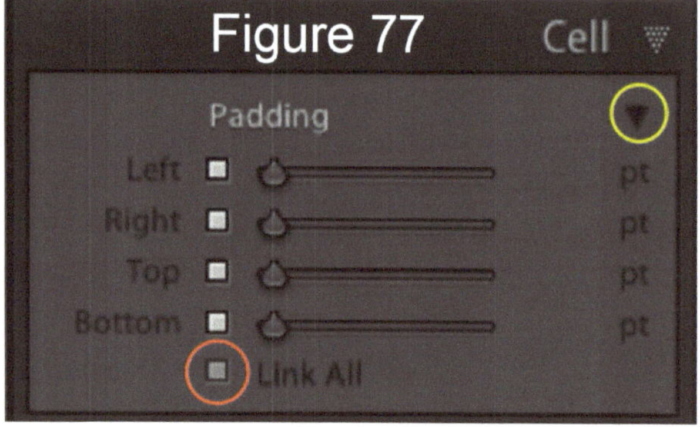


If your are in either the Spread view or the Single Page view, the zoom slider will be present at the top of the page allowing you to zoom in on the image and then move it around on the page.

## Saving the Book

With the images placed in the layout and cropped and padded the way you want them, it's a good idea to save the Book. Before you save your book take the time to go through the images one more time to make sure you have taken care of all of the problems with all of the images. This would include spot removal, noise reduction, anything that will detract from the image. Now you are ready to save your book. If you look at the upper left corner of the work area, you will see the words "Unsaved Book". Even though Lightroom® has a bit of a memory for what you've accomplished in organizing and placing your images in your book, you want Lightroom® to remember all the settings you created in addition to image placement and organization, so, saving it is still something you want to do on a regular basis. Your book will be saved to the Collections panel. There are four ways to create a saved book, they are as follows:

- Click with the cursor on the "Create Saved Book" Button at the top right of the work area.
- Click on the plus (+) sign in the header bar of the Collections panel.
- From the Book menu at the top of the screen, select "Create Saved Book".
- Use the keyboard shortcut, hold down the Command (Macintosh), Control (PC) key and press the S key on the keyboard.

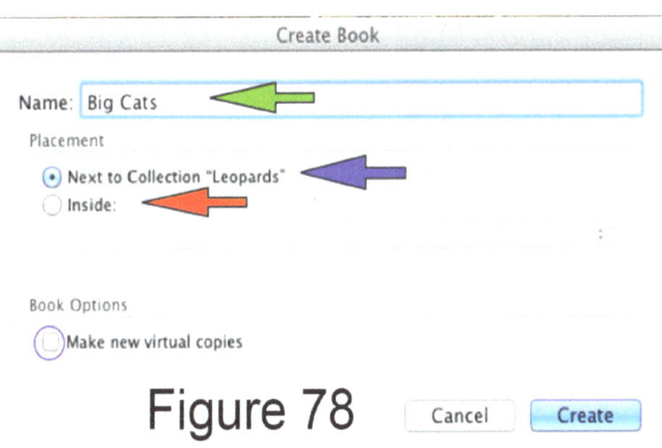

Figure 78

All of these methods will bring up on screen the Create Book dialog box. (Figure 78) In the top blank, (Green arrow, Figure 78)give your book a generic name, not the name for the final book. If you created a Collection Set for books, place the new book inside that Collection Set (Red arrow, Figure 78)and in the Collections panel on the left side of the work area you will see your book in the Book Collection Set. If you did not create a Book Collection set, your book will be saved as a Collection in the Collections panel. (Blue arrow, Figure 78) When you are in the Library module, if you go to the Collections panel and hover the cursor over the book to highlight your book, a right pointing arrow will show up to the right of the generic name of the book. Clicking with the cursor on that right pointing arrow will open your book in the Book module.

Another option you have in the Create Book dialog box is to Make new virtual copies. You will find a checkbox in the bottom section of the Create Book dialog box. (Blue circle, Figure 78) If you click with the cursor in this check box, when you create your book, Lightroom® will convert all the images in the book to Virtual Copies. The advantage to doing this is that should you work on an image that is in the book in the Develop module for another purpose, to print it for example, any develop settings you place on that image will also be placed on the image in the book if it is the Master Copy of the original image. The image will not be affected if it is a Virtual Copy.

## The Caption Panel

To add some extra interest or insight to your book you may want to place titles or captions on your images. This is done in the Captions panel. (Figure 79) There are two sections to the Captions panel, the top section is for adding a title or caption to a selected photo. If you have a photo layout with multiple photos you can add a title to each photo. The bottom section is for adding a title or caption to the page. Starting with the top section, there are two ways you can add a title or caption to an image. The first way is in the Book module. To add a title or caption in the Book module, do the following.

- Select the photo to which you want to add a title or caption.

- When you select the photo, the Captions panel becomes active.
- Place a check mark in the box in front of the words "Photo Caption" by clicking in the box with the cursor. (Red circle, Figure 79)
- A text field will appear on the page beneath the image. (Blue arrow, Figure 80)
- Type a title or caption in this text field.
- Be aware, that whatever you type in the text field will only apply to the book module.

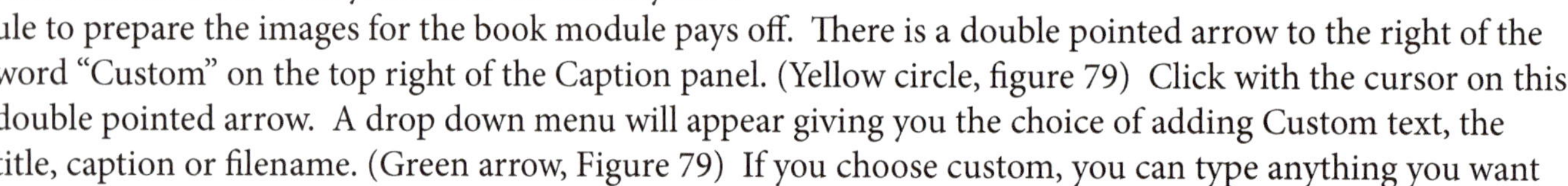

The second way to add a title or caption to an image is where all the hard work you did in the Library module to prepare the images for the book module pays off. There is a double pointed arrow to the right of the word "Custom" on the top right of the Caption panel. (Yellow circle, figure 79) Click with the cursor on this double pointed arrow. A drop down menu will appear giving you the choice of adding Custom text, the title, caption or filename. (Green arrow, Figure 79) If you choose custom, you can type anything you want in the text field, but if you choose any of the latter three, Lightroom® will pull the title, caption or filename from the metadata and place it in the text field. If you did not place captions, titles, etc. on your images in the Library module, you can go back to the Library module and fill in the title and captions blanks in the Metadata panel so they will show in the Book module. The advantage to filling out the title and captions in the Metadata panel in the Library module is that the information will stay with the image in all the modules. Any custom information you place on an image in the Book module will only be available in the Book module. So, it's worth it to prepare the images in the Library module before moving the Collection to the Book module.

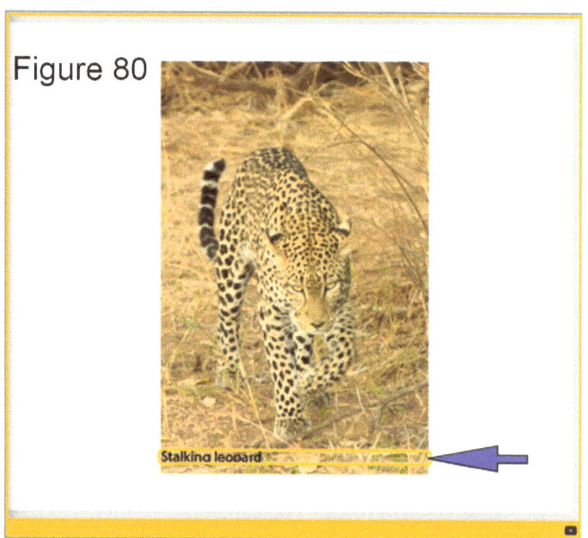


You can place the text field with the title, caption, filename or custom text above, below or over the image by clicking with the cursor on the appropriate button at the bottom of the first section of the Caption panel. You can also offset the text field by clicking on the Offset slider bar and moving the text field up or down. Placing a check mark in the box labeled "Align With Photo (White circle, Figure 79)will place the text inside the borders of the image. (Blue arrow, Figure 80)

The second section of the Caption panel is for placing a Page Caption. Page Captions can be useful if you have a multi-image layout and you want to make a page caption that includes all the images on the page. Make sure you select an image and then place a check mark in the box in front of the words "Page Caption" to activate the captions panel. A text field will appear below the image. You can place this text field at the top or bottom of the image by clicking with the cursor on the appropriate button at the bottom of the Page Caption section of the Caption panel. You can also offset the Page Caption by sliding the slider on the offset slider bar in the Page Caption section of the Caption panel.

## The Type panel

In the Type panel, (Figure 81) you can use one of the Lightroom® font presets or choose your own font and font style. The top blank in the Type panel has the name of a font with a double pointed arrow to the right of it. Clicking with the cursor on the double pointed arrow (Yellow circle, Figure 81) will bring up a drop down menu from which you can choose any of the available fonts. The second blank also has a double pointed arrow to the right. (Red circle, Figure 81) Clicking with the cursor on this double pointed arrow will bring up a drop down menu from which you can choose a font style, Italic, Bold, Bold Italic, etc. Below the blanks for font and font style is a color picker box (Blue ellipse, Figure 81) from which you can pick a color for you type. Below the color picker box are two sliders for changing the size and opacity of the type and a bottom section for aligning and placing the text. Intially, these are the only type effects available. However, to the right of the color picker box is a left pointing arrow. (White circle, Figure 81) Clicking with the cursor on this arrow will turn the arrow down and expand the Type panel, adding slider bars which give you the opportunity to change, in addition to the size and opacity of the type, the tracking, baseline, leading and kerning of the type. There is also a slider bar for changing the number of columns from one to three. Once you have added a second or third column, the last slider bar becomes active and allows you to change the size of the gutter between the columns. At the bottom of the type panel are a four icons which allow to align text to the right, center, left or justify it and three icons which allow you to place the text at the top, center or bottom.

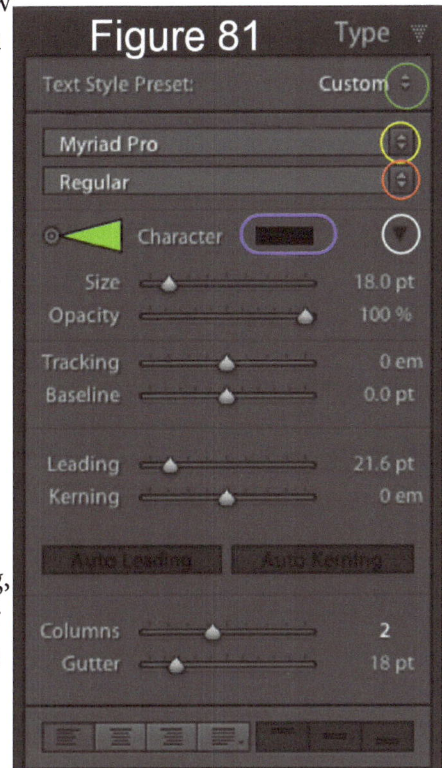


After setting the type the way you want it, you can save your settings as a new preset. To save your type settings as a new preset, click with the cursor on the double pointed arrow on the right side of the top section of the Type panel, labeled "Type Style Preset". (Green circle, Figure 81) A drop down menu will appear on screen. From that menu select "Save Current Settings as New Preset". A pop up New Preset dialog box will appear on screen. In the top blank of this dialog box name your new Type preset and click with the cursor on the Create button at the bottom right of the New Preset dialog box. Later, if you want to change a Type preset you can go back and change it. To change a Type preset, do the following:

- Click with the cursor on the double pointed arrow on the right of the Type Style Preset section at the top of the Type panel.
- Choose the Type preset from the resulting menu.
- Make the changes to the Type preset.
- Click with the cursor on the double pointed arrow to the right of the Type Style Preset
- From the resulting menu choose "Update Preset", the bottom choice.
- You can also delete a Type preset, restore the default presets and rename a Type preset from this menu.

## The Front and Back Cover

The front cover of your book is probably the most important in making people want to open your book, so a lot of thought needs to go into it. You might want to design the cover first, before organizing and placing your images in the book. You can always change the cover as you place your images, but having a book cover might make it seem like you have a goal, one that will orient you towards the images you place in the book. To start designing your front and back cover, look first at the default layout to see if it works for you. (Figure 82) The default layout has an image on the front and back with a spine in between. Getting your image(s) on the front and back cover is exactly the same as placing them on the spreads or pages, select the image and drag it to the cover. You may only want an image on the front cover with a title and your name and an image on the back cover. You might want text on the front and back cover along with the images. So, before you decide, do the following:

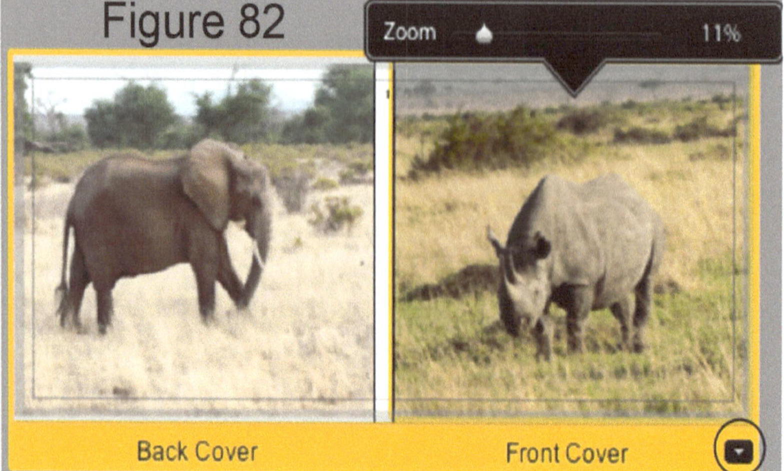

Figure 82

- Click with the cursor on the down pointing arrow at the bottom right of the front cover. (Black circle, Figure 82)
- The Modify Cover dialog box will appear with all the possible layouts for the front and back covers. (Figure 83)
- Place the image(s) you want on the front and back cover.
- Click with the cursor on other layouts in the Modify Cover dialog box and Lightroom® will change the front and back covers on screen.
- Scroll through and try various layouts from the Modify Cover dialog menu and choose the one that works the best.
- If you choose a cover layout with text boxes, place the text in those boxes.
- Use the Type panel to change the size, opacity, keening, etc. of your type.
- After you have placed the images and type you can go back to the Modify Cover dialog box and choose another cover to see how it works.

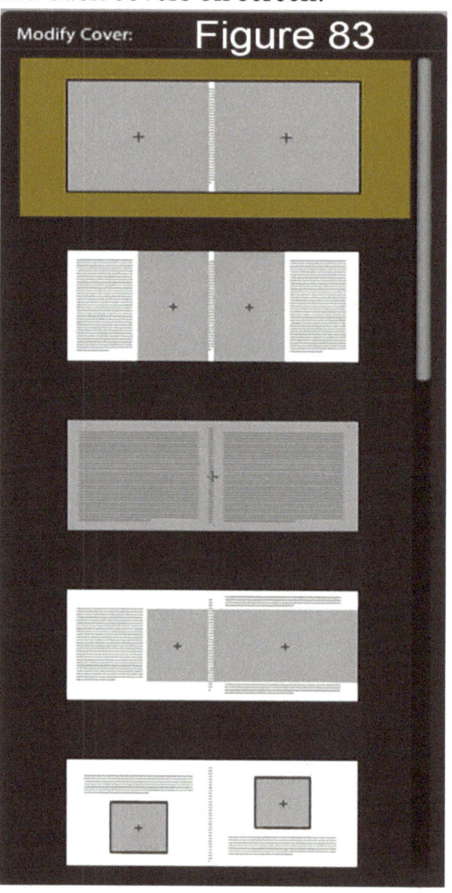

Figure 83

TIP: If you choose to have text boxes on the front and/or back cover, it is a good idea to create that text ahead of time, even in another program and then copy and paste the text into the text boxes on your covers. It will save time.

As with the images or spreads, the Page Caption is available for the front and back cover in the Caption panel. However, the Photo Caption is grayed out and not available for the front and back covers in the Caption panel.

## The Background Panel

The final panel in the right column of panels is the background panel. (Figure 84) You have several choices for how your background is applied behind your images. If you want the background to be the same for all your images then place a check mark in the box in the top section of the Background panel labeled “Apply Background Globally”. (Yellow circle, Figure 84) If you only want the background applied to one image or you want different backgrounds for different images, then leave the check box in front of “Apply Background Globally” unchecked. In the second section of the Background panel is a blank for a graphic and a check box in front of the word “Graphic”. Here you have two choices, you can insert an image from your Filmstrip or you can insert a graphic from one of the Lightroom® presets. To the right of the blank for the image or graphic, is a down pointing disclosure arrow. (Blue circle, Figure 84) When you click with the cursor on the down pointing disclosure arrow, the “Add Background Graphic” menu will appear with three Lightroom® presets, Photos, Travel and Wedding. If you select Photo, you can drag one of the images from the Filmstrip to the blank in the Background panel. If you want to select one of the graphics from either the Travel or Wedding presets, clicking with the cursor on either preset will open up a series of graphics from which you can choose. (Figure 85) Choose a graphic and click on it with the cursor. Lightroom® will place it in the background of your image or images. To add an image from the Filmstrip, all you have to do is select the image in the Filmstrip and drag it to the blank space in this second section. If you only want to add a color for the background, leave the box in front of the word Graphic unchecked and in the bottom section of the Background panel is a color picker box for applying a color to the background. (White ellipse, Figure 84) To apply a background color, do the following:

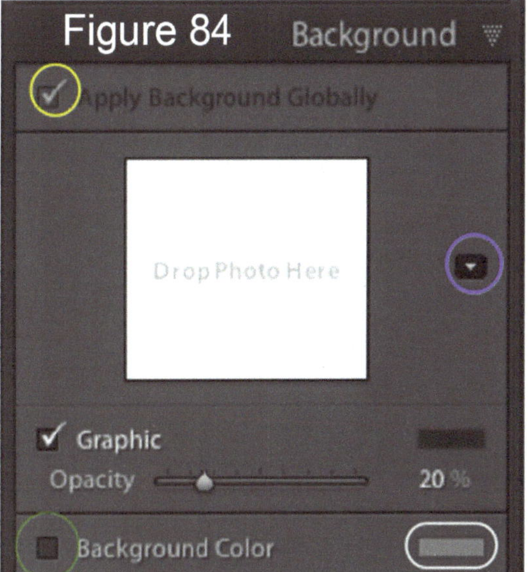


- Click with the cursor in the box in front of the words "Background Color" to activate this section.
- Click with the cursor in the color picker box to the right side of this section of the Background panel to open the color picker box.
- The cursor turns into an eye dropper with which you can choose the color for the background in the color picker box.
- Click with the eyedropper cursor on a color in the color picker box.
- Once chosen, the color will be applied to the background of the images.
- In addition, if you have placed a graphic in the background, the color will also be applied to that graphic.

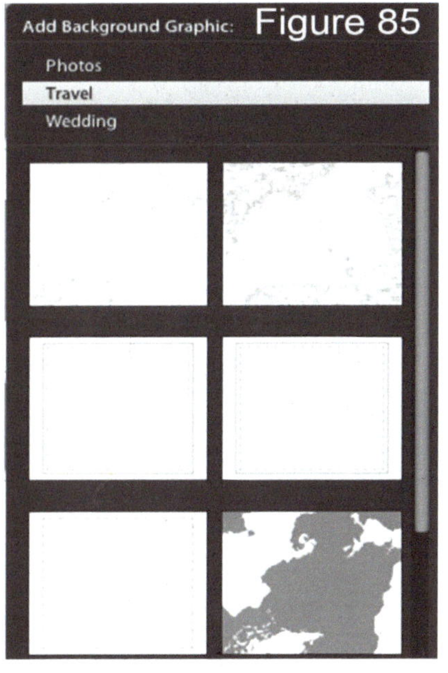


## Creating a Saved Book

With your book set up the way you want it, the next option is to create a saved book. Looking at the top left of the screen in the work area, you will see the text "Unsaved Book". This is to remind you that you need to save your book. If you have already saved your book as you created it and given it a generic name, this text will not be there. On the right side of the top of the screen in the work area is the text "Clear Book" and "Create Saved Book", if you have saved your book periodically as you went along creating it, this text will not be there either. Of course, after all the hard work you put in to the final book, you want to save it. To save the book, do the following:

- Go to the Collections panel on the left side of the screen and highlight the previously saved version of your book.
- Click with the cursor on the minus (-) sign in the header bar of the Collections panel.
- A pop up dialog box will appear on screen asking you if your really want to delete your previously saved book.
- Click with the cursor on the Delete button at the bottom right of this pop up dialog box.
- The collection of the previously saved book will disappear from the Collecitons panel.
- Now on the left side of the work area screen the "Unsaved Book" text will be back and the "Clear All" and "Create Saved Book" text will be back on the top right side of the work area.
- The final copy of your book will still be in the work area ready to be created.

If you want to start over, then click with the cursor on "Clear Book", but if you want to save all the settings then click with the cursor on "Create Saved Book". The Create Book dialog box will appear on screen in which you can name the final version of your book, pick a place on your computer to save your book and again create Virtual Copies of the images in your book. What you are really doing by creating a saved book is creating another Collection that is specific to the Book module. The saved book will be found in the Collections panel and will have a book icon on it. (Yellow circle, Figure 85A) If you are in the Library or Develop module and hover your cursor over this book collection, a right pointing arrow will appear at the right side of the collection. Clicking with the cursor on this arrow will take you to the book module with your book open. If you are in any other module the right poointing arrow will not appear when you hover your cursor over the book in the Collections panel, but if you click with the cursor on the book, it will open in the Book module.

## Printing Your Book

When you are done with you book you have three choices for printing it. You can print it as a JPEG or PDF or you can upload it to Blurb®. All of this is accomplished in the Book Settings panel at the top of the right column of panels in the Book module.

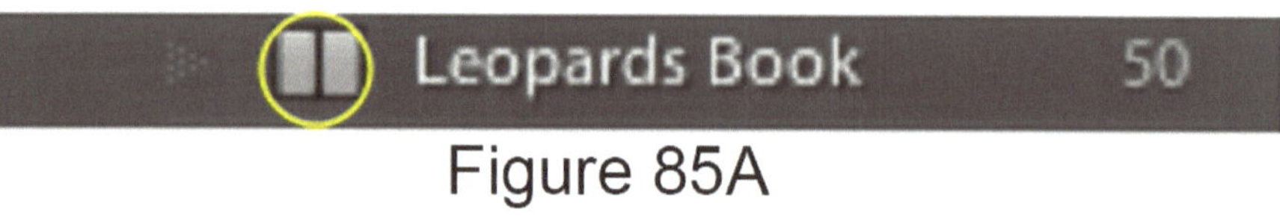

Figure 85A

## Saving a Book as a JPEG

If you want to export your book to JPEG, then do the following:

- In the top section of the Book Settings panel, click on the double pointed arrow on the right side of the Book section (Yellow circle, Figure 86) and from the menu that appears, choose "JPEG".
- Choose the Size and Cover in the second section of the Book Settings panel. (This step is not necessary if you are just going to view the book on a monitor)
- In the third section select the JPEG quality, color profile, resolution, amount of sharpening and media type.
- At the bottom of the right column of panels on the screen, click with the cursor on the Export Book to JPEG button.
- A Save dialog box will pop up in the work area.
- Type in a name for the book in the top blank.
- Navigate to the place on your computer where you want to save you book and highlight it by clicking on the location with the cursor.
- Click with the cursor on the Save button at the bottom right of the dialog box.
- Click with the cursor on the Export book to JPEG button at the bottom of the right column of panels.
- You also have the choice to save the book as JPEG images in a PDF format by clicking on the Export Book as PDF button at the bottom of the left column of panels.
- The images will be saved as JPEG images in a folder at the chosen location.

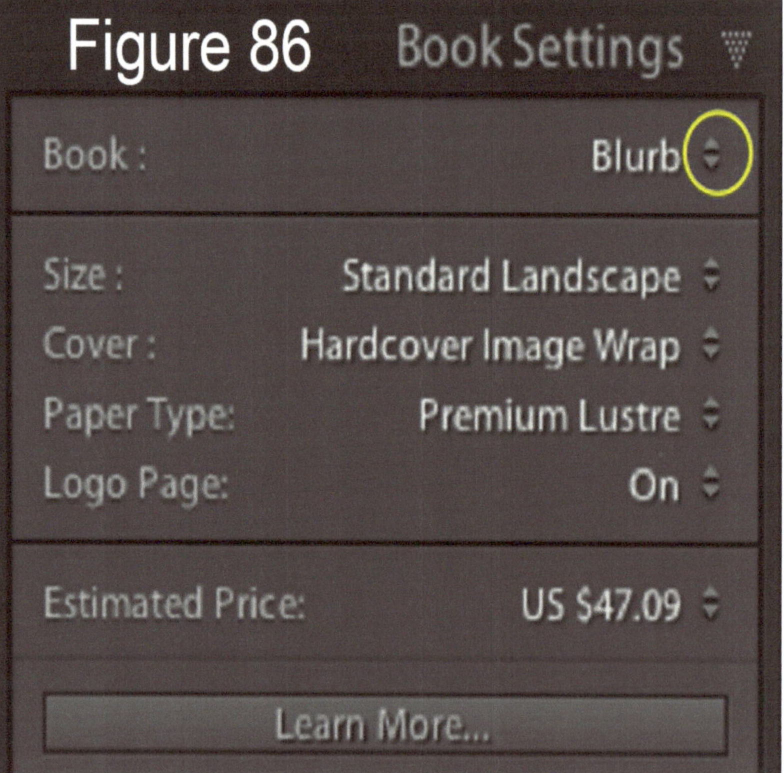
Figure 86

## Saving a Book as a PDF

To save your book as a PDF, do the following:

- From the top section of the Book Settings panel, click with the cursor on the double pointed arrow on the right side of the "Book" section (Yellow circle, Figure 86), choose PDF.
- Make the appropriate choices for size, cover etc. in the second panel of the Book Settings panel.
- Click with the cursor on the "Export Book to PDF" button at the bottom of the right column of panels on the screen.
- The Save dialog box will appear on screen
- Name your book in the top blank.
- Choose a location on your computer to save your book.
- Your book will be saved in the chosen location as two PDFs, one for the front and back covers and one for the images.

You can now send you book to a printer as a JPEG or PDF.

## Sending the Book to Blurb®

To send you book to Blurb®, you first need to create an account with Blurb®. To create an account, click on the "Send Book to Blurb®" button at the bottom of the right column of panels on the screen. In the dialog box that pops up on screen, click with the cursor on the words "Not a member?" at the bottom left of the dialog box. A new dialog box will pop up on screen for you to fill out to become a member. Fill in the appropriate blanks and register. Once your account is active you will be able to upload your book to Blurb® by clicking with the cursor on the "Upload Book" button at the bottom right of the dialog box.

## Neat Lightroom® Tricks

While the entire Book module is a neat Lightroom® trick there are a couple of things, that if you are aware of them will help you get your book ready to publish.

## The Targeted Adjustment Tool

There is a Targeted Adjustment tool in the Type panel with which you can change the leading. To use it, do the following:

- Highlight all the text in which you want to change the leading.
- Click with the cursor on the Targeted Adjustment tool icon in the type panel (Green arrow, Figure 81, page 161)
- Place the Targeted Adjustment tool cursor over the last line of the highlighted text.
- Click with the cursor on the text (The cursor disappears) and move it up and down to change the leading.
- The Leading slider in the Type panel will move left or right as you move the Targeted Adjustment tool up and down.
- When you release the cursor the Targeted Adjustment cursor will reappear.
- Click with the cursor on the Targeted Adjustment tool icon in the Type panel to turn it off.

## Avoiding Duplicate Images in the Book

After you finish placing and organizing your images as well as placing captions, titles and text in text boxes

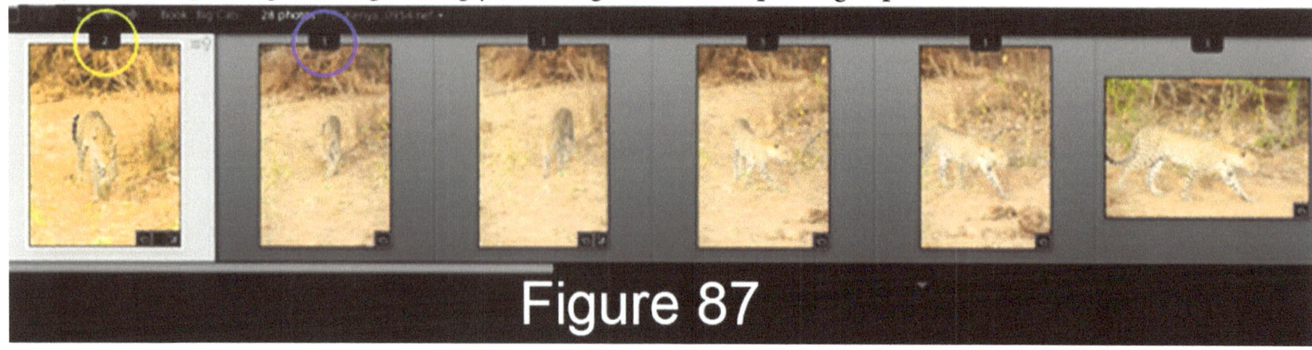
Figure 87

you should carefully check the entire book to make sure everything is as you want it to be. One of the things you probably want to avoid is duplicate images. Lightroom® helps you avoid duplicates very easily. When an image is placed in a spread, Lightroom® places the number 1 in a badge on top of that image in the Filmstrip. (Blue circle,Figure 87) If the same image is placed in another spread, that image will have the number 2 on it in the Filmstrip. (Yellow circle, Figure 87) So when you review the book after finishing it all you have to do is check the Filmstrip for the numbers. If there are duplicate images, you will have to search to book to find both of them to eliminate the duplicate. As of now there is no easy way to click on an image in the Filmstrip and have it highlighted in the multi-image view in the book. It is possible that you might use an image twice in a book. For example, if you used the full sized image on one page and used the zoom to fill slider to crop it on a second page the number 2 would be on that image in the Filmstrip. In that case with the numbers on the Filmstrip, it is easy to check to see if the images are different.

## Creating a Custom Layout in the Print Module

While it is hard to imagine that with all the page layouts available in the book module, there would be a need for another one. However, you can create a custom layout template in the ***Print module*** for use in the Book module. To create a custom layout template, do the following:

- In the ***Print module*** start in the top panel, Layout Style, and choose Custom Package.
- In the Layout panel set the page size to the same size as the pages in your book.
- Move down to the Cell panel and click with the cursor on "Clear Layout" at the bottom of the "Add to Package" section of the Cell panel.
- If you know the dimensions of the images you want to place, click with the cursor on any of the six buttons in the "Add to Package" section and select the dimensions you want. (This technique will be discussed further in the Print module)
- When you click on a selection it will be placed on the page in the work area.
- Once you have the number of images and the dimensions you want on the page, you can drag the blank frames around to any position.
- Save the new layout as a print template by clicking on the plus (+) sign in the Template Browser header bar of the ***Print module.***
- Name the new print template in the pop up menu and click with cursor on the Create button at the bottom right of the dialog box.
- With your layout compete, drag images into the cells.
- Go to the "Print panel" and select "Print To: JPEG File" in the top section.
- Set the print resolution to 300 dpi.
- Set the Custom File Dimensions to the dimensions of the pages in your book.

- Select Pro Photo RGB for the color space
- Turn off Print Adjustment.
- Click with the cursor on Print and save the file to one of the folders that is in Lightroom® or to your desktop, someplace easy to find.
- If you saved the file to a folder in Lightroom®, Control (Macintosh), Right (PC) click with the cursor on that folder and from the pop up menu choose "Synchronize Folder"
- Lightroom® will find the new file and add it to the folder.
- If you saved the file to your desktop or some where else, Import the file into Lightroom® and after import, add the file to the book collection.
- Now you can drag the file to a page on the book.

TIP: If you saved the new layout as a print template, you will be able to repeat the process and use the layout again in the Book module.

## The Print Resolution

For images that you have cropped using the zoom to fill slider bar on a page, Lightroom® makes sure the resulting resolution from cropping will be adequate to print the image. The recommended resolution for printing is 200 ppi. If the resolution is less than the recommended resolution, Lightroom® places a small, white exclamation point on a black background in the upper right corner of the image. (Black circle, Figure 88) This allows you to change the resolution to ensure the images will look good in your book. It seems like Lightroom® always has your best interests in mind, doesn't it?

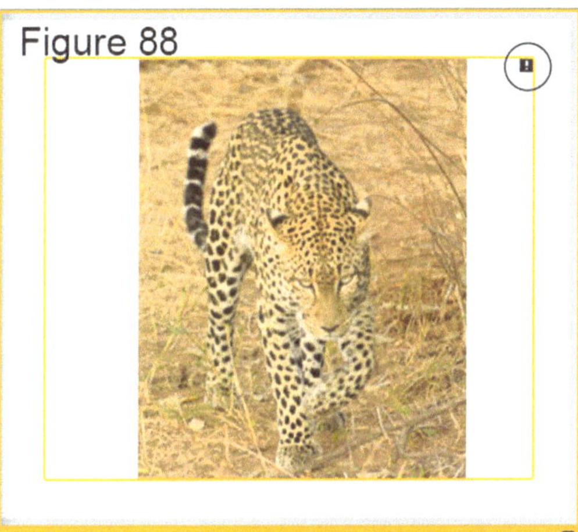
Figure 88

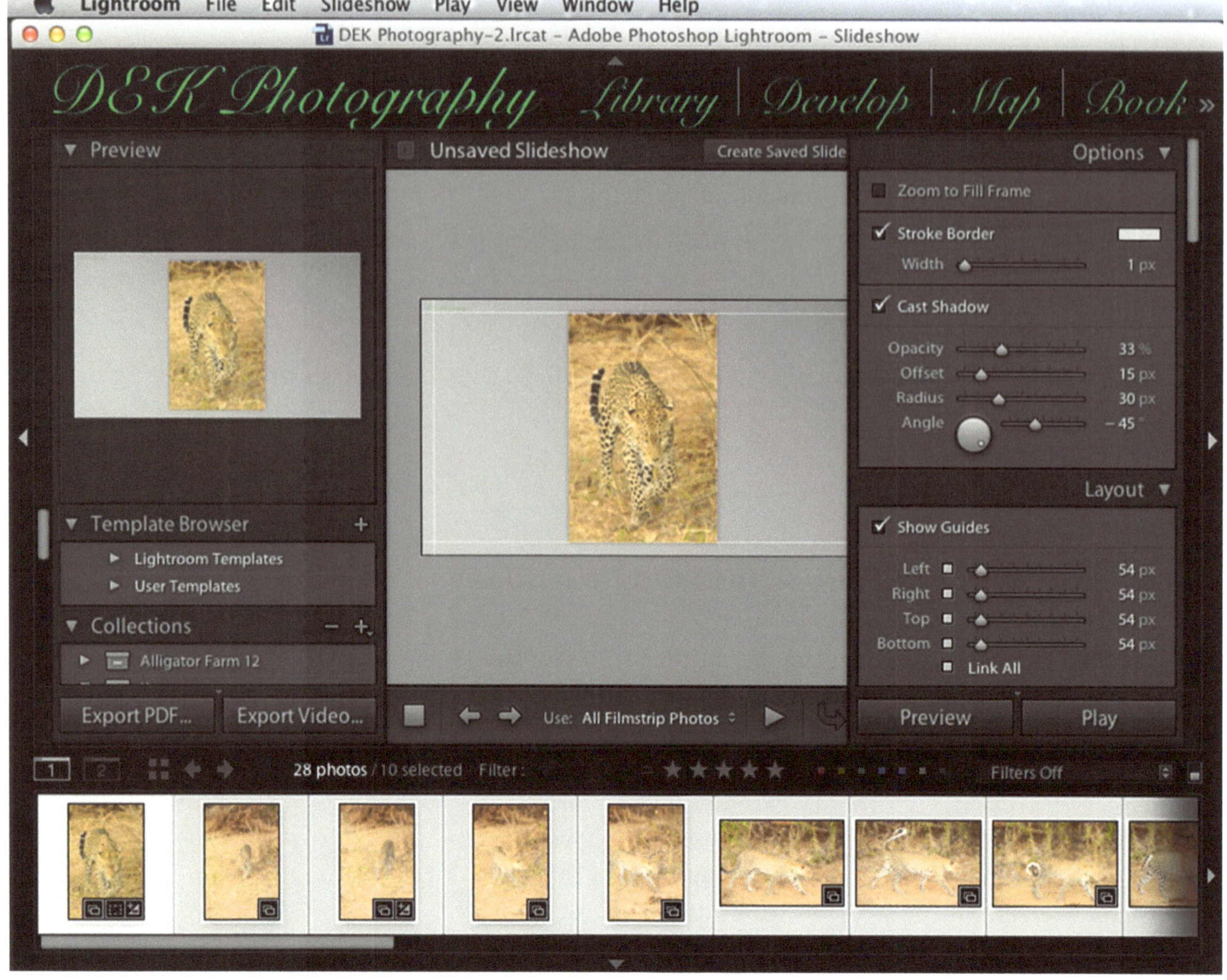


# The Slideshow Module

Like the Book module to create a Slideshow, you need to spend some time in the Library module organizing your images into a Collection. Again, it isn't a bad idea to create Virtual Copies of all the image you want to use in a Slideshow. If you use the Master copy in the slide show and then change it in the Develop module, any new develop settings you place on the Master copy will show up in the Slideshow. That includes renaming the image. For example, if you use a color Master copy in the Slideshow and then later change the Master copy to black and white, the image in the slideshow will also be black and white. If you use Virtual Copies in your Slideshow that will not happen, the images will remain as you left them in the Slideshow.

The easy way to do this is to do the following:

- Choose the images you want in the Slideshow.
- Place those images in a Collection.
- Place a check mark in the box labeled "Make new virtual copies"
- From the edit menu drop down menu choose "Select all, OR
- Use the keyboard shortcut, hold down the Command (Macintosh), Control (PC) key and press the A key on the keyboard.

You are now ready to move your Collection to the Slideshow module.

## The Screen Setup

The menu bar at the top of the screen is similar to menus in the Book module, except that a Slideshow menu has replaced the Book menu. In the left column of panels, the Preview window is still there, but there are no choices for magnifying the image. Below the Preview window is the Template Browser in which there are five Lightroom® templates and below those templates are any user templates you create. If you just want to set up a quick Slideshow, you can try out the different Lightroom® templates by selecting one and then scrolling through your slides to see how they look on screen. Below the Template Browser panel is the Collections panel which is the same in all of the Lightroom® modules. At the bottom of the left column of panels are two buttons, Export to PDF... and Export to Video... The Work area and Filmstrip remains unchanged from other modules, but the Toolbar has changed. (Figure 89) The following are now available in the Toolbar starting at the left side of the Toolbar, you will find:

- A square icon, clicking on this icon with the cursor will take you to the first slide in the slideshow.
- A left pointing arrow, clicking with the cursor on this arrow will take you to the previous slide.
- A right pointing arrow, clicking with the cursor on this arrow will take you to the next slide.
- The word "Use" which will give you a choice of which images you use in the Slideshow. The default is All Filmstrip Photos, but if you click with the cursor on the double pointed arrow to the right of this choice you will see a drop down menu giving you the choice of using Selected Photos or Flagged Photos in addition to the choice of using All Filmstrip Photos.
- A right pointing arrowhead, the clicking on of which will show you a preview of the Slideshow.
- Two curved arrows that will allow you to rotate images clockwise or counter clockwise.
- The letters ABC, clicking with the cursor on these letters will place a blank labeled Custom Text, to the right of the ABC letters in which you can add text to the slide.
- At the right side of the Toolbar is text telling you the number of the current slide in the Slideshow, the total number of slides in the Slideshow and the length of time of the slide show. If you hover your cursor over this text, the cursor turns into a hand with one finger up and a left and right pointed arrow. Clicking with this cursor on the text will allow you to view the images in the Filmstrip on screen in the work area without having to scroll through the Filmstrip.

Figure 89

The right column of panels contains six panels for use in creating the attributes of your slide show.

## Setting up the Slideshow

Before you get to the right column of panels you should select the template you want to use from the Template Browser panel at the top of the left column of panels. When you make your first Slideshow, it might be a good idea to start with the default template. After setting up the slide show and making changes, you can save the result as a new user template.

## The Options Panel

Starting at the top of the right column of panels, the first panel, the Options panel, (Figure 90)has three sections that allow you to set up how the image appears on screen. In the first section, you can set the image to zoom to fit the frame. This option works pretty well with horizontal images, but it crops vertical images and often does not work well. Place a check mark in the box in this section and see how you like it. If you don't like the result, uncheck the box.

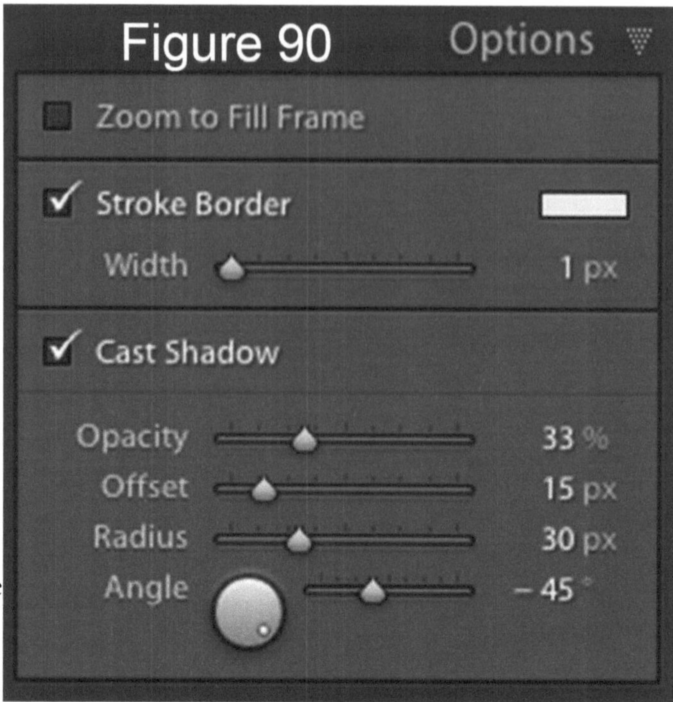


In the second section of the Options panel you can add a stroke border around the frame of the image by checking the box in this section. If you decide to place a stroke border around the image, Lightroom gives you two options for the stroke border. You can change the width and color of the stroke border. Change the width with the slider bar in the Stroke Border section. Change the color by clicking with the cursor on the color picker box to open it in this section and selecting a color with the eye dropper cursor which appears when you hover your cursor over the color picker box. The color picker box is works the same as the color picker boxes in the Develop module.

The third section of the Options panel allows you to place a drop shadow around the image. With the slider bars in this third section, you can increase or decrease the Opacity, Offset, Radius and Angle of the drop shadow. If you keep the default black background, you will not be able to see the drop shadow, however if you change the background to a lighter color you will be able to see the drop shadow.

## The Layout Panel

The Layout panel (Figure 91) is almost exactly the same as the Padding section of the Cell panel in the Book module and the Layout panel in the Print module. How the image looks on screen is based on a frame and these panels allow you to change the frame size and position of the image in the work area. The Layout panel shows the guides for all four sides, left, right, top and bottom and when you first open the Layout panel, all four sides are linked together. If you move one of the sliders, all four sides move towards the center of the image an equal amount. If you unlink the guides by unchecking the Link All box, you can off-set the image to the right, left or top or bottom. The difference between the Cell panel in the Book module and the Layout panel in the Slideshow module is that in the Book module you can have multiple images on a page and place padding in between the images, whereas in the Slideshow module you can only have one image at a time on the screen. The ability to off set the image in the slide show will come in handy if you want to place some information such as your copyright or contact information on one side of the image. However you choose to set the guides, make sure you check how both a horizontal and vertical image will appear in the slideshow.

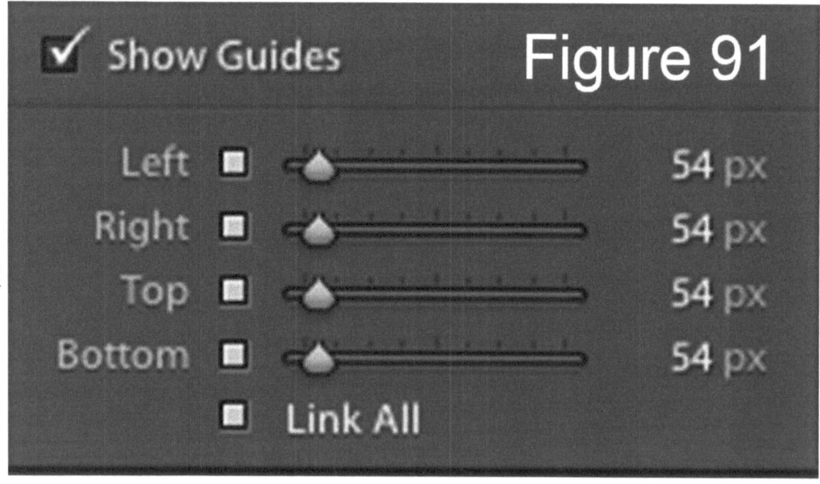

## The Overlays Panel

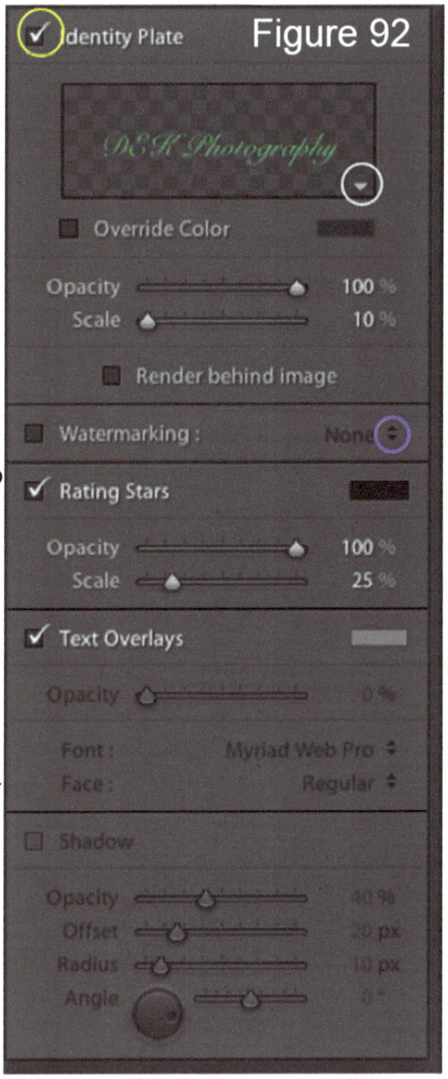

The third panel down, the Overlays panel, (Figure 92) is where you can place text on the images in your Slideshow. At the top of the panel is a section for the Identity Plate. If you created your Identity Plate when you first started using Lightroom®, it is available to place on your images in the Slideshow. To place your Identity Plate on the images do the following:

- Place a check mark in the box in front of the words " Identity Plate at the top of the Overlays panel. (Yellow circle, Figure 92)
- The Identity Plate will appear at the top right of the image on screen.
- To move the Identity Plate to another position on screen, click with the cursor on the Identity Plate and drag it to a new position. As you move the Identity Plate around the image, you will see it snap to different locations.
- One nice thing about the location of the Identity Plate is that if you locate it at the bottom left of a Landscape oriented image, it will also be located at the bottom left of a portrait oriented image.
- The Identity Plate can be located either inside or outside the image.
- You can override the color of your Identity Plate if you want to by placing a check mark in the box labeled "Override Color". Then click with the cursor in the color picker box to the right of the Override Color text and selecting a new color for the Identity Plate.
- Increase or decrease the opacity of the Identity Plate with the Opacity slider.
- Increase or decrease the size of the Identity Plate with the Scale slider.

Figure 92



If you did not create an Identity Plate, here is your opportunity to do it. Click with the cursor on the down pointing arrow in the box for the Identity Plate.(White circle, Figure 92) A pop up menu will appear on screen. From this menu choose "Edit". This will bring up the Identity Plate Editor dialog box. You can create a new Identity Plate as described at the beginning of this book or edit your existing one in this dialog box and save it. Once you have your new Identity Plate you can use it in your Slideshows.

The next section of the Overlays panel is the Watermarking section. If you have created and saved a Watermark you can apply it to the slide show by doing the following:

- Click with the cursor in the box in front of the word "Watermarking"
- To the right of the word "Watermarking" is the word "None" by default. There is a double pointed arrow to the right.
- Click with the cursor on this double pointed arrow to bring up any Watermarks, text or graphic you have created in Lightroom®. (Blue circle, Figure 92)
- Choose a Watermark from the list by clicking on the Watermark with the cursor and the Watermark will be applied, by default to the center of the image.
- The last choice from the drop down menu is "Edit Watermarks".
- Clicking with the cursor on "Edit Watermarks" will bring up the Watermark Editor dialog box, allowing you to edit an existing Watermark or Create and save a new Watermark.

TIP: Slideshows are usually about showing your work at its best and Watermarks can interfere with that. So, you might want to think about not using a Watermark in your slideshow.

Below the Watermarking section of the Overlays panel is a section that allows you to include any rating stars you applied to your images. If you place a check mark in the box in front of the words "Rating Stars", any rating stars you place on the image will be placed at the top left of the image. However, by default they will be black and might be difficult to see on the image. If you want the Rating Stars to be easily seen on the image, do the following:

- To the right of the words "Rating Stars is another color picker box, click with the cursor the color picker box to open it.
- Choose a bright color that will be easily seen on the image.
- Move the Opacity slider in this section to the right.
- Move the Scale slider in this section to the right.
- The Rating Stars will appear in the top left of the image.
- Click with the cursor on the Rating Stars and move them to any position you want in the image.

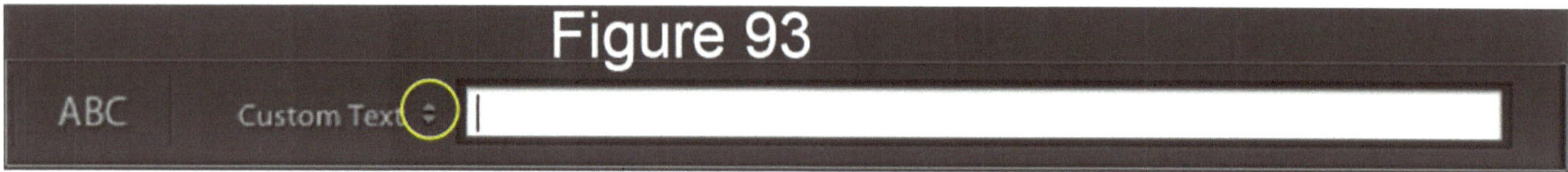

Figure 93

The next section down in the Overlays panel is the Text Overlays section. (Figure 93) To add text to the images in the Slideshow, do the following:

- Click with the cursor on the "ABC" icon in the toolbar.
- The words "Custom Text will appear to the right of the icon along with a text blank.
- After the words "Custom Text" will be a double pointed arrow. (Yellow circle, Figure 93)
- Click with the cursor on this double pointed arrow to bring up a menu from which you can choose the type of text you want inserted. Your choices are Caption, Date, Equipment, Custom Text, Exposure, Filename, Sequence, Title and Edit. (Figure 94)
- Other than "Custom Text", Lightroom® will pull the information from the metadata of the image.
- The Caption and Title will only be inserted if you placed them in the metadata in the Library module.
- If your choice is "Custom Text", type the custom text into the blank to the right of the "ABC" icon on the Toolbar.
- The text overlay will appear at the bottom left corner of the image.
- You can click on the text box with the cursor and move it to a new position on the image and like the Identity Plate it can be located inside or outside the image.
- There is also a color picker box to the right at the top of the Overlays panel from which you can choose a color for the text overlays.
- Finally, in the last section of the Overlays panel you can place a drop shadow on the text overlays.

Figure 94

Custom Settings

Caption
✓ Custom Text
Date
Equipment
Exposure
Filename
Sequence
Title

Edit...

## The Backdrop Panel

Lightroom allows you to change the way the area behind your slide looks in the Backdrop panel. (Figure 95) This is called the Backdrop and unless you placed a check mark in the Zoom to Fill Frame box in the Options panel there will be a backdrop behind your image. The top section of the Backdrop panel is for placing a Color Wash on the Backdrop of your image. To place the Color Wash, do the following:

- Click with the cursor in the box in front of the words "Color Wash", this will activate the Color Wash panel.

- Choose the color for the Color Wash by clicking with the cursor in the color picker box to the right of the words "Color Wash".
- There will be a gradual color wash applied from the upper right to the lower left in the backdrop.
- Use the sliders on the slider bars in this section of the Backdrop panel to change the Opacity and Angle or direction of the Color Wash.

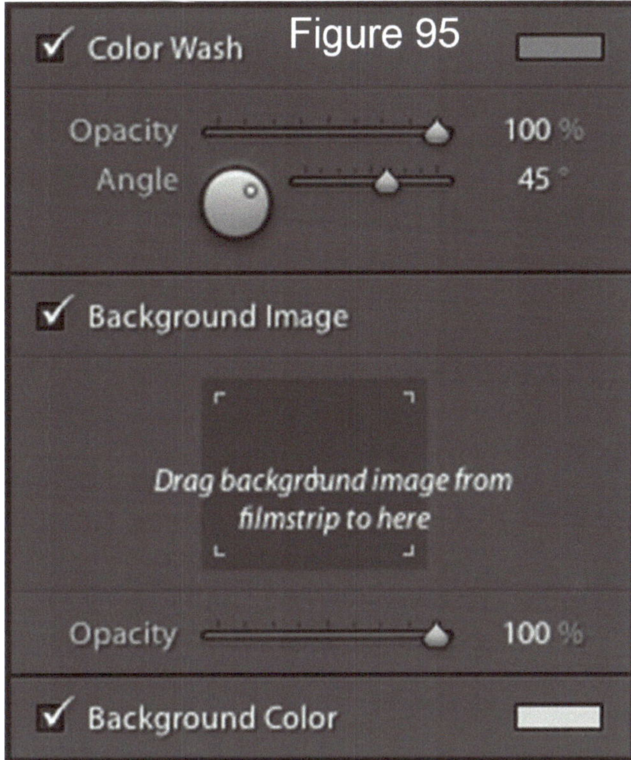

Figure 95

The second section of the Backdrop panel allows you to place an image from the Filmstrip in the Backdrop. If you have a pattern or landscape image you would like to use as the backdrop for your images, place a check mark in the box in front of "Background Image". Select the image in the Filmstrip and drag it to the blank in this section of the Backdrop panel. Below the blank for the image is an Opacity slider with which you can change the pattern or image in the Backdrop. Finally, in the bottom section of the Backdrop panel you can change the color of the Backdrop. To change the color of the Backdrop, do the following:

- Place a check mark in the box in front of the words "Background Color". Doing this will activate the color picker box to the right of the words "Background Color".
- When you hover your cursor over the color picker box it turns into an eye dropper cursor.
- Select the color by clicking with the eye dropper cursor on it and the background will take on that color.
- You can increase or decrease the saturation of the color by dragging the eyedropper cursor up or down.
- If you have placed a pattern or image on the Backdrop, that will also take on the color.

## The Titles Panel

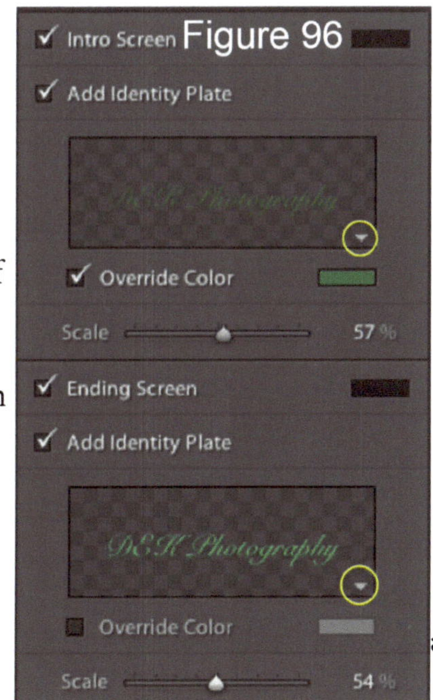

Figure 96

The Titles panel (Figure 96) has two identical sections, one for the introductory screen and one for the ending screen. The Intro screen shows for approximately five seconds when the slideshow starts and the Ending screen shows for approximately five seconds after the slideshow ends or for the duration you set the slides to be on screen in the Playback panel. To activate either section, Intro or Ending, place a check mark in the box in front of each title by clicking in the box with the cursor. To the right of both the Intro Screen and Ending Screen is a color picker box that allows you to choose the color of the screen background. Simply click on the color picker box with the cursor and choose the color you want the screen background to be with the eye dropper cursor. The default color for both the Intro and Ending screens is black and you can leave it that way. Below the Intro and Ending Screens you can add the Identity Plate to the center of the screens. Add the Identity Plate by clicking with the cursor in the box in front of the text "Add Identity Plate". Your main Identity Plate will be added into the blank. You can change the color by placing a check mark in the "Override Color " box beneath the Identity Plate box. Placing a check mark in this box activates the color picker box to the right and you can use the same procedure to change the color of your Identity Plate. You can change the size of the Identity Plate on either the Intro or Ending screens by using the Scale slider bar at the bottom of either the Intro or Ending screen sections. Lightroom® will help you determine how you want the screens to look because every time you make a change in the Titles panel to the Identity Plate, the Intro or Ending screen will appear for about five seconds in the work area.

The Titles panel is an excellent place to introduce your slide show and place credits at the end. You can have as many Identity Plates as you want, so, for example if you are a wedding photographer you might create an identity plate with the name of the bride and groom for the Intro screen or if the slideshow is about a trip, create an identity plate with the location of the trip in the Intro screen. For the ending screen you can create an identity plate that says something like "Photography by your name or business name and phone number or you could use a graphical identity plate, a logo for your business if you have one. The possibilities are endless. To create an identity plate for this purpose, do the following:

- Click with the cursor on the down pointing arrow at the bottom right of the box in which the Identity Plate is placed (Yellow circles, Figure 96)
- A pop up menu will show all your Identity Plates as well as the opportunity to edit Identity Plates.
- Click with the cursor on "Edit"
- The Identity Plate Editor dialog box will appear on screen.
- Type the Intro screen Identity Plate text into the box.
- Choose the font, color and font size from the appropriate boxes.
- Click with the cursor on the double pointed arrow at the end of the blank that says "Custom" on the bottom left side of the Identity Plate Editor dialog box.
- Choose "Save As" in the drop down menu.
- In the pop up "Save identity Plate" dialog box, name the new Identity plate and click with the cursor on the Save button.

The procedure is exactly the same for the Intro or Ending Screens, the new Identity Plates are now ready to be placed in the Intro or Ending screen.

## The Playback Panel

The final panel is where you reap your reward for all the hard work you did preparing your Slideshow, but first there are a couple of things to do to really finish it off. In the top section of the Playback panel (Figure 97) you can add music to your slide show. To add a Sound track to your Slideshow, do the following:

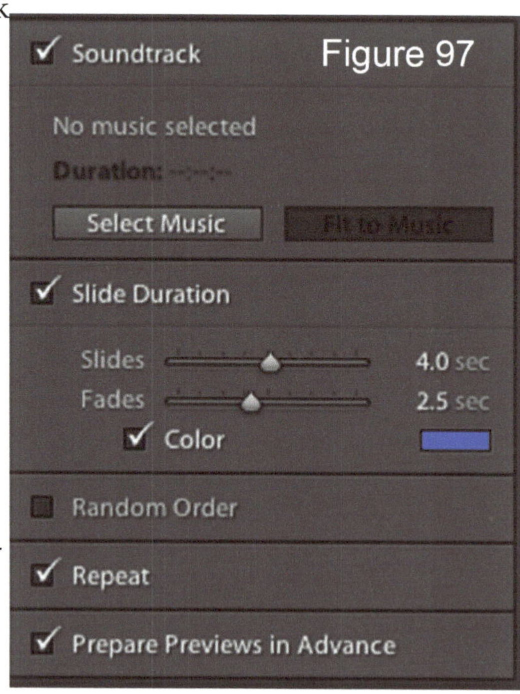


- Click with the cursor in the box in front of the word "Sound track" to place a check mark in the box. This will activate the Sound track section.
- Click with the cursor in the box in front of the words "Slide Duration" to activate this section of the Playback panel.
- Click with the cursor on the button that says "Select Music" in the Sound track section.
- Lightroom® will show you where the music is located on your computer in the Finder (Macintosh), Explorer (PC).
- Choose the music and Lightroom® will place the title and indicate the length of the song above the Select Music button.
- Click with the cursor on the "Fit to Music" button to the right of the "Select Music" button.
- Depending on how many slides are in the Slideshow, Light-

room® will determine how long each slide will play on screen and how long the fade in between slides should be.

- The default for the Fade is 2.5 seconds, which seems a little long. You might want to change the Fade to be closer to 1.0 seconds, it will make the slideshow run smoother.
- If you do not click with the cursor on "Fit to Music", and instead select how long each slide stays on the screen and how long each fade is, then if the slideshow is longer than the duration of the song, the song will restart and play over again.

TIP: In the Slide Duration section, below the Sound track section, you can change the slide duration and the Fade time using the sliders in this section. For example, if you want the slide on the screen longer then lengthen the slide time and shorten the Fade time using the sliders. After you have done this, again click with the cursor on the "Fit to Music" button.

If you don't plan to use a sound track with the Slideshow, then in the Slide duration section do the following:

- Set the time you want the slides on the screen using the Slides slider or click in the scrubby slider box at the right end of the slider bar and type in a duration in seconds.
- Use the Fade slider to set the time between slides or type a time in seconds in the scrubby slider box at the right end of the Fade slider bar.
- The default color that appears on screen during the Fades is black, but you can change it to any color by placing a check mark in the box in front of the word "Color" and clicking with the cursor in the color picker box to the right of the word "Color".
- Between slides, the screen will turn to whatever color you picked in the color picker box during the fades.

TIP: You may want to set the slide duration and fade time first, because knowing how many slides you have in your Slideshow and how long you want each slide on the screen as well as how long you set the fades, Lightroom® will tell you how long the Slideshow will be. Look at the right side of the Toolbar and there you will find the number of slides in the Slideshow, what number the current slide is and how long the Slideshow will play. You can then look for music close to that time to place as the sound track.

You can also set the Slideshow to play the slides in random order by clicking with the cursor in the box in front of the words "Random Order". Placing a check mark in the box in front of the word "Repeat" will let the Slideshow start over after it finishes. Finally, place a check mark in the last box at the bottom of the panel to Prepare Previews in Advance. Your Slideshow is now ready to play. You can preview it in the work area on screen by clicking with the cursor on the "Preview" button, the left button at the bottom of the right column of panels. Alternatively use the keyboard shortcut, hold down the Option key and press the Return key (Macintosh) or hold down the Alt key and press the Enter key (PC). To play the Slideshow full screen click with the cursor on the "Play" button at the bottom of the right column of panels. Alternatively, use the keyboard shortcut, press the Return key (Macintosh), Enter key (PC). Pause the Slideshow by pressing the Space bar. With the slideshow paused, you can move through the slides, forward or backward using the left and right arrow keys. Restart the Slideshow by again pressing the Space bar. Stop the slide show by pressing the Esc button on the keyboard.

Even though your Slideshow is ready to play, you're not done yet. If you look at the top left of the work area, you will see the words "Unsaved Slideshow". This is there to remind you that your Slideshow needs to be saved. At the top right of the work area are the words "Create Saved Slideshow". Your Slideshow will be saved in the Collections panel in the left column of panels. To save your Slideshow do the following:

- Click with the cursor on "Create Saved Slideshow" at the top right of the work area, OR
- Click on the plus (+) sign in the header bar of the Collections panel and select "Create Slideshow from the pop up menu

- With either method, a Create Slideshow dialog box (Figure 98) will appear on screen.
- Name your Slideshow in the top blank of the Create Slideshow dialog box.
- In the Placement section of the Create Slideshow dialog box decide if you want to place the Slideshow as a stand alone Collection or inside a Collection Set.
- If you did not bring your images into the Slideshow module as Virtual Copies, place a check mark in the box in front of the text "Make new virtual copies" in the Slideshow Options section of the Create Slideshow dialog box. (Red circle, Figure 98)
- Click with the cursor on the Create button at the bottom left of the Create Slideshow dialog box.

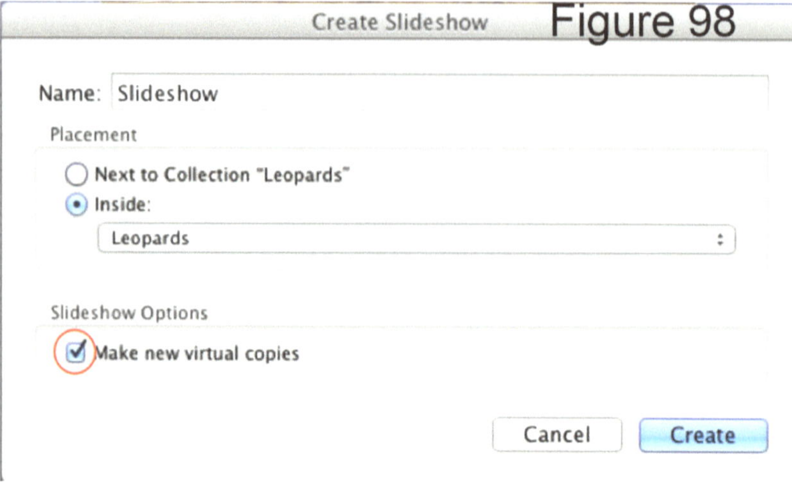

Figure 98

Your Slideshow will be saved in the Collections panel and will have a Slideshow icon to the left of it. (Yellow circle, Figure 98A) The Collections panel is available in all seven modules of Lightroom®. If you hover your cursor over a slideshow in the Library or Develop module a right pointing arrow will appear after the number of slides on the right side. Clicking with the cursor on the right pointing arrow or the name of the slideshow will take you to the Slideshow module and open the slideshow. In the Book, Print and Web modules, the arrow does not appear when you hover your cursor over the name of the slideshow, but clicking with the cursor on the slideshow name will also take you to the Slideshow module and open the slideshow.

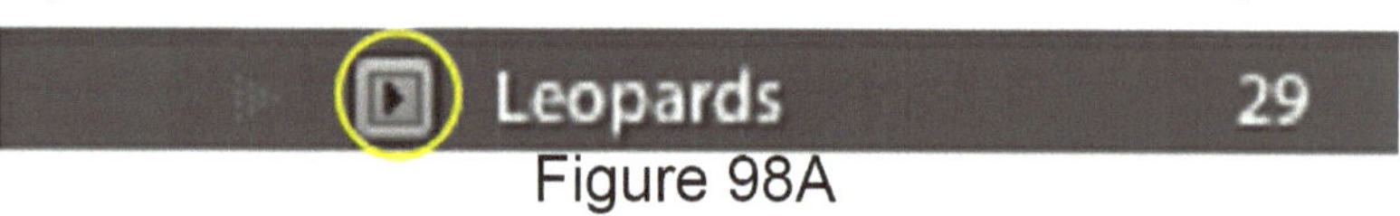

Figure 98A

If you are happy with your Slideshow settings, you can save them as a template. To save your settings as a new Slideshow Template, do the following:

- Click with the cursor on the plus sign (+) in the header bar of the Template Browser panel at the top of the left column of panels in the Slideshow module.
- In the New Template dialog box that appears on screen, give the new template a descriptive name.
- Click with the cursor on the Create button at the bottom left of the New Template dialog box.
- Your new Slideshow template will be stored under the User Templates in the Template Browser panel.

You can also choose to create a new folder for your templates and store your templates in that folder. (Actually, this can be done in any panel. To create your own folder for your templates, do the following:

- Control (Macintosh), Right (PC) click with the cursor on either the Lightroom® Templates or User Templates header bar.
- From the pop up menu select New Folder.
- In the New Folder dialog box that appears on screen, name the new folder (Dave's Templates).
- Now, instead of saving your templates in the User Templates, you can store them in your own named folder.

Guess what? You're not done with the Slideshow panel yet. You probably want to share your beautiful work with others or maybe force it on them. So, you can export your Slideshow, attach it to and email and send it to them. At the bottom of the left column of panels in the Slideshow module there are two buttons with which you can export your Slideshow. One button says "Export PDF..." and the second one says "Export Video..." Actually, there are three ways to export your Slideshow. If you hold down the Option (Macintosh), Alt (PC) key the PDF button changes to "Export JPEG". So JPEG is the third way to export the slide show. The reason you might want to export the slides as JPEGs is, if you are going to use them in another program such as Power Point or Keynote.

The reason you might want to export your Slideshow as a PDF is, if you just want to send some one your images. For example, if you have fifty or a hundred slides you want to send, exporting them all to a PDF is a very efficient way to send them, rather than sending fifty or a hundred individual images. To Export the Slideshow as a PDF or JPEGs, do the following:

- Click with the cursor on the Export PDF button at the bottom left column of panels in the Slideshow module.
- In the Export Slideshow to PDF dialog box (Figure 99) that appears on screen, name the Slideshow in the blank at the top of the dialog box.
- Choose a destination for the Slideshow.
- In the bottom section of the Export Slideshow to PDF, set the quality with the Quality slider.
- By default, the size is set to Screen and the width and height are indicated in the boxes above the word "Screen", but you can change the width and height by clicking with the cursor on the double pointed arrow next to the word "Screen" and selecting a different width and height. You can also choose to have the Slideshow automatically play full screen by placing a check mark in the appropriate box.

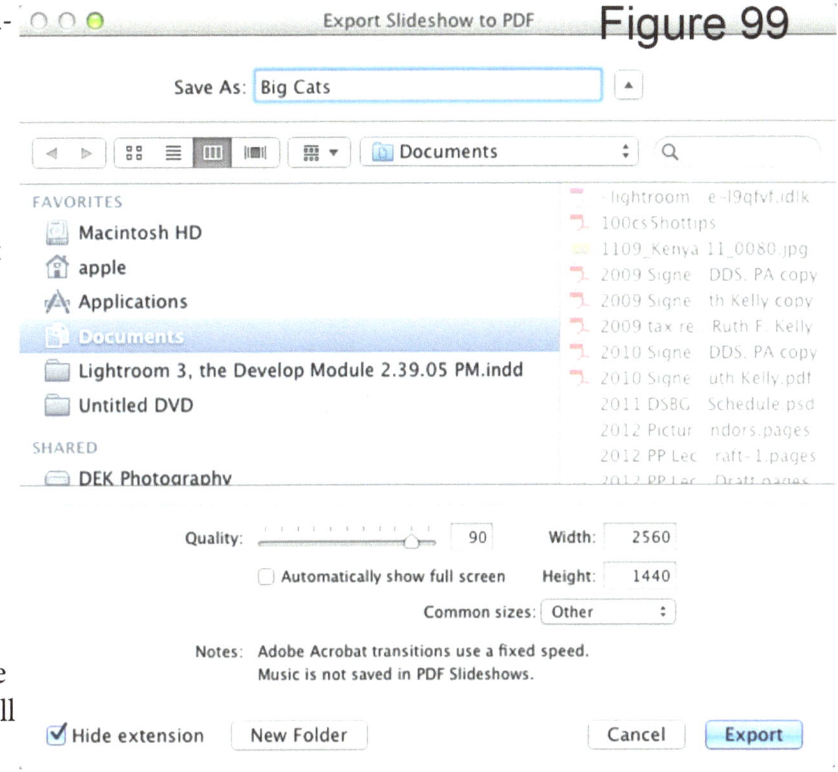

Figure 99

- A note at the bottom of the dialog box informs you that transitions play at a fixed speed and music is not saved with the PDF.
- This message is not present when exporting as JPEGs, because the slides will be exported to a Folder and be available for use in another program.
- Click with the cursor on the Export button at the bottom right of the dialog box.

The best way to export your Slideshow is to video because everything, all your settings will be exported. You can then share your Slideshow by emailing it or put it up on You Tube or show it on a high definition monitor. To export your Slideshow to video do the following:

- Click with the cursor on the Export Video button.
- The Export Slideshow to Video dialog box will appear on screen. (Figure 100)
- From the Export Slideshow to Video dialog box that appears on screen, name the Slideshow in the top blank labeled "Save As".
- Choose a destination for the video Slideshow in the second blank.
- In the bottom section of the Export Slideshow to Video dialog box choose a Video Preset from the choices in the blank to the right of the words "Video Preset".

- Click with the cursor on the Export button at the bottom right of the dialog box.

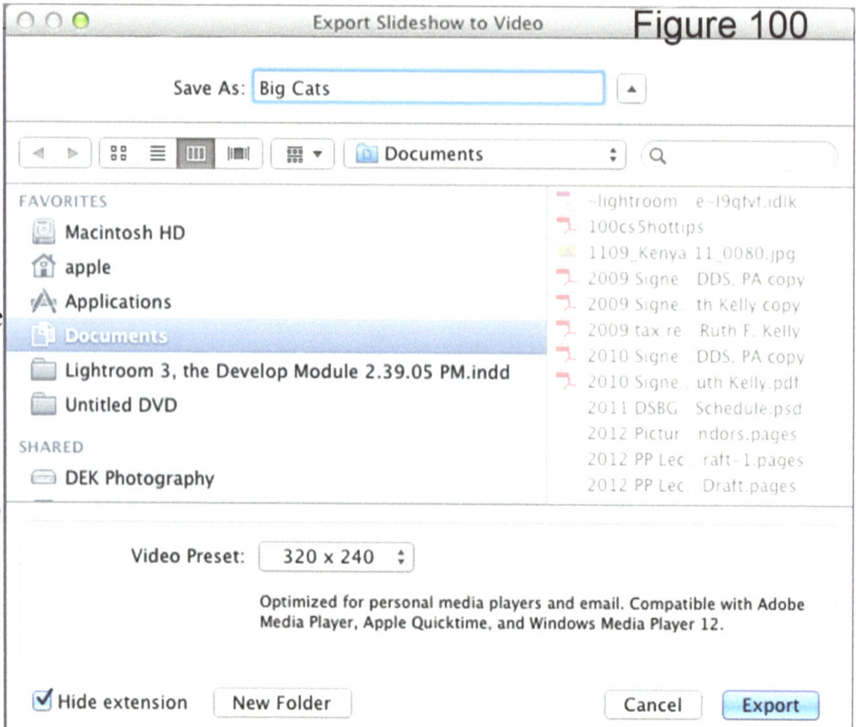


TIP: Each time you click on a Video Preset, Lightroom® will show you a message at the bottom of the Export Slideshow to Video dialog box telling you for what kind of device each of the different presets are optimized. For example, if you choose the 720p video preset you can put your video up on You Tube or use the Publish Services in the Library Module to put the video up on social media sites such as Facebook® or Flickr®. Choosing the 1080p preset will allow the slideshow to be shown on high definition units. The 480x320 preset is adequate for smart phones, Adobe® media player, Apple® Quicktime and the Windows® media player.

So, showoff, you can use your fantastic slideshows to communicate with all kinds of people, thanks to the Slideshow module of Lightroom®4.

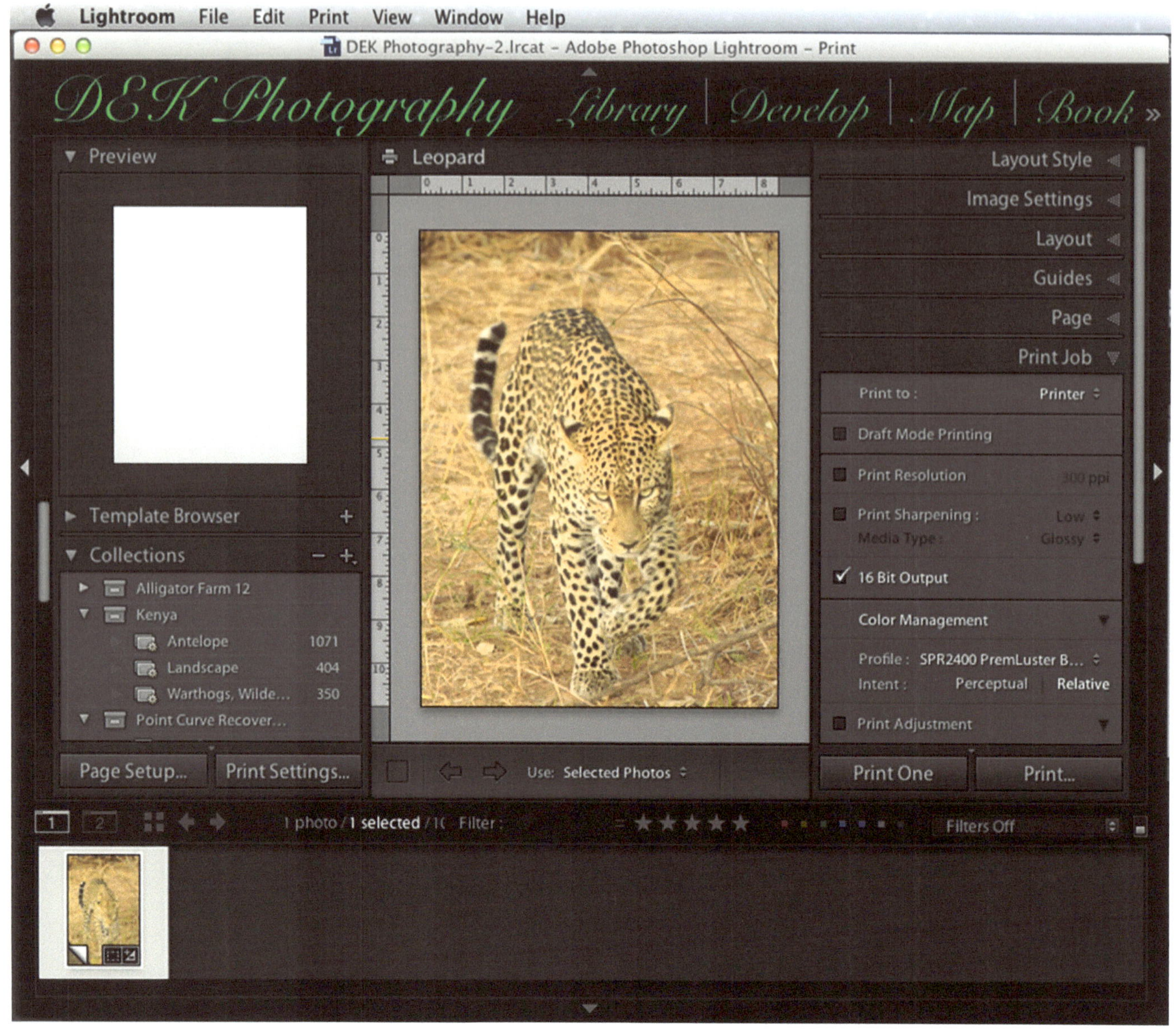


# The Print Module

Printing your picture is the culmination of all your hard work. You came upon a scene, created the image in your mind before you created it in the Camera. You knew exactly what you wanted so you got the right exposure and composition. Then you imported it into Lightroom® and because it was a RAW file you put the perfect develop settings on it to bring out the best in the image, or else you got a lucky shot, it happens. Either way the next thing to do is soft proof the image and take it into the Print module of Lightroom®

One thing you might think about doing if you have several images you want to print, is create a Print Collection Set or a Print Collection. Once you start printing it will be easier to print one image after another from the Print Collection than going back to the Develop module, developing another image and taking it back to the Print module for printing. Once you get your monitor calibrated and the print settings just right it is better to print all the images in the collection instead of going back and forth between modules preparing images. To create a Print Collection Set, do the following:

- Open the Print module without any images selected.
- In the Print module, click with the cursor on the plus (+) sign in the header bar of the Collections panel.

- From the menu that appears on screen, select "Create Collection Set...".
- In the Create Collection Set dialog box that pops up on screen, name the Collection Set something like "Prints" in the top blank.
- Place the Collection Set as a top level Set.
- The Print Collection Set will show up in the Collections panel with a Set icon to the left. (Yellow circle, Figure 101)
- Now when you bring an image into the Print module, click with the cursor on the "Create Saved Print" button at the top right of the work area.
- In the "Create Print" dialog box that appears on screen (Figure 102), name the print in the top blank.
- Place the print inside the Prints Collection Set.
- Click with the cursor in the box in front of "Make new virtual copies".
- Click with the cursor on the "Create" button at the bottom right of the Create Print dialog box.

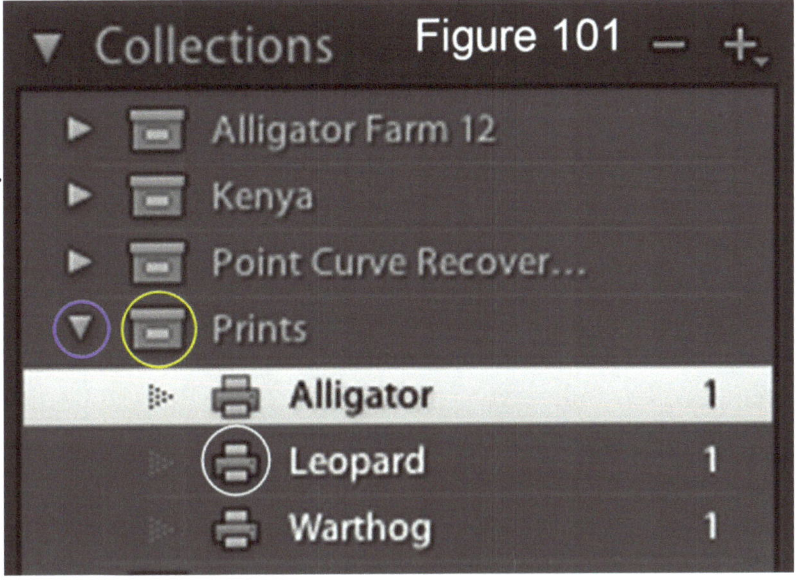


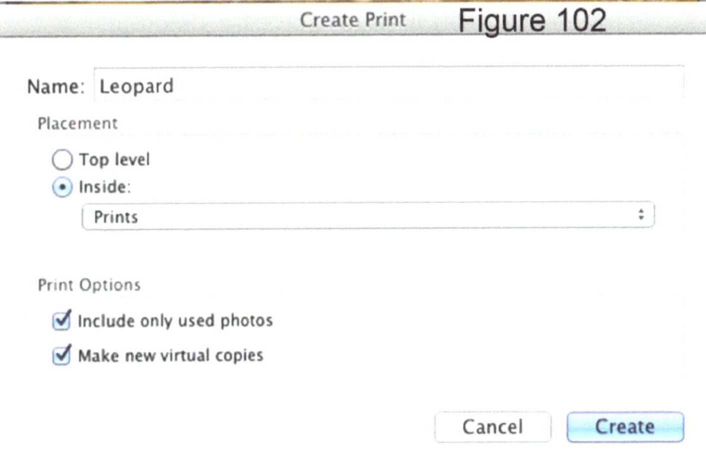


Using this setup, each time you add an image to be printed to the Prints Collection set, it will be listed in alphabetical order, separately inside the Prints Collection Set with a printer icon to its left. (White circle, Figure 101). You will be able to see all the images to be printed in the Collections panel. You can close the Prints Collection Set by clicking with the cursor on the down pointing arrow to the left of the Prints Collection Set (Blue circle, Figure 101)to save room in the Collections panel. If you click with the cursor on the Print Collection Set when it is closed in the Library module, the Print Collection Set with all the images inside it will open in either the Grid or Loupe view. All the images will be in the Filmstrip across the bottom of the screen. If the Print Collection Set is open in the Library, Develop or Map module, when you hover your cursor over an individual image, a right pointing arrow will appear to the right of the image. Clicking with the cursor on this right pointing arrow will open the Print module and only the one image will be in the Filmstrip and on screen for printing.

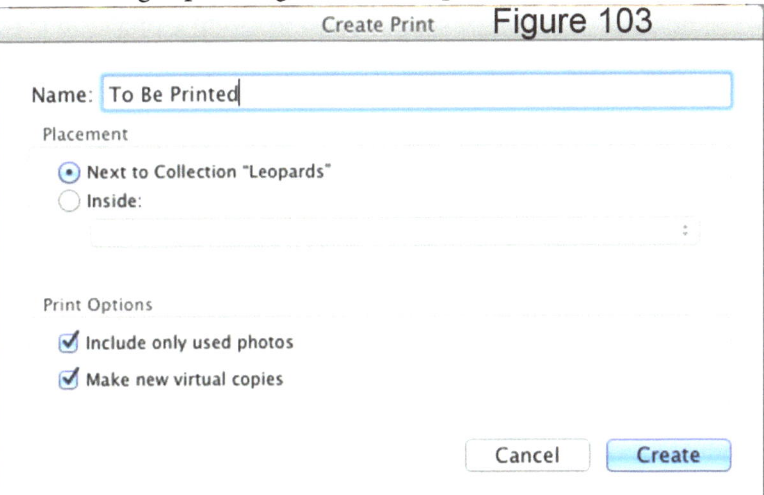


If you would rather just have one Prints collection to which you can add images, do the following:

- Select an image and open the Print module.
- Click with the cursor on the "Create Saved Print" button at the top right of the work area.
- Alternatively, click with the cursor on the

plus (+) sign in the header bar of the Collections panel and choose "Create Print" from the menu that appears.

- Name your Print collection in the top blank. (Figure 103)
- Leave this Print collection as a top level collection.
- Check the "Make new virtual copies" box by clicking in it with the cursor.
- Click with the cursor on the Create button at the bottom right of the Create Print dialog box.
- The Print Collection will show up in the Collections panel as a top level Collection with a printer icon to its left. (Yellow circle, Figure 104)

Using this setup, you can add images to the Print Collection by dragging them into it. The number of images in the Print Collection will be indicated on the right side of the Print Collection, but you will not be able to see what the images are without opening the Print Collection.

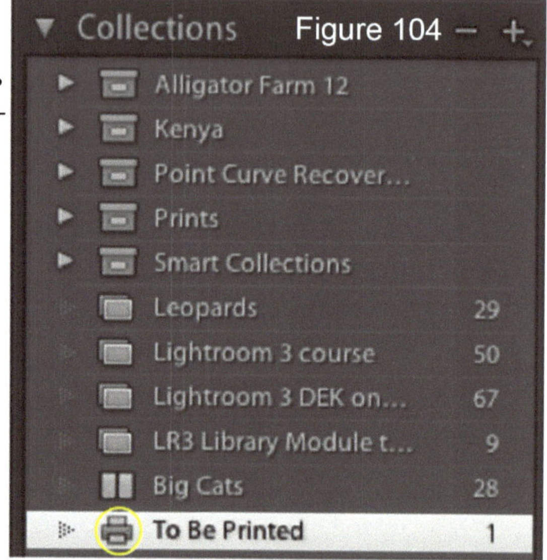


The Print collection will be in the Collections panel in all modules and will have a printer icon to the left of it so you know it is your Print collection. Once you have finished placing develop settings on an image and soft proofing it, you can drag it to the Print collection. When you decide to print images they will be waiting for you in the Print collection when you move to the Print module. Just remember to make any images you move to the Print Collection Virtual Copies. Make the Virtual Copy in the Print module and then move the virtual copy into the Print Collection.

The reason you want Virtual Copies in the Print collection is that the images here should be as you want to print them. If you place a master copy in your Print collection and then change the develop settings in the develop module, those new develop settings will also be reflected in the image in the Print collection, whereas they will not if the image is a Virtual Copy in the Print collection.

## Getting to the Print Module

Once you have finished applying develop settings to your image, you should soft proof the image in the Develop module and then move it into the Print module. To get to the Print module, do one of the following:

- From the Window menu at the top of the screen, select Print (Use this method if you have a lot of time)
- Click with the cursor on Print in the module picker at the top right of the screen.
- Use the keyboard shortcut, hold down the Option and Command (Macintosh), Alt and Control (PC) keys and press the 6 key on the keyboard.
- Use a better keyboard shortcut, hold down the Command (Macintosh), Control (PC) key and press the P key on the keyboard.

Any of these methods will open the Print module, so pick your favorite.

### The Screen Setup

In the menus at the top of the screen there is, as you would expect a new Print menu. The work area in the center of the screen is unchanged. In the left column of panels there is now only a Preview window with no magnification levels. There are two panels below the Preview window, Template Browser and Collections, the same as in the Slideshow module. The Template Browser consists of twenty-seven Lightroom® templates and a User Templates section for any print templates you create.

The Collections Panel is the same as it is in all the modules. At the bottom of the left column of panels on the Macintosh, there are two buttons, Page Setup. and Print Settings. On the PC there is only one Print Settings button. These will be discussed shortly. The Filmstrip is unchanged but the Toolbar has some changes. The following are the contents of the Print module Toolbar starting at the left side:

- A square icon, that will take you to the first of the images to be printed. (Yellow square, Figure 105)
- A left pointing arrow, the clicking on of which will take you to the previous page of images to be printed. (White ellipse, Figure 105)
- A right pointing arrow, the clicking on of which will take you to the next page of images to be printed. (White ellipse, Figure 105)
- Text that says "Use" with a selection following it.(Red circle, Figure 105) If you click with the cursor on the double pointed arrow to the right of the text (Blue circle, Figure 105), you will have a choice of "All Filmstrip Photos", "Selected Photos" or "Flagged Photos". for printing.
- On the right side of the toolbar is text informing you of how many photos are to be printed and what number the current image in the work area is out of the number to be printed. (Green arrow, Figure 105)

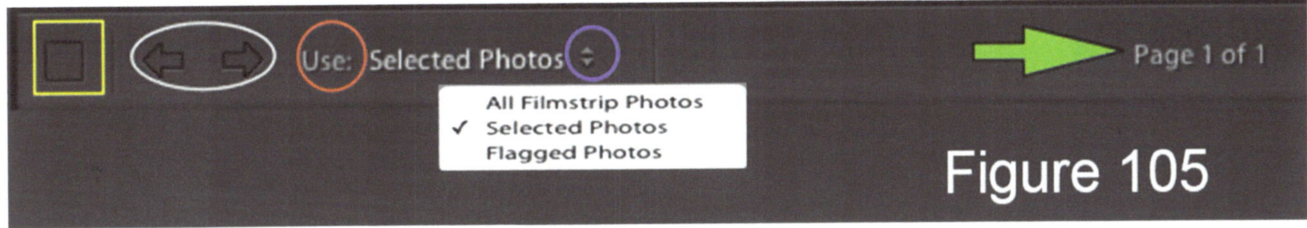

Figure 105

The right column of panels is where the print setup is accomplished.

## Page Setup

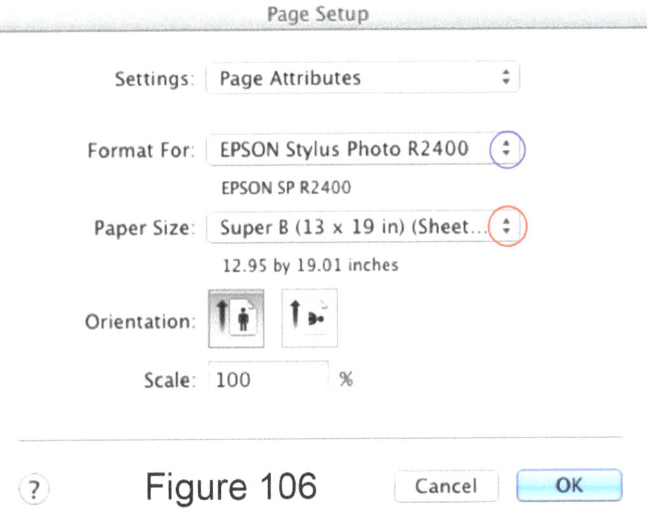

Figure 106

Once in the Print module with an image selected for printing, the first thing you should do is setup the page. So, click with the cursor on the Page Setup button at the bottom of the left column of panels. This will bring up the Page Setup dialog box on screen. (Figure 106) The first thing you need to do is tell Lightroom® what printer you are going to use. In the second blank down, titled "Format For" click with the cursor on the double pointed arrow on the right side of the blank. (Blue circle, Figure 106) Lightroom® will show you the available printers connected to your computer and you can choose one. The next thing to do is select the paper size in the third blank down. Click with the cursor on the double pointed arrow at the right side of this blank (Red circle, Figure 106) and from the menu of paper sizes choose the one you want. Next select the orientation for the print, portrait or landscape by clicking on the appropriate icon in the orientation section. With the printer selected and the page setup done, you are ready to prepare your image for printing, that's done in the right column of panels.

## Print Settings

The second thing necessary to get ready to print an image is to setup the Print Settings. On the Macintosh, there is a separate button for Print Settings at the bottom of the left column of panels. On the PC all the settings are under one button. To setup the Print Settings, do the following:

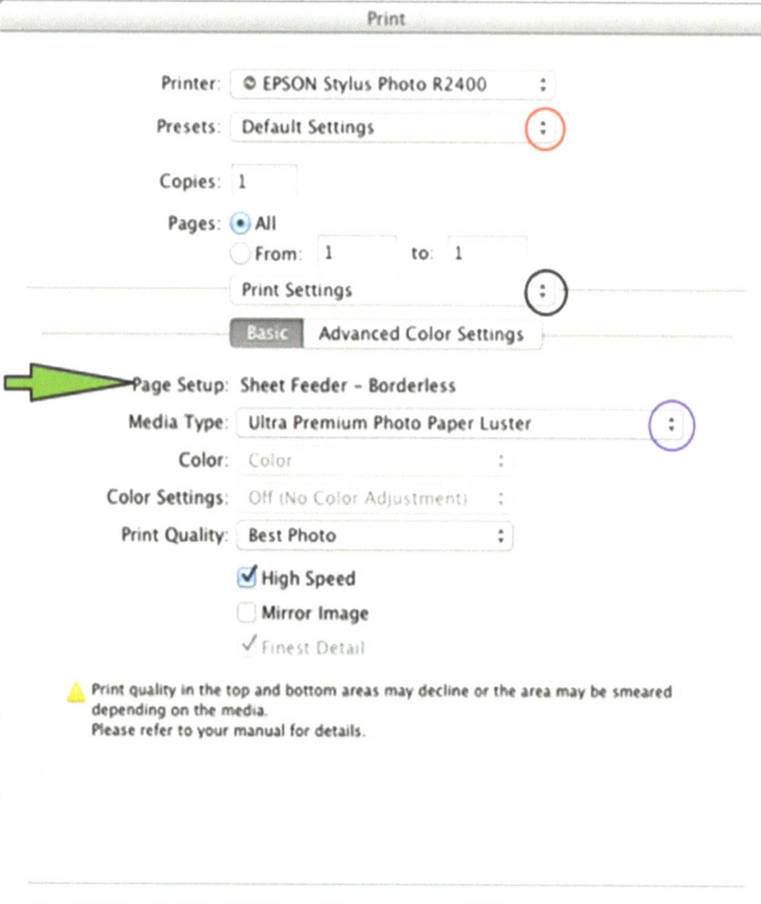

Figure 107

- On the Macintosh click with the cursor on the Print Settings button at the bottom of the left column of panels.
- In the center of the Print dialog box that opens on screen is a blank that says "Layout" with a double pointed arrow to the right of it. (Black circle, Figure 107)
- Click with the cursor on this double pointed arrow and from the resulting menu select "Print Settings".
- The bottom section of the Print dialog box will expand to show you the Print settings.
- In the bottom section, make sure the Page Setup selection is correct, the same as the one you chose in the Page Setup dialog box. (Green arrow Figure 107)
- Click with the cursor on the double pointed arrow at the right side of the Media Type blank. (Blue circle, Figure 107)
- All of the available types of paper will appear in a pop up menu.
- Choose the paper type on which you want to print.
- If your printer requires different kinds of ink, for different paper types (Matte, Glossy, etc), make sure the correct ink is installed for the type of paper on which you are going to print.
- Click with the cursor on the double pointed arrow at the right side of the blank labeled "Presets"
- From the Preset menu that appears select "Save Current Settings as Preset"
- In the dialog box that appears on screen, name the new print preset and indicate if it is for only the current printer or all your printers.
- Click with the cursor on the OK button at the bottom right of the dialog box.
- Click with the cursor on the Save button at the bottom right of the Print dialog box.

Set up print settings for each type and size of paper on which you print. It will save you time in the Print module.

## The Right Column of Panels

### Layout Style

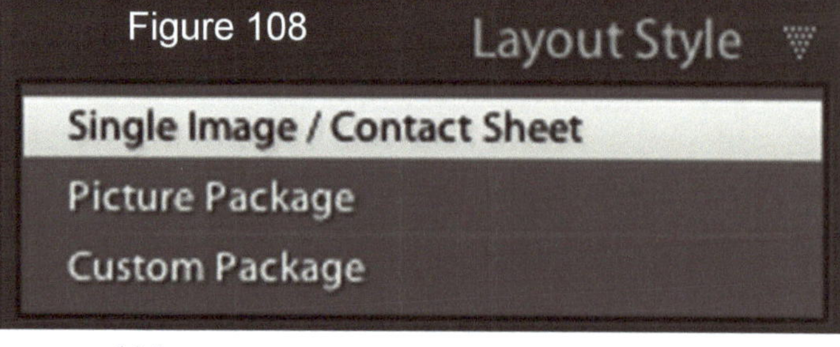

Figure 108

The top panel in the right column of panels is the Layout style. (Figure 108) There are three choices for the style, Single image/Contact Sheet, Picture Package and Custom Package. Single Image is pretty much self explanatory. With Picture Package, you can choose a template and place one image on the page at different sizes. The Custom Package allows you to choose a template and then place multiple images of different sizes on the same page. The Contact Sheet, Picture Package and Custom Package are where the Template Browser really comes in handy. Regardless of which Layout Style you choose, you will need to spend time in the other panels on the right side of the work area.

## Single Image Layout Style

When you select the Single Image layout, the image selected in the Filmstrip will show up on screen. There are four single image templates in the Template Browser and you can customize all of them. For Example, if you choose the 5x7 template, the image will show up in the center of the work area as a 5x7 image in landscape mode. What you then need to do is work in the other panels to get the image ready to print. Each of the panels on the right side of the screen will be discussed separately, so what follows is a brief discussion of what is possible in the various Layout styles. In the Image Settings panel, you can place a check mark in the box in front of Zoom to Fill and the image will fill the space, but may be cropped at the sides. If you have zoomed the image to fill, when you place your cursor over the image it will turn into a hand cursor. Click with the hand cursor on the image and you will be able to move the image around inside the frame. Placing a check mark in the other boxes in the Image Settings panel will allow you to rotate the image to Fit better on the paper size. This might work well when you have a landscape orientation image for which you have chosen Zoom to Fill. You can add a stroke border and you can also change the color of the stroke border by clicking with the cursor on the color picker box to the right of the text "Stroke Border". The choice of "Repeat One Image per Page" really doesn't apply to the Single Image layout.

In the Layout panel, you can change the margins to make room on one side or the other for information in an Identity Plate. Since you are only printing one image, there is no need to change the Page Grid or Cell Size.

In the Guides panel, you can turn on Rulers, Page Bleed and Dimensions if you want to know that information.

In the Page panel you can change the background color for your image if you place a check mark in the box in front of the text "Page Background Color" and use the color picker box to the right of that text. You can also place an Identity Plate on the image and move it around to any position you want. If you changed the margins in the Layout panel to make room for the Identity Plate you can place it outside the image in the area you cleared for it. You can have as many Identity Plates as you want, so you can edit an Identity Plate as described in the Titles panel of the Slideshow module to provide information and place it anywhere on the print. For example:

- In the Layout panel move the bottom margin up with the slider to make room for the Identity Plate.
- Edit an Identity Plate to provide information about the image, set the opacity and scale with the sliders.
- Place a check mark in the Identity Plate box to activate it and place it on the image.
- Click with the cursor on the Identity Plate and move it outside the image to the bottom of the print.

You can also place a watermark on your image by placing a check mark in the appropriate box. You can also place page numbers, info and crop marks. If you choose to place a watermark on your image to be printed, you can also edit your watermarks by clicking with the cursor on the double pointed arrow at the right side of the Watermarks bar and choosing "Edit Watermarks" from the resulting menu. If you would like to place Photo Info on the image, placing a check mark in the box in front of this text will place the Photo Info at the bottom of the image. Your choices for photo info are caption, custom text, date, equipment, exposure, filename sequence and title. With the exception of custom text, all of the other information is pulled by Lightroom® from the image metadata. You can also edit any text and change the font size in the Page panel.

The next panel down in the right column of panels in the Print module is the Print Job, but since the choices in the Print Job panel are the same for all the Layout Styles, the different Layout Styles should be discussed first.

## Contact Sheet Layout Style

Probably the easiest Layout Style to create is the Contact Sheet. There are four contact sheet templates in the Template Browser and there is not really a need for any others because they can all be customized using the Layout panel in the Print module. The numbers in front of each Contact Sheet template refer to the number of columns and rows in the contact sheet template. To create a Contact Sheet, do the following:

- Create a Print Collection of images in the Library module you would like to print if you have not already done so.
- Move to the Print module.
- Select all the images in the Collection (Hold down the Command (Macintosh), Control (PC) key and press the A key on the keyboard.
- Click with the cursor on the "Create Saved Print" button at the top right of the work area to create a Print Collection.
- Click with the cursor in the check box in front of "Make new virtual copies"
- Select a contact sheet template from the Template Browser.
- Lightroom will automatically populate the cells in the Contact Sheet template.

Depending on how many images you have you can customize the contact sheet template by doing the following in the Layout panel:

- Use the page grid sliders in the Layout panel to increase or decrease the number of rows and/or columns.
- Use the sliders in the Cell Spacing section to increase or decrease the vertical or horizontal cell spacing.
- Use the sliders in the Cell Size section to increase or decrease the height or width of the cells.
- Make all the cells square by placing a check mark in the box at the bottom of the panel.

In the Image Settings panel you can zoom the image to fill the cell, rotate the image to fit the cell and increase or decrease the stroke border. The option for repeating one image on a page is also available, but then it is not a contact sheet of multiple images anymore.

In the Page panel there are several useful options. You can change the background color of the template, add a watermark and photo info. In the case of the watermark, it will be added to each image on the page. Photo info such as exposure can be selected from the drop down menu that appears when you place a check mark in the box in front of the text "Photo Info" and click with the cursor on the double pointed arrow on the right side of this section. The text will appear at the bottom of each image.

When you are done creating your contact sheet, if you have put a lot of effort into making changes in the template, you can save it as a new User Template. To create a new User Template for your contact sheet, do the following:

- Click with the cursor on the plus (+) sign in the header bar of the Template Browser.
- Alternatively, use the keyboard shortcut, hold down the Command (Macintosh), Control (PC) key and press the N key on the keyboard.
- If you have a lot of time, from the Print menu at the top of the page, select "New Template".
- In the New Template dialog box that pops up on screen, give the new template a descriptive name.
- Place it in the User Templates folder unless you want to create a new folder for templates.
- Click with the cursor on the Create button on the bottom right of the New Template dialog box.

## Picture Package Layout Style

The Picture Package Layout Style allows you to place one image of different sizes or the same size on a page. You can start by selecting a template from the Template Browser and Lightroom® will place an image in the cells in the template you have chosen. There are many options for creating your Picture Package layout style. The following are what can be accomplished to create exactly the Picture Package layout you want:

- Delete any cell in the template layout by clicking with the cursor on it and pressing the Delete (Macintosh), Backspace (PC) key.
- Alternatively delete a cell by Control (Macintosh), Right (PC) clicking on it and from the menu that appears selecting "Delete Cell"
- Rotate a cell by Control (Macintosh), Right (PC) Clicking on it and selecting "Rotate Cell" from the resulting menu.
- Go to the Cell panel and add any size cell to the layout by clicking with the cursor on the dimensions you need.
- Create a custom dimension cell by clicking with the cursor on the double pointed arrow in the header bar of any cell size and selecting "Edit" from the resulting menu. Type in the new dimensions and Lightroom® will place the custom cell on the page.
- Move any cell to a new position on the page by clicking on it with the cursor and dragging it to a new position.
- Increase or decrease the spacing between cells by using the Cell Spacing sliders in the Layout panel.

TIP: When moving cells to new positions in Picture Package, the last cell placed will be in front of any previous cells. You cannot take a previously placed cell and move it on top or in front of a cell that has been placed on the page after it.

TIP: As you add cells to a page, if there is no room for the new cell, Lightroom® will automatically add a new page and place the new cell on it.

TIP: If you have selected zoom to fill in the Image settings panel, in order to move the image around in the frame you will need to hold down the Command (Macintosh), Control (PC) key which will turn your cursor into a hand cursor when you hover it over a cell. Clicking with the hand cursor on the image will allow you to move the image around in the cell.

After completing the Picture Package cell layout you should add it to the User Templates in the Template Browser for future use.

## Custom Package Layout

The Custom Package layout is far more versatile and easier to create. What follows is the simplest way to create a Custom Package layout:

- In the Layout Style panel at the top of the right column of panels select the Custom Package layout.
- The last template you used in creating a Custom Package layout will appear on screen.
- Open the Cell panel and click with the cursor on the "Clear Layout" button to clear all the images and cells and leave a blank page.

You now have two options for creating a Custom Package layout.

First Option:

- Chose the images you want in the Custom Package layout.
- Select an image in the Filmstrip and drag it onto the page. By default it will have approximately a 2x3 in aspect ratio with handles at the corners and midpoint on all four sides.
- Continue dragging images onto the page.
- Open the Cells panel.
- If you want to maintain the 2x3 aspect ratio place a check mark in the box in front of the text "Lock to Photo Aspect Ratio". (If you leave the box unchecked, you can drag the aspect ratio to what ever you want.)
- To change the size of an image on the page, select the image by clicking on it with the cursor and click with the cursor on any one of the handles and drag the cell to the size you want it.
- You can also adjust the size of the cell by clicking with the cursor on the slider bars or in the scrubby slider box at the end of the slider bars in the "Adjust the Selected Cell" section of the Cells panel and dragging left or right to increase or decrease the cell size.
- Alternatively, you can click with the cursor in the scrubby slider box and type in a dimension.
- Place as many images on the page as you can, change the dimensions and move the images around on the page to create the Custom Package layout.
- You can place an image on top or inside another image and move it to the back or front , rotate or delete it by Control (Macintosh), Right (PC) clicking on the image and choosing where you want the image to be on the page from the resulting menu.
- If you like the Custom Package layout after you have completed it, save it as a User Template in the Template Browser panel.

Second Option:

- In the Cells panel, select an aspect ratio from the buttons and click with the cursor on it.
- The blank cell with the chosen aspect ratio will appear on the page.
- Continue to place blank cells of various aspect ratios on the page, change the aspect ratio and move the cells around on the page until you have the Custom Package layout the way you want it.
- From the Filmstrip, select an image and drag it to the cell where you want to locate it.
- Re-arrange the cells on the page.
- After finishing the layout for your Custom Package, save it as a User Template in the Template Browser panel.

## The Image Settings Panel

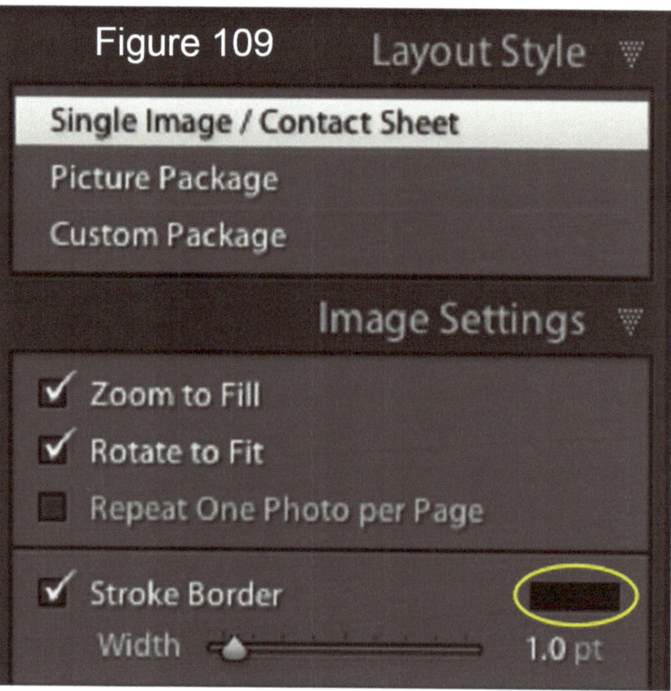


The options available in the Image Settings panel (Figure 109) are different depending on which Layout Style you choose in the top panel. If you choose the Single Image/Contact Sheet, (Figure 109) the options in the Image Settings panel are as follows:

- Zoom to Fill, which allows you to fill the frame with the image, but may cause some of the image to be cropped.
- If you choose Zoom to Fill, when you hover your cursor over the image it turns into a hand cursor. Clicking with the hand cursor in the frame allows you to move the image around in the frame.
- Rotate to Fit, which is valuable depending on whether your image is landscape or portrait ori-

entation. If you have an image with landscape orientation and the frame is a portrait orientation, choosing "Rotate to Fit" will allow you to print the whole image.
- Repeat One Photo per Page really doesn't apply to the Single Image/Contact Sheet Layout Style because either you have only a single image or if you choose Contact Sheet and then "Repeat One Photo per Page it is no longer a Contact Sheet. Instead it is a Picture Package.
- You can Add a Stroke Border and use the slider bar beneath the Stroke Border selection or the scrubby slider box at the end of the slider bar to control the size of the Stroke border. A Stroke Border is a line outside the perimeter of the image the size and color of which can be changed.
- You can also change the color of the Stroke Border by using the color picker box to the right of the Stroke Border selection. (Yellow ellipse, Figure 109)

The options in the Image Settings panel for the Picture Package Layout style are as follows:
- Zoom to Fill and Rotate to Fit are still present in the top section. (Figure 110)
- Repeat One Photo per Page is no longer a choice because by definition, Picture Package only has one image per page.
- In the second section of the Image Settings panel for Picture Package, you can add a Photo Border, which is the same as a Stroke Border. The difference between a Stroke Border and a Photo Border is the Stroke Border width is limited to 20 pt and the Photo Border width can be up to 36 pt.
- You can control the width of the Photo Border with either the slider bar or the scrubby slider box at the end of the slider bar.
- You can also add an Inner Stroke to each image on screen using the Inner Stroke slider bar or the scrubby slider box at the end of the slider bar. An Inner Stroke causes the image to be smaller in size because it compresses the image inside the frame. An Inner Stroke width is limited to 20 pt.
- You can change the color of the Inner Stroke using the color picker box to the right of the section. (Yellow circle, Figure 110)

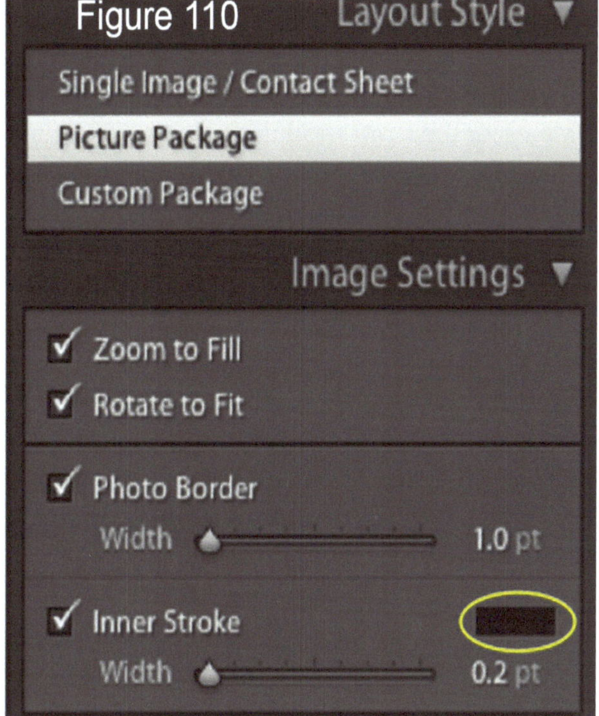


The options in the Image Settings panel for the Custom Package Layout Style (Figure 111) are only slightly different than those of the Picture Package Layout Style. They are as follows:
- There is no Zoom to Fill choice in the Custom Package Layout Style.
- The Rotate to Fit option is still present and again valuable for landscape and portrait orientated images.
- The Photo Border option is still present and the width limitation is 36 pt.
- The Inner Stroke option is still available and the width is limited to 20 pt.
- You can also change the color of the Inner Stroke using the color picker box. (Yellow ellipse, Figure 111)

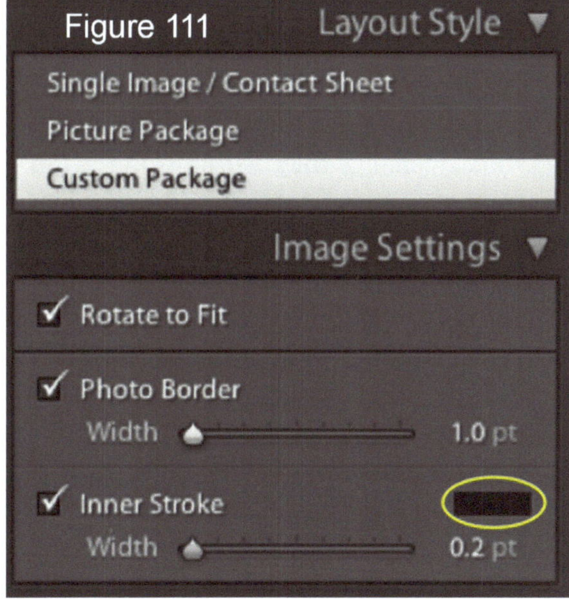

With the Custom Package Layout Style you have more versatility in setting up the layout of your images. However, with the Zoom to Fill option missing you have to tell Lightroom® how much of the image to show by cropping the image in the Develop module.

## The Layout Panel

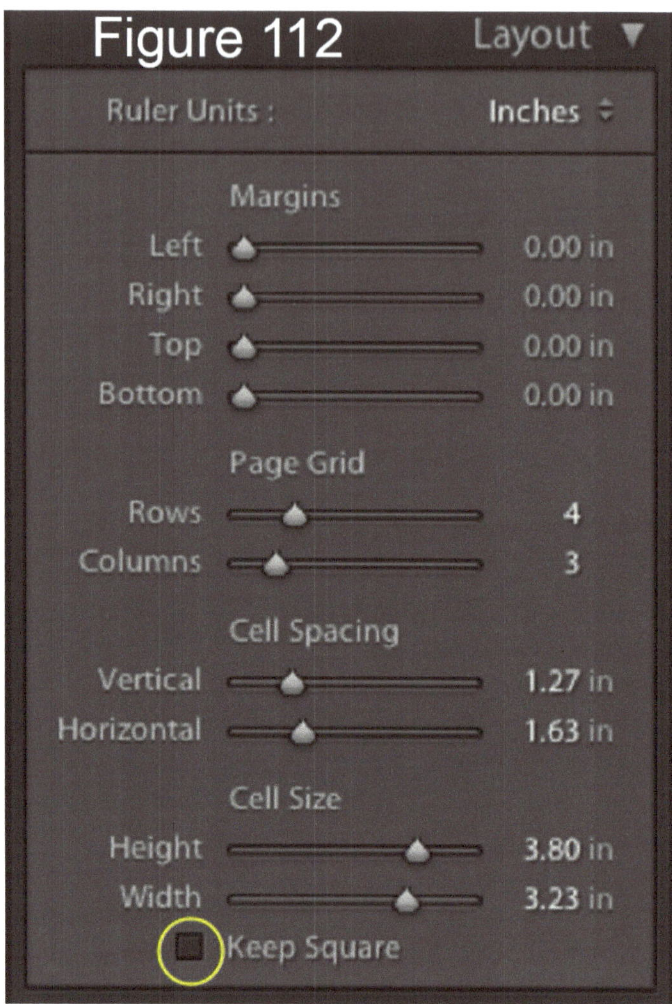


The Layout panel is only available when Single Image/Contact sheet is chosen for the Layout Style. (Figure 112) Any time you open the Print module, it will open with last template you used to print an image or images. If the last time you printed an image or images, you used the Custom Package Layout Style, the Print module will open with that custom template on screen, but with no images in the frames even if you have images selected in the Filmstrip. If the Picture Package Layout Style was the last template used, the Print module will open with the last Picture Package template used and the frames will be filled with image that is selected in the filmstrip. When the Print module opens, the last Layout Style used will be indicated in Layout Style Panel. Once the Print module is open, if you select a template from the Template Browser that has more than one image, the Print module will open the Picture Package Layout Style and the Layout panel for the Single Image/Contact sheet will disappear. The same will happen if you select a Custom template in the Template Browser, Lightroom® will open the Custom Layout Style and the Layout panel will disappear. Therefore, if you want to print just one image, you must select the Single Image/Contact Sheet Layout Style in the Layout Style panel or one of the single image templates from the Template Browser. Making this selection will open the Layout panel beneath the Image Settings panel on the right column. (Figure 112) Before you use the Layout panel for a single image, make sure you have chosen the printer with which you want to print the image in the Print Settings dialog box. Also, make sure the correct paper size is chosen in the Print Settings dialog box. If you want to print a 13x19 image and in the Print Settings, 8x10 is chosen, the Layout panel will limit you to the 8x10 aspect ratio. The following are the options available for printing a single image in the Layout panel:

- You can change the ruler units in the top section from inches, which is the default to centimeters, millimeters, points or picas.
- In the second section, you can change any of the margins using the slider bars or the scrubby slider box at the right side of each slider bar.
- The default margin is .25 inches, but you can change that to zero or to within about .25 inches of whatever the limit of your image width and height is.
- In addition to changing the margins with the slider bars and/or scrubby slider box, you can hover your cursor over a margin on the image in the work area and it will turn into a double pointed arrow. Click with the cursor on the margin and you can slide it left or right or up and down depending on which margin it is over which the cursor is hovering. The Cell Size Height and width slider bars will move correspondingly and indicate the size changes in the scrubby slider boxes to the right of the slider bars.
- You can change the on screen size of the image by moving the sliders on the Cell Size Height and Width

sliders on the slider bars or by using the scrubby slider box at the end of the height and width slider bars.
- If you want to print a borderless image, set all the margins to zero.

There are several more options in the Layout panel for Contact Sheets. A single image layout can be turned into a contact sheet layout simply by choosing one of the contact sheet templates from the Template Browser. If you do this, the single image that is on screen will show up in the top left cell of the contact sheet. If you then go to the Filmstrip and select a series of other images, Lightroom® will place them in the other cells on the contact sheet. Other options available for Contact Sheets are as follows:

- You can change the number of rows and columns by using the slider bars or the scrubby slider boxes at the end of the slider bars in the Page Grid section of the Layout panel.
- You can change the vertical and/or horizontal spacing between the cells by using the slider bars or scrubby slider boxes at the end of the slider bars in the Cell Spacing section of the Layout panel.
- A second way to change the vertical or horizontal spacing between the cells in a Contact Sheet is to hover your cursor over either the vertical or horizontal margin of one of the cells. The cursor turns into a double pointed arrow. If you click with the double pointed arrow cursor on one of the margins you can slide it up or down or left or right depending on which margin you clicked on. As you move the cursor up and down or left and right, the vertical or horizontal space between the cells will increase or decrease.
- You can change the size of the cells up to a certain amount, depending on how many cells are on the Contact Sheet by using the sliders or scrubby slider boxes at the end of the sliders in the Cell Size section of the Layout panel.
- You can keep cells square by placing a check mark in the box in front of the text "Keep Square" at the bottom of the Layout panel. (Yellow circle, Figure 112)

To use the scrubby slider boxes, either click with the cursor in the box, hold the cursor down and move the one fingered hand cursor right or left. Moving to the right increases the number, to the left decreases the number of rows or columns. The number of rows and columns can also increased or decreased by clicking once in the scrubby slider box and typing a number into the scrubby slider box at the right side of the slider bars in the Page Grid section of the Layout panel.

The space between the images can be increased using either the cell spacing or cell sizing slider bars or the scrubby slider box at the right side of the cell spacing or cell sizing sections of the Layout panel. Finally, the images can be kept square by clicking with the cursor in the box in front of the text "Keep Square" at the bottom of the Layout panel.

## The Guides Panel and the Rulers, Grids & Guides Panel

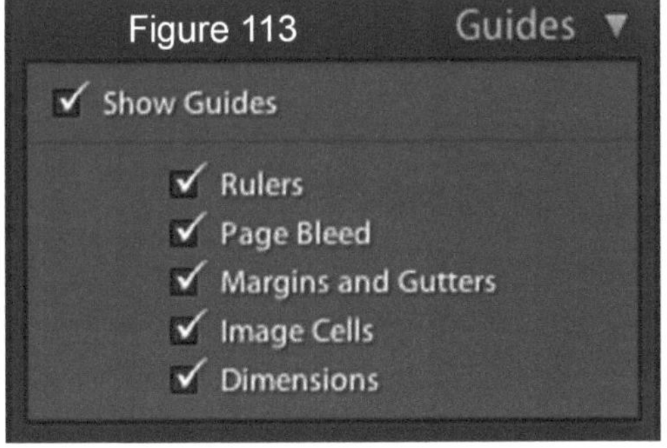


When the Single Image/Contact Sheet Layout Style is selected the Guide panel has only one section. (Figure 113) All of the options in the Guide panel are grayed out until you place a check mark in the box in front of the text "Show Guides". With the guides turned on, in this section you have the following options:

- You can make visible the rulers at the top and left side of the screen by placing a check mark in the box in front of the text "Rulers".
- You can turn on the Page Bleed by clicking with the cursor in the Page Bleed box, but there is usually no visible difference on screen.
- You can turn on the Margins and Gutters by clicking with the cursor in the box in front of that selection. Light gray vertical and horizontal lines will appear between the cells. The Margins and Gutters are seen better when there are no images in the cells.

- Placing a check mark in the box in front of the text "Cells" will show all the cells on screen with black outlines.
- Placing a check mark in the box in front of the text "Dimensions" will show you the dimensions of the cells at the top of each cell.

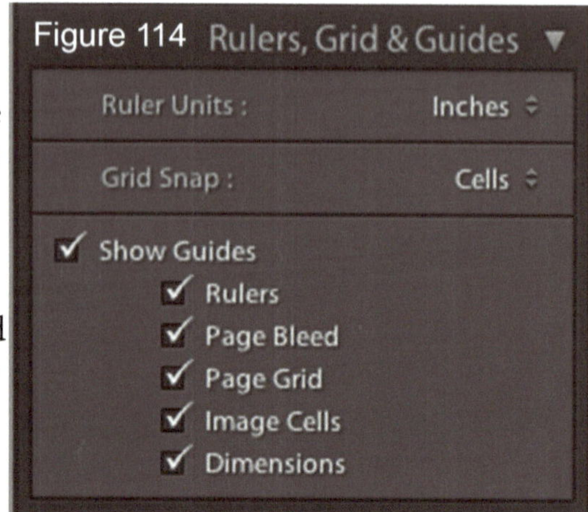


When Picture Package or Custom Package is selected as the Layout Style, the Layout panel disappears and the Guides panel is replaced by the Rulers, Grids & Guides panel. (Figure 114) The difference between this panel and the Guides panel for the Single Image/Contact Sheet Layout Style is that two sections have been added. The top section is now the same as the top section in the Layout panel for the Single Image/Contact Sheet Layout Style, a section for changing the Ruler Units has been added. The second added section in the Rulers, Grid & Guides panel is a section for Grid Snap has been added for the Picture Package and Custom Package Layout Styles. There is only one difference in the Rulers, Grids & Guides panel between the Picture Package Layout Style and the Custom Package Layout Style. The difference is that in the Picture Package Layout Style, the default in the Grid Snap section is "Cells", whereas in the Custom Package Layout Style the default for the Grid Snap section is "Off". The options available in the third section of the Rulers, Grids & Guides panel are the exactly the same as the options available in the Guides panel for the Single Image/Contact Sheet Layout Style. In order to activate the options, you need to place a check mark in the box labeled "Show Guides". The options are then activated by clicking with the cursor in the box in front of each option. When you click with the cursor in the box in front of "Dimensions", the image dimensions appear at the top of each cell. The units of measure will be what you selected in the top section of the Rulers, Grids & Guides panel. Your choices are inches, centimeters, millimeters, points or picas.

## The Cells panel

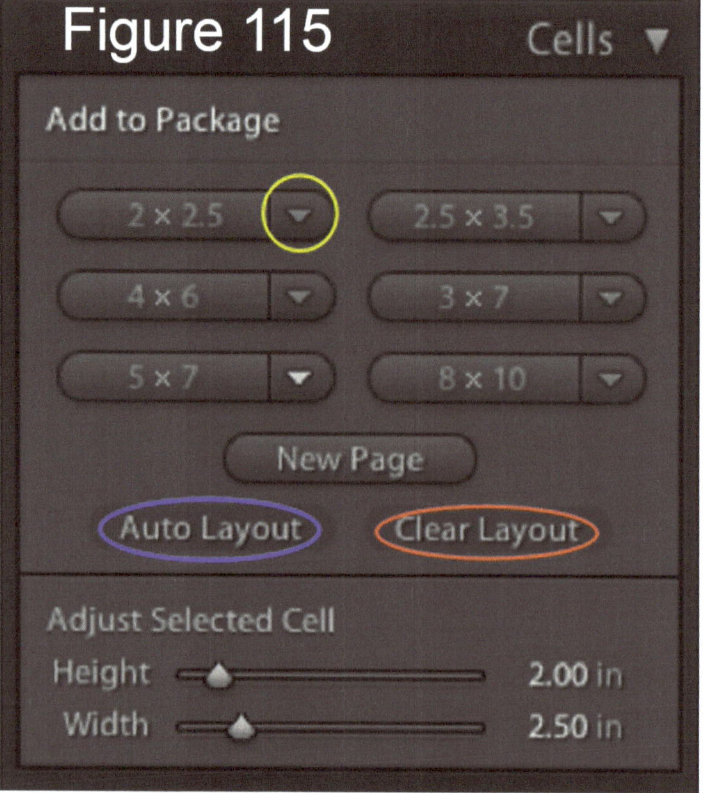


The Cells panel is only available in the Picture Package and Custom Package layout style. In the Cells panel you can create a custom layout for either the Picture Package or Custom Package Layout Styles. The top section of the Cells panel is for adding cells to the layout. There are six buttons in this section, each one of which is labeled with a different cell dimension or aspect ratio (Figure 115) Each button has a down pointing arrow to the right of the dimensions. (Yellow circle, Figure 115) It is kind of a mystery that there are six buttons, when clicking with the cursor on the down pointing arrow on the right side of the button brings up a menu that includes of all the other standard aspect ratios from which to choose and the opportunity to create a cell with your own custom dimensions. (Figure 116) You can use the same button to place all the cells with different dimensions on the page. To create your own custom layout for either the Picture Package or Custom Package Layout Styles, do the following:

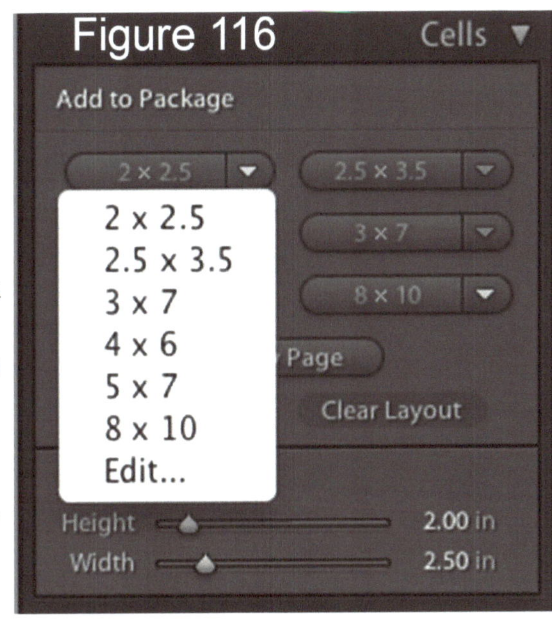


- Select either the Picture Package or Custom Package Layout Style. Whatever the last layout or template you used for either of the Layout Styles will appear on the page on screen. If it is a Picture Package layout the cells will be filled with an image. If it is a Custom Package layout the cells will be blank.
- Click with the cursor on the "Clear Layout" button (Red ellipse, Figure 115) to clear the layout and give you a blank page.
- Click with the cursor on a button with the aspect ratio you want for your first cell.
- A cell with the chosen aspect ratio will appear on the page on screen.
- If none of the standard aspect ratios are what you want for a cell, click with the cursor on the down pointing arrow at the right side of one of the buttons (Yellow circle, Figure 115) and from the resulting menu choose "Edit".
- A "New Custom Size" dialog box will pop up on screen. (Figure 117) Type in the dimensions you want and click with the cursor on the "Add" button at the bottom right of the New Custom Size dialog box.

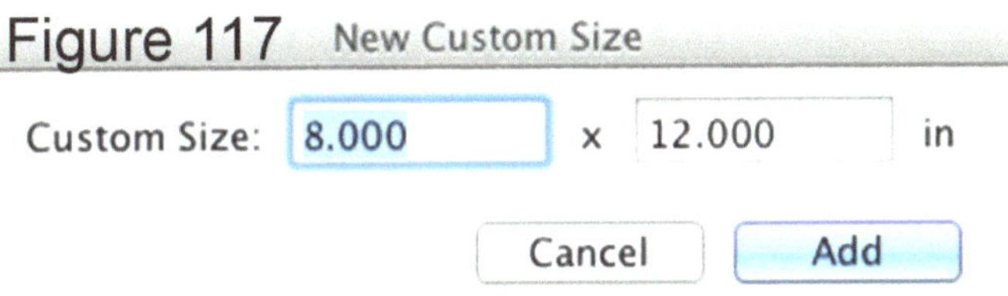


- The custom sized cell will appear on screen and the new custom size will be added to the menu choices of which ever button was used to create the new custom size.
- Continue to add cells to the page until you have it the way you want it.
- After placing the cells on a page, you can select a cell and change the width and height by using the width and height slider bars or scrubby slider boxes in the bottom section of the Cells panel.
- You can also hover the cursor over one of the borders of a cell, selected or not and the cursor will turn into a double pointed arrow allowing you to move the border and change the width and/or height of the cell.
- If you like the custom layout when you are finished, save it as a template by going to the Print menu at the top of the screen and selecting "New Template".
- In the New Template dialog box that appears on screen, name the new template and click the create button at the bottom right of the New Template dialog box.

Each time you place a cell on the page, if you click with the cursor on the "Auto Layout" button, (Blue ellipse, Figure 115) Lightroom® will arrange the cells on the page for you to create the greatest amount of space for more cells. If there is not enough room on one page, Lightroom® will automatically open another page. You can add another page by clicking with the cursor on the "Add a Page" button. (Figure 115)

TIP: The Custom Package Layout Style is a very easy way to create a composite image.

## The Page Panel

It is with the options in the Page panel (Figure 118) that you can add important and/or interesting information to your print. Regardless of which Layout Style you have chosen, some or all of the options can be used. The following are the options available in the Page panel:

- Change the color of the background by clicking with the cursor in the box in front of the text "Page

Background Color" and then picking a color from the color picker box available at the right side of this section.
- Add an Identity Plate to the page or to every image on the page.
- You can create an identity plate for what ever information you want show on the page or on each image on the page.
- To place the Identity Plate on each image, click with the cursor in the check box in front of the text "Render on every image" at the bottom of the Identity Plate section of the Page panel.
- Override the color of the Identity Plate by placing a check mark in the box in front of the text "Override Color" beneath the Identity Plate box and then pick a color from the color picker box to the right of that text.
- Change the opacity and size of the Identity Plate by using the opacity and scale sliders or the scrubby slider boxes at the end of the slider bars.
- Place a Watermark on every image by clicking with the cursor in the box in front of the text "Watermarking".
- By default the blank to the right of "Watermarking" says "None". Click with the cursor on the double pointed arrow to the right of "None" (Yellow circle, Figure 118) and you will be given the opportunity to select any of the watermarks you have already created, edit those watermarks or create a new watermark.

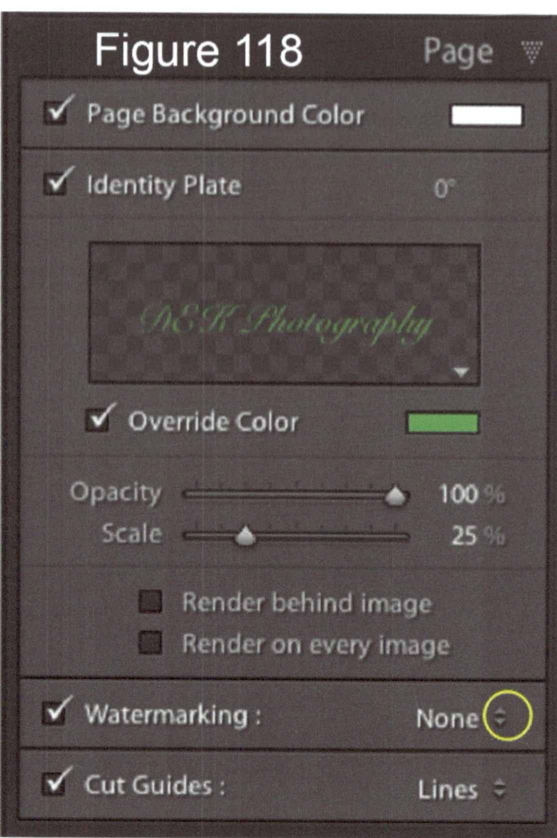


When the Single Image or Contact Sheet layout style has been selected, there are a couple of sections in the Page panel not available in the Picture Package or Custom Package layout styles. When Single Image/Contact Sheet Layout is selected, these three panels are added at the bottom of the Page Panel. (Figure 119)These sections are entitled "Page Options", "Photo Info" and "Font size". These sections allow you to do the following on a single image or contact sheet:

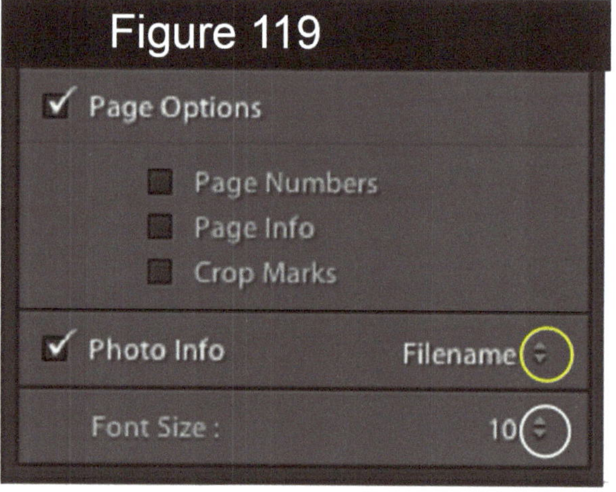


- Place information on the Single Image or Contact Sheet layouts in the Page Options section. The information that can be placed on the page to be printed is page numbers, page info and crop marks. The page info consists of the information about sharpening that is to be done, the ICC profile and the Printer name.
- To place the Page Options on the page, first click with the cursor in the check box in the box in front of "Page Options" and then place check marks in the appropriate boxes in this section.

The section below Page Options allows you to place Photo Info on the individual images. The Photo Info is information Lightroom® pulls from the metadata of each image.
- The choices for Photo info are found by clicking with the cursor on the double pointed arrow on the right side of the Photo Info header bar (Yellow circle, Figure 119)and include Caption, Custom Text, Date, Equipment, Exposure, Filename, Sequence, Title and Edit...
- Choosing "Edit..." from the Photo Info menu will bring up the Text Template Editor dialog box on screen.
- In the Text Template Editor dialog box you can create a template with a combination of any IPTC and/

or EXIF metadata as well as custom text. Creating Text Template is very similar to creating a new filename template. Select the IPTC or EXIF metadata in their respective blanks and click with the cursor on the insert button to the right of the blank. As you insert each choice, Lightroom® will pull the choice from the image metadata and place it in the Example blank. Above the blank will be an example of the new Text Template. (Green arrow, Figure 120)[1]

- After creating a new Text Template, click with the cursor on the double pointed arrow to the right of the Preset blank at the top of the Text Template Editor dialog box (Blue circle, Figure 120) and from the drop down menu choose "Save Current Settings as a New Preset".
- In the New Preset dialog box, name the new text preset and click with the cursor on the Create button at the bottom right of the New Preset dialog box.
- The new Text preset will now be available in the drop down menu of the Photo Info section of the Page panel.

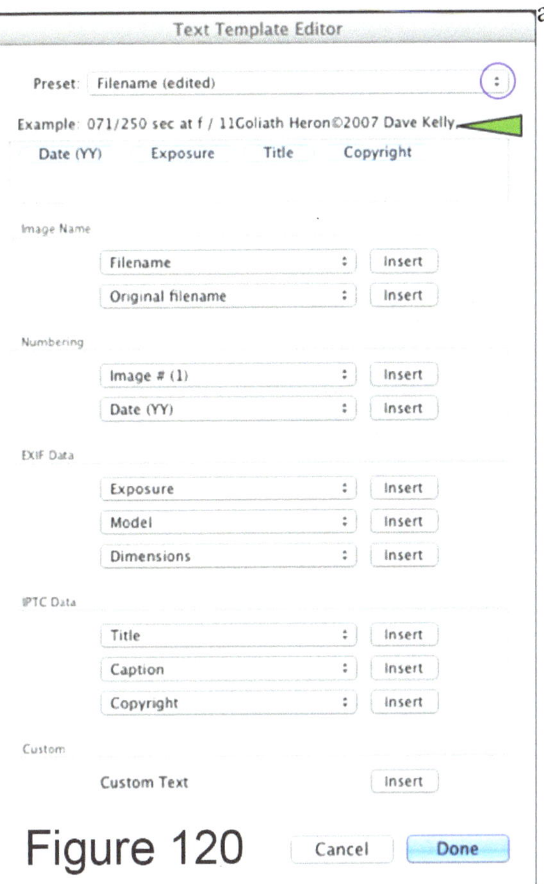


Figure 120

In the last section of the Page panel you can change the size of the Photo Info text on the image(s). To change the font size, click with the cursor on the double pointed arrow to the right of the font size (White circle, Figure 119)and the available font sizes will pop up on screen.

## Print Settings

When the Print module was originally opened, you were supposed to open the Page Setup and Print Settings and tell Lightroom® what printer you were using and what size and type paper you are using. If you did not do that, then now is the time to do it. So, just to review, with the page setup complete, if you are using a Macintosh, click with the cursor on the Print settings button at the bottom of the left column of panels. If you are using a PC, this information is included in the Page Setup, so click with the cursor on Page Setup to get to Print Settings. With the Print Settings dialog box on screen, (Figure 107, page 189) select your printer in the top blank and then go to the blank in the center of the Print dialog box which by default says "Layout". Click with the cursor on the double pointed arrow at the end of the blank that says "Layout". From the resulting menu choose "Print Settings". The print settings for different printers can be different. Some printers have multiple ways to handle different types of paper, some have only one way to handle paper. In the bottom section of the Print dialog box the first choice you will have to make is how the paper is fed into the printer. This depends on whether you are using a roll of paper or sheets of paper of a certain size. If your printer has multiple ways to feed paper to the printer, click with the cursor on the double pointed arrow to the right of the blank under Page Setup and choose how you want the paper fed into the printer. Next, choose the type of paper in the blank labeled "Media Type". It will be important to remember the type of paper because you will need to tell Lightroom® which ICC profile to use when you get to the Print Job. In the next blank down, choose whether you want the print to be color or black and white. Next, turn off the color management in the next blank down. You want Lightroom® to manage the color not the printer and if you leave the color management turned on you may get a double color management done. What you want to have happen is for Lightroom® to convert the image from the color space you are using in Lightroom® to the color space of the printer profile. Depending on your printer, you may not have all these choices or there

1

may be other choices to make. Finally, click with the cursor on the Save button at the bottom right of the Print dialog box. Later you can use these saved settings in setting up a Print Template.

## The Print Job Panel

Finally you get to the last panel in the right column of panels in the Print module, the Print Job. (Figure 121) The top section of the Print Job panel, "Print To:" by default, is set to Printer, because most of the time you are going to be sending the image to be printed. However, you can select to print to a JPEG file (more on this later). The second section of the Print Job panel is for selecting Draft Mode printing. This is a lower quality of printing and should be left unchecked.

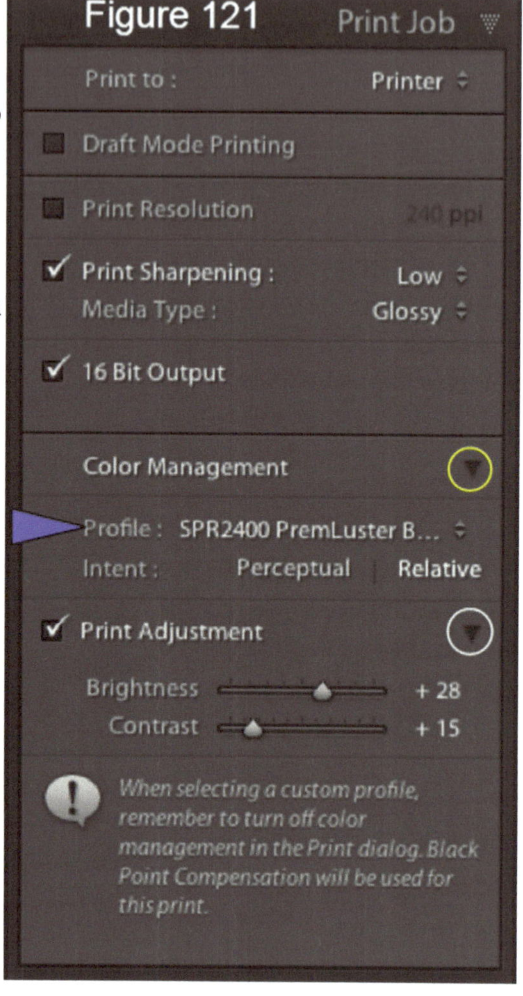


The next section in the Print Job panel has to do with Print Resolution. You can leave this box unchecked because Lightroom® can look at the image and see the image size and know the resolution at which you want to print the image and it will interpolate up or down to give you the correct Print Resolution. The only reason to change the Print Resolution is if you have taken the image to Photoshop and sharpened it at a certain resolution. If that is the case place a check mark in the box in front of Print Resolution and then type in the resolution in the scrubby slider box to the right of Print Resolution.

The next two choices in the Print Job panel are Sharpening and Media Type. To select the media type, click with the cursor on the double pointed arrow to the right. Your choices are Glossy and Matte. Click with the cursor on your choice. Choosing the sharpening you want may take some experimentation on your part to get the print you want. Depending on what type of image you are printing, you may want to choose Low, Standard or High for the sharpening.

If your printer is capable of 16 bit printing, then turn that option on in the next section.

The last section in the Print Job panel concerns color management and is the most important of the sections in the Print Job panel. By default, the Profile is set to "Managed by Printer". That is definitely not what you want. What you want is to match the Media Type you selected in the Print Settings dialog box. Each printer and/or paper manufacturer have created specific profiles for their printers and for their paper types. These profiles are called the ICC profiles and are available as downloads from the manufacturer's website. So, if you have not done it already, go to the website of the printer/paper manufacturer and download the ICC profiles for the printers/paper types. To set up the color management correctly, do the following:

- Click with the cursor on the double pointed arrow to the right of "Managed by Printer".
- Any ICC profiles you have previously used to print an image will be listed in the pop up menu that appears, along with the word "Other"
- If the ICC profile for the paper on which you want to print is listed, select it by clicking on the profile with the cursor.
- The ICC profile for the paper you chose will now be listed as the Profile in the Color Management section. (Blue arrow, Figure 121)

- If the ICC profile for the paper is not listed, then click with the cursor on "Other".
- A list of all the ICC profiles you have downloaded from the manufacturer's websites will pop up on Screen.
- Click with the cursor on the ICC Profile for your paper choice and it will now appear as the choice in the Profile blank.
- Lightroom® will now convert the color space you were using in the application to the proper printer color space for printing the image.

The next choice in the Color Management section is Perceptual or Relative. These are rendering intents and have to do with how Lightroom® handles out of gamut colors. These are the same rendering intents found in the Soft Proofing section of the Develop module and it is here in the Print Job panel of the Print module that you have to commit to one or the other. However, it is in the Soft Proofing section of the Develop module you should make the choice between Perceptual or Relative.

Finally, Adobe has added the ability to adjust your prints as the last step in the Color Management section of the Print Job panel. If your print comes out too light or dark you can use the Brightness slider or scrubby slider box to make it brighter or darker. If the print appear washed out or flat, you can use the Contrast slider or scrubby slider box to increase the contrast. To activate the Print Adjustment section of the Color Management section, place a check mark in the box in front of the text "Print Adjustment". If the Brightness and Contrast sliders are not visible, click with the cursor on the down pointing black arrow on the right side of the panel. (White circle, Figure 121) You will not be able to see the results of using these effects in the image on screen, like the print sharpening, they are added on output, so it will take some experimentation to get the print to look the way you want it. If you have calibrated your monitor and printer, you may not need these adjustments.

## Printing to JPEG

The second choice in the Print To section at the top of the Print Job panel is to print to a JPEG. (Figure 122) There are a couple of reasons you might want to print to a JPEG. If you have a blog and want to include images in the blog would be one reason. Another might be that you want to export the images so you can use them in a Power Point or Keynote presentation.

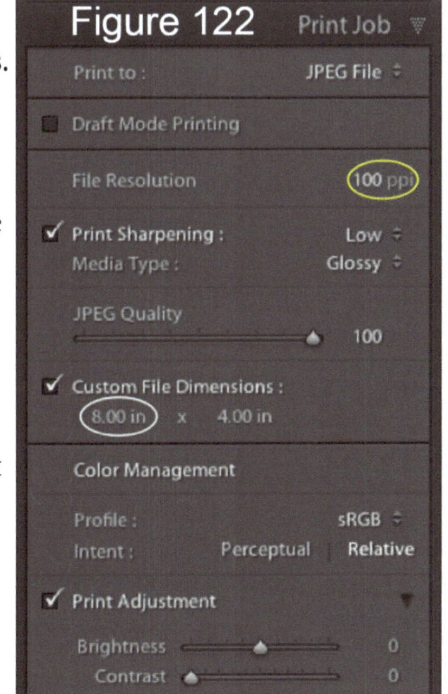


When you choose to print to a JPEG, the Print Job panel options changes. The main option you should pay attention to is Custom File Dimension which will determine the size of the image on screen. The Custom File Dimensions are in the unit of measure you chose in the first section of the Layout panel. Most of the time you are going to want the image to be a certain number of pixels on the longest side. To get the dimension you want,do the following:

- In the Custom File Dimension boxes, select the length of the longest side. The first box is for width, the second box for height.
- Set the Print Resolution scrubby slider box to 100 ppi.
- Example, if you want the image to be 800 pixels on the long side set it at 8 inches (If inches is your unit of measure). Setting the Print resolution at 100 pixels per inch will give you 800 pixels on the long side.
- Set the JPEG Quality to 100.

In the Color Management section of the Print to JPEG section, select the color space depending on where the image will be viewed. If it will only be viewed on screen then select the sRGB color space. The remaining choices are the same for images to be printed on a printer.

## Printing

When you are ready to print all you need to do is click with the cursor on the "Print One" button at the bottom right of the screen. If you click with the cursor on the "Print..." button, it will bring up the Print Settings dialog box with all the settings you have already made. If you chose "Print One", make sure that in the Toolbar, "Selected Photos" is the choice in the "Use" blank and that only the photos you want printed are selected. If you have All Filmstrip Photos selected or images selected that you don't want printed, then Lightroom® will print one copy of every selected image or every image in the Filmstrip.

## Create a Saved Print

After you have completed getting your print the way you want it, especially if you have set up a custom template and it is a print you feel you will be printing several times or a project for a client, there is one final thing to do in the Print module. If you did not do it when it was discussed at the beginning of the Print module, then now is the time to Create a Saved Print. This is different than saving a Print Template. A Print Template can be used with any collection of images. You just have to drag the images into the frames on the template. With a Saved Print, the images are fixed to the layout. So, just to review, the steps to take to create a saved print are as follows:

- Create a Collection Set titled something like "Saved Prints" (If you haven't already done so)
- Click with the cursor on the "Create a Saved Print" button at the top right of the work area.
- In the Create Print dialog box that appears on screen, give the print a descriptive name in the top blank.
- Place the print inside the Saved Prints collection set.
- In the Print Options section place a check mark in the box in front of the text "Make new virtual copies" if your images are not already virtual copies.
- Click with the cursor on the Create button at the bottom right of the Create Print dialog box.
- Your print will be saved as a print collection in the Saved Prints Collection Set and will be available to print any time in the future.

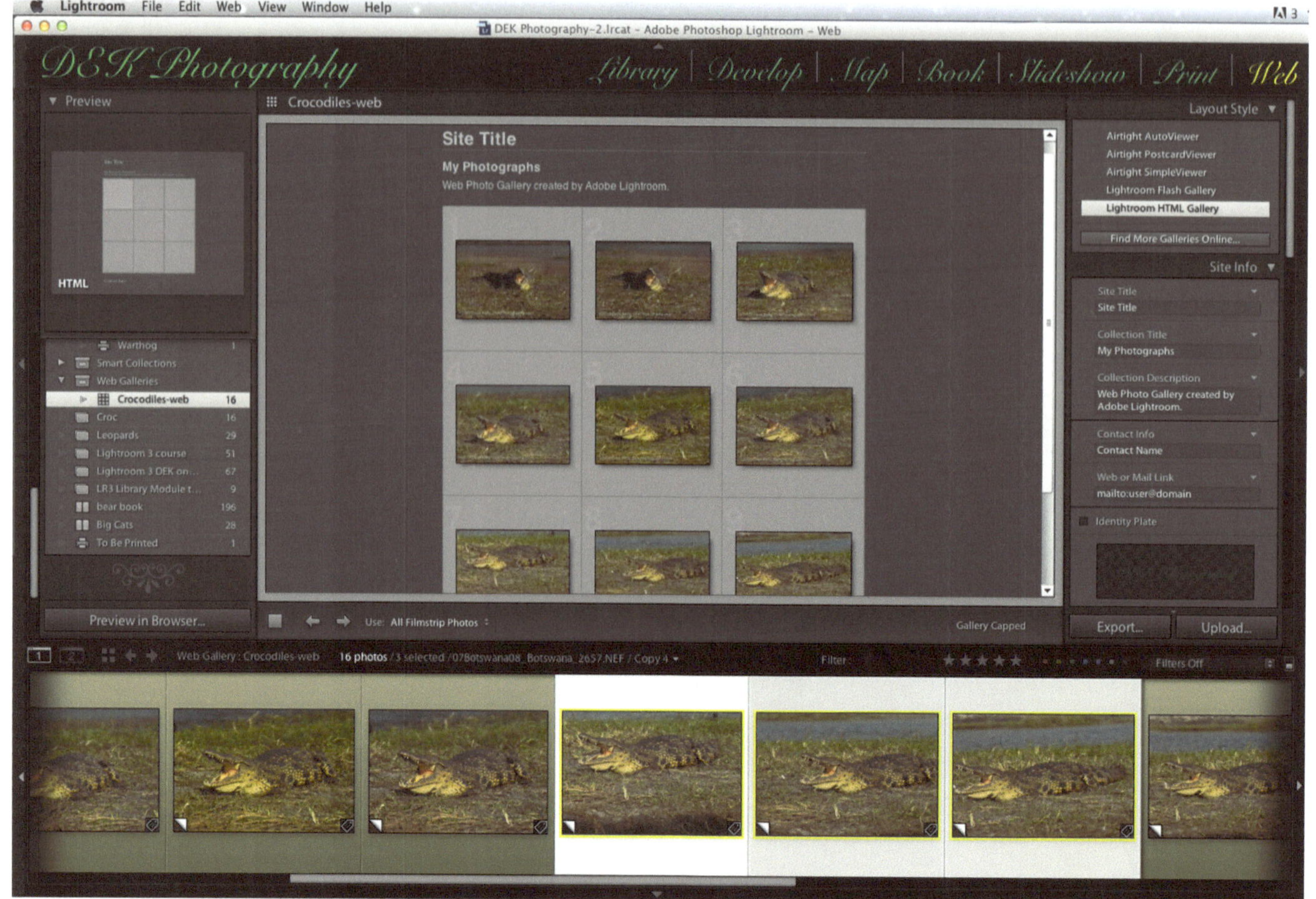


# The Web Module

Before you get started creating a web gallery, it's a good idea to get a domain name and hosting package. You can get both of these from a web hosting company of which there are many. Some have all the bells and whistles and can be very expensive, others are cheap and not very good. So, before you decide who will host your website, do a little research to find a company that meets your needs at a reasonable price. Once you decide on a company, buy your domain name and hosting package from them.

With your domain name secured, decide what you want your web gallery to be about. Do you want it to be a place to display your images in the hope of attracting clients or a place where you can share pictures with friends and family or an educational website where people can learn techniques, tips and tricks about photography. Whatever you decide will influence which images you choose to put in your web gallery. The best place to start creating your web gallery is in the Library module and the best way is to create a Collection of the images you want to display. Using Flagged images as an example, you might want to create a portfolio of your best images. This is where all the hard work you did in the Library module pays off (If you did it). If you bothered to create a Smart Collection of flagged images when you were flagging, rating and/or labeling your images then you are all set. Just select the flagged collection and open the Web module. If you did not create a Smart Collection of flagged images, but you did flag your best images then all you have to do is go to the Library Filter Bar and in the Attributes section select "Flagged" (that is if you bothered to go through all your images and flag, rate or label them). These should be your best images and they should be on screen. The procedure should be as follows:

- Open the Web module with your collection of images.
- If you plan to have multiple web galleries, click with the cursor on the plus (+) sign in the header bar of

the Collections panel and choose "create a Collection Set from the pop up menu. (Figure 123)

- Name the Collection Set "Web Galleries".
- Make sure all the images you want in the Web Gallery are selected in the Filmstrip.
- Create a Web Gallery by again clicking with the cursor on the plus sign (+) in the header bar of the Collections panel and selecting "Create Web Gallery" from the resulting menu. (Figure 123)

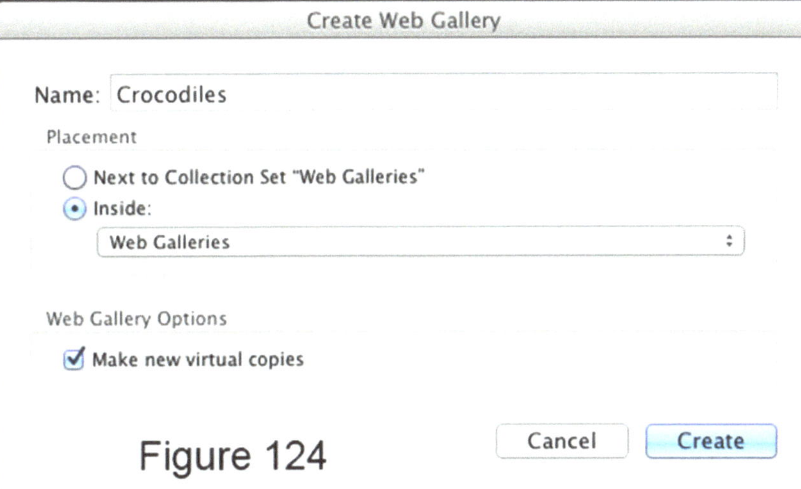

Figure 123

Figure 124

- Alternatively, click with the cursor on the "Create Saved Web Gallery" button at the top right of the work area.
- In the Create Web Gallery dialog box that pops up on screen, (Figure 124) name the Web Gallery in the top blank.
- Place the Web Gallery inside the Web Galleries Collection Set.
- In the Collections Options section of the Create Collection dialog box make sure you place a check mark in the box in front of the text "Make new virtual copies".
- The new Web Gallery will be listed in the Collections panel inside the Web Galleries Collection Set and will have a Web icon to the left. (Yellow circle, Figure 125)

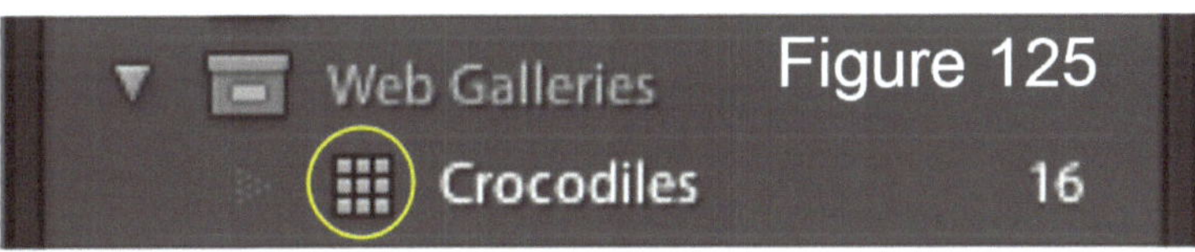

Figure 125

TIP: The advantage to creating a web gallery collection is that there is some functionality to it. When you hover your cursor over a web gallery collection in the Library, Develop or Map module a right pointing arrow appears to the right of the number of images in the collection. Clicking with the cursor on this arrow opens the web gallery in the Web module. When you hover your cursor over the web gallery in the Book, Slideshow or Print module, the right pointing arrow does not appear, however, clicking with the cursor on the web gallery will still open the web gallery in the Web module.

TIP: In the Create Web Gallery dialog box that pops up on screen, Lighroom® will not let you give a web gallery the same name as another collection, so add "-web" to the name.

## Web Screen Setup

The only difference in the menus at the top of the screen in the Web module is that the Web menu has replaced the menu for the previous module. In the left column of panels the Preview window is present, but without the ability to zoom in on the image in the work area. There are two panels present, the Template Browser and the Collections panel. At the bottom of the left column of panels is a "Preview in Browser" button that will let you see what your web gallery will look like when it is on line. The work area is the same as is the Filmstrip at the bottom of the screen. The Toolbar is only slightly changed from the toolbar in the Slideshow module. It has the icons for going to the first image in the collection (Yellow circle, Figure 126), left and right pointing arrows for going to a previous or next image (Blue ellipse, Figure 126)and a "Use" option for choosing

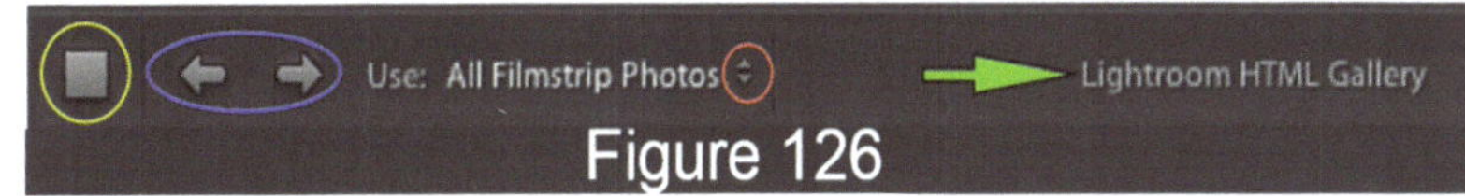

Figure 126

which images in the Filmstrip will be used in the Web Gallery. If you click with the cursor on the double pointed arrow to the right of "Use" (Red circle, Figure 126) a menu will appear from which you can choose to use all Filmstrip Photos, Selected Photos or Flagged Photos. The only other text on the Toolbar is at the right side and it tells you the name of the web template on screen. (Green arrow, figure 126) The column on the right side of the screen has seven panels for setting up and uploading your web gallery. Finally there are buttons for Export and Upload at the bottom of the right column of panels.

## Selecting a Web Template

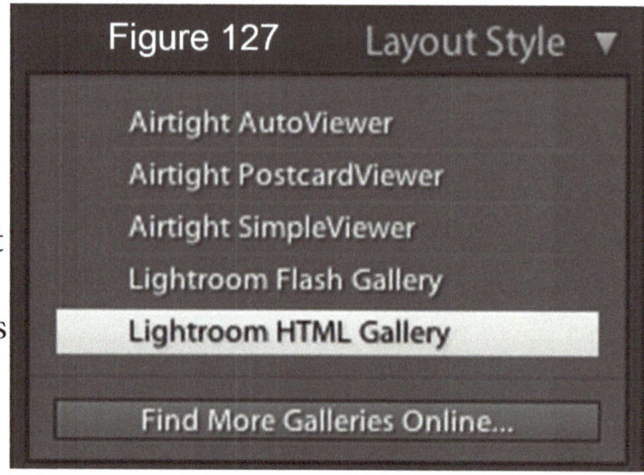


Before you select a template for your web gallery, make sure all the images you want to use in the Filmstrip are selected. Even though there are thirty-six web templates in the Template Browser panel, that is probably not the best place to start. The best place is in the Layout Style panel at the top of the right column of panels. (Figure 127) There are five layout styles listed in this panel. Along with the default HTML and default Flash layout styles there are three Airtight layout styles available, which are pretty interesting. By default, the Lightroom® HTML gallery is selected, so when you open the Web module with the images in the Filmstrip selected, the Lightroom® HTML gallery will be populated with the images from the Filmstrip. Clicking with the cursor on any of the other four layout styles will show you that layout style with your images inserted in the gallery. All of the layout styles are completely functional, all of the buttons, arrows or text will work.

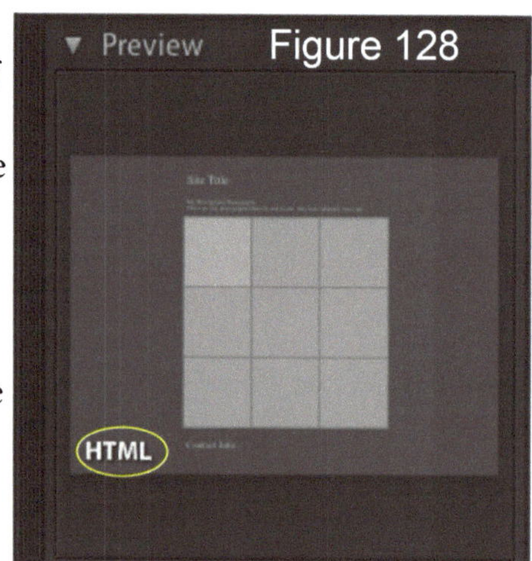


If the none of the Layout Styles are what you are looking for in a web gallery then go to the Template Browser in the left column of panels. If you hover your cursor over the name of a template, you will be able to see what the template looks like in the Preview window at the top of the column. Lightroom will also tell you if the gallery is a flash or HTML gallery in the bottom left corner of the Preview window. (Yellow ellipse, Figure 128) If you click with the cursor on a gallery, Lightroom® will open the gallery in the work area with your images loaded into the frames. Experiment with the different layouts and templates to find the one in which your images look the best.

In making the decision as to whether you want an HTML gallery or a Flash gallery you should think about where your web gallery is going to be viewed. The advantage to a Flash gallery is the images are loaded quickly and there are easy transitions in delivering the images to the screen. The disadvantage to a Flash gallery is they are not supported on mobile/smart phones or tablets such as the iPad. So you should think about where your gallery will be viewed.

## Customizing the Web Gallery

Regardless of the layout style or template you select, you are not stuck with it as is. You can customize any layout or template with the panels in the right column.

## The Site Info Panel

In the top section of the Site Info panel you have the opportunity to type anything you want into the blanks in the panel. There are two ways you can name your site, describe the images and provide some information about the images. The first way is to click with the cursor directly into the blank on the template in the work area and enter text. (Figure 129) The second way is to click with the cursor on the blank in the Site Info panel (Figure 130) and type in text. Either way will put the text into the template. In the top blank, (Yellow arrow, Figures 129 & 130) "Site Title", name the site or page. If it is part of a larger website, you may want to name the page for what it contains rather than putting your company name in the blank. In the second blank, (Blue arrow, Figures 129 & 130) "Collection Title", you can provide the name of the Collection for the images in the web gallery. The third blank, (Red arrow, Figures 129 & 130) "Collection Description", which, by default, says "Web Photo Gallery Created By Adobe Lightroom®", can be left as is, used to provide more information about the site or removed. To remove a blank, simply click inside the blank and then press the delete (Macintosh), Backspace (PC) key to remove the text and then press the Return (Macintosh), Enter (PC) key on the keyboard and the text and blank will disappear from the template. All of these choices have a down pointing arrow at the right of the of the blank. (Yellow circles, Figure 130) Lightroom® will remember any text, titles, etc. you have previously used in any of these blanks. Clicking with the cursor on any of the blanks will bring up a menu with all the previously used information from which you can choose to fill the blank. In the Site Title section, for example, Lightroom® has a memory of all the previous site titles you have used. Clicking with the cursor on this down pointing arrow will bring up a menu with all of the previous site titles as options from which you can choose. The bottom selection in this menu is to "Clear the list". The same is true for the other blanks is this section, Collection Title and Collection Description.

Figure 129



Figure 130

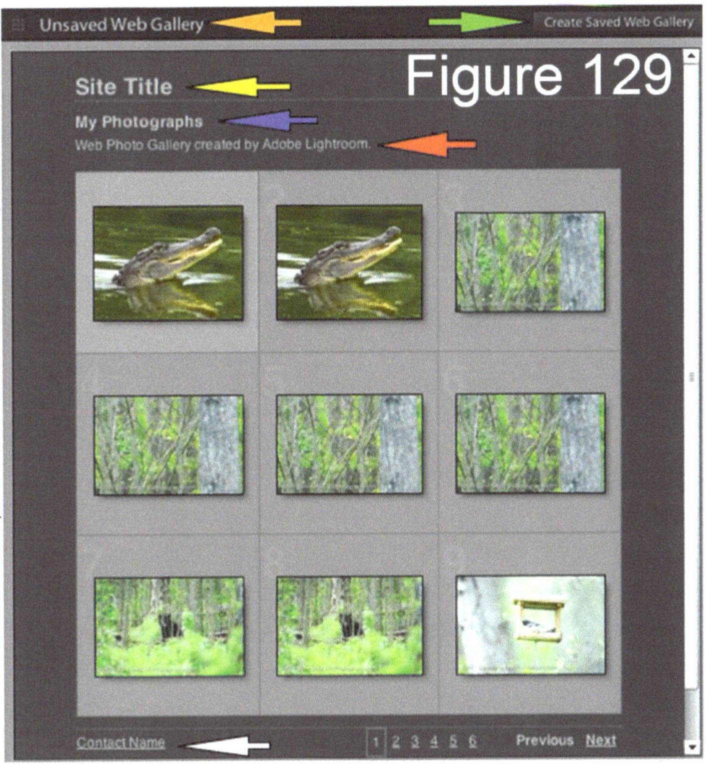

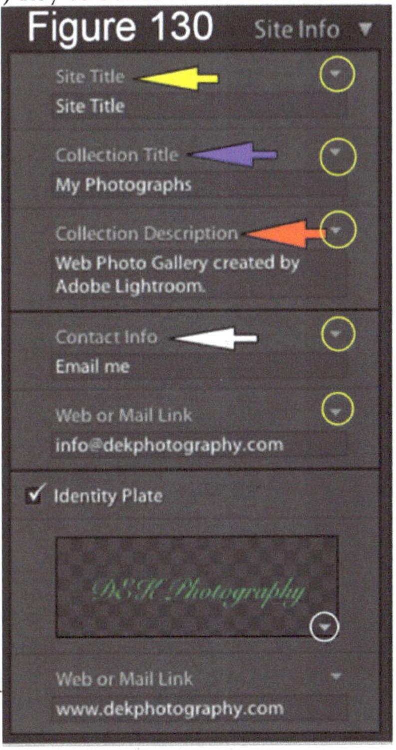

The second section of the Site Info panel is for contact information. You can type your name in this blank or something like "Contact me" or Email me". (White arrow, Figure 130) Again there is a down pointing arrow at the end of the Contact Info bar with options you have previously used from which you can choose. The next blank down, Web or Mail Link is for your contact email link or website URL. This information shows up at the bottom of the Web Gallery, (White arrow, Figure 129) below the images, so that when some one clicks on the email link it will automatically open an email blank addressed to you.

In the final section of the Site Info panel you can use an Identity Plate to replace the Site Title. There are a couple of advantages to doing this because you can edit an Identity Plate and use it to provide more information about your web gallery. There is no limit to the number of Identity Plates you can have and Lightroom® remembers all of the Identity Plates you create. Therefore, you can use an Identity Plate you created in another module, create a specific one for the web gallery or create and use a graphical Identity Plate. All of the previously created Identity Plates and the ability to edit or create a new one are found by clicking with the cursor on the down pointing arrow at the bottom right of the Identity Plate blank. (White circle, Figure 130)

Finally, in the Site Info panel you can add a link to your email or to another website or to a blog in the blank at the bottom of the panel. If you place a link to a website or blog, when a viewer clicks on the Identity plate, they will be taken to the website or blog in the blank. If you place your email address in this blank, when a viewer clicks on the Identity Plate, an email message blank will open up on screen with the message addressed to you.

## The Color Panel

To continue customizing your web gallery, you can use the Color Palette, the next panel down. In this panel you can change the colors of the background, text, header, cells, border, and controls. The choices for what you can change are different for an HTML gallery (Figure 131) and a Flash gallery (Figure 132), but the process is the same. On the left side of the panel is a list of what can be changed in both the flash and HTML galleries. To the right of each element of the gallery that can me changed is a color picker box that works exactly the same as all the color picker boxes in Lightroom®. To change the color of any element in a web gallery, do the following:

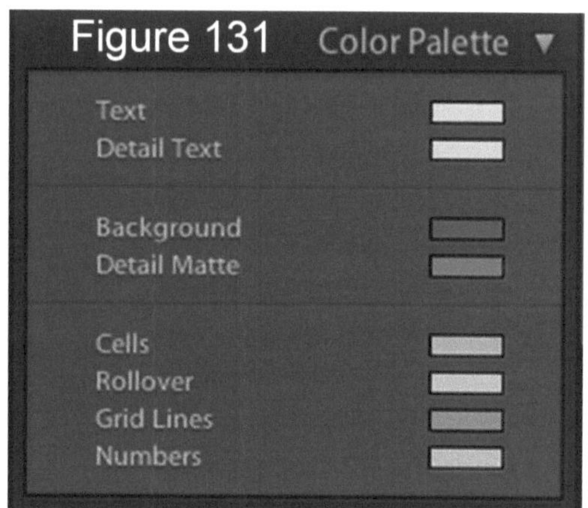


- Click with the cursor on a color picker box to open it.
- When you hover your cursor over the color picker box, it changes into an eye dropper cursor.
- Click the cursor and hold it down and move the eye dropper cursor left to right or right to left over the colors in the color picker box and the element that is to be affected will change color in the web gallery template.
- Moving the cursor up and down will change the saturation of the color in the web gallery template. At the top of the color picker box the saturation of the color will be one hundred percent and decrease as you move the eye dropper cursor down.
- When you find the color you want for the element, release the cursor.
- Click with the cursor on the X at the top left of the color picker box or anywhere outside the color picker box to close it.

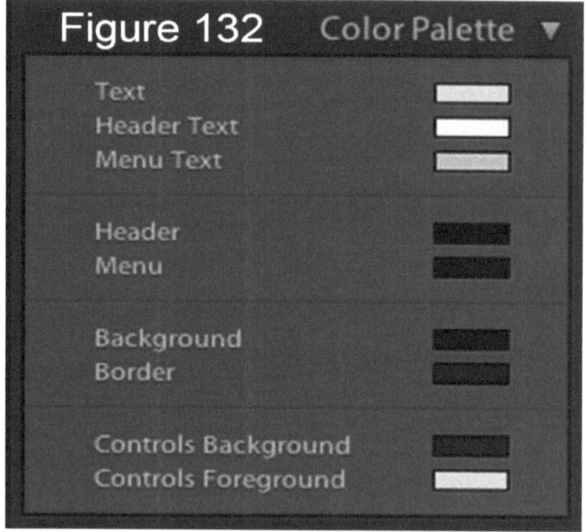


TIP: For the background color, use a color that will make your images stand out. If you have very colorful images, do not pick a bright background color to compete with the images.

### The Appearance Panel

The options for customizing your web gallery in the Appearance panel depend on whether you choose an HTML web gallery or Flash web gallery. Starting with the HTML web gallery templates (Figure 133), the following are things you can do to customize it:

- The first choice is to add a drop shadow to the photos. This is done by clicking with the cursor in the box in front of this choice.
- The second choice is to change the color of the section borders. These are the lines at the top and bottom

of the template that separate, for example, the Identity Plate from the Site Title text. Use the color picker box to the right of the section to change this color.

- The third section allows you to change the Grid Pages. You can increase or decrease the number of rows and columns of the cells. The default is nine cells, three rows and three columns. To change the number, hover the cursor over the bottom right corner of the cells and drag right and/or down to increase the rows or columns (Yellow arrow, Figure 133). As you move the cursor the new number of cells will be come a lighter gray. When you have the number of cells desired, click with the cursor on the bottom right cell and the template on screen will change to that number of cells.
- You can show the Cell Numbers or not by checking or unchecking the box in front of this choice.
- Finally, you can change the color of the photo borders by placing a check mark in the box in front of Photo Borders and choosing a color using the color picker box to the right.
- The last section allows you to make changes to the individual image pages. Change the size of the image on the screen using the Size slider bar or the scrubby slider box to the right. Change the width and color of the Photo Borders by placing a check mark in the box in front of "Photo Borders" and then using the color picker box to the right to select a color for the border. Change the width using the Width slider bar or the scrubby slider box to the right.

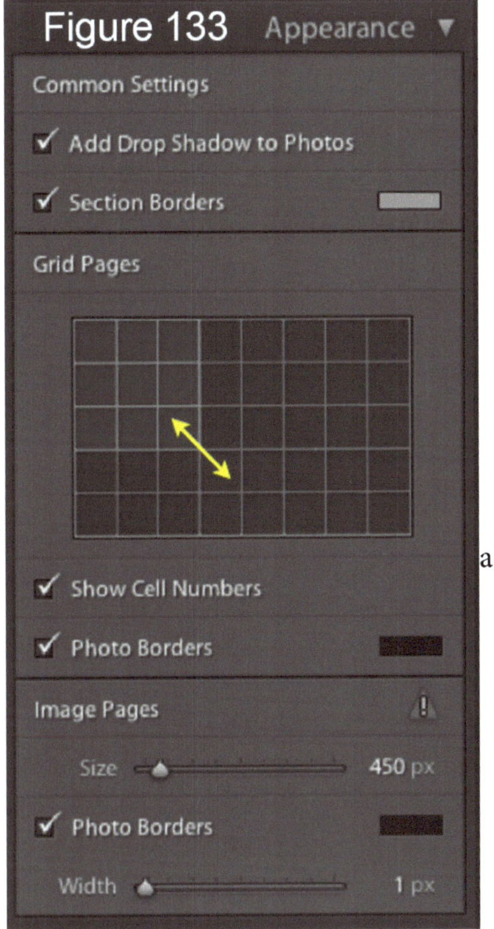


The options for a Flash gallery are more limited. (Figure 134) In the top section, titled "Layout", you can determine where you want the thumbnail images, across the bottom, on the left side or eliminate them from the screen and have just the large image on screen. In the Layout section, click with the cursor on the double pointed arrow at the right of the section (Yellow double arrow, Figure 134) and choose how you want the Thumbnail images to appear. Choose "Scrolling" to place them across the bottom beneath the large image. Choose "Left" to place them in a single column on the left side of the large image. Choose "Paginated" to place them in multiple columns on the left side of the large image. Finally, choose "Slideshow" to hide the small thumbnail images and have only the large image on screen.

In the second section of the Appearance panel for a Flash gallery you can choose to show an Identity Plate at the top of the screen by placing a check mark in the Identity Plate box. Of course, you have the choice of any previously created Identity Plate, editing an Identity Plate or creating a new one by clicking with the cursor on the down pointing arrow at the bottom right of the Identity Plate box. (White circle, Figure 134)

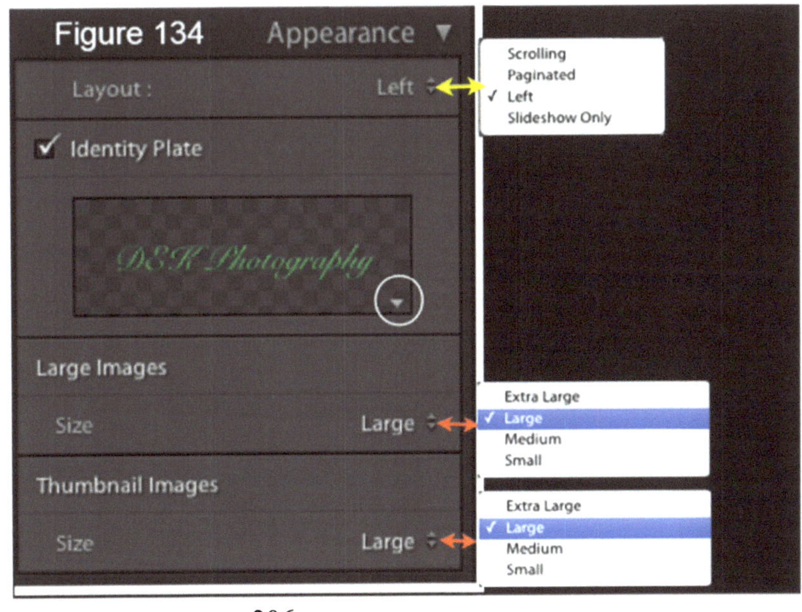


The last two sections of the Appearance panel for a Flash gallery allow you to choose the size of the large on screen image and small thumbnail images. To the right of each of these sections is a double pointed arrow, the clicking on of which will give you a choice of small, medium, large or extra large. (Red double arrows, Figure 134)

## The Image Info Panel

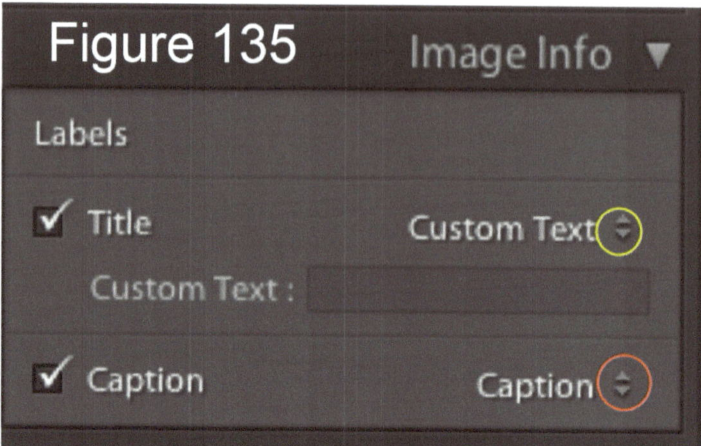


The Image Info Panel (Figure 135)allows you to place any of the metadata or some custom text on each image in your web gallery. The information you can place is the same for a Flash or HTML gallery. The default labels are "Title" and "Caption". In order for Lightroom® to place either the title or caption on the image in the web gallery you first have to place a check mark in each of the boxes in front of these choices. If you added a title and caption to the metadata when you were creating the collection in the Library module, they will show up on the image. If you did not add the title and caption to the metadata then you need to go back to the Library module, open the Metadata panel on the right side of the screen and type in a title and caption in the appropriate blanks. However, you are not limited to the title and caption, you can click with the cursor on the double pointed arrow to the right of the title or caption (Yellow and red circles, Figure 135) and from the menu that appears choose any of the metadata to show in the labels. (Figure 136) One of the choices is "Custom Text". If you choose "Custom Text", a blank will appear beneath the title or caption. Click with the cursor in the blank to activate it. The blank will turn white and you can enter any text you want to show on the image.

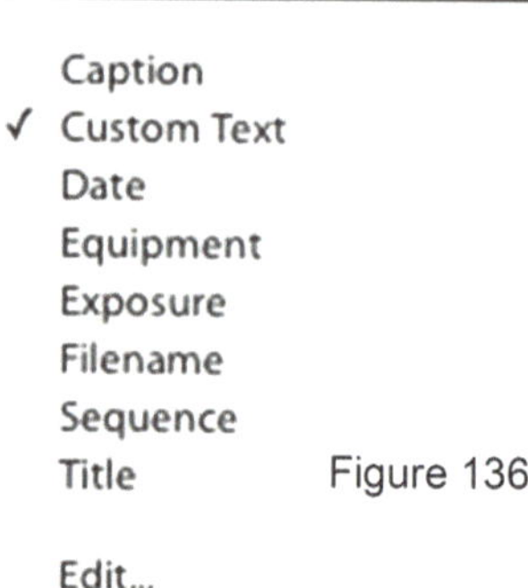


Figure 136

## Saving Your Custom Web Gallery Template

After you have put in your time customizing your web gallery template, it's a good idea to save it as a template. This is especially true if it is only one page in a website and you want all the pages to have the same settings. To save your web gallery settings as a template, do the following:

- From the Web menu at the top of the screen, choose "New Template" or use the keyboard short cut, hold down the Command (Macintosh), Control (PC) key and press the N key on the keyboard or click with the cursor on the plus (+) sign in the header bar of the Template Browser.
- The New Template dialog box will pop up on screen.
- Name the new template in the top blank.
- Select the location for the new template, User Templates is the default.
- Click with the cursor on the Create button at the bottom right of the New Template dialog box.

With your new template selected in the User Template panel of the Template Browser, the next time you bring in a collection of images for a web gallery, they will automatically appear on screen populating you customized template. The only thing you will need to do to get the web gallery ready to upload to the web is add any customized text.

## Output Settings

This is the panel in which you get your images ready to go up on the web. (Figure 136) There is really not much to do here. You need to set the Quality with the top slider. By default it is set at 70, which is about right. The second decision is how much metadata do you want to accompany the image onto the web? The third decision is do you want to put a watermark on your images to protect them? If your web gallery is just for family, friends and fun, you probably don't need a watermark. If the images are your best, a watermark is not a bad idea. The last decision is how much output sharpening do you want Lightroom® to do? The default for sharpening is "Standard" and is usually adequate. The options are the same for both Flash and HTML web galleries.

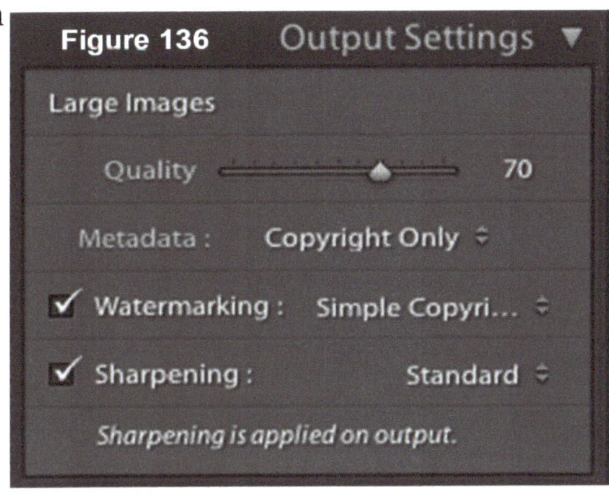


## Upload Settings

With all the settings determined, it is time to upload the web gallery to your server. In order to do that, you need to type in some custom settings. Here's how you do that:

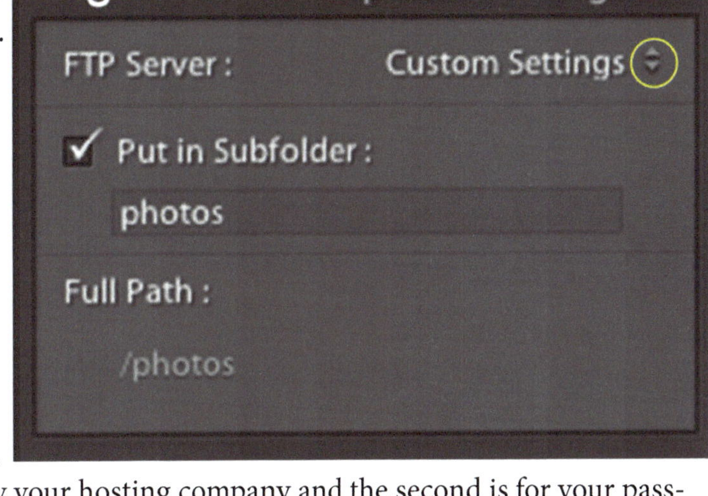


- In the Upload Settings panel, click with the cursor on the double pointed arrow at the right of the first section labeled "FTP Server:". (Yellow circle, Figure 137)
- From the menu that appears, select "Edit".
- The Configure FTP File Transfer dialog box will pop up on screen. (Figure 138)
- In the top blank of the second section type in the Server, your hosting company.
- Below the blank for the Server are two blanks, one is for your user name which is supplied by your hosting company and the second is for your password. Type your user name and password into the blanks.
- To make sure you have entered the correct user name and password, click with the cursor on the Browse button at the right side of the blank labeled "Server Path". (Red ellipse, Figure 138)
- Clicking with the cursor on the Browse button will take you to your server where you can select the correct folder. It should be HTML.
- If everything is correct then click with the cursor in the box below password to store your password inside of Lightroom®. (Black circle, Figure 138)
- Next, type in your Server

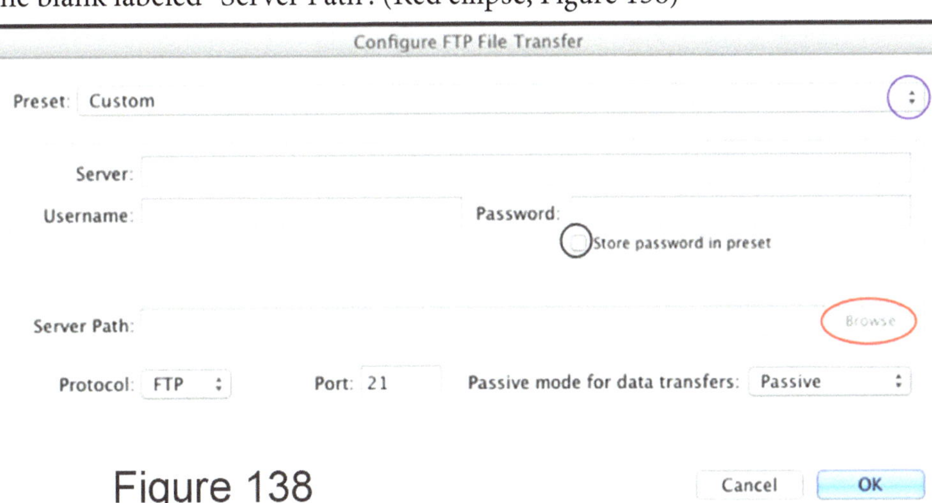


Figure 138

Path in the next blank down. Your Server Path will be given to you by your hosting company.

- Save your settings as a preset. Click with the cursor on the double pointed arrow at the right side of the blank labeled "Presets" and from the resulting menu select "Save Current Settings as a New Preset".
- The New Preset dialog box will pop up on screen. Name the new preset in the blank and click with the cursor on the Create button at the bottom right of the New Preset dialog box.
- Finally, click on the OK button at the bottom right of the Configure FTP File Transfer dialog box.

The next step is to go back to the Upload Settings panel (Figure 137) and put your web gallery in a subfolder. To put your web gallery in a subfolder, place a check mark in the box labeled "Put in Subfolder". The blank immediately below the "Put in Subfolder" text becomes active and you can type in the name of a subfolder.

Finally, you are ready to upload your web gallery. All you need to do now is click with the cursor on the Upload button at the bottom of the right column of panels. Now you can check to see if everything worked by opening your browser and typing in the full URL. In this case it would be www.dekphotography.com/lions/. If you've done everything correctly, your web gallery will open up on the web. Now you can email this full URL as a link attached to an email to friends and family to see your images online.

### Neat Lightroom® Tricks

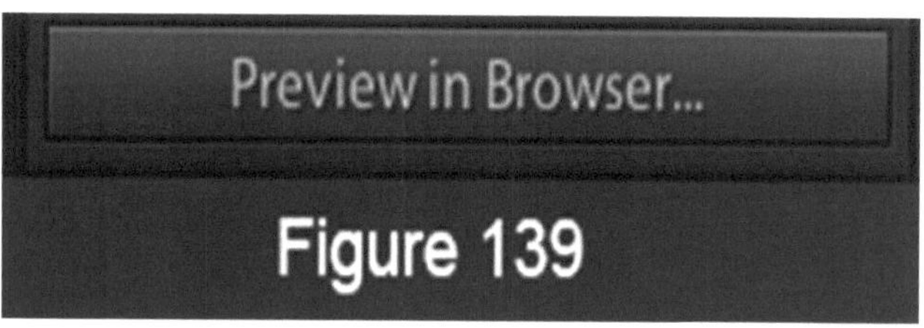

Figure 139

There really is only one neat Lightroom trick in the Web module. However, it is a very helpful, very important trick. As you go through the process of customizing your web gallery, you can check to see how it will look in a browser. To do this, click with the cursor on the "Preview in Browser" button at the bottom of the left column of panels in the Web module. (Figure 139) It is probably a good idea to do this after you finish with each of the panels in the right column, but it is especially important to do it often when you are working in the Color Palette and changing colors of the background or cells. You will want to know how the final settings will look. It is just as important when working in the Appearance panel. If you change the size of the Thumbnail images, you will want to know if they will be too small when viewed on the web. Clicking on the Preview in Browser button will not upload your web gallery to the web, but it will show you what it will look like on the web. In addition, all the buttons will be functional so you can move through the images and see how you like your work to that point.

# Final Thoughts

There you have it, a fresh look at and a tour through Adobe Photoshop Lightroom® 4. I tried to make it as easy as possible for you to follow along with the bullet points. While I tried to be as thorough as possible, I believe there are plenty of as yet undiscovered options available in Lightroom®4 and will be many more in the next version. So, I'd appreciate any feedback on things you find confusing or things you wish I'd covered in more detail or anything you discovered on your own. Thanks

Dave Kelly
info@DEKPhotography.com

# Index

## Symbols

## A



## B



## C



## D



## E

## L



## M



## N



## O

## P

www.ingramcontent.com/pod-product-compliance
Lightning Source LLC
LaVergne TN
LVHW070117110826
845147LV00002B/142

* 9 7 8 0 6 1 5 6 9 2 6 0 9 *